INNOVATION DIFFUSION

A NEW PERSPECTIVE

LAWRENCE A. BROWN

METHUEN

LONDON AND NEW YORK

First published in 1981 by
Methuen & Co. Ltd
11 New Fetter Lane, London EC4P 4EE

Published in the USA by
Methuen & Co.
in association with Methuen, Inc.
733 Third Avenue, New York, NY 10017

Printed in the United States of America

British Library Cataloguing in Publication Data
Brown, Lawrence A
Innovation diffusion.
1. Innovations
I. Title
301.24'2   80-49706

ISBN 0-416-74270-X

CONTENTS

ACKNOWLEDGEMENTS

The author and publishers would like to thank the following for permission to reproduce material:

'The Cones of Resolution Problem in Diffusion Research', p. 37–45:This section contains material from Semple, R.K. and Brown, L.A. (1976) 'Cones of resolution in spatial diffusion studies: a perspective', *Professional Geographer,* 28, 8–16 (reprinted with the permission of the Association of American Geographers).

Chapters 3 and 4, pp. 50–151: These chapters contain material from Brown, L.A., Brown, M.A. and Craig, C.S. (1981) 'Innovation diffusion and entrepreneurial activity in a spatial context: conceptual models and related case studies', in Sheth, J.N. (ed.) *Research in Marketing, Vol. 4,* Greenwich, Conn., JAI Press (copyright 1981) (reprinted with the permission of JAI Press). They also contain material from Brown, L.A. (1975) 'The market and infrastructure context of adoption: a spatial perspective on the diffusion of innovation', *Economic Geography,* 51, 185–216 (reprinted with the permission of the Editor).

'The Case of Friendly Ice Cream', pp. 63–8: This section contains material from Meyer, J.W. and Brown, L.A. (1979) 'Diffusion agency establishment: the case of Friendly Ice Cream and public sector diffusion processes', *Socio-Economic Planning Sciences,* 13, 241–9 (copyright 1979) (reproduced with the permission of Pergamon Press Ltd).

'The Case of Bank Credit Card Services', pp. 74–9: This section contains material from Brown, L.A. and Malecki, E.J. (1977) 'Comments on landscape evolution and diffusion processes', *Regional Studies,* 11, 211–23 (reprinted with the permission of the Editor).

'The Case of Cable Television', pp. 79–86: This section contains material from Brown, L.A., Malecki, E.J., Gross, S.R., Shrestha, M.N. and Semple, R.K. (1974) 'The diffusion of cable television in

Ohio: a case study of diffusion agency location processes of the polynuclear type', *Economic Geography*, 50, 285–99 (reprinted with the permission of the Editor).

'The Case of the Planned Parenthood Affiliate', pp. 87–91: This section contains material from Brown, L.A. and Philliber, S.G. (1977) 'The diffusion of a population related innovation: the Planned Parenthood Affiliate', *Social Science Quarterly*, 58, 215–28 (reprinted with the permission of the Editor).

'Commercial Dairying in Aguascalientes, Mexico: A Theoretical Perspective on Infrastructure-Constrained Diffusion in Developing World Settings', pp. 215–25: This section contains material from Brown, L.A. and Lentnek, B. (1973) 'Innovation diffusion in a developing economy: a mesoscale view', *Economic Development and Cultural Change*, 21, 274–92 (reprinted with the permission of the University of Chicago Press).

'Structural Characteristics and Diffusion: Agricultural Cooperatives in Sierra Leone', pp. 244–51: This section contains material from Brown, L.A., Schneider, R., Harvey, M.E. and Riddell, J.B. (1979) 'Innovation diffusion and development in a Third World setting: the case of the cooperative movement in Sierra Leone', *Social Science Quarterly*, 60, 249–68 (reprinted with the permission of the Editor).

'Social Science Research, Public Policy Formulation and Programs of Innovation Diffusion', pp. 285–303: This section contains material from Brown, L.A. (1980) 'The innovation diffusion process in a public policy context', in Agnew, J.A. (ed.) *Innovation Research and Public Policy*, Syracuse, University of Syracuse Geographical Series (reprinted here with permission).

PREFACE

This book examines innovations and the processes by which they spread across the human landscape, but little attention is given to the creative process from which either material or conceptual innovations spring. Accordingly, it seems fitting to address this topic through my experiences in spawning the ideas presented here, as a final gesture to the book and to the many persons and events that have been a part of its evolution.

There seems to be at least a superficial similarity in the creative process involved in designing a new product or technique, discovering a scientific principle, writing a novel or articulating a social science paradigm. Thus, just as the novelist claims to be taken over by the characters being created, I often found myself compelled to pursue and develop specific ideas, even before they had crystallized in my mind. In this respect, a given idea, like a character in a novel, was like an embryo beating on the walls of its shell to see the light of existence. Similarly, the articulation of one idea often led with a rush to the birth of a related idea. In surveying the product of my efforts, however, I can see how much more could be done, and conclude, therefore, that the completion of a book only represents the limits of one's energy rather than the exhaustive articulation of a topic. Thus, the dialectic of creation goes on.

To be more specific about the genesis of this book, its embryo may be traced to my PhD dissertation, completed in 1966. In that, I chanced to apply the then prevailing model of spatial diffusion, as articulated by Torsten Hagerstrand, to the situation of diffusion within an urban system. In doing so, I found an anomaly, to use Kuhn's (1970) terms, between Hagerstrand's paradigm and the empirical reality of diffusion at the regional scale. With what seemed at the time like a tremendous and brilliant effort, I accounted for that anomaly in *two* pages of my dissertation! Little did I realize that twelve years later those two pages would be expanded to the nearly four hundred that are presented here. In retrospect, then, my sophomoric naivete seems comical, even though it is probably an inherent part of the creative process.

There are some other, less explicit roots that underlie this book. One is my background in the ways of business and the world of commerce, derived from my family. With this as a guide, it was only a short step to conclude that the traditional social science models of diffusion, which focus upon adoption behavior, are wanting in not considering the role of the entrepreneur in propagating innovations. And once this was realized, my upbringing also provided the tools for initiating the articulation of the entrepreneurial perspective presented in this book.

A sense of social justice and a concern with equality and welfare issues is another outgrowth of my childhood. However, this sense lay dormant with regard to innovation diffusion until I read Yapa's (1976) essay on 'Innovation diffusion and economic involution', which triggered what is termed here the development perspective.

Another root of this book stems from the work of Richard Chorley on general systems theory and research design. I can still remember the explosion of excitement and awareness that accompanied my first reading, as a graduate student, of his well-known 'Geomorphology and general systems theory' and 'Geography and analogue theory'. Chorley's epistomological framework for merging empirical reality, conceptualization, theory and research design is very much present in my thinking of today.

Finally, one cannot discount the serendipity of science which results in a coalescence of seemingly unrelated tasks. Who would have thought, for example, that my work on locating day-care centers, completed in the rush of social consciousness of the early 1970s, would ever be relevant to a conceptualization of innovation diffusion?

The work more directly underlying this book began in 1973 with a grant from the Social Sciences Division of the National Science Foundation. Supplementary funds have been provided by the College of Social and Behavioral Sciences and the Graduate School of the Ohio State University. This support is gratefully acknowledged. Even more appreciated, however, is the confidence in my abilities expressed by the segment of the Geography community that reviewed my (perhaps) overly ambitious 1973 proposal and by Howard Hines, then the Director of the Social Sciences Division. I have felt a responsibility and obligation to that confidence and tried not to dissappoint it. I also appreciate the support of Patricia

McWethy, who came on board towards the end of the NSF grant as
the Director of their newly formed Geography and Regional Science
Program.

Realizing the vision of the 1973 proposal and going beyond it
involved the efforts of many persons, for which I am deeply indebted.
Broadly represented in this book are the contributions of Marilyn A.
Brown, now of the University of Illinois Department of Geography,
and Edward J. Malecki, now of the University of Oklahoma
Department of Geography. Lyn and Ed were the principle graduate
research associates on the NSF project and participated directly and
indirectly in most of its aspects. Other persons whose contributions
are significantly reflected here include C. Samuel Craig, now of the
New York University Graduate School of Business Administration;
Ron Garst, now of the University of Maryland Department of
Geography; Susan G. Philliber, now of the Center for Population and
Family Health of Columbia University; R. Keith Semple, now of the
University of Saskatchewan Department of Geography; and Kevin
R. Cox and Matthew Sagers of the Ohio State University Depart-
ment of Geography. There also are several persons who read most of
this manuscript and offered suggestions that considerably improved
its content. Particularly helpful in this regard were Vijay Mahajan of
the University of Pennsylvania Department of Marketing, Anne S.
Macke of the Ohio State University Center for Human Resource
Research, and Rickie Gilliard and Rita Schneider of the Ohio State
University Department of Geography. Finally, the completion of this
book has been enhanced by the academic milieu and support of
research activity provided by the Department of Geography under
Ned Taaffe and John Rayner, the former and present chairperson,
respectively.

Another set of acknowledgements is for those who assisted in the
production of this book, which the fledging author quickly discovers
to be every bit as important as the ideas developed and the writing
itself. Many aspects of manuscript production were handled by the
Editorial and Printing Services Department of the Ohio State
University Research Foundation which, under the direction of Chet
Ball and Alan Evans, has been incredibly helpful throughout the
research reported here. Typing and formating of the manuscript were
done on the programmable world processing system of the Kenneth
Thompson Academy. The figures were meticulously drawn by Rita
Schneider of the Ohio State University Department of Geography.
The efforts of the Methuen staff in bringing this book to reality also
are appreciated.

In addition to the above persons and the many others who worked in various ways on the research underlying this book, I would like to render a special acknowledgement to two others.

One of these is Torsten Hagerstrand. His work, completed in 1953, was years ahead of comparable efforts in Geography and Social Science. As such, it has served as a beacon that many have followed, including myself, and I have tried to mold this book in accord with his precepts.

I also would like to give a special acknowledgement to Everett Rogers. His *Diffusion of Innovations,* published in 1962, was a benchmark study that, like Hagerstrand's, set the pace for much of the future work on the topic. I am indebted to this, and its 1971 revision, for enhancing my grasp of the social science understanding of innovation diffusion. These, together with Rogers' books on family planning (1973) and development and modernization processes (1969, 1976), indicate Rogers' broad scope of ideas and, more impressively, a willingness to view his previous work critically, even though it is, for many, the basis of his reputation. This is a rare and enviable quality in our world of scholars.

Finally, an essential ingredient in the creation of this book has been the personal support and encouragement received from so many friends and colleagues: especially, the staff of my National Science Foundation project, who willingly took over the responsibility for getting things done when necessary; Angelika and the beautiful daughter she has raised, who have provided grounding and a sense of continuity throughout this entire effort; and Anne, who saw me through the writing of the manuscript.

This book is dedicated to my daughter Arnika who, as noted in the dedication, has been an innovation in my own life.

LIST OF ILLUSTRATIONS

TABLES

1

INTRODUCTION

Accounts of the rise, relative prosperity and fall of mankind's various civilizations are replete with references to the critical role of innovation. Thus, we are taught as children that the innovation of domestic agriculture paved the way for the advent of civilized society as we know it today, that innovations in administrative organization enabled the Roman Empire to control then vast portions of the earth's surface, that the industrial revolution which so changed the face of organized society was in fact an aggregation of many individual technological and organizational innovations, and that the Second World War ultimately ended because of the atomic bomb. We also are taught that one of the pillars of European and North American foreign policies since the 1950s has been the export of technology to developing nations.

In learning about the above examples, the emphasis generally was upon invention and refinements leading to the innovations becoming practical. However, innovations do not immediately appear over the entire earth's surface once they are perfected. Some groups of people and some places have immediate access to the innovation, some gain access later and some never do. Accordingly, the distributional characteristics associated with innovations also are important for study. These characteristics change over time, rather than remaining static, and the process by which such change occurs, that is, by which innovations spread from one locale or one social group to another, is called *diffusion*.

This book is about the diffusion of innovations. The term innovation is used broadly and may encompass a new product, new technique, new practice or a new idea. Contemporary examples include space travel, transistor circuitry, cable television, the bank credit card, a new brand of toothpaste, or clothing fashions. Further, the fast food outlet, color television or bicycle may be an *innovation* in a Developing or Third World nation, even though they would not be considered such in the United States.

Accordingly, an item classified as an innovation might be *intrinsically new* or it might only be new to the setting in which we find it. Consistent with this observation is the following definition from E.M. Rogers and Shoemaker (1971: 19)

An innovation is an idea, practice, or object perceived as new by an individual. It matters little, so far as human behavior is concerned, whether or not an idea is objectively new as measured by the lapse of time since its first use or discovery. It is the perceived or subjective newness of the idea for the individual that determines his reaction to it. If the idea seems new to the individual, it is an innovation.

Even with Rogers and Shoemaker's definition, there remains a question of how new is new or the degree of newness, that is, some things are just barely new and others are dramatically so. To this point, Robertson (1971: 7) states

The critical factor in defining a new product should be its effect upon established patterns of consumption. A continuum may be proposed . . . . A *continuous* innovation has the least disrupting influence on established consumption patterns. Alteration of a product is almost always involved, rather than the creation of a new product. Examples include fluoride toothpaste, menthol cigarettes, and annual new model automobile changeovers. A *dynamically continuous* innovation has more disrupting effects than a continuous innovation. Although it still generally does not involve new consumption patterns, it involves the creation of a new product or the alteration of an existing one. Examples include electric toothbrushes, electric haircurlers, and the Mustang automobile. A *discontinuous* innovation involves the establishment of new consumption patterns and the creation of previously unknown products. Examples include television, computers, and the automobile.

Both Rogers and Shoemaker, and Robertson are referring to innovations adopted by individuals or households, sometimes termed *consumer innovations*. There also are *firm* or *technological innovations* which are

new production inputs, machines, processes, and techniques adopted by firms or entrepreneurs for their own use. (Malecki, 1975: 1)

Studies of these two types of innovation generally have proceeded separately with little if any crossreferencing. Hence, the distinction between consumer and technological innovations is common in the research literature. Yet some technological innovations are adopted by households, as in an agricultural setting where the firms are single family units, or by individuals, as in the medical profession. Further, the diffusion processes for each of these two types of innovation are more similar than is generally recognized. The elaboration of this communality is one of the topics addressed in this book (Chapter 5). More generally, attention is given to both consumer and technological innovations, although more to the former, and to the articulation of a conceptual model at least partially applicable to both.[1]

THE INNOVATION DIFFUSION PROCESS: A SYNOPSIS

With regard to the processes by which innovations diffuse, research has been addressed to three areas. One of these concerns *inventive activity* or the transformation of an idea into a marketable product or service (Myers and Marquis, 1969; Gruber and Marquis, 1969; Mansfield, 1968a, 1968b; Utterback and Abernathy, 1975; Rossini and Bozeman, 1977; Levy, 1972). It is generally agreed that the initial idea or design concept arises from a fusion of technical feasibility with the recognition of a need or demand, and that the idea is carried into invention by research and development activity (Figure 1.1). A related geographical question is the location of inventive activity, which has tended to be concentrated in larger and more industrialized cities (Pred, 1966, 1973b, 1977; Feller, 1971, 1975).

The Economic History Perspective

The above aspects of inventive activity are not directly concerned with diffusion (Figure 1.1) and, hence, will not be addressed in this book. A concern related to inventive activity that will be given attention, however, is the way(s) in which innovation is *adapted* to the needs and situations of potential adopters, which is seen here to constitute one aspect of the *preconditions for diffusion*. This has been primarily studied by economic historians in the context of technological innovations, but there are considerable implications for the diffusion process in general. Specifically, the *economic history perspective* (Chapter 6) posits that innovation is a *continual* process whereby the form and function of the innovation and the environment into which it might be adopted are modified throughout the life of the innovation, and these changes affect both the innovation and its market. Thus, the computer, while still called a computer, has undergone almost yearly changes since the first Univac was made commercially available some thirty years ago. Newer computers are dramatically faster, have extensive storage capacity and rely upon solid state integrated circuitry rather than vacuum tube systems. Other innovations have gone through more subtle changes. Color

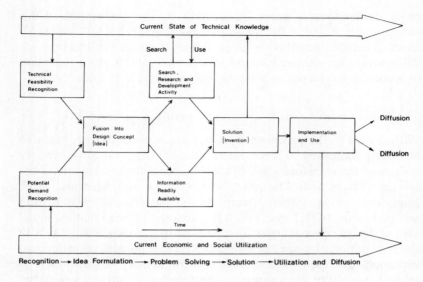

Figure 1.1   The Innovation Process
Adapted from Myers and Marquis, 1969: 4

television, for example, now costs less, has better color and better programming. However, whether the changes are dramatic or subtle, those innovations which are successful typically become more *adapted* to the market and are, therefore, likely to be *adopted* by an increasingly wider range of persons or organizations.

Isolation of the Diffusion Process

A second major area of research has directly focused on the *diffusion process* itself, generally under the assumption of an unchanging innovation. All members of the population of potential adopters do not adopt simultaneously and some never adopt. Further, the progression of innovation diffusion through a given population takes place with some regularity. Thus, a comparison of the adopters with the non-adopters of a given innovation generally would reveal systematic differences in the economic, social, locational and demographic characteristics of each group. Such differences also would be observed were one to examine the characteristics of those who adopted soon after the innovation was made available, those who adopted at some intermediary time and those who lagged in adoption. Maps showing the locations of each of these three groups of adopters, for example, would look quite different, and the spatial patterns might well appear as a series of waves emanating from some central point (Figure 1.2). A great deal of research attention has been given to such differences, reflecting a general interest in the correlates, temporal trends and spatial patterns of innovation diffusion. Another concern of diffusion research, representing a more critical question in this author's opinion, is *why* such differences occur, or *what are* the *underlying generative processes*.

These concerns have been addressed by several disciplines, some of which have a long-standing tradition of diffusion research. In anthropology and geography, for example, the research tradition dates from the early 1900s with the question of the role of diffusion as compared to evolution in the formation and change of cultures. Sociologists, on the other hand, trace their concern to Tarde's (1903) book on imitation behavior. A focus upon innovations *per se* rather than upon generalized diffusion process or culture indices is more recent, dating perhaps to the 1930s as represented by the work of Bowers (1937, 1938), McVoy (1940), Pemberton (1936, 1937, 1938) and Ryan and Gross (1943). Other disciplines more recently engaging in diffusion research include economics, marketing, political science, communications and education (E.M. Rogers and Shoemaker, 1971: 44–70).

The Adoption Perspective: The Traditional Approach to Diffusion Studies. The dominant and most completely developed area of research on the diffusion of innovations, representing an effort spanning about forty-five years, focuses upon the process by which adoption occurs, or the *demand* aspect of diffusion. Until recently, in fact, the *adoption perspective* was coincident with what people referred to as innovation diffusion research.[2] It is also that concern which has had the most direct input into policy. This is evidenced by its heavy utilization in the design of programs of the United States Cooperative Extension Service, family planning programs in Third World nations and development programs of the United States Agency for International Development, among others. Virtually billions of dollars are spent annually on such programs, and by this measurement, the adoption perspective on innovation diffusion may be one of the most successful of all social science paradigms![3]

The adoption perspective is best summarized by Rogers (E.M. Rogers and Shoemaker, 1971), and is represented in geography by the work of Hagerstrand (1953, 1967a).[4] The basic tenet of this conceptualization of the spread of innovation across the landscape is

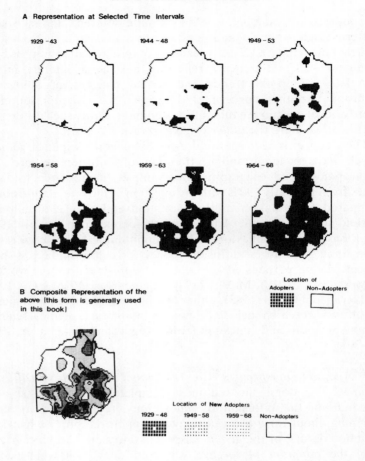

Figure 1.2   The Wave-Like Effect of Innovation Diffusion:
Commercial Dairying in Aguascalientes, Mexico
    Note: For further analysis of this diffusion, see Chapter
7, pages 215–25.

that the adoption of an innovation is primarily the outcome of a
learning or *communications* process (Figure 1.3). Accordingly, a
fundamental step in examining the process of diffusion is identification of factors related to the *effective* flow of information and of the
characteristics of information flows, information reception and
resistances to adoption. An important aspect of resistance is an
individual's general propensity to adopt innovation, or his *innovativeness*. Another important aspect of resistance is the congruence

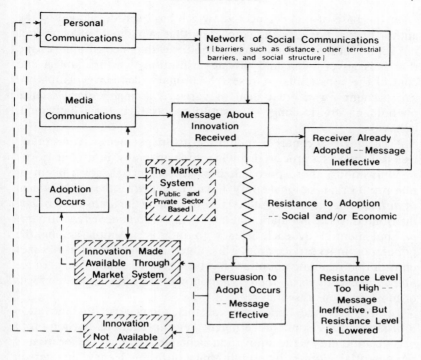

Figure 1.3   A Flow Diagram of the Adoption Perspective on Innovation
  Diffusion (after Hagerstrand) with Modifications Reflecting More Recent
  Work on the Market and Infrastructure Perspective
      Note: Dotted lines and shaded boxes indicate aspects of the market and
  infrastructure perspective.

between the innovation and the social, economic and psychological
characteristics of the potential adopter.

The Market and Infrastructure Perspective. The now traditional
approach to innovation diffusion, the adoption perspective, implicitly
assumes that all have an equal opportunity to adopt, and focuses,
therefore, upon individual characteristics to explain differences in the
actual times of adoption. By contrast, the *market and infrastructure
perspective* (Chapters 3, 4 and 7) takes the stance that the opportunity
to adopt is egregiously and in many cases purposely unequal.
Accordingly, focus is upon the process by which innovations and the
conditions for adoption are made available to individuals or
households, that is, the *supply* aspect of diffusion.

At the base of this perspective, which has been developed by the author of this book, is the conviction that individual behavior does not represent free will so much as choices within a constraint set and that it is government and private institutions which establish and control the constraints. A research corollary of this view is that we can account for a great deal of variance in many social science phenomena by looking at institutional, rather than individual, behavior.

Accordingly, the market and infrastructure perspective conceptualizes diffusion as a process involving three activities. For the majority of innovations, those propagated by a commercial, government or non-profit organizational entity, the *initial activity* is the *establishment of diffusion agencies* (or outlets) through which the innovation will be distributed to the population at large. As a *second activity*, a strategy is implemented by each agency to induce adoption among the population in its service area. This, together wih the actions of other entities that facilitate adoption, has been termed *establishment of the innovation*. Only *third,* then, is *adoption* of the innovation, the focus of most previous research.

To illustrate the importance of this perspective on innovation difusion, unless some government, entrepreneurial or non-profit organization makes the innovation available at or near the location of the potential adopter, by establishing a diffusion agency, that person or household will not have the option to adopt in the first place. Even then there are at least two other considerations which pertain to diffusion agency strategy in propagating the innovation. First, each potential adopter may or may not know of the innovation (or may know about it in varying degrees). This would depend upon the agency's promotional communications strategy. Second, each potential adopter may or may not have access to the innovation (or will have access to it in varying degrees). One factor in this would be the price of the innovation; another is the potential adopter's ability to obtain financial resources such as a loan. Also important might be the potential adopter's proximity to infrastructure relevant to using the innovation such as energy, service or delivery/collection systems. In general, knowing about the innovation and having access to it pertain to the broader consideration of the ways in which resources are made available or allocated to different individuals, both by propagators of innovations and by society at large. Also pertinent is the individual potential adopter's ability to utilize these resources, which itself may be a societal product.

Thus, conceptually recognizing the supply side of diffusion shifts attention to the diffusion agency instead of the adopter. The locations of these agencies and the temporal sequencing of their establishment determine where and when the innovation will be available. This provides the general outline of the spatial pattern of diffusion. Further detail is contributed by the operating procedures of each agency. These create differing levels of access to the innovation depending upon a potential adopter's economic, locational, social and demographic characteristics. The establishment of diffusion agencies and the operating procedures of each agency are, more generally, aspects of marketing the innovation. This marketing involves both the creation of infrastructure and its utilization. Thus, the characteristics of the relevant public and private infrastructures— such as service, delivery, information, transportation, electricity or water systems—also have an important influence upon the rate and spatial patterning of diffusion. Accordingly, both within the agency service area and the larger region of which it is a part, the diffusion is shaped by what has been termed the *market and infrastructure context of innovation adoption and diffusion*. As illustrated in Figure 1.3, however, this perspective is complemetary to, rather than exclusive of, the adoption perspective.

The Development Perspective

In addition to a concern with inventive activity and the diffusion process itself, a third major area of research has been the *impact* of innovation diffusion, such as its effects on economic development, social change and individual welfare. However, the reverse question also is of concern, that is, the ways in which diffusion is affected by aspects of the overall level of development. Specific studies have examined the negative and indirect effects of public programs of diffusion; the redesign of such programs so they are more effective, both in diffusing innovations and in bringing about suitable impacts in the social and economic arenas; the nature of the diffusion component in the evolution of the urban and regional landscape; the ways in which the adoption of one innovation may influence the adoption of another and enjoyment of its attendant benefits; and the role of social norms and public infrastructure, manifestations of the level of development, as preconditions affecting the rate and spatial patterning of diffusion.

In part, the *development perspective* (Chapters 7 and 8), which is articulated for the first time in this book, is a logical extension of the market and infrastructure perspective. This is so in that the latter calls attention to the importance of access to resources and public infrastructure in innovation diffusion. Thus, the numerous shortcomings of government and privately operated diffusion programs, many of which rely on the adoption model, are readily apparent from the vantage point of the market and infrastructure perspective.

More generally, however, the development perspective represents a reaction to a discontinuity between belief and fact. Traditionally, the belief has been that innovation diffusion has a positive impact upon individual welfare and, collectively, economic development and social change. The facts, however, present a somewhat different picture. In Third World nations, for example, the diffusion of technological innovations has not led to significant economic development and improvement in individual welfare so much as it has tended to increase regional inequalities, widen the disparities between social and economic classes and increase élitist entrenchment. Likewise, we have become acutely aware of the systematic disenfranchisement of minorities in our own country through subtle mechanisms such as credit availability and educational opportunity. Also contributing to this awareness are questions such as the wisdom of our government allocating money to space program innovations instead of to innovations related to better education or to encouraging entrepreneurship among the disadvantaged population groups. Such awareness is even found in popular news magazines. For example,

The [agricultural] mechanization controversy asks these basic questions: Technology for what? For whom? And at what cost? Similar questions are being raised in a variety of contexts, including the building of nuclear power plants and the proliferation of pesticides suspected of causing cancer and birth defects. The traditional willingness of Americans to refer such decisionmaking to a narrow group of 'experts' has been repeatedly shaken. Increasingly, people are recognizing that the social consequences of applied technology must be considered before enormous sums of public funds are allocated. (Meyerhoff, 1980: 11)

The Complementarity of the Various Perspectives on Innovation Diffusion

As is evident from the above discussion, the development perspective provides unique insights into the innovation diffusion process. Likewise, so do the economic history, adoption, and market and infrastructure perspectives. Further, each of these perspectives addresses in varying degrees the three major areas of research on the topic—invention and transformation into innovation, diffusion and impact. Procedurally, however, this work has been characterized by a *six-blind-men-and-the-elephant* approach to knowing; that is, each of these perspectives or themes has been developed rather independently of the others with little if any crossreferencing. Nevertheless, in considering them together it is clear that the four perspectives are in fact complementary and provide a comprehensive view of the innovation diffusion process. The nature of this fit is portrayed in Figure 1.4.

THE PURVIEW OF THIS BOOK

The concern of presenting a multifaceted, yet integrated picture of the innovation diffusion process will be found throughout this book. Chapter 2 considers the antecedents of the present work. This includes a review of the various traditions of diffusion research in geography and an indication of how these reflect the broader trends of the discipline and social science in general. Chapters 3 and 4 present the market and infrastructure perspective, the first of these focusing on diffusion agency establishment, the second on diffusion agency strategy and innovation establishment. The structure of both these chapters is one that alternates a conceptual or theoretical statement with an illustrative case study from the United States. Specific innovations examined in this context include Friendly Ice Cream Shops, cable television, the bank credit card, Planned Parenthood affiliates and four agricultural innovations. Chapter 5 briefly summarizes the conceptual framework pertaining to the diffusion of innovation among firms. More importantly, it also draws upon the market and infrastructure perspective to demonstrate communalities in the diffusion of technological and consumer innovations, and raises a new set of questions pertaining to the way in which technological innovations are made available to potential adopters. A review of the economic history perspective is presented in Chapter 6. Chapter 7, the first dealing with the development perspective, demonstrates the applicability of the market and infrastructure perspective in a Developing or Third World setting. Two case studies are used in this respect: one on the diffusion of several crop innovations in an area of Kenya; another on the diffusion of commercial agriculture in an area of Mexico. Chapter 8 articulates the development perspective in a more conceptual manner, dealing among other things with equity aspects of innovation diffusion, particularly as they pertain to individual welfare and

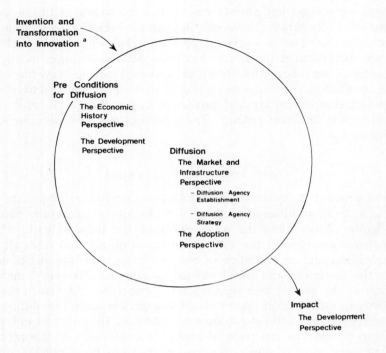

Figure 1.4   The Innovation Diffusion Process in Terms of the
Perspectives From Which It Has Been Studied
[a]For references on invention and its transformation into
innovation, see Levy (1972), Myers and Marquis (1969),
Schmookler (1966) and Rossini and Bozeman (1977). Other
aspects of this diagram are treated in this book.

regional disparities. One case study of the diffusion of cooperatives in
Sierra Leone also is presented. The concluding ninth chapter presents
a brief summary of the material in this book and addresses its policy
implications.

Before addressing these topics, brief consideration should be given
to a related issue. The orientation of this book is towards the spatial
aspects of innovation diffusion. However, for many persons, particularly those actually diffusing innovations, the *rate* and *speed* of
diffusion is a matter of more primary concern. It is important to note,
therefore, that these concerns are closely, perhaps inextricably,
linked. Said another way, they are two sides of the same coin in that
every spatial pattern of diffusion has its temporal expression, and

every temporal pattern its spatial expression. To illustrate, in seeking to maximize the rate of diffusion, the early efforts of the diffuser probably should be concentrated on those locales where adoption is most likely. Such locales might be characterized by more effective diffusing organizations, by a more extensive development of that public infrastructure needed to implement the innovation, or by populations with a clear need for the innovation. Similarly, to increase the rate the diffuser probably should choose a stragegy that maximizes the contagion element of diffusion, which often manifests itself in a wave-like or neighborhood effect spatial pattern. This might be accomplished by targeting diffusion strategy on more densely populated areas or ones with more effective communications infrastructure.

More generally, however, the spatial aspects of diffusion are not the only domain of applicability for the framework presented in this book, only that which the author has chosen to develop and a reflection of his disciplinary affiliation. Accordingly, it is hoped that readers will view this material not only in terms of how it is directly applicable, but also in terms of how it might be *extended* to their own domains of interest. This exhortation is made with considerable conviction that the material presented here has widespread implications for both academic and policy issues.

The rationales for this statement are two. First, is the belief that supply and access considerations account for an extremely high, if not predominant percentage of the variance in the temporal rates and spatial patterns of diffusion. Second, so much attention has been given to the demand or adoption side of diffusion that we may well be in a situation of diminishing returns to research effort, whereas the supply side is virtually virgin territory for academic and applied investigation. While the first of these points is arguable, and there surely would be sharp differences of opinion on the matter, the second is not. It is hoped, therefore, that future research will evidence a shift towards the issues addressed in this book and towards further integrating the various perspectives on innovation diffusion, as in Figure 1.4.

1 Significant attention also has been given to innovation diffusion within organizations (Zaltman, Duncan and Holbeck, 1973; E.M. Rogers and Agarwala-Rogers, 1976) and innovation adoption by communities (Bingham, 1976; Perry and Kraemer, 1978; Agnew, Brown and Herr, 1978; and Feller, Menzel and Kozak, 1976). These concerns are not elaborated in the present book, but aspects of them are occasionally alluded to in making a point.

2 In the field of marketing, for example, innovation diffusion is seen as a topic in *consumer behavior* (Robertson, 1971; Midgley, 1977), rather than as a topic in *distribution* and *logistics* which pertain to supply considerations, the concern of this book.

3 Success of this sort is the result of a social and political process, as well as of intellectual merit, and it would be extremely interesting to trace the history of the application of the adoption paradigm, with the goal of illuminating this facet of social science effectiveness. Work somewhat related to this type of question is Littlewood's (1977) study of population policies in the United States. Other illustrations of this point include the tenacity in the Soviet Union of Lysenko's theory that acquired characteristics could be passed on to future generations through birth, and the difficulties associated with acceptance in the United States of Darwin's theory of the evolution of the human race. For a general discussion on the intermixing of scientific and societal concerns, see Rich (1979).

4 For other reviews see Jones (1967); Katz, Levin and Hamilton (1963); Robertson (1971); Midgley (1977); and Chapter 2 of this book. More current and sometimes jaundiced views of diffusion research can be found in Feller (1979); Kelly and Kransberg (1978); and Radnor, Feller and Rogers (1978).

2

DIFFUSION RESEARCH IN GEOGRAPHY: A THEMATIC ACCOUNT

While geographers have studied diffusion processes throughout most of this century, the focus of that effort has shifted over time, mirroring the broader concerns of the discipline as a whole. Many of these shifts have entailed dramatic departures from the prevailing norm of diffusion research and a change in the course of study. The work of Hagerstrand in the early 1950s is an example. As a consequence, diffusion studies of the cultural geographer early in this century are hardly recognizable as being of the same genre as more recent studies which focus on the role of entrepreneurial agents in the diffusion of innovation.

The object of this chapter is to provide a historical perspective on our study of diffusion, giving particular attention to the developments set in motion by the work of Hagerstrand. In part the concern is with what we have learned, but just as important is how such knowledge has been gained and what research problems (questions) have been deemed worthwhile.

This chapter is divided into six major sections. The first deals with the cultural geography tradition of diffusion study, an antecedent of the chapter's central focus. Attention then turns to the work of Hagerstrand, wherein both his operational and conceptual contributions are summarized. The next two sections trace the research trends in the twenty-five plus years since Hagerstrand, focusing first upon efforts related to operational models of diffusion and then upon efforts related to the conceptual model of diffusion. The fifth section takes a broader view of spatial diffusion research in terms of a philosophy of science perspective and the overall trends of the geography discipline. The chapter concludes by discussing ambiguities in diffusion research which result from confounding geographic scale, process and form. The skeleton of the ensuing discussion is presented in Figure 2.1, which summarizes the progress of diffusion research in geography.

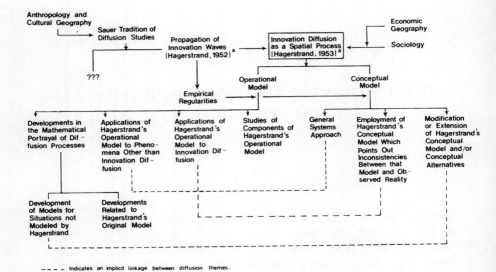

- - - - Indicates an implicit linkage between diffusion themes.

Figure 2.1   Diffusion Research in Geography: Themes and Their Interrelationships
[a]These refer to particular works by Hagerstrand.

THE CULTURAL GEOGRAPHY TRADITION OF DIFFUSION RESEARCH

Diffusion has been the subject of geographic enquiry for several decades. The spread of a phenomenon, idea or technique throughout a population or region incorporates basic geographic elements of distance, direction and spatial variation, and thus forms a valid field of geographic interest. The most immediate approach from which present-day work descends was generated within the context of cultural geography, whose research goal is

to identify environmental features characteristic of a given culture and if possible to discover what role human action plays or has played in creating and maintaining given geographic features. (P.L. Wagner and Mikesell, 1962: 1)

Culture and the human or cultural *landscape* are the main concern, and diffusion studies are relevant in so far as they clarify questions concerning culture origins, the spatial configuration of culture areas and culture-related or culture-influenced features on the earth's surface. Carl Sauer is generally recognized as the central figure in this approach, which tends to be closely aligned with and complementary to some concerns of anthropology (Mikesell, 1967, 1978).

Many studies within this framework, such as those of Bobek (1962) and Stanislawski (1949), are formulated within the context of the controversy regarding the relative importance of *diffusion* or *simulta-*

neous invention in the development of the cultural landscape. They demonstrate a strong bias towards an empirical, inductive approach with emphasis upon landscape development in prehistory and over a considerable period of time. Often the investigation considers a single phenomenon, which is seen as a culture trait, and attempts to explain its observed spatial distribution as the outcome of a process unfolding over space and time.[1] A typical procedure is to examine a phenomenon's spatial distribution at different times or its frequency of occurrence at different locations at a single time. From these observations inferences are drawn regarding origins, means, and routes of dispersal of both the observed phenomenon and the culture traits, ideas or techniques for which it is a surrogate (Sauer, 1952; Edmonson, 1961; Seidenberg, 1960; Hagerstrand, 1952; Harlan and Zohary, 1966). Attention also is given to the particular cultural and environmental conditions necessary for the adoption of a particular phenomenon (Stanislawski, 1949; Seidenberg, 1960).

In stressing the role of diffusion in the development of the human landscape, however, many studies within the cultural geography tradition proceed further to consider the indirect effects of the culture trait innovation on the physical and cultural environment. A notion basic to their discussion is that the diffusing item is both a stimulus to new innovation and itself subject to modification as it spreads from its point of origin. The relation between diffusion, the item being diffused and the human landscape is therefore complex and subject to continual change. One result of this view is an emphasis upon describing these ever-changing relationships, rather than upon understanding the specific processes by which the item moves from one location to another.

The directions of contemporary diffusion research in the cultural geography tradition are not apparent to this author. Hence, they have been indicated by a series of question marks in the flow diagram of the themes of diffusion research in geography (Figure 2.1). It is noteworthy, however, that the recent study by Hannemann (1975) on the diffusion of the Reformation in south-western Germany from 1518 through 1534 touches on many of the themes of concern to other geographers currently carrying on diffusion research, and Mikesell (1978: 10) indicates that this may be typical.

HAGERSTRAND ON THE DIFFUSION OF INNOVATION

Sauer's counterpart in the research of primary concern to this review is Torsten Hagerstrand, whose work of the early 1950s initiated a shift in focus towards the generative processes underlying diffusion. Since this focus is not inconsistent with Sauer's conceptualization of diffusion, it is interesting to speculate why it was not a major topic of research at an earlier date. One reason may be that the identification and definition of specific processes controlling locational change are less feasible in the sparsely documented situations studied by cultural geographers.[2] Second, and perhaps more important, the main impact of Hagerstrand's work was on researchers trained in economic and urban geography who were primarily concerned with location and locational processes rather than landscape. Whatever the reason, however, the shift has been extensive. Illustrative of this is Haggett's (1965: 10–13) classification of research workers of the Sauer school as predominantly *landscapists* or *ecologists* and research workers of the Hagerstrand school as *locationalists*.[3]

Hagerstrand's research (1952, 1953, 1965a, 1965b, 1967a, 1967b) focuses upon the diffusion of manufactured innovations (where the word 'manufactured' is used to distinguish the diffusion of, say, tractors from the diffusion of ideas or behavior patterns). His first study, *The Propagation of Innovation Waves* (1952), is an evident continuation of the earlier cultural geography tradition (Figure 2.1) by its use of a primarily inductive approach and its concern with diffusion patterns rather than diffusion processes. However, empirical study at a somewhat later date (1953) led Hagerstrand to observe that

The spatial order in the adoption of innovations is very often so striking that it is tempting to try to create theoretical models which simulate the process and eventually make certain predictions achievable. (Hagerstrand, 1967b:7)

This statement is indicative of a change of emphasis in Hagerstrand's work from description and inductive generalization to a more deductive approach focusing on generative processes. Concomitant with this we observe a willingness to draw broad, general conclusions from one or a few empirical examples that did not characterize the cultural geographers.[4] The basic work in this shift is Hagerstrand's PhD dissertation, completed in 1953 and translated into English under the title *Innovation Diffusion as a Spatial Process* (1967a) (Figure 2.1).

Hagerstrand made three contributions that even today, more than twenty-five years later, play a role in ongoing research activities. These are (1) a conceptualization of the diffusion of innovation process, (2) the development of a technique for operationalizing that conceptualization and (3) the identification of empirical regularities in diffusion (Figure 2.1). Brief consideration is now given to each of these contributions.

Hagerstrand's Conceptualization of the Diffusion Process

The basic tenet of Hagerstrand's conceptualization of the spread of innovation across the landscape is that the adoption of an innovation is primarily the outcome of a learning or communications process.[5] This implies that factors related to the *effective* flow of information are most critical and, therefore, that a fundamental step in examining the process of diffusion is identification of the spatial characteristics of information flows and resistances to adoption.

In Hagerstrand's conceptualization (Figure 1.3) information originates in the form of messages from the mass media or from existing adopters.[6] He posits that the destination of personal messages depends upon the sender's network of interpersonal contact or his *network of social communications*, and that the configuration of this network is primarily dependent on the presence of various social and terrestrial barriers which impede, divert and channel communications. Particular attention is given to terrestrial barriers such as lakes, forests, difficult terrain and the geographical distance separating two potential communicants.[7]

The conceptualization further recognizes that resistance levels differ from one individual to another, as a function of both personal and group characteristics, and that higher levels of resistance require more information for adoption to occur. Hagerstrand's discussion leads to a dichotomy of resistance as either the result of values which are inconsistent with adoption of the innovation (*social* resistance) or the result of practicalities which make adoption difficult or impossible (*economic* resistance).

Finally, to address the problem of diffusion at different geographical scales, a hierarchy of networks of social communication is posited. As an example, one network may operate locally and another regionally. The first of these would control diffusion among farmers in a single locale whereas diffusion at the central place level of aggregation might utilize a regional network comprised of persons in different central places that communicate with one another. The superimposition of these two levels would provide a comprehensive picture of diffusion in the area represented.

In summary, Hagerstrand's conceptualization proposes a transformation of a population from one with a low proportion of adopters to one with a high proportion of adopters by means of information dissemination through media and interpersonal contact. In a spatial frame of reference the principal mechanisms of this transformation are the networks of social communication which are characterized by biases and distortions that are reflected in the spatial patterns of innovation diffusion.

Hagerstrand's Methodological Framework

To implement the above conceptualization Hagerstrand used Monte Carlo simulation. Three models of varying complexity were developed. In the third, which is the most complex and best portrays Hagerstrand's conceptual model, only interpersonal communications are considered.[8] Adoption takes place after a specified number of messages are received, the specified number varying according to an individual's resistance to adoption.[9] Time is treated in discrete units of equal interval and each past adopter sends a message in every time interval. The destination of each message is dependent on the probability of contact between teller and potential receiver. This probability is a function of the distance between them unless water or forest barriers intervene. For the case in which distance only is considered, a distance decay function is employed to compute the probabilities of interaction between each of twenty-five cells in a five by five cell grid and the center cell of that grid, using the centers of each cell to compute the intervening distance (the probabilities within this grid sum to one).[10] The resulting grid of probabilities is termed the *mean information field* (MIF). It is employed with a map which is gridded in a similar manner, but with many more than twenty-five cells, by being centered over a map cell containing an adopter of the innovation at time t. A random number is then drawn to determine which of the twenty-five surrounding map cells receives a message to adopt in time $t+1$.[11] If the message passes over a water or forest barrier, it is either nullified or a new random number drawn, depending upon the nature of the barrier. This procedure is repeated for every adopter and for every time interval. If a previous adopter receives a message, the message is lost, that is, it has no effect and is not repeated; if a message is received by a non-adopter who, owing to his resistance level, requires more than one message before adoption, the message is stored until sufficient messages for adoption are accumulated (Figure 1.3).

Empirical Regularities in Diffusion

Three patterns generally have been associated with diffusion processes (Figures 2.2A, 2.2B, 2.2C). Over time, a graph of the cumulative level of adoption is expected to approximate an *S-shape*.

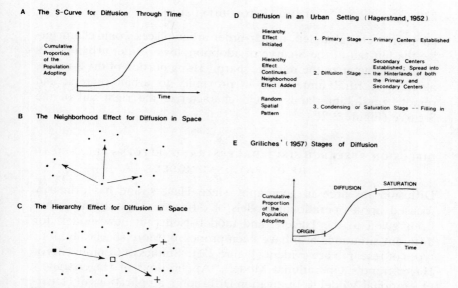

A The S-Curve for Diffusion Through Time

Cumulative Proportion of the Population Adopting

Time

B The Neighborhood Effect for Diffusion in Space

C The Hierarchy Effect for Diffusion in Space

D Diffusion in an Urban Setting (Hagerstrand, 1952)

Hierarchy Effect Initiated — 1. Primary Stage -- Primary Centers Established

Hierarchy Effect Continues Neighborhood Effect Added — 2. Diffusion Stage -- Secondary Centers Established; Spread into the Hinterlands of both the Primary and Secondary Centers

Random Spatial Pattern — 3. Condensing or Saturation Stage -- Filling in

E Griliches' (1957) Stages of Diffusion

Cumulative Proportion of the Population Adopting

ORIGIN   DIFFUSION   SATURATION

Time

Figure 2.2 Empirical Regularities in Diffusion
Note in E the congruence of Griliches' schema with that of Hagerstrand in D.

In an urban system, the diffusion is expected to proceed from larger to smaller centers, a regularity termed the *hierarchy effect*. Within the hinterland of a single urban center, diffusion is expected to proceed in a wave-like fashion outward from the urban center, first hitting nearby rather than farther-away locations, and a similar pattern is expected in diffusion among a rural population. This third regularity is termed the *neighborhood* or *contagion effect*.

While Hagerstrand (1952, 1967a) was not the first social scientist to identify these regularities, he is credited with introducing these concepts to the geography discipline.[12] He also provides a framework which makes evident the interrelationships among these regularities. For diffusion in a central place or urban system context, this posits three phases (Hagerstrand, 1952): a *primary* stage during which the initial diffusion centers are established; a *diffusion* stage during which neighborhood-type diffusion occurs in areas near diffusion centers and secondary diffusion centers are established in lower order urban places; and a *condensing* or *saturation* stage during which filling-in occurs and diffusion eventually ceases (Figure 2.2D).

This framework thus illustrates the complementarity of the hierarchy and neighborhood effects and their temporal positioning within the diffusion process. It also implies that, if the locales of

adopters were tabulated, higher-order urban places would characterize the left tail of the S-curve of adoption; lower-order urban places
would characterize the middle, sharply rising portion of the S-curve,
along with rural hinterlands in proximity to urban centers; and
remote rural hinterlands would characterize the right tail of the
S-curve (Figure 2.2E).[13]

DIFFUSION RESEARCH SINCE HAGERSTRAND: EFFORTS RELATED TO THE OPERATIONAL MODEL

Diffusion research in geography since Hagerstrand has primarily
focused upon operational models of diffusion. Most attention has
been given to the Hagerstrand model itself, but new models for
different situations also have been proposed. More specfically, four
types of research are evident (Figure 2.1): 'Studies of Components of
Hagerstrand's Operational Model', 'Applications of Hagerstrand's
Operational Model to Innovation Diffusion', 'Applications of Hagerstrand's Operational Model to Phenomena Other Than Innovation
Diffusion', and 'Developments in the Mathematical Portrayal of
Diffusion Processes'. Each of these is now considered.

Studies of Components of Hagerstrand's Operational Model

The mean information field (MIF) is the component of Hagerstrand's
operational model which has received most attention. Perhaps this is
because the MIF embodies the spatial dynamics of the model, being
the mechanism by which diffusion impulses are relocated from a
point of origin to a point of destination. One set of concerns has been
mechanistic. These have focused on the procedures for creating an
MIF from raw data, on the best mathematical function to represent
the attenuation of spatial interaction with distance or the *distance
decay* effect, and on the estimation of the goodness of fit between a
simulation produced by the MIF and its real world counterpart
(Morrill and Pitts, 1967; Marble and Nystuen, 1963; Shannon, 1970;
L.A. Brown and Moore, 1969; Haggett, Cliff and Frey, 1977: 244–
7).[14] The computer programming of the Hagerstrand model also has
received attention (Pitts, 1963), resulting in a number of software
packages that primarily vary only in their treatment of the MIF
mechanism (Pitts, 1965, 1967; Marble, 1967; Marble and Bowlby,
1968; Marble, Hanson, Huff, Manji and Pacheco, 1970). These
programs have, of course, made the Hagerstrand model readily
accessible and perhaps account in part for its widespread use.[15] Also

enhanced by programming developments are efforts to examine in an experimental setting the various diffusion patterns that result from different initial or ongoing conditions (Yuill, 1964; Morrill and Manninen, 1975; Haggett, Cliff and Frey, 1977: 242–4).

Substantive questions with regard to the MIF also have been raised. One of these concerns the type of surrogate to use in calibrating an MIF (Morrill and Pitts, 1967; Mayfield, 1967; Mayfield and Yapa, 1974; Shannon, 1970). Hagerstrand used telephone call data. Some other options explored are the distances between the pre-marriage residences of husbands and wives; distances between acquaintances; migration distances; and the distances of bus, commuting or shopping trips. Another substantive question concerns the nature of barriers other than geographic distance which shape the MIF and distort its symmetry. Yuill (1964) suggests that two properties of barriers are relevant: their shape (for example, parallel barriers, bar barriers with end gaps or bar barriers with a center gap) and their permeability (for example, absorbing, reflective or permeable). Directional distortions also have been investigated, particularly for urban contexts where a bias could be introduced by the location of an urban place or the central business district (Marble and Nystuen, 1963).

Application of Hagerstrand's Operational Model to Innovation Diffusion

The extent of the attention given to particular aspects of Hagerstrand's model is reflective of its importance and utility in the geography discipline of the 1960s. Not surprisingly, then, there are many examples of its application, both to the diffusion of innovation and to other diffusion or diffusion-like situations.[16]

Examples of studies dealing directly with innovation diffusion include Shannon (1970) on the diffusion of a community health care plan within Detroit, DeTemple (1971) on the diffusion of Harvestore storage systems in north-east Iowa, Johansen (1971) on the diffusion of strip cropping in south-western Wisconsin, Misra (1969) on the diffusion of agricultural innovations in Mysore, India, and Bowden (1965) on the diffusion of irrigation wells in the Colorado High plains.

To illustrate the approach of this line of research consider the Bowden study. This employed both a local communications field, based upon the distances traveled to attend a free barbecue in Yuma, Colorado, and a regional communications field, based upon long-distance telephone calls from Yuma. These were combined to form a single MIF, of circular rather than square shape, with possible contacts ranging from 1 to 40 miles. In addition, a ceiling on adoption or saturation level of sixteen wells per township was employed. Except for these minor variations, the model used by Bowden is similar to that of Hagerstrand. However, the fit of the similated diffusion pattern with the real diffusion pattern was quite good. Bowden was thus able to project the future adoption of irrigation wells and to estimate the rate of depletion of groundwater resources, a demonstration of the practical utility of the Hagerstrand model.

Applications of Hagerstrand's Operational Model to Phenomena Other Than Innovation Diffusion

In applying the Hagerstrand operational model to phenomena other than innovation diffusion, modification of the model generally has been slight, similar to the type of changes Bowden made and not such as to constitute a significant alteration. Phenomena examined in this way include migration (Hagerstrand, 1957; Cobb, 1971; Moore, 1966), the spread of the black ghetto (Morrill, 1965c) and the urban fringe (Morrill, 1965a), the spread and growth of urban centers in a settled area (Morrill, 1965b) and in a frontier area (Bylund, 1960; L.A. Brown and Albaum, 1971), intraurban travel (Nystuen, 1967) and transportation network growth (Garrison and Marble, 1965).

With regard to these efforts, L.A. Brown and Moore (1969: 143) have noted

most have applied the structure of Hagerstrand's operational model directly to their own problem, without significant modification to reflect the peculiarities of the process being studied. The result has been that relatively little has been learnt about the particular structure of each situation. The models contain sufficient parameters such that the observation that the simulated pattern is similar to the real world diffusion pattern can only lead to the conclusion that the suggested structure provides a *plausible* explanation of the real world processes . . . . Clearly, the research findings would be of greater interest if an attempt were made to determine if alternative structures are also plausible in the sense that they can be made to approximate the real world patterns.

In essence, then, the applications of the Hagerstrand model, either to innovation or to other diffusion phenomena, were accomplished without raising the question of whether the substantive assertions of the model (for example, that the process involved information flow or spatial interaction) were in conformance with the substantive reality of the processes being modeled.[17]

Developments in the Mathematical Portrayal of Diffusion Processes

Some developments in the mathematical portrayal of diffusion processes also have been directly concerned with the operational model of Hagerstrand. These efforts have been directed towards a more mathematically formal statement of the model, and often have involved the borrowing or restatement of models developed in the physical or biological sciences (D.L. Anderson, 1970, 1971; L.A. Brown, 1965, 1968b, 1970; Gale, 1972; Zeller and Brown, 1976). The majority of efforts, however, have focused upon diffusion involving urban places. Accordingly, they have proposed models that differ in operational structure from that of Hagerstrand, although the tenets of Hagerstrand's conceptual model generally are left unaltered.

The usual procedure in mathematical modeling since Hagerstrand is to take one or more of the empirical regularities as given and then to create a model which, as at least one outcome, will reproduce that regularity.[18] D.L. Anderson's (1970) model of local diffusion and Webber's (1972: 222–63) more general model, for example, produce an S-shaped curve which is cited as partial verification. Similarly, Morrill's (1968, 1970) wave model of diffusion utilizes the neighborhood effect regularity related to diffusion outward from an urban center, as do Casetti and Semple (1969) and Webber (1972: 222–63). For diffusion in an urban system, Boon (1967) utilizes the hierarchy effect regularity, while Berry (1972), Hudson (1969b) and Pedersen (1970, 1975) utilize the combination of hierarchy effect and neighborhood effect postulated earlier by Hagerstrand (1952).

To illustrate this line of research more extensively, consider the model of Berry (1972: 109–17) for diffusion among a set of urban places (or within an urban system). This is designed to account for the time at which an innovation first appears in a given town j, relative to the time of its appearance in other towns. This time order of diffusion, indicated by the magnitude of F in equation (2.1) below,

is a function of its [a town's] own rank [or population] in the urban hierarchy, and the force exerted on it [through communications or otherwise] by virtue of its location relative to other centers in the hierarchy that have already adopted the innovation. (Berry, 1972: 114–15)

The model itself, in population form, is

$$K'P_j \sum_{i=1}^{n} P_i(1/e^{\beta s_{ij}}) \geqslant F \qquad (2.1)$$

where

P_j is the population of town j
s_{ij} is the distance between towns i and j
K' is a scale parameter
x, β are parameters reflecting the effect (or friction) of distance
F is the threshold level of force (through communications or otherwise) pertaining to the innovation.

In this model, the force exerted on j from other centers i through interaction is indicated by the term $P_i(1/e^{\beta s_{ij}^x})$, a variation of a gravity model formulation. Thus, if the parameter x and/or β is very large, there is a high friction of distance, the interaction effect is diminished, diffusion is largely on the basis of the rank of j (indicated by P_j in equation (2.1)), and a hierarchical pattern would be observed. Alternatively, if x and β are at or near zero, interaction becomes a significant force in the diffusion, the pattern of which would then exhibit a combination of hierarchy and neighborhood effects. Note, however, that the variance in possible outcomes is considerably increased if interurban contact is not assumed to follow a gravity model formulation, a modification well supported by recent empirical evidence and conceptual arguments pertaining to innovation diffusion (L.A. Brown, 1975; Pred, 1973b, 1975a) and elaborated in this book.

A second interesting aspect of Berry's model is its link with urban systems theory. The value of F, for example, sets a threshold limit below which diffusion would not occur. This relates to the threshold concept of central place theory, and accordingly, higher values of F would be expected for higher-order innovations and visa versa. Berry's model can be more directly linked to the mathematical theory of urban systems by replacing P_i and P_j with their rank size rule equivalent, $P_r = K(1/r^q)$, where P_r is the population of a town of rank r. This yields

$$(K'K^2)(1/r_j^q) \sum_{i=1}^{n} (1/r_i^q e^{\beta s_{ij}^x}) \geq F \qquad (2.2)$$

Finally, rather than dealing in relative time as indicated by the order of adoption, Berry demonstrates how his model could be linked to real time. This can be accomplished by fitting a logistic function to the actual S-curve of diffusion, and then employing this function to generate the number of adoptions for any given real time interval such as a single year.[19]

Concern with the operational model dominated diffusion research of the 1960s. While the contributions of this work to modeling techniques in geography were considerable, it led at best to a modest increase in our substantive knowledge of diffusion processes. In 1970 the accepted conceptual model was still that of Hagerstrand, proposed nearly twenty years earlier. Since then, however, there has been a dramatic shift towards substantive and conceptual concerns (Figure 2.1). That shift is documented in this section. The first topic is the effort to set diffusion within a general systems framework. Attention then turns to largely empirical research which suggests a number of inconsistencies between observed reality and the Hagerstrand model. The final topic of this section is work that addresses those inconsistencies and proposes conceptual alternatives and/or modifications to the Hagerstrand paradigm.

General Systems Approach

A general systems perspective is evident in L.A. Brown's (1968b) observation that many different phenomena involving movement (for example, innovation, migration, travel, trade or industrial movements) may be examined within a diffusion framework.[20] The framework he proposes is based on the isomorphism that all such situations consist of six basic elements: (1) an area or environment, (2) a temporal dimension, (3) an item being diffused, (4) places in which the item is located at the start of a time interval (nodes of origin), (5) places in which the item is newly located at the end of a time interval (nodes of destination), and (6) paths of movement, influence or relationship between origin places and destination places (edges).

The last four elements are represented as a dynamic graph set in a temporal geographic space (the first two elements). This is illustrated in Figure 2.3 for *relocation-type diffusion,* in which some members of the population change their locations from times t to $t+1$, and for *expansion-* or *contagion-type diffusion,* in which new members are added to the population between times t and $t+1$ and locate so as to alter the population's locational pattern. It is suggested that a relatively small set of characteristics of each of the six basic elements and a few general principles may prove satisfactory for the analysis of diffusion processes as well as other types of movement in geographic

Relocation - Type Diffusion

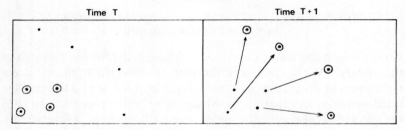

Expansion - Type Diffusion

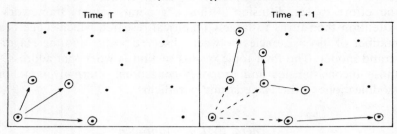

• Indicates a potential location of the diffusing phenomenon

⊙ Indicates an actual location of the diffusing phenomenon during the time indicated

•——➤• Indicates that during the indicated time a stimulus passed from the node at the origin end of the arrow to the node at the destination end, and resulted in location of the diffusing phenomenon at the destination node

•– – ➤• Indicates that the stimulus represented in •——➤ • passed during a time period previous to the one indicated

Figure 2.3   Diffusion Portrayed as a Dynamic Graph

space, thus providing a basis for a general theory of spatial diffusion or movement.

Inconsistencies Between Observed Reality and the Hagerstrand Model

The general systems approach outlined above leads to the expectation of a coalescence in the work of geographers studying diffusion and those studying the dynamic aspects of other phenomena. This has in fact occurred, though not in the way envisioned (L.A. Brown, 1968b), and one outcome has been to point up inconsistencies between observed reality and the Hagerstrand model.

One strand of the coalescence is comprised of work which employs diffusion theory in another, usually broader context such as growth pole and regional development processes (Berry, 1972; L.A. Brown,

1974; Morrill, 1974; Thomas, 1974; Riddell, 1970), spatial decision-making (Wolpert, 1964), and urban system development (Pred, 1973a, 1973b; Robson, 1973: L.A. Brown and Malecki, 1977). To illustrate, the diffusion of technical innovations and of entrepreneurial or other organizational entities have been seen as an important element underlying differential growth rates among urban areas (Pred, 1966). This has then led to accounting for and modeling the evolution of the urban landscape by drawing upon the conclusions of diffusion research that hierarchy and neighborhood effects characterize the diffusion of entrepreneurial and other organizational entities; that information transfer is a critical element underlying these diffusions; and that models incorporating population and distance components, such as the gravity model, suffice to account for the patterns of spread (Robson, 1973). Recently, however, L.A. Brown and Malecki (1977: 222) suggest that

to account for the diffusion underpinnings of landscape evolution, the simplistic population and distance notions of traditional diffusion models are not adequate . . . [instead] it appears certain that we must look toward the organizational decision making process, which often involves turning to the unique institutional setting in which such decisions are made.

This topic will be given further attention in Chapter 8.

A second strand of the coalescence in the work of diffusion researchers and that of geographers studying the dynamic aspects of other phenomena originates in the *time geography* of Hagerstrand and his research associates (Pred, 1973c: 36–50; Carlstein, Parkes and Thrift, 1978a, 1978b, 1978c; Hagerstrand, 1974; Carlstein, 1978). This notes

Innovations affect the use of resources in space and over time. Some innovations serve to increase capacity and release a certain resource, while other innovations require additional inputs of human time, settlement space(-time), water and energy, and so on. And each of these resources is made available in certain time-space locations. (Carlstein, 1978: 149)

Accordingly, an *activity systems* perspective is advocated wherein adoption is viewed in the context of the time budgets and the social, economic and personal resources characterizing the milieu or locale of the potential adopter(s), and the innovation's impact upon or congruence wih these is a critical element in diffusion. From the time geography perspective, then, innovation diffusion research of the past has tended to be narrow in its focus upon single innovations and communications processes related to adoption.

Several examples of the application of this perspecive are provided by Carlstein (1978: 150–8). The introduction of formal schooling to an agrarian society is a *time-demanding* innovation that takes children away from their tasks in the village production process, so that acceptance should be inhibited. However, if electric light, which is *time expanding* in that it extends the day, also were introduced, the school would compete less with the scarce production time resource, and acceptance would be more likely. Alternatively, grinding mills, which replace manual grinding of grain into flour, also are *time expanding* in that they allow completion of other tasks by freeing up daylight time. Also important is both the *synchronization* and *synchorization* of resource inputs related to an innovation, that is, resource inputs must be available both *when* and *where* they are needed. Finally, some innovations, such as the motor car, create *flexibility* in time and space, which increases their likely impact upon time-space systems.

Finally, a third strand of coalescence in the work of diffusion researchers and that of geographers studying the dynamic aspects of other phenomena originates from empirical research on diffusion itself. This finds a number of situations for which Hagerstrand's conceptual model is at best a partial explanation, and ultimately leads to the consideration of factors other than information flows. Wilbanks (1972), for example, raises the question of whether interpersonal communications or transportation infrastructure is more important in accounting for innovation diffusion at the regional scale in India. Later, this question is addressed directly by L.A. Brown and Lentnek (1973), using a Mexican example, with the conclusion that infrastructure is more important. Likewise, Shawyer's (1970, 1974) examination of the establishment of purchasing cooperatives in rural Britian, along with the studies of Yapa (1975) and Hudson (1972), provides evidence that the communications process in innovation diffusion is not spatially patterned in the way suggested by Hagerstrand's conceptualization.

L.A. Brown (1968a, 1969) goes yet one step further by suggesting that the shopping trip behavior of potential adopters and the marketing strategy of the propagators of innovation are more important determinants of diffusion patterns at the regional scale. Related to this latter suggestion are studies of the diffusion of organizational entities that disseminate innovations (Y.S. Cohen, 1972; Sheppard, 1976; Webber and Joseph, 1977; Pedersen, 1970, 1975; Hanham and Brown, 1972) and the strategies employed in their location (Meyer, 1975). Berry (1972: 112–13), for example, observes

Several possible reasons for hierarchical filtering can be posited, among them a *market-searching* process in which an expanding industry exploits market opportunities in a larger-to-smaller sequence, a *trickle-down* process in which an activity faced with rising wage rates in larger cities moves to smaller cities in search of cheaper labor, and *imitation* process in which entrepreneurs in smaller centers mimic the actions of those in larger cities, or a simple probability mechanism in which the probability of adoption depends upon the chance that a potential entrepreneur residing in a given town will learn of the innovation, a probability which declines with size of town.

Together, these raise the prospect that diffusion patterns may in large part be explained by entrepreneurial actions rather than social interaction. This latter point is argued explicitly by L.A. Brown, Malecki and Spector (1976) and by L.A. Brown and Cox (1971) who also question the degree to which the S-curve, hierarchy effect and neighborhood effect are in fact pattern regularities associated with innovation diffusion.

Modification and Extension of Hagerstrand's Conceptual Model

The identification of inconsistencies between observed reality and the Hagerstrand model has led to two distinct conceptual developments in innovation diffusion research (Figure 2.4). One of these, the *market and infrastructure perspective,* is concerned with the diffusion process itself on the supply side. In particular, focus is upon the potential adopter's access to innovations or the way in which innovations are differentially made available to various social, economic or locational categories of potential adopters. The concatenation of this perspective with the adoption perspective of Hagerstrand is diagramed in Figure 1.3. The second line of conceptual thinking, the *development perspective,* is concerned with the impact of diffusion processes, particularly upon individual welfare, economic development and social change, as well as the ways in which the level of development itself affects innovation diffusion.

Since these recent developments are discussed in great detail in the remaining chapters of this book and were summarized in Chapter 1, they will not be elaborated further at this point. Before closing this chapter, however, it is useful to consider how the developments in diffusion research, documented above, are a mirror of the discipline as a whole.

DIFFUSION RESEARCH IN GEOGRAPHY AS A MIRROR OF THE DISCIPLINE

The above discussion indicates that diffusion research in geography since Hagerstrand primarily has been concerned with the operational

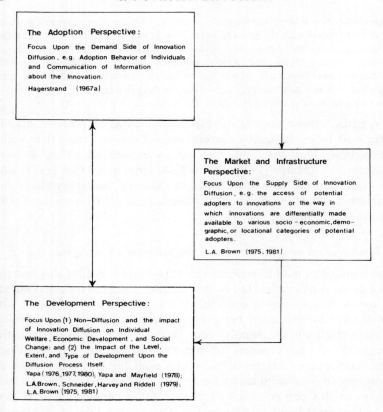

The Adoption Perspective :

Focus Upon the Demand Side of Innovation Diffusion , e.g. Adoption Behavior of Individuals and Communication of Information about the Innovation.

Hagerstrand   (1967a)

The Market and Infrastructure Perspective :

Focus Upon the Supply Side of Innovation Diffusion , e.g. the access of potential adopters to innovations or the way in which innovations are differentially made available to various socio − economic, demo- graphic, or locational categories of potential adopters .

L.A. Brown   (1975 , 1981)

The Development Perspective :

Focus Upon (1) Non—Diffusion and the impact of Innovation Diffusion on Individual Welfare , Economic Development , and Social Change; and (2) the Impact of the Level, Extent, and Type of Development Upon the Diffusion Process Itself.
Yapa (1976 ,1977, 1980); Yapa and Mayfield (1978); L.A.Brown , Schneider , Harvey and Riddell (1979) ; L.A. Brown (1975, 1981)

Figure 2.4   Dimensions of Contemporary Geographical Work on Innovation Diffusion

model of diffusion. This focus coincides with a broader trend in geography and other social science disciplines characterized as the *quantitative revolution*. Recognizing this fosters the observation that diffusion research was also an important medium of the *revolution*. Futher, the recent shift towards the conceptual model of diffusion coincided with a disciplinary shift towards a concern with substantive reality, relevance and societal utility (Taaffe, 1974; King, 1976, Peet, 1975; D. Harvey, 1974).[21] These shifts and their manifestations in day-to-day research are illustrative of the research process itself.

To elaborate this point, it is useful to employ Kuhn's (1970) idea about *paradigms* and their importance to *normal* science. These foster a coherent tradition of scientific research by suggesting which experiments or intellectual exercises are worth performing, by directing research towards given goals, and by providing both a set of rules and standards for scientific practice and a consensus that eliminates the unproductive work of dealing with controversy about the legitimacy of the paradigm. In Kuhn's own words,

The success of a paradigm . . . is at the start largely a promise of success discoverable in selected and still incomplete examples. Normal science consists in the actualization of that promise, an actualization achieved by extending the knowledge of those facts that the paradigm displays as particularly revealing, by increasing the extent of the match between those facts and the paradigm's predictions, and by further articulation of the paradigm itself. (1970: 23–4)

Yet, the existence of a paradigm also implies the existence of barriers to the development of alternative paradigms

To a great extent these are the only problems that the community will admit as scientific or encourage its members to undertake. Other problems, including many that had previously been standard, are rejected as metaphysical, as the concern of another discipline, or sometimes as just too problematic to be worth the time. A paradigm can, for that matter, even insulate the community from those socially important problems that are not reducible to the puzzle form, because they cannot be stated in terms of the conceptual and instrumental tools the paradigm supplies. (Kuhn, 1970: 37)

How, then, does change occur in science?

they [discoveries] are not isolated events but extended episodes with a regularly recurrent structure. Discovery commences with the awareness of anomaly, i.e. with the recognition that nature has somehow violated the paradigm-induced expectations. . . . It [discovery] then continues with a more or less extended exploration of the area of anomaly. And it closes only when the paradigm theory has been adjusted so that the anomalous has become the expected. (Kuhn, 1970: 52–3)

Thus, the paradigm incorporates a mechanism for its own replacement or alteration by providing expectations that are also the background against which anomaly is recognizable. In this way, the scientist learns to see nature in a different way.

Kuhn's framework is best applied to physical science, but, while not doctrinaire, his ideas can be stretched to encompass the social science efforts reviewed in this chapter. Thus, the quanitative revolution embracing the tenets of logical positivism may be seen to represent a *paradigm* about the research procedure itself, dictating matters pertaining to research tools, the questions asked and substantiation required (Amedeo and Golledge, 1975; Burton, 1968). On a lesser scale, the Hagerstrand model may be seen to represent a *paradigm* pertaining to a segment of substantive reality. The Sauer school of diffusion study also embraces a *paradigm*, although one that has not been set out in explicit terms as have the Hagerstrand model and quantitative geography.

To illustrate the shifts among these foci of diffusion studies, Table 2.1 compares articles epitomizing the Sauer school, the transition from that to the Hagerstrand tradition, the Hagerstrand tradition itself and the market and infrastructure perspective. The critical change, illustrative of the *paradigm* shift on the substantive level, is in the dominant process posited, discussed in earlier sections of this chapter. But changes representative of the methodological shift of the discipline also have occurred, and are manifest in the research methods employed and the type and the generality of findings. There also are shifts in the type of situation studied.

Without Kuhn's view of normal science, and with the *benefit* of hindsight, the extensive work embracing the Hagerstrand model might be deemed myopic and ill directed. However, the effort seems reasonable when viewed as an elaboration of the dominant paradigm, which required the discovery of an anomaly (between that model and substantive reality) before the research direction could be altered. How is anomaly discovered?

In the case of the shift to the market and infrastructure model, the anomaly was recognized by trying to apply the Hagerstrand conceptual model to diffusion at a regional scale (L.A. Brown, 1968a: 30–42; 1969: 189–95). Using a hypothetical situation it was concluded that

as the result of circumstances . . . not considered by current spatial diffusion theory . . . an understanding of innovation adoption must . . . consider the shopping trip behavior of the potential adopter. Furthermore, it must also consider the distribution policies of the propagator of the innovation, since it is necessary to know whether a market utilized by the potential adopter is one chosen as a distribution point by the propagator. (L.A. Brown, 1969: 192)

Later, Hanham and Brown (1976: 70) draw upon empirical evidence to note

it seems improbable that the speed of information transfer could have accounted for the fact that it took three or four years for the diffusion wave to reach areas between 20 and 30 kilometers from the original centers.[22]

Nevertheless, it was at least a full six years after the observation of this anomaly that the perspective of the market and infrastructure model came to be accepted. In part, this period represents the *extended-exploration-of-the-area-of-anomaly* step of the paradigm

Table 2.1   A Comparison of Articles Epitomizing the Major Foci of Diffusion Research in Geography

	Sauer school of diffusion study (Stanislanski, 1949; Harlan and Zohary, 1966)	Transition (Hagerstrand, 1952)	Hagerstrand tradition of diffusion study (Hagerstrand, 1953, 1967a)	Market and infrastructure context of innovation adoption and diffusion (L.A. Brown, 1975)
Type of situation studied	Ancient, e.g. the Grid-pattern town and wild wheats and barley	Modern, e.g. the automobile	Modern, e.g. bovine tuberculosis vaccine plus others	Modern, e.g. market products and services
Research methods employed	Qualitative analysis of available documents and cartography	Cartography	Cartography, statistical analysis and mathematical modeling	Qualitative analysis via case studies, economic analysis, cartography, statistical analysis and mathematical modeling
Type and generality of findings	Findings pertain to both diffusion pattern and diffusion process, but applied only to the phenomena being considered	Findings pertain to diffusion pattern only, but seen to apply in general to innovation diffusion in urban systems	Findings pertain to both diffusion pattern and process, and are seen to apply in general to innovation diffusion at all spatial scales	Findings pertain to both diffusion pattern and process, and are seen to apply in general to innovation diffusion at all spatial scales
Dominant process posited	None	None	Communications	Marketing and infrastructure development

shift process, and overcoming the expected resistance to change. However, this period also corresponds with the broader shift in disciplinary focus from the quantitative revolution to a concern with relevance or societal utility and substantive reality (Taaffe, 1974; King, 1976).

Thus, the market and infrastructure model can be seen to play a role in the present focus of the discipline, just as the Hagerstrand model can be viewed as a medium of the quantitative revolution. It is likely, in fact, that such a congruency was a prerequisite to the widespread acceptance of either model, that is, that the extensive elaboration of the market and infrastructure paradigm that has recently taken place would not have occurred without the concomitant shift in disciplinary focus.

Another consideration is illustrated by the shift from the cultural geography paradigm of diffusion to that of Hagerstrand. It appears to this author that this had less to do with the study of innovation adoption *per se* than with the quantitative revolution, and that serendipity played a role. In March through June 1959, Hagerstrand spent an academic quarter at the University of Washington with William Garrison and his students, Morrill, Getis, Marble, Nystuen, Bunge, Tobler and Dacey, among others. These were economic and urban geographers who would later be largely responsible for the quantitative revolution. In this context, one might speculate what would have happened to diffusion research and the *revolution* had Hagerstrand instead visited Berkeley, the seat of cultural geography and largely substantively oriented diffusion research.

One final note. In this section and throughout this chapter there has been a tendency to refer to the various models or perspectives as though they were discontinuous and mutually exclusive of one another, the earlier being replaced by the latter. While this is convenient for expository purposes, in reality the process of change is more one wherein the new development represents a reaction to the old but also incorporates it. To illustrate, the market and infrastructure pradigm may be seen as a reaction to that of Hagerstrand, but in actuality the former offers an alternative explanation for innovation diffusion that defines the domain of the Hagerstrand model rather than replaces it. The result is two complementary models, each primarily applicable at different geographic scales (Figure 1.3). Likewise, the development perspective provides an elaboration of both the Hagerstrand and market and infrastructure models.

What we look for eventually, of course, is a truly integrated model that combines all three perspectives. This task will be addressed in the remainder of this book, but first it is necessary to sort out some ambiguities related to the way in which our ideas on diffusion have evolved. Specifically, these ambiguities result from a confounding of geographic scale, process and form, which may in part be traced to the disciplinary preoccupation with *pattern* or *form* in the quantitative revolution era and with *process* or *substantive reality* in the current era. Attention now turns to this topic.

THE CONES OF RESOLUTION PROBLEM IN DIFFUSION RESEARCH

The diffusion of innovation is the product of a number of human decisions. These decisions are attributable to entities such as individuals, households, diffusion agencies, corporation managements or governmental bodies and have manifestations in the form of spatial patterns of diffusion appearing at local, regional, national or other spatial scales. From the geographer's perspective, therefore, scale in diffusion research takes on at least *two* dimensions: the *functional*, reflecting decisions made by different aggregations of individuals, and the *spatial*, reflecting manifestations of these decisions as may be observed within a spatial context. This distinction (or dichotomy) has not always been recognized in the geographic literature, with the result that our notions of scale in diffusion of innovation contain a number of inconsistencies. This section aims at a clarification of the concept of scale as it relates to the spatial diffusion of innovation, and resolves existing inconsistencies by articulating a framework within which the broad spectrum of innovation diffusion situations may be placed.

The Concept of Scale

Recent spatial diffusion research has utilized the terms 'macro', 'meso' and 'micro' scale. Distinguishing scale differences such as these is seen by Beer (1968) to be a normal activity of scientific investigation, which he terms the *cones of resolution* problem. He argues that all complex systems are composed of a variety of subsystems, each of which is composed of a multitude of details, and that the key in scientific research is to identify meaningful scales of analysis so as to enable focusing on those aspects of the system which will lead to a more complete understanding of the overall process. However, the application of this approach in spatial diffusion research has resulted in confusion as to whether the *functional scale*, *spatial scale*, or both is being referenced.

Gould (1969: 25–68), for example, discusses recent diffusion studies in terms of Beerian cones of resolution defined by a *spatial* perspective. The scales involved vary from the individual or micro scale to the national/international or macro scale.

The micro scale is exemplified in Gould (1969: 26–38) by the diffusion of pasture improvement subsidies and TB control of dairy cattle in central Sweden, by tractors in rural America spreading from the flat wheat lands of North Dakota, by the spread of hybrid corn from Iowa through the entire corn belt and by the spread of irrigation wells in Colorado.

As one moves up the cones of resolution and examines diffusion processes at larger *spatial* scales, individual effects tend to be blurred and smoothed (Gould, 1969: 41). For example, while the diffusion of pioneer settlement over an area is the result of a myriad of individual decisions, there is considerable regularity and order in the aggregate pattern, and we find similar patterns of movement of people across Pennsylvania at different times, going as far back as the colonial era (Gould, 1969: 45–7). Another example comes from northern Tanzania where cotton-marketing cooperatives spread rapidly over a fifteen-year period and then became a conduit for political ideas that eventually led to independence (Gould, 1969: 47–50).

A further shift in *spatial* scale could bring us to the national and international. Gould (1969: 50–5) cites as examples the innovations of domestic agriculture, the railway, and Rotary International moving to surrounding nations from hearth areas in, respectively, Asia Minor, England and the United States. Examples at the national level (Gould, 1969: 55–68) include the diffusion of radio broadcasting, banking, classical town names, presidential sufferage for women and divorce reform throughout the United States; the spread of local governmental administration and modernization in Sierra Leone; and the spread of roads in Ghana.

Brown (L.A. Brown, 1968a, 1969, 1975; L.A. Brown and Cox, 1971; L.A. Brown and Lentnek, 1973), on the other hand, stresses consideration of the mechanisms generating the various diffusions. Two types of decision are noted: those pertaining to the establishment of diffusion agencies and those pertaining to the strategies by which the diffusion agency reaches the individual adopter. In the context of reported empirical research the first primarily relates to studies of diffusion across nations and within urban systems, and the second primarily relates to studies of diffusion within the hinterland of a single urban center. Consequently, Brown also employs the terms 'macro scale' and 'meso scale' and views as 'micro scale' processes directly related to individual adoption decisions. Examples include the diffusion of commercial dairying within the rural hinterland of a single urban center (L.A. Brown and Lentnek, 1973) as meso scale, and the diffusion of hybrid corn throughout the United States (L.A. Brown and Lentnek, 1973) and of television receivers through a central place system in Sweden as macro scale (L.A. Brown, 1968a, 1969).

Thus, Brown and Gould differ in the basis for distinguishing between macro, meso and micro scales—for Brown the *functional* aspect is critical; for Gould, the *spatial*. Were there a perfect correlation between the spatial and functional scales, the difference would not be a problem, but this is not the case. We find, for example, agency establishment processes operating in a range of spatial scales—in single urban hinterlands, among towns in a localized area, among towns nationally and among nations. Further illustration of the importance of distinguishing the *functional* and *spatial scales* is provided by three examples from the recent spatial diffusion literature.

First, Gould (1969: 25–6) portrays the micro scale as involving

spread through a social communications network linking individuals to one another.

or as when

the innovation and ideas diffuse from individual to individual.

Thus, the diffusion of tractors and hybrid corn are designated as micro scale phenomena because they involve individual decisions, and the spread of banking is presented as macro scale because it swept the entire nation. Yet, all three innovations—tractors, banking and hybrid corn—spread to all parts of the nation, and the adoption of each of the three also involves individual decisions.

Second, to speak of the meso scale problem as one that involves the hinterland of a single urban center (L. A. Brown and Lentnek, 1973) does not consider the fact that the center could be Tokyo with its world-wide hinterland as well as a Midwestern farm community with its more localized hinterland. Likewise, with regard to the macro scale, the diffusion of an innovation across the United States is not necessarily functionally the same as diffusion across Sweden or Sierra Leone.

Finally, neighborhood effect diffusion patterns have been most often associated with a communications process at the micro scale. The same pattern also may appear at the macro or meso scale, but there it has been associated with marketing strategies that constitute an entirely different process (L.A. Brown and Lentnek, 1973; L.A. Brown, 1975).

These examples illustrate the importance of articulating a framework within which ambiguities such as those noted can be resolved. Doing so involves separating considerations of pattern and process, and asking how the various spatial patterns—neighborhood, hierarchical or random—interrelate with elements of both the spatial and functional scales. Attention now turns to this task.

An Alternative Framework for Viewing Cones of Resolution in Diffusion Studies

As noted, geographers (as well as other social scientists) have articulated two perspectives on innovation diffusion. The first is the *functional perspective* which encompasses the mechanisms and decisions that drive the diffusion process to its various outcomes. The second is the *spatial perspective* which encompasses one manifestation of the functional.[23] These are indicated in Figure 2.5, where cells with a letter designation F are associated with the functional perspective and those with S the spatial perspective.

The Functional Perspective.[24] L.A. Brown and Cox (1971) argue that innovation diffusion situations may be subdivided into two major categories according to whether (or not) there is a propagator with an interest in the rapid and complete diffusion of the innovation, observing that this distinction is consistent with behavioral realities (cells F.PS and F.NPS of Figure 2.5). Propagator-supported innovations, which constitute the focus of this book, are typified by commercial products and services such as Volkswagen, Harvestore Silo or BankAmericard. Non-propagator-supported innovations are typified by culture traits.

An important behavior of propagators is the establishment of agencies and related strategies in order to channel innovations to potential adopters and expedite diffusion. Thus, two distinct subprocesses may be identified: the establishment of diffusion agencies and the establishment (or distribution) of the innovation itself. These may be viewed in a supply-demand framework. In particular, institutional or entrepreneurial propagators in effect have a supply of agencies for which potential agents have a demand. The interactions at the interface between the propagator and the agent lead to agency locations. Further, diffusion agencies, once estab-

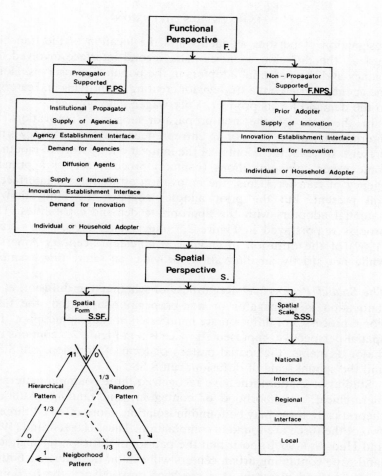

Figure 2.5 Cones of Resolution in the Innovation Diffusion Process

lished, become suppliers of the innovation with the task of both stimulating and responding to the demand of individuals in their market or service area who are potential adopters. This constitutes the innovation establishment interface.

This two-stage propagator-supported process is represented in Figure 2.5 under cell F.PS. It may be illustrated by franchise operations such as Volkswagen which was a significant innovation in the United States in the late 1940s and 1950s. The first stage or interface involved Volkswagen corporate executives and the potential franchise agents. Here, decisions were made regarding the designation of persons as agents and the location of the franchise outlets, the diffusion agencies. The second interface involved the agency and the potential adopters in the population it serves. Here, the agency carried out a strategy for creating, identifying and catering to the demand for its product, Volkswagen automobiles.

In the case of the non-propagator-supported innovation, an intermediary in the form of an entrepreneurial agent or agency is not present. Instead, the adopter of the innovation, by word of mouth or some other communications (contact) process, acts as a primary agency of transfer. Thus, the innovation establishment interface is still present, but the prior adopter supplies the innovation to potential adopters with the appropriate demand capabilities. This process is portrayed in Figure 2.5 under cell F.NPS. Pyle's study (1969) of the diffusion of cholera in nineteenth-century America, while not strictly an innovation, provides an interesting example.

The Spatial Perspective. Regardless of whether the diffusion of an innovation is propagator or non-propagator-supported, the functional processes of diffusion are manifested in geographic space. The spatial perspective, represented by cells S in Figure 2.5 contains two major elements: the spatial pattern or form of diffusion, cell S.SF, and the spatial scale of diffusion, cell S.SS.

Studies of spatial form have recognized three common patterns— hierarchical, neighborhood or contagion, and random. Although theoretically these may be found in isolation, more often all three or two of the three are found in combination. Thus, Hagerstrand (1952) and Hudson (1969b) posit that the pattern of diffusion throughout a landscape containing urban centers will exhibit the influence both of contagion and hierarchy as a result of, respectively, the friction of distance and urban-size filtering. That various pattern combinations are possible is represented by the triangular graph under cell S.SF of Figure 2.5.

Berry's (1972) example of the diffusion of television broadcasting through an urban system is an example in which the hierarchy effect dominates, and thus it may be associated with the upper portion of the triangular graph. Other studies focus on the hierarchical pattern but also include elements of the other two spatial forms. Examples other than Hudson (1969b) and Hagerstrand (1952), previously noted, are Bell's (1965) study of the diffusion of radio and television in the United States, L.A. Brown (1968a, 1969) on television in Sweden, Pedersen (1970, 1975) on various entrepreneurial innovations in Chile, Hanham and Brown (1972) on cremation in Sweden, and Eiden (1968) on nursing homes, community hospitals, swimming pools, and municipal fluoridation in North Dakota.

The second spatial form discussed extensively in the diffusion literature is the neighborhood pattern represented along the bottom side of the triangular graph, under cell S.SF of Figure 2.5. Hagerstrand's (1967a) classic study of the diffusion of agricultural innovation among Swedish farmers is almost solely concerned with this and thus would be represented at the extreme left of that bottom side. Other examples include Zelinski (1967) on classical town names in the United States from their origins in upper New York State, Griliches (1957) on hybrid corn in the United States from an origin point in Iowa, Casetti and Semple (1969) on tractors from the Dakotas throughout the central agricultural regions of the American Midwest, and Cox and Demko (1968) on agricultural riots that originated in south-western Ukraine at the turn of the century.

Although geographers in search of *spatial regularities* have focused their attention on hierarchical and neighborhood effects, in many cases *no* spatial regularities are obvious. Such a finding is reported by Tornqvist (1967), for example, with regard to the diffusion of television receivers in a localized area of Sweden. Also, strong random effect components appear in the diffusion pattern for artificial insemination among a sample of Swedish farmers (Hanham, 1973) and for cable television stations in Ohio (L.A. Brown, Malecki, Gross, Shrestha and Semple, 1974). In the observation of random effects, however, one must be careful that the opportunity set (Moore, 1970) is properly defined. For example, if the spread of a teaching innovation is being examined, the pattern might appear random if the population of reference is the whole academic community, whereas it might appear neighborhood or hierarchical if the members of the population are differentiated into sets according to the relevance of the innovation to the activities of each academic person. Thus, although more difficult to discern, order may be present in an apparently random pattern of diffusion.[25]

These patterns of diffusion—hierarchical, neighborhood, or random—may appear at any level of spatial aggregation or spatial scale, arbitrarily designated as local, regional and national under cell S.SS of Figure 2.5. For example, the neighborhood effect has been observed at a national level in the diffusion of hybrid corn (Griliches, 1957), at a regional level in the diffusion of cable television (L.A. Brown, Malecki, Gross, Shrestha and Semple, 1974), and at a local level in the diffusion of Bovine TB control (Hagerstrand, 1967a).

An interesting illustration of this, as well as of the role of opportunity set principles, is Hagerstrand's (1967a) schema depicting diffusion as occurring through a hierarchy of networks of social communications (Figure 2.6). The national, regional and local levels of spatial aggregation each contain a network within which neighborhood effect principles of contact operate. Further, a node on one level network will have contact with nodes on another level, thus providing a conduit or interface for the filtering of contacts between levels, presumably in a hierarchy effect fashion. Finally, the nodes on each level can be seen to represent an opportunity set. Thus, if only the national scale opportunity set is considered, a neighborhood effect pattern would be observed, whereas were the nodes on all three levels considered together the pattern could well seem hierarchical or random.

This illustration of Hagerstrand also brings up the question of how an innovation moves through spatial scales as it proceeds through time and over space, which in turn may have implications for the functional perspective. One common pattern, for example, is for an innovation to begin in a local area, spread regionally, and then filter back downwards to (other) local areas in the region while at the same time spreading to other regions. Each of these shifts in spatial scale is accompanied by changes in organizational structure and decision-making systems.

In summary, the main point of the discussion of this section is the importance of separating the various types of cones of resolution in diffusion studies. Thus, we ought to speak of cones of resolution for the functional perspective as distinct from those for the spatial perspective. Further, within those major rubrics we ought to distinguish between cones of resolution for propagator-supported innovations as distinct from non-propagator-supported, and cones of resolution for spatial form as distinct from spatial scale. While this may seem obvious, the literature on diffusion of innovation is replete with confusions and contradictions because these distinctions have not been recognized. The use of terms 'macro', 'meso' and 'micro' scale as well as the many attempts to infer a communications process of diffusion from a neighborhood effect pattern of diffusion, as even done recently by M. E. Harvey and Greenberg (1973), bear witness to this.

Having established these distinctions, a clearer understanding of the linkages between the functional and spatial aspects of inquiry must be achieved. A step in that direction with regard to propagator-supported innovation is presented in the following two chapters which examine the agency establishment and the innovation estab-

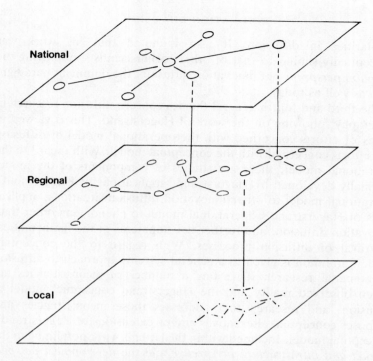

Figure 2.6   Schematic Portrayal of Diffusion Viewed at Different
   Spatial Scales

lishment interfaces (portrayed under cell F.PS of Figure 2.5). As indicated by Figure 2.5, however, this is only a portion of the overall task.

OVERVIEW

This chapter examines the themes of diffusion research in geography, portrayed in Figure 2.1. A historical approach is taken in an effort to understand how these themes relate to one another and to the broader concerns of the discipline, as well as the nature of the themes themselves.

The first general theme is the cultural geography tradition which studied diffusion as an element in the broad evolution of the cultural landscape. Attention then turns to Hagerstrand whose work more immediately set the stage for contemporary diffusion research. His contributions were in three areas: conceptualization of the innovation diffusion process, operationalization of that conceptualization through mathematical modelling, and identification of empirical regularities in diffusion. It also is noted that his work was conceptually similar to that of other social scientists employing the *adoption perspective* of innovation diffusion, the dominant paradigm then as well as today.

The third and fourth general themes concern diffusion research in geography following on the work of Hagerstrand. This is viewed in terms of efforts concerned with the operational model of diffusion and efforts concerned with the conceptual model. With regard to the operational model, there are studies of components of the model originally developed by Hagerstrand, applications of Hagerstrand's operational model to other innovation diffusion situations, applications of Hagerstrand's operational model to phenomena other than innovation diffusion, and further developments in the mathematical portrayal of diffusion processes. With regard to the conceptual model, attention is given to a general systems approach to diffusion phenomena, research suggesting a number of inconsistencies between observed reality and the Hagerstrand conceptual model of diffusion, and research that addresses those inconsistencies and proposes conceptual alternatives and/or extensions of Hagerstrand's conceptual model. Included within the latter is work pertaining to the *market and infrastructure perspective* and the *development perspective,* to be elaborated in the remainder of this book.

The fifth general theme examined in this chapter is that of diffusion research in geography as a mirror of the discipline. This demonstrates that the development of the various research themes was related to broader themes in the discipline as a whole. Particular attention is given to the quantitative revolution and the more recent disciplinary shift towards a concern with substantive reality, relevance and societal utility. In both cases diffusion research can be seen as a medium through which these disciplinary concerns were made manifest. This section of the chapter further demonstrates that the development of the various research themes of diffusion also relate to a broad philosophy-of-science model of paradigm dominance, shift and replacement with an alternative paradigm.

Because diffusion research has been carried out over such a long time span and under several different philosophical regimes of geography, there are a number of ambiguities in the literature. These in part stem from confusing the nature of and the interrelationships between geographic scale, geographic process and the manifestation of process, geographic form. This problem and the related ambiguities, the sixth general theme of diffusion research, were addressed as the cones of resolution problem.

Having set the stage by discussing diffusion research of the past, attention now turns to diffusion research of the present.

NOTES

1 This is discussed in *The Science of Geography* (National Academy of Sciences/ National Research Council, 1965: 26) as the *developmental* approach.
2 Nevertheless, such questions have been addressed by recent cultural geography and anthropological research (Levison, Ward and Webb, 1973; Edmonson, 1961; Clarke, 1968; C.A. Smith, 1976a, 1976b; Renfrew and Cooke, 1979). The anthropological work of this type evidences considerable influence from Hager-strand and geography in general.
3 Students of diffusion have at times pointed to the methodological differences between research in the Sauer and Hagerstrand traditions (the former being largely qualitative; the latter quantitative) as being significant. In this writer's opinion, however, that difference is incidental to the more fundamental differences in the types of questions raised and the conceptualizations promulgated.
4 This tendency also is evident in *The Propagation of Innovation Waves* (1952).
5 This assumption is congruent with the predominant line of thinking in diffusion research to date. For a review see Chapter 1 above and Jones (1967); Katz, Levin and Hamilton (1963); Midgley (1977); Robertson (1971); or E.M. Rogers and Shoemaker (1971).
6 Primary attention is given to elaborating the mechanisms of interpersonal communication rather than those of the mass media flows of information. It is likely that this emphasis follows from Hagerstrand's concern with constructing an operational model of innovation diffusion and from the findings of sociologists (Katz, 1957) that interpersonal communications are more influential upon adoption than are mass media.
7 Since the work of Karlsson (1958) and Duncan (1957) suggests that social barriers (or social distance) are functionally similar to terrestrial barriers, social barriers also can be considered a part of Hagerstrand's conceptual model.
8 Although Hagerstrand's initial conceptualization is quite general, creation of an operational model requires the establishment of a simpler and therefore more restrictive set of assumptions. This constraint is evident in the models. For a more detailed and didactically oriented account of the model summarized here, see Gould (1969: 25–38) or Abler, Adams and Gould (1971: 409–22).
9 Five resistance levels were employed. The lesser level required one message; the greater level required five messages. Individuals were randomly assigned a resistance level, and both the probabilities underlying this assignment and the number of messages required for adoption in each resistance class were arbitrarily determined.
10 The distance decay function was computed from frequency distributions of short-range migrations and telephone calls over varying distances. Such a curve declines monotonically with increasing distance between potential interactants (or communicants) and is considered to apply symmetrically to the geographic space being studied (that is, no directional bias in interaction is taken into account).
11 The population of each cell would vary, reflecting the real world population distribution, so that adoption could occur several times in any given cell.
12 For an early statement of the S-curve, see Ryan and Gross (1943); for the hierarchy effect, see Bowers (1937); for the neighborhood effect, see McVoy (1940).
13 At a later date the economist Griliches (1957), apparently working independently, proposed three stages—origin, diffusion and saturation—which are parallel to Hagerstrand's stages. This also is illustrated in Figure 2.2E.
14 Goodness of fit is sometimes ascertained by a direct comparison of the actual and

simulated pattern. Another approach is to compare the S-curve, the hierarchy effect, or the neighborhood effect associated with the actual and simulated diffusion. Recently, Sopher (1979) and Meir (1979) propose and illustrate a disparity measure that also could be used to compare actual and simulated diffusions.

15 For an example of such use, see Shannon (1970).

16 Hagerstrand's work also has had a significant impact among social scientists other than geographers. Examples include Larouche (1965), a city planner studying residential growth in Montreal; Karlsson (1958), a sociologist concerned with the spread of information through social groups; Rainio (1961, 1962), a social psychologist whose models focus upon social interaction, imitation behavior and group learning; and Hanneman, Carroll, Rogers, Stanfield and Lin (1969), sociologists studying the diffusion of innovation.

17 This should not be taken to imply that the researchers carrying out this work were not aware of or concerned with the substantive aspects of the situations being studied. Morrill's (1965c) study of the Negro ghetto, for example, contains an excellent account of the characteristics of the ghetto, the forces that generated and maintain it and the processes of ghetto expansion.

18 An interesting exception is Day (1970). For a rural locale, this discusses several diffusion processes of a substantive nature, identifies the spatial patterning or sequencing associated with each, and, on the basis of those, formulates alternative models of the course of diffusion through time.

19 The model of Pedersen (1970, 1975), summarized in Chapter 3, pages 70–2, is conceptually and mathematically similar to that of Berry. Another interesting approach to their conceptualization has been articulated by Chappell and Webber (1970) who employ an electrical analogue algorithm. More recent studies in this genre include Ralston (1978) and Webber and Joseph (1978, 1979). For a general discourse on mathematical models of diffusion in geography, see Hudson (1972) or Haggett, Cliff and Frey (1977: 231–58).

20 This approach is summed up in the following (L.A. Brown, 1968b: 6–8)

the viewpoint is taken that processes controlling the spread of quite different phenomena may be structurally similar in several respects. Structural congruencies of this sort are called isomorphisms. One example of such is the structural similarity between a transportation network and an organization structure, even though the content of each (e.g. roads and chains of command) is quite dissimilar. . . . To focus upon isomorphism is not an uncommon approach in science. In physical science, for example, M.R. Cohen and Nagel (1934: 139) note that 'the formula of inverse squares applies to electrical attraction and repulsion as well as to the force of gravitation. This is possible because these different subject matters have an identical formal structure with respect to the properties studied. Physics also discovers that the same set of principles is applicable to the motion of planets, the dropping of a tear, and the swinging of a pendulum.'

As to the value of this approach, Cohen and Nagel also state:

'It is the isomorphism found in diverse subject matter which makes possible theoretical science as we know it today.'

On a more modest level, however, identification of isomorphism provides the opportunity to borrow methodology, ideas and concepts from one subject matter for application to another. Such borrowing frequently results in a new point of view which provides the researcher with insight into the problem being examined.

21 These different emphases are readily illustrated by comparing this review with one done eleven years ago by the same author (L.A. Brown and Moore, 1969). For a recent and more comprehensive discussion on this point, see Agnew (1979).

22 A similar process operated in the emergence of the development perspective. This was in part

a response to the fact that the diffusion of technological innovations generally has not led to significant economic development in Third World nations but, instead, has tended to increase regional inequalities and widen the disparities between social and economic classes. (L.A. Brown, 1977: 22)

23 In addition to the functional and spatial dimensions in studies concerning the diffusion of innovation, there is also the temporal. Since the functional and spatial characteristics of any system will shift over time, the temporal perspective also is important in analysis, but it is not treated here because it has not been associated with research ambiguities to the degree that the functional and spatial perspectives have.

24 An interesting article relative to this subsection is Redlich (1953), which presents a comparable scheme developed from an historian's perspective.

25 For general discussions of the relationship between opportunity sets and manifest patterns of spatial interaction, see Moore (1970), Moore and Brown (1970) and Griffith and Jones (1980).

3

THE MARKET AND INFRASTRUCTURE PERSPECTIVE I: DIFFUSION AGENCY ESTABLISHMENT ASPECTS OF INNOVATION DIFFUSION

As noted in Chapter 1, social scientists have traditionally viewed innovation diffusion as an area of inquiry pertaining to individual choice, focusing upon the individual or household adoption decision. Accordingly, research has emphasized the role of social networks, information flows, individual or household demographics and psychological variables such as innovativeness and resistance to adoption.[1] More recent research indicates that this perspective alone does not provide sufficient explanation if, as is the case for most contemporary innovations, the innovation is propagated by an entity motivated to bring about rapid and complete diffusion (L.A. Brown, 1968a, 1969, 1975; L.A. Brown and Cox, 1971).

In this setting the mechanisms through which innovations are made available to potential adopters are of equal if not greater importance; that is, it is necessary to consider *supply* as well as *demand* factors. In considering both, diffusion of innovation is no longer simply a consumer behavior phenomenon. It is instead a much broader topic requiring consideration of institutional behaviors, by public and private entities, which affect the individual's or household's access to the innovation or, said another way, which establish the constraints within which individual choice is made.

In general, then, the market and infrastructure perspective complements the traditional focus on innovation adoption by articulating the role of supply factors in the diffusion process. A central element of this framework is the *diffusion agency*—the public or private sector entity through which an innovation is distributed or made available to the population at large. Examples of entities that might perform such a function include retail and wholesale outlets, government agencies (for example, Cooperative Extension Service county offices) or non-profit organizations (for example, Planned Parenthood affiliates).

As noted in Chapter 1, the diffusion agency enters into the

diffusion process in two ways. On the one hand it provides a point of distribution for a given geographic area. Thus, the locations of the agencies and the temporal sequencing of their establishment determine where and when the innovation will be available and provide the general outline of the spatial pattern of diffusion. This is conceptualized as the *first* stage of the diffusion process, *diffusion agency establishment.*

The second way the diffusion agency enters into the diffusion process is by conceiving and implementing a strategy to promote adoption among the population in its market or service area. These *agency operating procedures,* the *second* stage of the diffusion process, contribute further detail to the spatial pattern of diffusion by creating differing levels of access to the innovation depending upon a potential adopter's economic, locational, demographic and social characteristics. The establishment of diffusion agencies and the operating procedures of each agency are, more generally, aspects of marketing the innovation. This marketing involves both the creation of infrastructure and its utilization. Thus, the characteristics of the relevant public and private infrastructure, such as service, delivery, information, transportation, electricity or water systems, also have an important influence upon the rate and spatial patterning of diffusion.

Together, then, these *market and infrastructure factors* comprise the *supply* side of diffusion and shape its course. These factors also affect the *demand* side of diffusion by establishing constraints within which *adoption,* the *third* stage of the sequence, occurs.

The steps of this framework—diffusion agency establishment, diffusion agency strategy, and adoption—are presented sequentially for heuristic purposes. In reality, however, they may not occur in order and may not be mutually exclusive. For instance, while existing diffusion agencies are implementing marketing strategies to induce adoption of a particular innovation, other agencies might be created. Further, while both these events are occurring, there is also adoption in the service areas of existing agencies. Finally, the agencies may themselves be the innovation (for example, the fast food outlet, the planned regional shopping center (Y.S. Cohen, 1972) and the department store in Japan (Tanaka, 1971).

This brings up the question of exactly what we mean by innovation and to which kinds of innovations this framework pertains. The examples above indicate that an innovation may be either a new product or service, such as quadraphonic stereo systems or credit card services, or a new way of providing an old product or service, such as 24-hour banking or the planned regional shopping center.

Furthermore, as noted in Chapter 1, each of these types of innovation may be *continuous,* involving alteration of an existing product such that consumers need not develop new consumption patterns; *dynamically continuous,* involving the creation of a new product or service or the alteration of an existing one such that consumption patterns are somewhat disrupted; or *discontinuous,* involving the creation of previously unknown products or services such that new consumption patterns must be established (Robertson, 1971: 4–7). The framework presented in this chapter and Chapter 4 is relevant to the diffusion of all these types of innovation.

The remainder of this chapter considers diffusion agency establishment, the first stage of the innovation diffusion process. Chapter 4 considers the second stage, the implementation of diffusion agency strategy to promote adoption within its service area. Both chapters discuss those factors which play a key role in the respective stages of diffusion, giving particular attention to implications for the spatial patterning of diffusion. Several case studies are woven into the discussion in order to illustrate the validity of the market and infrastructure framework and its translation into a real world setting.

DIFFUSION AGENCY ESTABLISHMENT

The majority of innovations are promoted by entities which are here termed *propagators.* These entities are profit- or non-profit-motivated organizations or government agencies acting to induce the rapid and complete diffusion of the innovation. One aspect of this endeavor is the choice of market area for distributing the innovation, a part of a broader *market penetration* strategy. This is treated in the present framework in terms of the decision of where and when to establish a diffusion agency. Other aspects of market penetration such as the selection of a specific site within the market area, size of outlet, design of outlet, or inventory will, at most, be only briefly discussed.[2]

An important consideration is the *locus of decision-making* with respect to diffusion agency establishment. At one extreme is a *centralized structure* wherein a single propagator (or several propagators acting together as one) determines the number of outlets to be established at any given time and their location, size and other characteristics. Thus, the gross pattern of diffusion is centrally controlled. At the opposite extreme is a *decentralized structure* in which each diffusion agency is established independently by a different entrepreneurial or non-profit-motivated entity, so that the

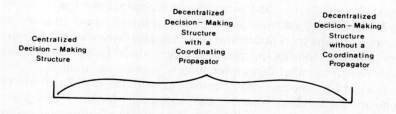

Figure 3.1   A Continuum of Diffusion Agency Establishment Situations

gross pattern of diffusion comes about solely through the aggregation of individual actions and decentralized decision making.

In between these two extremes is diffusion in a *decentralized structure with a coordinating propagator*. In this, each agency is established by a different entrepreneurial or non-profit-motivated entity, but some aspects of this are controlled and orchestrated by the coordinating propagator. Thus, the pattern of diffusion is *influenced, but not determined by*, the coordinating propagator. The degree of coordination may vary considerably, as indicated by the variety of franchise arrangements, so that this latter case really represents a continuum depending upon the extent of propagator control and orchestration of the diffusion (Figure 3.1). One thing that cannot be controlled, however, is the decision to establish an agency in the first place since, by definition, this must be done by the local, individual entrepreneur.[3]

In general, diffusion patterns and the relative importance of different variables varies according to the organizational structure of the diffusion. Market potential, profitability or economic factors, for example, are of paramount importance in the case of a centralized decision-making structure, operating to order the spatial sequencing of diffusion. However, these variables only serve as threshold conditions in the decentralized situation where information flow factors (among entrepreneurs) take on a greater importance. If the diffusion is in a decentralized structure with a coordinating propagator, the most common case, the relative importance of economic as opposed to information factors varies according to the arrangement between the propagator and the entities establishing diffusion agencies.

Empirically observed diffusions are not necessarily characterized by only one of these three prototypes. For instance, centralized and decentralized structures may occur simultaneously, as in the spread of Coca Cola in Ontario which resulted from the actions of one key firm, Coca Cola Ltd and numerous independent bottlers (Osleeb, 1974). Similarly, a diffusion may evolve from one type of structure to another. In fast food operations, for example, there was initially only one firm, McDonalds, operating in a centralized fashion, which was later joined by other firms after success became apparent.

From the perspective of one concerned with the spatial patterns of innovation diffusion, one of the important decisions in agency establishment is *whether to create a new network of diffusion agencies or to utilize an already existing one*. The consequences of this decision in terms of each of the three prototype situations are illustrated in Figure 3.2. This is now briefly elaborated.

If an *existing* distribution network is utilized, there are two basic possibilities. On the one hand, the *existing network* might consist of a series of *outlets* that are *linked together organizationally*. Thus, test marketing considerations aside, utilizing such a network generally results in a blanket coverage (national or regional) wherein the innovation is simultaneously made available over the range of locations or markets included in the network. For decentralized diffusion with a coordinating propagator, an example is the use of supermarket chains by large package foods manufacturers (for example, Proctor and Gamble) to introduce a new brand. For centralized diffusion (where the existing network would, by definition, be controlled by the propagator), an example is the introduction of a new model General Motors automobile through its dealer network.

An alternative to a distribution system that is organizationally linked is diffusion through *independently owned outlets* such as 'mom and pop' or locally owned furniture stores. This type of system would characterize decentralized diffusion without a coordinating propagator. The establishment of cable television systems in Ohio provides an example (L.A. Brown, Malecki, Gross, Shrestha and Semple, 1974). However, such a system also might be utilized by a coordinating propagator. For example, the bank credit card in Ohio was made available through local banks, each of which is independently owned (L.A. Brown and Malecki, 1977).

If an existing network of diffusion agencies is utilized, whether it is organizationally linked to the propagator or comprised of independently owned outlets, *the spatial patterns of diffusion will be constrained by and reflect the spatial pattern of the existing network.* Suppose, for example, that Federated Department stores were the sole outlets through which an innovation was distributed. These are found in only some regions of the United States and in some cities

Decision - Making Structure	Diffusion Agency Network	
	New	Existing
Centralized	Spatially Sequential Diffusion	Linked System of Agencies Controlled by Propagator and Blanket Spatial Coverage
Decentralized with a Coordinating Propagator	Spatially Sequential Diffusion	Linked System of Agencies Not Controlled by Propagator but Blanket Spatial Coverage or Unlinked Agencies with Spatially Sequential Diffusion
Decentralized without a Coordinating Propagator	Spatially Sequential Diffusion	Unlinked Agencies with Spatially Sequential Diffusion

Figure 3.2 Aspects of Diffusion Agency Establishment as a Consequence of the Decision to Establish a New Network of Diffusion Agencies or to Utilize an Existing One

within those regions. Accordingly, the spatial patterns of diffusion would be constrained to those locations irrespective of the actual distribution of potential adopters. Alternatively, there could be a close correlation between the spatial distribution of the existing network and that of the population of potential adopters. Examples of this would be an outlet network comprised of supermarkets or local banks. In this case, then, the diffusion pattern would closely approximate the distribution of potential adopters (*ceteris paribus*).

If a *new network* is established, whatever the organizational or decision-making structure of the diffusion, diffusion agencies are typically located sequentially in time and space (Figure 3.2). This is also true if the innovation is distributed through an existing network of *independently owned* outlets. In these cases, then, there is a more marked geographic problem. Attention now turns to elaborating this problem in terms of the three situations of diffusion agency establishment—through a centralized decision-making structure, through a decentralized structure without a coordinating propagator and through a decentralized structure with a coordinating propagator. Each of these is considered for a profit-motivated setting, but a final subsection turns to diffusion by government or non-profit-motivated entities.

Profit-Motivated Diffusion under a Centralized Decision-Making Structure

The most important single consideration for agency location in a centralized setting is the expected profitability associated with alternative urban areas (L.A. Brown and Cox, 1971).[4] Optimally, the markets would be ranked and then sequentially exploited; the most profitable first and the less profitable later, if at all. This occurs because of limited supplies of the innovation, the business uncertainty associated with the introduction of an innovation, limited capital and the consequent importance of obtaining maximum levels of performance from established diffusion agencies.

One critical factor in the profitability estimate is revenues. These can be estimated in terms of market potential, and (*ceteris paribus*) those areas with larger potential ought to be preferred. For many innovations market potential will vary directly with the number of persons in each urban area and its hinterland. That is not always the case, however. The market potential for agricultural innovations provides an obvious example.

Expenses also enter into the calculation of profitability. These would include the unit cost of the innovation, the costs of transporting it to the diffusion agency and of distributing it to adopters, the costs of advertising and otherwise promoting the innovation, and the costs of establishing, maintaining and operating each diffusion agency.

From a spatial perspective, the most important expenses are those related to the accessibility of a potential agency location to the parent entity.[5] This is primarily relevant to logistics aspects of propagation, such as servicing the agency and transporting the innovation to it (Kollat, Blackwell and Robeson, 1972; Kotler, 1972). Accessibility also enters in other ways, particularly because of the risk and uncertainty associated with innovation diffusion. Given limited resources for market research, nearby locations, especially those that are personally known to the propagator, can be better evaluated in terms of sales potential, the means of tapping that potential and the extent of various costs. Even without severe resource limitations, however, it is likely that more will be known about accessible locations, and further, it is reasonable to suppose that what is known will be perceived as more reliable. Finally, there are accessibility-related economies in innovation promotion and in agency maintenance and operating costs. With regard to the latter, accessible locations can be easily supervised by the propagator, thus reducing expenses and increasing control and the likelihood of success.

One conclusion of this general discussion of market selection under a centralized decision-making structure is that *market potential* and *accessibility* will be important factors underlying the locational priorities established by the propagator. These provide, respectively, hierarchy and neighborhood effect tendencies in the pattern of diffusion. The topic of pattern will receive more attention. First, however, this general discussion will be elaborated by considering its formal expression.

A Model. The establishment of diffusion agencies in a centralized decision-making structure is essentially a multiple facility location problem. The extensive literature on this problem (Lea, 1973a, 1973b; Hodgart, 1978) provides many models that may be adapted or directly applied to the innovation diffusion setting (for example, L.A. Brown, Williams, Youngmann, Holmes and Walby, 1974; Holmes, Williams and Brown, 1972; Kochen and Deutsch, 1969, 1972; Schneider and Symons, 1971a, 1971b; Scott, 1971; Teitz, 1968a, 1968b). Generally, however, these models do not portray the complexities of the substantive problem. More appropriate are the models presented in Kotler (1971: 302–23) or Craig and Brown (1974). These provide the basis for the following discussion.

The propagator in a centralized structure might evaluate alternative locations i in terms of establishing a single diffusion agency in each in time t.[6] A criterion for this can be provided by

$$\bar{Z}_{it} = \sum_{k=t}^{t+h} \frac{Z_{ik} - I_{ik}}{(1 + r)^k} \tag{3.1}$$

where

$\bar{Z}_{it}$ is the net present value in time t of anticipated profit from place i over the planning horizon h

Z_{ik} is the anticipated profit from place i in time k

I_{ik} is the out-of-pocket cost in time k related to establishing a diffusion agency in place i at time t, which would include debt service payments (principal and interest) as well as other out-of-pocket costs, if any

r is the discount rate per time interval k.

In this

$$Z_{ik} = (p_{ik} - c_{ik} - d_{ik})q_{ik} - m_{ik} - a_{ik} \qquad (3.2)$$

where

p_{ik} is the unit sales price of the innovation in place i at time k

c_{ik} is the unit cost of the innovation in place i at time k

d_{ik} is the unit cost of transporting the innovation from the point of production or warehousing to the diffusion agency(ies) in place i at time k

q_{ik} is the estimated unit sales of the innovation in place i at time k

m_{ik} is the cost of maintaining and operating the diffusion agency(ies) in place i at time k

a_{ik} is the advertising expenditure in place i at time k.

The estimated unit sales variable in equation (3.2), q_{ik}, requires further attention. For each place i there is a market potential for the innovation, Q_i.[7] The portion of this realized at a given time, however, will be limited by the degree of market penetration in place i. This effect may be traced by employing the cumulative first-time sales of the innovation in a functional form such as the logistic, for example,

$$w_{ik} = \frac{Q_i}{1 + e^{-(a+b\sum_{j=1}^{k-1} N_{ij})}} \qquad (3.3)$$

where w_{ik} is an estimate of unit sales in place i at time k on the basis of market potential (Q_i) and the degree of market penetration (N_{ij}).[8] Equation (3.3) also may be viewed as portraying the market response or the growth in demand for the innovation in place i.[9]

There are other factors in addition to the innovation's market potential and market penetration that affect its diffusion. Thus,

$$q_{ik} = f(w_{ik}, g_{ik}, p_{ik}, a_{ik}, h_{ik}, e_{ik}) \qquad (3.4)$$

where

g_{ik} is the general economic conditions in place i at time k, perhaps indicated by a surrogate such as unemployment

p_{ik} is the price of the innovation in place i at time k

a_{ik} is the advertising expenditure for the innovation in place i at time k

h_{ik} is the diffusion agency capacity in place i at time k

e_{ik} is the diffusion agency effectiveness in place i at time k.

General economic conditions would be taken account of in the planning of the propagator, but would not be in its control. However, decisions are made with regard to price, advertising expenditures and those diffusion agency characteristics that affect agency capacity and effectiveness.[10]

Given an estimate of sales in location i for each time period k (q_{ik}, equation (3.4)) and estimates of other variables in the profit equation (3.2), the net value of anticipated profit from place i over the planning horizon h ($\bar{Z}_{it}$) may be estimated by equation (3.1). Then, locating a given number and size of diffusion agencies, determined by capital or other constraints, simply consists of successively choosing the locations with the highest values of $\bar{Z}_{it}$.[11]

Spatial Patterns of Diffusion in a Centralized Decision-Making Structure. It has been noted that the elements operating in a centralized setting provide tendencies towards both hierarchy and neighborhood effects in the pattern of diffusion.[12] This now will be examined more closely, employing the model presented in the preceding section as a framework.

One important influence upon pattern is the market penetration strategy employed by the propagator.[13] The tools he uses include the price of the innovation, the advertising expenditure, and the locations, sizes and numbers of outlets or diffusion agencies (equation (3.4)). Combinations of the various decision points for these would relate to a scale of operations and to associated costs and revenues. Two situations that may face the propagator operating in a centralized decision-making structure are depicted in Figure 3.3. In one (Figure 3.3A), it is not possible to realize a profit because total revenue does not offset total costs at any scale of operation, but the latter would determine the level of loss. This situation would occur early in the diffusion when the market for the innovation is not sufficiently developed. Over time, however, total revenue should increase (equation (3.3)), so that the propagator eventually should be faced with a second situation (Figure 3.3B) in which realizing a profit is possible, and its magnitude varies with the scale of operations.

In either of these situations the propagator may implement a market penetration strategy with the intent of (a) minimizing costs, (b) maximizing profits (or minimizing losses) or (c) maximizing sales. As an illustration of the dynamics implicit in these strategies consider the Craig-Brown (1974) formulation of equation (3.4) (note 10 of this chapter). This indicates that the propagator can obtain greater sales by lowering price, increasing advertising, increasing the number of

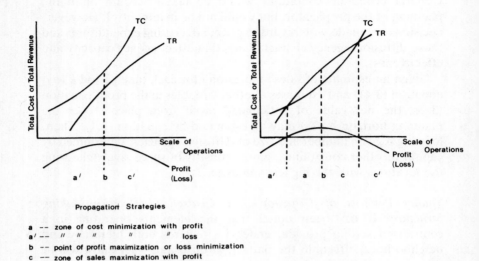

Propagation Strategies

a -- zone of cost minimization with profit
a′ --   ″   ″   ″   ″   ″   loss
b -- point of profit maximization or loss minimization
c -- zone of sales maximization with profit
c′ --   ″   ″   ″   ″   ″   loss

Figure 3.3 Propagator Strategies under a Centralized Decision-Making Structure for Two Hypothetical Situations

diffusion agencies, or some combination thereof. Since some (or perhaps all) of these sales would be first time, market penetration would be increased, and the time to develop full market potential would be decreased (equation 3.3). However, the balance between price and the variable and fixed costs (equation 3.2) will be adversely affected. Thus, a sales maximization strategy might be pursued while maintaining a profit margin (Figure 3.3B, zone c), but the margin will vary inversely with the increase in sales. Further, even greater sales are possible if a short-term loss is initially borne (Figure 3.3B, zone c′), perhaps justified by the longer-term gains from realizing full market potential more quickly.

The strategy that emerges depends in part upon the *capital available* to the propagator. Sales maximization is a viable option for the capital-rich propagator, whereas the capital-poor propagator would be more likely to follow a strategy of cost minimization until expansion capital is available.[14] In either case, after a level of success has been attained mixed strategies are likely. For example, sales maximization might be pursued in new markets at the same time that profit maximization is pursued in older markets.

The market penetration strategy affects diffusion pattern in a number of ways. The market developed by a sales maximization strategy, for example, would exhibit a higher rate of diffusion than one in which cost minimization was initially applied. Considering all markets together, under profit maximization each would be entered in an order reflecting sales potential and accessibility, and the former would play an even greater role under sales maximization. If *sales potential* varies directly with the market's total population, as in the widely used estimation method outlined in note 7 of this chapter, a hierarchy effect tendency would emerge. If *sales potential* is dependent upon other characteristics, such as the size of the farming population for agricultural innovations, the hierarchy effect is likely to be muted or eliminated.

Whatever the basis of *market potential*, its role will be reduced under a strategy of cost minimization. One option would be to enter markets in the same order as under a profit or sales strategy, but with facilities insufficient to tap their sales potential fully. It is more likely, however, that greater importance would be given to accessibility and other cost-related factors in selecting markets, resulting in either full or partial exploitation of markets of lesser size. Under the first option the hierarchy effect in the diffusion pattern may not diminish, but the rate of its development would be slower. However, the other, more likely behaviors would enhance neighborhood effect tendencies which generally derive from the cost structure of diffusion.

One element in this is the cost of maintaining and operating a diffusion agency, m_{ik}. A portion of m_{ik} relates to the management and control infrastructure of the diffusion agency system as a whole and would vary directly with distance from the home office and inversely with the number of diffusion agencies in a region. This cost would be particularly influential early in the diffusion when management and control infrastructure is being developed . Also enhanced by a spatial concentration of agencies are warehousing and inventory economies, another portion of m_{ik}; the effectiveness of advertising expenditures, a_{ik}; and the visibility of the innovation and ease with which it can be obtained by potential adopters, elements of diffusion agency effectiveness, e_{ik}. Further, if capital is limited, as it often is in the initial stage(s) of diffusion, locational decisions may rely heavily upon the propagator's knowledge instead of costly market surveys, leading to development in familiar areas near the home office rather than farther away. Finally, the cost of transporting the innovation from the point of production or warehousing to diffusion agencies, d_{ik}, varies directly with distance, thus favoring closer locations. An important characteristic here is that the per unit cost of transportation will remain more or less the same whatever the sales volume, unlike the per unit cost of factors such as maintenance and operation, m_{ik}, which will vary inversely with sales (equation (3.2)).

Factors such as those discussed in the preceding paragraph can be seen to comprise the *logistics* aspect of diffusion agency establishment. In general, these create spatial agglomeration economies that make accessibility of a place an important characteristic and provide tendencies towards a neighborhood effect in the pattern of diffusion and a strategy of region by region development. It has been noted that the degree to which these actually appear would depend upon whether the centralized propagator was operating to minimize costs, maximize profits or maximize sales. Also of significance is the relative importance of each of the logistics variables. To illustrate, if transportation costs are high relative to other costs, a strong neighborhood effect tendency is provided; a lesser effect is obtained if spatially variant elements of maintenance and operating costs dominate; and if neither of these is important there may be no neighborhood effect whatsoever.

Whether neighborhood, hierarchy or both tendencies are present, diffusion agency establishment will be limited to places with sales potential sufficient to support at least one agency. Thus, for a higher order compared to a lower order of (good) innovation, fewer places will have agencies and there will be fewer agencies in any given place.[15] With regard to the pattern of establishment, if agencies are identical, operate at full capacity and are taken as independent units rather than entities in a system, all places surpassing the threshold will provide the same sales and profit potential for the individual agency. The result would be locational indifference. Why then is there an impetus for hierarchically ordered locational priorities? One factor introducing a hierarchical tendency, discussed above, is the spatial agglomeration economies accruing to the diffusion agency that is part of an integrated system. A second factor devolves from the difference between the sales (profit) threshold required to operate an agency and its sales (profit) capacity, an index of the utility to the individual agency of areas with larger sales potential. The value of these factors would differ by innovation. It seems reasonable to hypothesize that higher-order innovations feature a higher *elasticity of agency profitability with regard to urban area sales potential*, and therefore a greater impetus towards hierarchically ordered locational priorities. However, the argument in this paragraph also implies that the hierarchical tendency should always be less than that expected by considering only place-to-place differences in sales potential.

To sum up, the critical factors for diffusion in a centralized decision-making setting are *capital availability, sales potential, logistics* and the *elasticity of agency profitability with regard to sales potential*. Although the expected pattern of diffusion would vary according to the mix of these characteristics in a given situation, the discussion provides little support for the hierarchy effect as a dominant tendency. To illustrate this further, Figure 3.4 considers situations comprised of idealized levels (for example, high/low capital availability) of these four characteristics. The hierarchy effect is a tendency in only six of the sixteen situations and is a singular force in only one, whereas the neighborhood effect appears thirteen times. Without knowing the frequency of occurrence of each characteristic, projective statements are tenuous, but there clearly is strong support for expecting neighborhood effects or no marked spatial bias in diffusion patterns in a centralized setting.

The Case of Friendly Ice Cream. An example of diffusion agency establishment under a *centralized decision-making structure* is the spread of Friendly Ice Cream shops, where the innovation or new product is largely the image presented by the Friendly shop.[16] The Friendly organization is highly centralized. The manufacture of ice cream and the processing of other foods sold in Friendly shops is carried on at Friendly's central processing plant in Wilbraham, Massachusetts, just outside of Springfield, the home of the founders of the *Friendly Concept*. Further, all market penetration and site selection decisions are controlled by corporate headquarters, as are decisions pertaining to product promotion and managerial training. Friendly also owns the land on which most of its shops stand, builds most of its free-standing shops and operates a fleet of trucks to supply all the shops from the central commissary. Virtually the only decisions made at the local shop level are how much to order from the central commissary, where to obtain fresh produce and milk locally and whom to hire as service personnel.

The conceptual model presented above suggests that the key determinants of the pattern of diffusion of Friendly shops ought to be the logistics of service, supply and control; market potential; the elasticity of outlet profitability with regard to market potential; and capital availability. Attention now turns to each of these factors.

With respect to *logistics* effects, the trucks delivering to Friendly shops from the central commissary have an overnight range of about 400 miles, creating a barrier to spread beyond that distance. Also, even within the 400-mile range, increased distances mean increased

Characteristics of the Firm	Characteristics of the Innovation							
	Market or Sales Potential Related to the Number of Persons in an Urban Area				Market or Sales Potential Not Related to the Number of Persons in an Urban Area			
	Logistics Effect							
	Significant		Minimal		Significant		Minimal	
	Elasticity of Agency Profitability							
	Sig	Min	Sig	Min	Sig	Min	Sig	Min
Low Capital Availability	Hierarchy Effect Constrained by a Neighborhood Effect	Neighborhood Effect	Hierarchy Effect Slightly Constrained by a Neighborhood Effect	Slight Neighborhood Effect	Neighborhood Effect with Random Element	Neighborhood Effect	Random Element Slightly Constrained by a Neighborhood Effect	Slight Neighborhood Effect
High Capital Availability	Hierarchy Effect Constrained by a Neighborhood Effect	Neighborhood Effect with Slight Hierarchy Effect	Hierarchy Effect	Slight Neighborhood and Hierarchy Effects	Neighborhood Effect with Random Element	Neighborhood Effect	Random Element	Slight Neighborhood Effect with Random Element

Figure 3.4 Expected Patterns of Diffusion under a Centralized Decision-Making Structure

Note: If a propagator used an existing network of diffusion agencies, it would channel the diffusion accordingly; but within that constraint, the same tendencies in pattern would be expected.

costs. Another logistical consideration is the relatively high degree of involvement of headquarters personnel in all aspects of the corporation's activity pertaining to individual shops. Thus, distance to the commissary or home office has been a critical consideration in the locational strategy for individual shops, suggesting that a neighborhood effect will be in evidence in the timing and location of shop openings.

The accuracy of this expectation is well illustrated by an isopleth map portraying the spatial dispersion of Friendly shops at selected years from 1936 through 1974 (Figure 3.5). The first shop was opened in Springfield in 1935; by 1951 there were ten shops in western Massachusetts and Connecticut; in 1965 the first Friendly shop was opened outside New England; and by 1974 Friendly Ice Cream had expanded as far west as Ohio. Further evidence of a neighborhood effect in the diffusion of Friendly Ice Cream is provided by a regression analysis in which log distance to Springfield explains 47 per cent of the variance in the year each of the Friendly shops was established.

Sales potential also is an important element in Friendly's locational strategy. While most of the variables used by Friendly to estimate this pertain to the site of the shop, and thus are not of interest in the present analysis, some are significant in choosing the urban place in which the shop is located. These are not *ordering* criteria, however, but *threshold* criteria of population size (more than 12,000 for 1970), median family income (above average) and community growth or rate of population change (above average). In actuality, only 32.2 per cent of the urban places with Friendly shops meet all three of the threshold requirements. Yet, 85.6 per cent meet the population requirement, 59.2 per cent the income requirement and 49.6 per cent meet the growth rate requirement. More significantly, only 1.7 per cent or six of the urban places, meet *none* of the threshold requirements.

One apparent reason why sales potential operates in a threshold fashion, rather than controlling the time order of Friendly shop establishment, is because the shops have a *low elasticity of profitability with respect to urban size*. Each Friendly shop provides essentially the same services, the same format, and has approximately the same capacity of ninety seats. While there is variation in their success, some operating at maximum capacity more often than others, this appears to be dependent upon site-related differences rather than upon differences among urban areas. Thus, locating the first shops in larger or faster growing cities would not be expected to provide significantly higher levels of profit. Together with the fact that Friendly stresses a solid, traditional, middle-class image which favors suburbs and smaller towns, these factors suggest that the pattern of Friendly shop openings will not exhibit a strong hierarchy effect, if any.

This expectation is confirmed by a step-wise regression analysis in which the year each Friendly shop was established is related to log distance from Springfield, to control for logistics effects, and the three sales potential variables of log population, median family

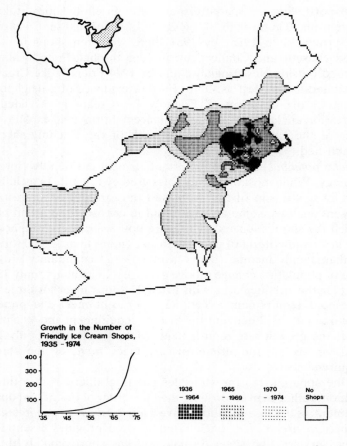

Figure 3.5   The Spatial Dispersion of Friendly Ice Cream
Shops for Selected Years, 1936–74.

income and percentage change in population. In general, the sales
potential variables are at best minimally related to the time order of
shop opening. Further, where one of these variables does enter the
equation, or where one of these variables has a noticeable zero-order
correlation with time of shop opening, the sign is generally in the
wrong direction. Considering this together with the evidence summarized above that 98.3 per cent of towns with Friendly shops meet at
least one of the basic requirements of population, disposable income
or community growth indicates that sales potential does function as a
threshold condition rather than as an ordering condition.

The last factor to be considered is *capital availability*. The theoretical discussion indicates that sales maximization is a viable policy for capital-rich propagators, whereas capital-poor propagators would be more likely to follow cost minimization until expansion capital is available.

Like many economic ventures, the Friendly Ice Cream Corporation began with limited capital and a significant infusion of entrepreneurial labor. Minimizing operating expenses was therefore important. Costs of delivery, supervision, control and market information had to be kept low in locating Friendly shops. It was important, therefore, to keep distance to the home office in Springfield at a minimum. As the corporation grew and capital availability improved, distance to Springfield became a less limiting factor. Even though logistical considerations still remained, decision-making and control were in part delegated to regional managers, and specialists in real estate took the responsibility for the development and siting of new shops.

The implication is that over time, as more capital becomes available, there should be a shift in the factors controlling the diffusion pattern. To test this, the regressions reported above were rerun for two separate time periods, 1936–64, the period prior to incorporation, and 1965–74. The most dramatic shift is in the role of logistics, which drops to explaining only 21 per cent of the variance in the second phase, less than two-thirds its importance in the first phase of Friendly's existence and less than half its importance overall. In both phases, however, sales potential variables are only minimally related to the time order of Friendly shop openings, suggesting that both phases are characterized by a low elasticity of shop profitability with urban size and by sales potential operating as a threshold rather than as an ordering condition.

There is, however, other evidence of a shift towards sales maximization in recent years. Friendly Ice Cream is currently expanding into a new market area, the Midwest, and spread in a wave-like or neighborhood effect pattern (by *osmosis* is their description of it) is still the policy. However, whereas this policy was initially justified only in terms of logistics costs, it is now justified in terms of market saturation and advertising benefits as well. Another indication of policy shift is the choice of Columbus, Ohio as the early locus of Midwest activity. Since all Ohio shops were initially serviced from Massachusetts, Cleveland would have been a more logical site for the first shops in terms of minimizing logistics and delivery costs to Wilbraham and in terms of its proximity to Troy, Ohio the site of

Friendly's new commissary. Columbus, however, has a greater potential for sales maximization. At the hub of interstate routes in central Ohio, it is better located for making all of Ohio aware of Friendly and for serving as a gateway to the rest of the Midwest.

In summary, the logistics of service, supply and control are critical factors in the market penetration behavior of Friendly Ice Cream, leading to a pattern of diffusion agency establishment with marked neighborhood effects. Sales potential differences among urban places act as a threshold for diffusion agency estblishment, but do not affect the sequencing of establishment because there is a low elasticity of Friendly shop profitability with regard to urban area size (or sales potential). Thus, a hierarchical component in the diffusion pattern is not evident. Capital availability also plays a role. A comparison of the years 1936 through 1964, preceding incorporation, with the years 1965 through 1974 indicates that diffusion in the earlier period occurred at a slower rate and in a more highly constrained neighborhood effect pattern. This is consistent with the expectation that cost factors would exert more control in a period of relatively scarce capital and that sales potential would become more important when capital was less scarce.

These findings are essentially those which would be hypothesized by considering the conceptual framework of diffusion agency establishment in a centralized decision-making setting together with the particular characteristics of the Friendly situation. Thus, support is provided for this portion of the market and infrastructure model of innovation diffusion. The case study also provides a qualitative sense of how the various relevant factors interact and play off with one another.

Profit-Motivated Diffusion under a Decentralized Decision-Making Structure

The previous discussion dealt with the single propagator who establishes a network of diffusion agencies. In the decentralized situation, on the other hand, each diffusion agency is established independently by a different entrepreneurial or economic entity, and it rather than a central propagator carries the burdens of risk, capital provision and decision-making responsibility. One implication is that the degree of success (or failure) of a single agency generally will be of limited concern to other agencies or to the coordinating propagator (if there is one), a fact reflected in the decentralization of decision-making responsibility.[17]

Thus, the agency location process in a decentralized setting will differ from the centralized. The profitability associated with a particular urban center will be important, but should operate primarily as a *threshold* for agency establishment rather than as a basis for ranking alternative locations. At most, a local entrepreneur will evaluate a small number of nearby centers; other locations will not usually be considered even though they may be more suitable for the diffusion agency.

The profitability threshold condition will be met by numerous locations. Within this set, where and when agencies are established will depend upon the entrepreneur learning about the innovation and about establishing an agency from which it may be propagated. In the diffusion of rural purchasing cooperatives in Britain (Shawyer, 1970, 1974), for example, individuals starting a new cooperative were previously in contact with one or more leaders of existing cooperatives. From these contacts they obtained evidence of the effectiveness and likely success of a cooperative, knowledge of how to establish and successfully operate a cooperative and moral support for the venture.

Characteristics of the entrepreneur also are important.[18] The entrepreneur must, for example, have sufficient capital to establish an agency, be capable of seeing the potential of the innovation, be willing to take the required risks and to expend the required effort, and possess certain promotional and management skills. The congruence of the innovation with the ongoing activities of the entrepreneur also may be important. Cable television systems, for example, frequently were established by store owners selling television receivers (L.A. Brown, Malecki, Gross, Shrestha and Semple, 1974). In terms of a place characteristic, then, those with human resources capable of being aware of and exploiting the innovation are more likely to receive diffusion agencies (Cochran, 1966).

A critical element in decentralized diffusion, then, is information linkages among places and related means of exposure to the innovation. If there is a coordinating propagator, a conscious strategy may underly the information flow pattern. If there is not a coordinating propagator, and often when there is, the information flow system is less explicit.

Perhaps relevant in this context is Hagerstrand's (1967a, 1967b) suggestion that flows may occur via a hierarchy of networks of social communication, although they should be seen to involve several types of communication, not just the social. Empirical work on regional contact systems is reported in Hagerstrand and Kuklinski (1971), Thorngren (1970) and Tornqvist (1970), but these works are primarily concerned with contacts between established businesses. More relevant is the work of Gould and Tornqvist (1971), Pred (1973a, 1973b, 1974a, 1974b, 1975a, 1975b, 1976, 1977) and Warneryd (1968), which are concerned with contact systems more applicable to the establishment of diffusion agencies. Nevertheless, our knowledge of regional contact systems is not sufficient to permit specification aside from crude surrogates such as the gravity model (Pedersen, 1970, 1975; Pred, 1973b: 229–38) or distance to a diffusion node. Clearly, then, more work must be done to identify which contact systems are relevant to diffusion in a decentralized setting and to determine their spatial characteristics.

Another important question concerns the strategy employed by a coordinating propagator in meting out information flows and incentives to prospective diffusion agents (agencies). Evidence indicates that expected profitability or gain would be the ordering criteria (L.A. Brown and Malecki, 1977; L.A. Brown and Philliber, 1977; L.A. Brown, Schneider, Harvey and Riddell, 1979; Nartowicz, 1977). Thus, many of the points made above with respect to diffusion under a centralized decision-making structure also apply to a coordinating propagator. One important difference, however, is that profitability for the coordinating propagator could well be defined on a narrower basis reflecting only that aspect upon which its return is calculated. For instance, franchisers typically profit from a one-time-only fee paid by each franchisee and from a percentage of the gross sales of each franchisee. Thus, their agency establishment strategy would *not* be based upon maximizing the profits of the agency system as a whole as in diffusion under a centralized decision-making structure (Zeller, 1978; Zeller, Achabal, and Brown, 1980).

A Model. An optimization approach was employed in modeling diffusion in a centralized setting, but the preceding discussion indicates that a stochastic model is more appropriate in the decentralized. A model that embodies this characteristic, as well as other aspects of diffusion under a decentralized decision-making structure, is that of Pedersen (1970, 1975). It contains three components to account for the time at which a diffusion agency first appears in a given town.

The first component is a threshold function pertaining to exposure to the innovation, defined as

$$I_i(t) = \sum_{j=1}^{n} [k(P_i P_j)/d_{ij}^b] A_j(t) > F \qquad (3.5)$$

where

$I_i(t)$ is the amount of information about the innovation in town i at time t

$P_i(t)$, P_j are the populations of town i and town j, respectively

d_{ij} is the distance between towns i and j

$A_j(t)$ is the time *since* the first diffusion agency was established in town j

F is the threshold level of information about the innovation

k, b are scale parmeters.

The second component is a threshold function pertaining to the ability of a town to support an agency distributing the innovation, defined as

$$P_i \geq L \tag{3.6}$$

where

L is the threshold level of population or market potential.

The third component is the probability that a town will have at least one entrepreneur who will establish a diffusion agency for the innovation, defined as

$$S_i = 1 - e^{-P_i q} \tag{3.7}$$

where

$P_i q$ is the expected number of entrepreneurs in town i who might establish a diffusion agency.

When threshold conditions with regard to exposure (equation (3.5)) and market size (equation (3.6)) are met, adoption occurs with probability S_i dependent upon the number of entrepreneurs in a town (equation (3.7)). To actually specify adopter and non-adopter towns and time of adoption, a Monte Carlo simulation algorithm could be appended to the model (Robson, 1973: 186–245). To make this model more directly comparable with that proposed for the centralized case, the threshold condition (equation (3.6)) could be defined in terms of profitability instead of market potential. Finally, this model could be adapted for the case of a coordinating propagator by altering the threshold function pertaining to exposure to the innovation (equation (3.5)) to reflect the expected profitability of the coordinating propagator which would guide its dispersal of information and other incentives for diffusion agency establishment.

One approach to formulating a model in accordance with this last suggestion has been developed by Zeller (1978; Zeller, Achabal, and Brown, 1980). This involves two separate linear programming models, one reflecting the locational objectives of a franchisor (the equivalent of a coordinating propagator) and the other of a franchisee (the equivalent of the local entrepreneur who might establish a diffusion agency). These individual models, particularly that for the franchisor or coordinating propagator, include many of the characteristics of the model for diffusion under a centralized decision-making structure, presented in pages 57–9 above. However, an entirely different and unique solution arises when the two models are concatenated into one to take account of the conflict in locational choices arising from differences between the objectives of the coordinating propagator, who is providing incentives for agency establishment, and the objectives of the individual entrepreneurs, who are actually establishing the agencies.

Spatial Patterns of Diffusion under a Decentralized Decision-Making Structure. Pred (1973b: 227–38) presents analysis pertaining almost exclusively to diffusion in a decentralized setting, although not designated as such. This includes a model that allows for hierarchical contact (and therefore diffusion) from larger to smaller towns, lateral contact between towns of similar size and reverse contact from smaller to larger towns. He concludes that diffusion agencies generally would be found in larger cities and their environs before smaller cities. Pedersen's model provides a similar conclusion.

Both Pred and Pedersen present an impressive number of empirical examples that support their findings.[19] However, studies of more recent diffusions indicate that patterns of diffusion dominated by neighborhood and/or random effects also are to be found. These have examined the diffusion of planned regional shopping centers in the United States (Y.S. Cohen, 1972), the department store in Japan (Tanaka, 1971), rural purchasing cooperatives in Britain (Shawyer, 1970, 1974), cable television systems in Ohio (L.A. Brown, Malecki, Gross, Shrestha and Semple, 1974) and Bank-Americard and Master Charge services in Ohio and West Virginia (L.A. Brown and Malecki, 1977). These examples point out that market potential for the innovation is sometimes dependent upon characteristics for which urban population is not a good surrogate, that information level may be proportional to the probability of agency establishment rather than functioning solely as a threshold, that more serious institutional constraints to agency establishment may be found in larger cities than in smaller ones, and that the organizational structure of a propagator may significantly affect the diffusion pattern.

In general, however, there is an ambiguity in these findings that indicates a need to specify more completely the decentralized model and to define diffusion pattern expectations in terms of those specifications. In doing this, the continuum from decentralized diffusion without a coordinating propagator to centralized diffusion becomes useful (Figure 3.1). As noted, there is no narration of information flows with regard to a diffusion agency establishment in the pure decentralized case. This dimension is present, however, with the introduction of a coordinating propagator. Moving further along the continuum, the coordinating propagator also might provide support packages, such as training programs for diffusion agency personnel or designed systems to be used by the diffusion agency in disseminating the innovation. Finally, the coordinating propagator's role may even extend to selecting locations for diffusion agencies, and at the extreme, there might be so much control that the diffusion can be viewed as centralized!

Now to address the deduction of expected spatial patterns, consider this continuum together with the four factors identified as important in centralized diffusions—capital availability, sales potential, logistics and the elasticity of agency profitability with regard to sales potential. The same kind of arguments used for the centralized case (pages 59–63) also apply to the decentralized, except that the relative role of each factor would be dependent upon the organizational setting (the continuum of which is represented in Figure 3.1), as well as upon the characteristics of the innovation itself.

To illustrate this dependency upon the locus of decision making with respect to agency establishment, consider sales potential and how it would be reflected in the pattern of diffusion. In the decentralized setting that approximates the centralized, sales potential would be used to rank alternative markets and agencies would be established accordingly. In a decentralized setting with a coordinating propagator, sales potential would be used to guide the dissemination of information and other incentives for agency establishment, but the local entrepreneurs who are the targets of this effort might or might not respond accordingly, thus introducing a random or, perhaps, neighborhood effect element to the diffusion pattern. Finally, in a decentralized setting without a coordinating propagator, sales potential would act predominantly as a threshold, and the response of entrepreneurs in locations meeting that threshold would exhibit a strong random element.

Thus, to portray the expected patterns of diffusion in a decentralized setting, one would need a series of diagrams such as Figure 3.4. Furthermore, as in the centralized case, the role of each factor would vary according to its relative importance for a given innovation, as well as according to the organizational structure of the diffusion. It is conceivable, then, that the same innovation in different decision-making settings would exhibit dramatically different patterns of diffusion, as might different innovations in the same decision-making setting! Also, however, the diffusion pattern of one innovation in a particular decision-making setting might be similar to the diffusion pattern of a different innovation in a different decision-making setting!

To illustrate these points further, attention now turns to two case studies: the diffusion of the bank credit card and of cable television systems. These represent diffusion under a decentralized decision-making structure with and without, respectively, a coordinating propagator.

The Case of Bank Credit Card Services. The spread of BankAmericard (BAC) and Master Charge services through Ohio and West Virginia provides an example of diffusion agency establishment under a *decentralized decision-making structure with a coordinating propagator.*[20] BankAmericard was the earliest national bank credit card system, first developed locally by the Bank of America in San Francisco in 1958. It remained a regional program in California until 1966, when national development was begun with the cooperation of five other banks including the City National Bank and Trust Company of Columbus, Ohio (CNB). Thus, Ohio and West Virginia were among the earliest states in which nationwide bank credit cards were available.

Master Charge is the name of the service of Interbank Card Association which first appeared in California in late 1966 in response to BankAmericard. This is actually a number of regional credit plans which are tied together as a national system via the Master Charge card. Master Charge services were not made available within the study area until early 1969.

Both systems involve a two-tier hierarchy of member banks who act as outlets (diffusion agencies) through which the credit card is made available to consumers. The higher level (Class A or Principal bank) is the card-issuing bank which extends credit to card-holders, collects fees from merchants and processes the paperwork for those banks it sponsors. The non-card-issuing banks (Class B or Associate banks) also maintain and service contracts with local merchants, but may or may not themselves participate in the credit operation.

Despite this apparent similarity, the two national systems differ in the structure and composition of their hierarchies. In the Bank-Americard system the Class A banks are licensed by an intermediary bank which is an agent for National Bank Americard Incorporated (NBI), and the Class A bank may in turn enroll Class B banks. The profits from merchant fees and consumer finance charges are shared with both NBI and its regional agent. CNB is the regional agent in Ohio and West Virginia.

In the Master Charge system, on the other hand, most Principal banks are tied together by a regional cooperative association that acts largely in a coordinative role. These banks do not pay licensing or profit-sharing fees to a parent entity, but are only obligated to cover the operating costs of the regional association. The Master Charge system, in contrast to BankAmericard, is actually controlled by the Principal banks, which are relatively few in number. In the study area there are thirteen Principal banks, linked together through BancSystems Association of Rocky River, Ohio.

The coordinating propagators of BAC and Master Charge in the study area, City National Bank and BancSystems Association, developed and implemented various propagation strategies.

CNB decided that the ideal initial coverage would be one Class A bank in each Ohio county, and the following strategy was developed for achieving this. (1) With the exception of the five or six least populous counties, one locally prominent bank in each Ohio county, usually located in the county seat, would be approached. (2) Since personal contact was believed to be the easiest and most effective method of approaching other banks, any business or personal ties by CNB executives would be utilized first, as well as institutional ties with correspondent banks.[21] (3) If there was more than one prominent bank in a given county, as was frequently the case, the most aggressive would be approached.[22] (4) All affiliates of the single bank holding company in the state (in 1967) would be avoided, due in part to local competition between CNB and another Columbus bank which headed the holding company. (5) The major metropolitan banks would be approached together at a formal presentation of the BankAmericard system to allow them to be the first to join.[23]

The pattern of diffusion that might have emerged from this strategy was thwarted by two unexpected events. First, before CNB had contacted any Ohio banks it was approached independently by three small correspondent banks interested in joining the BankAmericard

system. Second, the contacted metropolitan banks rejected Bank-
Americard at its formal presentation by CNB, largely because of
institutional factors. One of these factors was the perceived stature of
CNB relative to the larger and more prominent metropolitan banks.
Another institutional factor was the conservative attitude of the large
city banks and their orientation toward business and real estate
concerns rather than toward the individual consumer.[24] Thus, a
hierarchical pattern of diffusion taking place from larger to smaller
towns did not occur.

BancSystems did not draw up a detailed strategy for disseminating
Master Charge as CNB had done for BankAmericard. However, the
bank credit card principle was widely accepted by 1969 when Master
Charge got underway, and their fee arrangement also seems to have
played a role since it allowed for several Principal banks and provided
each with a greater profit incentive. Together with competition
effects, then, these factors resulted in a rather rapid rate of diffusion
and state-wide coverage for Master Charge. With regard to the
spatial pattern of this, the structure and composition of the Master
Charge system favors large banks as Principals, and these generally
would be located in larger cities, thus inducing a hierarchy effect
tendency.

Now turning to the composite patterns of diffusion (Figure 3.6),
the most noticeable aspect as of June 1968, when only BAC was
available, is an absence of patterns traditionally associated with diffusion (Figure 3.6A). Thus, we find *no* pronounced neighborhood effect around Columbus, *no* adoption by banks in the larger urban
areas of the state and *no* other evidence of a hierarchical component.
This reflects (1) CNB's reliance upon its correspondent banking network and the criterion of state-wide coverage in the diffusion strategy
and (2) CNB's rejection by the large city banks on institutional
grounds. Both these factors led to a spatial pattern of diffusion with
strong random components and early adoption in less urbanized
areas that would not be considered *innovative* by traditional criteria.[25]
Also noticeable is an absence of adoption in West Virginia, an area
not included in CNB's initial propagation strategy.

By March 1969, just before the introduction of Master Charge, the
diffusion of BankAmericard had already encompassed banks in
forty-one Ohio counties (Figure 3.6B). Some large city adoption
begins to be evident here, having taken place in Canton, Dayton,
Toledo and Akron. However, these are not the largest cities in the
state, and even among this subset the pattern is in the order of
smaller places first and larger places later.

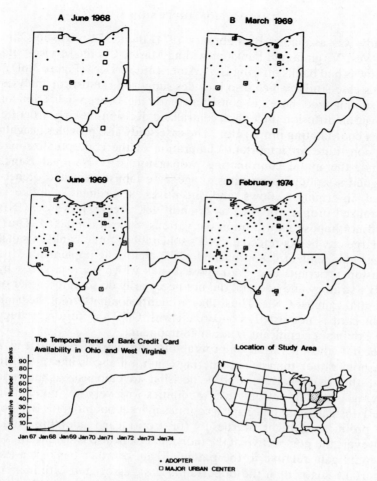

A June 1968

B March 1969

C June 1969

D February 1974

The Temporal Trend of Bank Credit Card
Availability in Ohio and West Virginia

Location of Study Area

Cumulative Number of Banks

90
80
70
60
50
40
30
20
10

Jan 67 Jan 68 Jan 69 Jan 70 Jan 71 Jan 72 Jan 73 Jan 74

• ADOPTER
□ MAJOR URBAN CENTER

Figure 3.6   The Spread of Bank Credit Card Services in
Ohio and West Virginia

The early pattern of Master Charge was very different from that of
BankAmericard. Between March and June 1969, sixty-seven Ohio
towns and two in West Virginia obtained Master Charge services
(Figure 3.6C). More significantly, there was immediate adoption by
banks in all major urban areas, that is, Akron, Canton, Cincinnati,
Columbus, Dayton, Cleveland and Toledo.

After July 1969 the pattern of diffusion seems most reflective of
competition effects rather than of the strategies of the coordinating
propagators. Most of the banks newly offering the bank credit card
service are located in towns where either BAC or Master Charge

already was available. By February 1974, then, 154 towns in Ohio and West Virginia had banks providing Master Charge services and 203 towns had banks offering BankAmericard services (Figure 3.6D).

This case study, which also includes supporting statistical analyses not summarized here, is consistent with the conceptualization of innovation diffusion under a decentralized decision-making structure with a coordinating propagator. The case study also provides insights that constitute an important elaboration of the conceptualization.

First, the initial coordinating propagator, City National Bank, designed a strategy pertaining to agency establishment and orchestrated information flows and incentives accordingly. Unlike a centralized propagator such as Friendly Ice Cream, however, CNB could not impose its will upon the various banks it contacted. Thus, the large city banks rejected CNB's solicitation, three banks in small towns independently approached CNB before it implemented its diffusion program, and even those banks which were targeted by CNB's strategy and adopted did not necessarily do so in the order of potential gain for CNB. Thus, the early diffusion pattern of the bank credit card is not strictly concordant with CNB's diffusion strategy and exhibits a significant random component.

Second, the operation of profitability and market potential as a threshold rather than as an ordering condition also is illustrated. In part, this derives from CNB's decision to emphasize state-wide coverage, leaving out only a few counties with very low population levels, instead of emphasizing a county's market potential for BAC or the profit that might accrue to (or from) each adopting bank. However, the perspective of the individual bank also is significant. Its potential gain relative to the potential gain of other banks is a less important factor than the opportunity costs associated with making the bank credit card available and the conditions of competition with other, nearby banks.

Third is the importance of institutional factors which previously have been given negligible attention in diffusion theory. An element of this is the different organizational structures of the BankAmericard and Master Charge systems leading to differences at the Class A or principal bank level in the amount of control and potential profit. A second element is the institutional stature relative to the large city banks of CNB at the time it became the regional propagator of BankAmericard. A third element is the disparity between the concept of credit embodied in the bank credit card plans and that of traditional banking. This appears to have particularly affected adoption by large city banks that were more conservative and more oriented toward business and real estate clienteles than toward individual or household consumers. Fourth, there is the reliance of CNB upon its correspondent bank network and the fact that this network has no noticeable spatial characteristics, which is typical of many organizational structures through which communications might flow (Pred, 1974b, 1975a, 1975b, 1976).

Finally, this case study indicates that the expectation of empirical regularities in the pattern of diffusion, such as the neighborhood and hierarchy effects, and the simplistic population and distance notions of traditional diffusion models do not constitute a sufficient level of understanding. For diffusion under a decentralized decision-making structure a more complex model is required. One variable in this would be *market potential* for the innovation; another would be *exposure* to the innovation, whereby a bank finds out about BankAmericard and Master Charge, the way in which it may become a diffusion agency for either and the gain from doing so. These are considered by the conceptualization presented above. Not considered, however, are *institutional characteristics* and *firm characteristics* pertaining to *management aggressiveness and innovativeness* whereby a bank would be exposed to the innovation early, would evaluate it as a significant venture and would be capable of responding by adopting the service and successfully promoting it. There is, however, a problem in measuring such factors for inplementation purposes. On the one hand, the case study material demonstrates that many of the common surrogates, such as distance from the coordinating propagator for exposure or information flows, are not suitable. On the other hand, knowing what the significant variables are does not in itself provide a solution. For example, management aptitude, management innovativeness and financial resources are known to be significant firm characteristics, but they are difficult if not impossible to measure, even with interview data (Malecki, 1975, 1977).

The Case of Cable Television. The establishment of cable television systems in Ohio is an example of diffusion agency establishment under a *decentralized decision-making structure without a coordinating propagator.*[26] Cable television may be distinguished from broadcast television in that it distributes signals to subscriber viewers by means of a system of cables and in-line amplifiers instead of electromagnetic waves. Signals are received and modified for distribution by an antenna and associated hardware (together called the *head-end*), and often, to expand the distance from which broadcast signals are received, microwave links also are employed. In addition to distributing existing broadcast signals, cable television originates some programming.

An important year in the development of cable television was 1948 when the Federal Communications Commission (FCC) imposed a freeze on new television broadcast facilities (A.J. Miller, 1967: 53). At that time broadcast facilities were only in sixty-one cities, primarily the larger urban centers of the United States (Berry, 1972). Since broadcast television signals are received well only within 50 to 100 miles of a radiating antenna and since this range is reduced in rough terrain, many areas of the United States were effectively left without television (Sloan Commission on Cable Communications, 1971: 11–12).

The lack of broadcast television coverage was a stimulus to the development of cable television. Initially, it functioned as a master antenna system, performing a task similar to that of the home reception antenna (Cooper, 1966: 9).[27] In 1949 a cooperative system serving residents of Astoria, Oregon was built (Taylor, 1951: 42–3), and in 1950 the first commercial system was established in Lansford, Pennsylvania, approximately 65 miles from the nearest broadcast facilities in Philadelphia (Seiden, 1972: 21; Steiner, 1973: 9). By the end of 1950 there were sixteen systems in seven states—Pennsylvania, Illinois, Kentucky, Ohio, Oregon, Washington and West Virginia (Zoerner, 1966: 38–9). Generally, the early entrepreneurs were either neighbors acting in cooperation or appliance dealers using the cable operation to stimulate television receiver sales (Zoerner, 1966: 4–5).[28] Thus, although a frequently cited reason for the emergence of cable television is public demand (Phillips, 1972: 3–4; Cooper, 1966: 71), the television dealers' motivation to turn latent demand into sales also must be seen as important.

The lifting of the FCC freeze on new television broadcast facilities in 1952 might have obviated the need for cable and given rise to new broadcast stations in small towns. But the proliferation of small town stations was prevented by the high investment requirements of broadcasting and by the nature of the FCC's channel allocations. In an effort to have stations in as many cities as possible, the FCC provided for hundreds of smaller one- or two-station markets. However, most of the new allocations, in these markets as well as larger city markets, were on ultra high frequency (UHF) channels, whereas most television receivers, then and for many years later, were built only with very high frequency (VHF) capabilities. Thus, the UHF channels often were unprofitable and went unutilized. In addition, households wanted to receive all three major networks, but town size often was not sufficient for that number of stations to be allocated. These factors resulted in many peripheral areas with little potential for suitable reception unless cable systems were constructed. Further, if an area could pick up all three major networks but only with marginal reception, it also was an ideal cable region. Thus, the lifting of the freeze on new television broadcast facilities and related FCC actions stimulated rather than deterred cable television growth (LeDuc, 1970: 84; Seiden, 1972: 11–19; Tate, 1971: 113–22).

By 1956 the cable industry had reached a plateau in its growth. Broadcast television was approaching the limit of its profitable market area and many favorable fringe communities were already wired for cable (LeDuc, 1970: 90). New growth was encouraged by two developments. First, color television created a need for the better quality reception that cable could supply (Sloan Commission, 1971: 26; Tepfer, 1964: 87). Second, viewers came to desire more options in their television fare, including non-network programming, enabling a cable system to profit in communities already receiving one or more broadcast stations (Tepfer, 1964: 40; Seiden, 1972: 21).

Until the 1960s cable television grew without official restrictions other than the franchise terms of individual communities. In 1962, however, the FCC permitted broadcasters to protest an application for a cable system if its approval and implementation would be detrimental to the broadcaster's operation (A.J. Miller, 1967: 54), and the next year the FCC ruled that cable systems could not transmit a broadcast show for fifteen days after origination if so requested by the broadcaster (Chase, 1969: 9). In 1965 the regulation of microwave gave the FCC increased control of cable television growth, and by 1966 Commission approval was necessary for establishment of a cable system located in any of the top one hundred markets of the nation.[29]

Under new rules effective in 1972, cable systems in the top one hundred markets are required to provide public access channels, to carry all significantly viewed signals and to provide certain minimum service.[30] In addition, systems with 3500 or more subscribers are required to carry at least twenty-four hours per week of locally originated programming (Federal Communications Commission, 1972: 60–1; Carey, 1971: 38). These regulations make operation in the larger cities more difficult but, judging by recent developments, not prohibitive (Steiner, 1973: 45–77; Tate, 1971: 39–70).

The diffusion of cable systems has occurred primarily under a decentralized decision-making structure. Early cable systems were locally established by a single entrepreneur or group of residents (Steiner, 1973: 9–10). Thus, their decision primarily pertained only to the construction of such a system, not to the community in which it would be located. Multiple system operating companies that engage in a centralized-type decision process have emerged. To date, however, they have grown primarily by buying out existing systems, rather than establishing systems in new areas.

The pattern of diffusion of cable television in the United States now can be summarized. In the early 1950s cable primarily existed where broadcast reception was marginal and where there was sufficient population to support a system. Particularly significant development in this era occurred in the populated, mountainous areas of the eastern United States where terrain obstructed broadcast signals (Zoerner, 1966: 39). After 1956, when microwave relay equipment became more readily available, cable service was extended to more remote locations, notably to populated pockets in the West (LeDuc, 1970: 93). In the late 1950s cable also entered the larger cities, impelled by the increasing demand for diversity in programming and the increasingly poorer quality of reception in growing urban places.[31] The 1970 distribution of cable systems in the United States (Figure 3.7) reflects these trends of early development in eastern mountain areas and of more recent growth in the south-west, west, and larger cities.[32]

The stages of development of cable television in the United States are mirrored in Ohio. Its temporal sequence of diffusion (Figure 3.7) is parallel to that of the United States as a whole and generally conforms to the traditional S-curve trend. Development began in Ohio in 1950 at a relatively brisk pace. In 1954 it leveled off, reflecting a plateau in the industry's overall growth nationwide. This plateau gave way to very rapid expansion in 1965 that still continues.

This temporal pattern suggests that division into two phases— before and after 1965—is appropriate. Support for this division also is to be found in the development of the cable industry. The year 1965 marks the beginning of extensive FCC regulation of the cable television industry. In addition, none of the top one hundred market cities in Ohio had cable service prior to 1965, an indication of a difference in market focus. Another difference lies in the role of cable television. Initially cable was seen as a means of providing some television reception to remote communities. Later the role shifted to providing improved reception and a greater variety of programming than that provided by broadcast television.

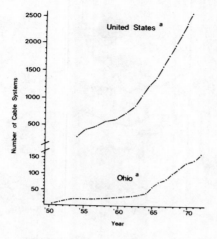

Alabama	60	Louisiana	32	Ohio	114
Alaska	7	Maine	25	Oklahoma	55
Arizona	22	Maryland	26	Oregon	87
Arkansas	55	Massachusetts	22	Pennsylvania	296
California	255	Michigan	48	Rhode Island	1
Colorado	29	Minnesota	42	South Carolina	24
Delaware	8	Mississippi	50	South Dakota	13
Florida	76	Missouri	48	Tennessee	44
Georgia	54	Montana	30	Texas	173
Hawaii	9	Nebraska	44	Utah	5
Idaho	45	Nevada	6	Vermont	25
Illinois	50	New Hampshire	20	Virginia	52
Indiana	40	New Jersey	26	Washington	102
Iowa	29	New Mexico	26	West Virginia	129
Kansas	59	New York	140	Wisconsin	46
Kentucky	90	North Carolina	32	Wyoming	23
		North Dakota	7		

Figure 3.7   Number of Cable Television Systems in the United States and
Ohio by Year, and in each State as of March 1970
[a]Note different scales for the United States and Ohio graphs.

These aspects of the development of cable television also are seen
in the spatial pattern of diffusion in Ohio (Figure 3.8). Early
development occurred in two areas of the Appalachian Plateau
portion of Ohio, areas of rather rugged terrain. In central eastern
Ohio a system was established at Glenmont in 1950, followed the
next year by systems at nearby Millersburg, Dover and New
Philadelphia. In the same year, 1951, systems were established in

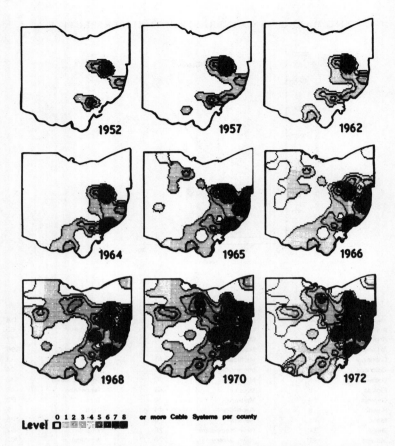

Level 🔳 0 1 2 3 - 4 5 6 7 8   or more Cable Systems per county

Figure 3.8   Spread of Cable Television Systems in Ohio for Selected
Years

south-eastern Ohio at Athens, The Plains and Murray City. Through
1964, the termination of Phase I, the location of new systems
generally follows a neighborhood effect pattern nucleated around
these two areas, resulting in a broad zone of cable service across the
Appalachian Plateau section of eastern and south-eastern Ohio.

In 1965, the beginning of Phase II, more systems were established
than in any previous year, and they are located in new and widely
separated areas. The shift to north-western Ohio is particularly
noticeable, occurring in the towns of Kenton, Piqua, Fostoria,
Bowling Green, Findlay, Tiffin and Wauseon. However, this shift is
not accompanied by the spatial clustering that characterized the
initiation of Phase I.

These trends continue for the whole of Phase II. By 1972 cable systems were located throughout the entire state with the exception of the large metropolitan centers, but density of service remained greatest in the Appalachian Plateau areas. Further, although some medium-size cities in the top one hundred market areas received cable during Phase II—Steubenville in 1965, Toledo and Canton in 1966 and Akron in 1969—development in the state's largest metropolitan areas such as Cincinnati, Cleveland and Columbus is only currently taking place.

To further evaluate the spatial pattern of cable system establishment in Ohio, statistical analyses were carried out using independent variables pertaining to market potential and exposure to cable television whereby entrepreneurs learn that a system may be established, how that is accomplished, and that doing so may be profitable or advantageous in some other way. Variables employed to measure market potential primarily pertain to the quality of television reception without cable; those employed to measure exposure were distances from Glenmont in eastern Ohio, Athens in south-eastern Ohio and Kenton in north-west Ohio. These represent the earliest established cable systems in each area and were taken to be diffusion nodes.

In general, both market potential and exposure are significantly related to the year in which a cable system is established, but the exposure variables are somewhat less important in Phase II. There are also some interesting differences in distinguishing between towns that established a cable system in Phase I, those in Phase II and towns that had not established such a system at all. Phase I adopter towns have significantly higher levels of market potential and are located closer to the original nodes of the diffusion in eastern Ohio than are Phase II adopter towns. In comparing Phase II with non-adopter towns the differences are not as marked and are even inconclusive for several variables.

Taken together, these analyses support the conceptualization of diffusion agency establishment under a decentralized decision-making structure without a coordinating propagator. Both *market potential* and *exposure* were important factors. That Phase II adopter towns were not so different from non-adopter towns underlines the additional importance of a factor akin to *firm characteristics pertaining to management aggressiveness and innovativeness*. In contrast to the bank credit card which was taken on by sizeable firms (banks), however, cable television systems were generally established by single entrepreneurs. Thus, the variable(s) to capture this factor should pertain to the local pool of entrepreneurial ability or the level of individual innovativeness. In the model for the decentralized case, presented on pages 70–2, this factor is represented by the probability that a town will have at least one entrepreneur who will establish a diffusion agency for the innovation.

Another interesting comparison is the random pattern characterizing the diffusion of the bank credit card and the neighborhood effect pattern characterizing cable television. It seems that this difference occurs because of the different mechanism of exposure in the two cases. City National Bank employed a formal network, its correspondent banking system, that had no marked spatial characteristics. By contrast, cable television spread *naturally,* without the orchestration of a coordinating propagator, through a grass roots system of interpersonal contact and local spatial interaction among towns. It is anticipated that such differences should be common in comparing cases with and without a coordinating propagator. More generally, however, comparing these two examples demonstrates how the *organizational structure* of diffusion directly affects the diffusion pattern and who has access to the innovation (thus permitting adoption) at any given time.

Finally, there is the role of *institutional* factors. These operated both in the establishment of cable television systems and in the bank credit card case. In the latter instance, the diffusion agency establishment efforts of the propagating bank were resisted by larger banks of greater institutional stature, which also were more conservative and more oriented toward business and real estate clienteles than toward individual or household consumers. By contrast, the institutional factors operating in the diffusion of cable television were external to the agency establishment decision, that is, they pertained to creating the conditions for diffusion rather than to the interactions between the various actors in the system.[33]

Diffusion Agency Establishment in Non-Profit-Motivated Settings

The centralized-decentralized distinction also carries into non-profit-motivated diffusion. The most prevalent centralized propagators of this type probably are the various federal, state and local governments. The county-based offices of the Cooperative Extension Service, for example, are diffusion agencies. Examples of agency establishment in a decentralized setting with a coordinating propagator include Montessori schools (Meyer, 1975) and Planned Parenthood family planning clinics (L.A. Brown and Philliber,

1977). Examples where there is not a coordinating propagator would include drug crisis centers, legal aid societies and buyer cooperatives.[34]

A detailed consideration of the processes involved in non-profit-motivated diffusions will not be attempted at this time. It is thought, however, that these may correspond to a surprising degree with those processes posited for profit-motivated diffusions.[35] A major difference is the absence of a profit criterion, a single index for assessing diffusion agency locations. However, non-profit-motivated diffusions can employ cost–benefit indices such as the number of persons assisted per dollar of agency expense.[36] If this kind of index is not used, the costs involved in serving a given need or demand must be weighed subjectively against the need or demand itself. These are not directly comparable, and proportionally more emphasis probably would be given to need or demand, with costs entering primarily in terms of the limits imposed by finite budgets. Nevertheless, this procedure has been shown to implicitly invoke and maximize a cost–benefit index, at least in one instance (L.A. Brown, Williams, Youngmann, Holmes and Walby, 1974).

This suggests that an appropriate model for non-profit-motivated diffusion agency establishment in a centralized decision-making setting would be a location allocation format in which facilities are located so as to maximize total service subject to a budget constraint (Lea, 1973a, 1973b; Hodgart, 1978), and that a model such as that presented on pages 70–2 above would be suitable for non-profit-motivated diffusion agency establishment in a decentralizing setting.

The similarity in the profit- and non-profit-motivated situations is further illustrated by the following.

The Case of the Planned Parenthood Affiliate. The Planned Parenthood Affiliate is an outlet through which family planning information and services are provided to the public. The establishment of these in United States cities provides an example of diffusion agency establishment under a decentralized decision making structure with a coordinating, *non-profit-motivated* propagator.[37]

The evolution of the present system of Planned Parenthood affiliates has occurred under a number of different organizations. Initially, the major force was the American Birth Control League, founded in 1921 (Kennedy, 1970: 94).[38] This merged with the Clinical Research Bureau in 1939 to form the Birth Control Federation of America, which in 1942 became the Planned Parenthood Federation of America (Kennedy, 1970: 256–7). In general, these private non-profit organizations provided family planning information and services to persons who did not have access to these elsewhere.

Ostensibly, affiliation has always begun at the local level as a result of local demand. Sometimes originating as interest clubs, charity groups, or as part of another organization such as a church, community members interested in the provision of family planning services at low cost may then request affiliation from the national Planned Parenthood organization. After certain standards are met, this affiliation may be granted, but fund raising continues to be the responsibility of the local affiliate.

Some examples from Ohio illustrate this pattern. The Columbus affiliate began in 1932 as the Mothers' Health Clinic of Columbus, not officially becoming a Planned Parenthood affiliate until 1943. The Maternal Health Association was the original name of the Youngstown (1934), Cleveland (1928) and Toledo (1937) affiliates, while Cincinnati's (1929) was the Committee on Maternal Health. Youngstown joined the Planned Parenthood Federation in 1944; the others may be assumed to have replicated this pattern. The founding women of these clinics were in all cases recognized community leaders.

This description seems to indicate that the initiation of Planned Parenthood affiliation was largely a grass roots movement. Indeed, support for this could be found in the Columbus, Ohio affiliate's newsletter of January 1968.

The same year (1934) members of our board helped start clinics in Springfield and Dayton. A few years later, clinics in Toledo and Youngstown were also given advice and assistance by members of our board.

This suggests a locally based process by which communities became exposed to the innovation.

However, Kennedy (1970) argues that the birth control movement was one of many women's reform projects taken up by

respectable matrons of the middle class

many of whom participated in several such efforts and were tied into a national network of reformers. He suggests that these women brought to the birth control movement the techniques of organization and propaganda that had been learned in efforts such as the temperance and suffrage movements (Kennedy, 1970: 105–6). Thus, the American Birth Control League carried on a systematic program of conferences, salaried speakers and fieldworkers who

canvassed the country organizing affiliated local leagues and soliciting the support of such groups as women's clubs and social work organizations. (Kennedy, 1970: 100–1)

These efforts apparently proceeded with an eye to the greatest likelihood of success in establishing an affiliate. Further evidence that centralized strategies were used in the birth control movement is found in an internal memorandum proposing a detailed promotional plan, based upon an analysis of 7309 'mothers' ' letters received by the American Birth Control League and Margaret Sanger in 1931 and 1932.[39] These were analyzed with regard to their place of origin, the types of persons writing and their content (Boughton, 1933). In general, the strategy suggests concentration of effort in communities that were larger in population size, less Catholic and of higher educational and income levels (Kennedy, 1970: 100).[40]

Another important promotional element was the National Committee on Federal Legislation for Birth Control. To bring pressure on Congress the Committee carried on an educational program much like that of the American Birth Control League, but organized and directed more tightly along regional, state and local lines (Kennedy, 1970: 228–9). As an indication of the resoluteness of these efforts, Kennedy notes

If a particular body resisted the persuasion of the lecturer and the importuning of the field worker, Mrs Sanger called upon her old radical lessons and counseled discreet 'boring from within': the field worker should join the organization and work quietly but tenaciously to bring it into line. (1970: 229)

While these strategies of the National Committee were not directed toward the organization of local birth control clinics, they probably had an influence in that direction. Further, it seems reasonable to assume that the Planned Parenthood Federation of America maintained at least some centrally directed and integrated developmental practices similar to those of its predecessors, outlined above.[41] The general picture, then, seems to be one of a central organization (or propagator) perceiving and fertilizing small seeds of local interest, which culminated in the establishment of a Planned Parenthood affiliate or diffusion agency.

The growth in the number of Planned Parenthood affiliates has experienced three rather distinct stages (Figure 3.9). During the first the number of affiliates increased from the initial Margaret Sanger clinic in 1916 to about eighty in 1939, corresponding with the change-over from the American Birth Control League to the Planned Parenthood Federaton of America. A period of very slow growth, perhaps representing a consolidation phase and formalization of standards for affiliation, followed from 1940 through 1960 with the

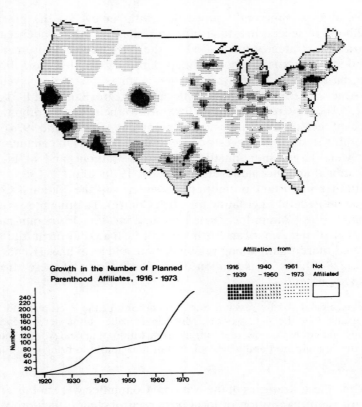

Figure 3.9 The Geographical Spread of Planned Parenthood
    Affiliates in the United States

number of affiliates increasing by only twenty-six. Another period of
very high growth followed from 1961 through 1973, when 137
affiliates were added.

With regard to geographical spread, the earliest Planned Parenthood affiliates were located in the largest cities: New York, Syracuse,
Detroit, Chicago, Dallas, Houston, Phoenix, Denver and the like
(Figure 3.9). Those formed from 1940 to 1960 generally were
spatially contiguous to these early affiliates; only in California and
Washington are new affiliates established without an apparent spread
from nearby places. In the 1961–73 stage the contagion pattern
dominates as the areas covered by the first and second stage affiliates
are widened. The overall spatial pattern, then, is one of initial
establishment in the large regional centers across the United States,

followed by a wave-like spread outward from these smaller urban centers and a general east-to-west and north-to-south trend.

Statistical analyses employed variables pertaining to a community's need for family planning services, its potential exposure to Planned Parenthood creating awareness of the innovation, and the presence of persons and organizations that might found an affiliate. These relate, of course, to the market potential, exposure, and firm characteristic factors of the conceptual model of diffusion agency establishment in a decentralized decision-making structure with a coordinating propagator.

Both the quantitative and qualitative analyses indicate that all these factors operated in this non-profit-motivated diffusion. Specifically, through community, organizational and interpersonal contact patterns community members came to be aware of the need for family planning services, the Planned Parenthood organization, and the way an affiliate might be implemented as a workable solution to a local problem. Further, in so far as this contact involved conferences, speakers and fieldworkers supported by the parent organization or major affiliates, costs would be incurred, and the observed patterns are consistent with operating in a manner that minimizes those costs. With regard to other factors, it seems clear that the American Birth Control League and Planned Parenthood narrated their organizational efforts towards communities where need, organizational capability and therefore the likelihood of affiliate adoption were greatest. The fourth factor of the general model, institutional factors, was not included in the statistical analyses, but their importance is strongly supported by the historical account of the evolution of the Planned Parenthood affiliate system. Like the cable television case, institutional factors here operated primarily in creating the conditions for diffusion, both at a national and community level.

OVERVIEW

This chapter has examined the process by which diffusion agencies are established. It is through these agencies that the innovation is made available to potential adopters, and hence, the timing and order of their establishment sets the broad outlines of the diffusion pattern. There are several diffusion agency establishment processes, rather than only one, and each is characterized by a different organizational structure. Thus, we speak of a continuum bounded by *diffusion under a centralized decision-making structure* and *diffusion under a decentralized decision-making structure without a coordinating propagator*. In between these poles are a series of situations termed *diffusion under a decentralized decision-making structure with a coordinating propagator*. The factors which are important in each of these cases are more or less the same, although their roles differ across the continuum portraying the organizational structure of diffusion.

Three approaches were employed to examine these situations. First, abstract conceptual models were formulated and the logical implications of those, in terms of spatial patterns, were deduced. Second, operational models, which reflect the conceptualization, were formulated. These provide a means of implementation for future research and a tractable structure for discussion. Third, case studies were carried out. These amplify and help establish the validity of the conceptual and/or operational models.

In diffusion under a centralized decision-making structure, a single propagator determines the number of diffusion agencies to be established and their location, size and other characteristics. Optimally, the various markets would be ranked according to their expected profitability and then sequentially exploited, the most profitable earlier and the less profitable later, if at all. The critical factors in this process are capital availability, sales potential, logistics and the elasticity of agency profitability with regard to sales potential. Traditionally, the pattern of diffusion associated with a set of urban places is a hierarchical one with the largest receiving the innovation earlier. Our analysis, however, finds little support for this and in fact provides a somewhat stronger case for expecting a neighborhood effect pattern or one with no marked spatial bias.

In diffusion under a decentralized decision-making structure each diffusion agency is established independently by a different entrepreneurial or economic entity, and it rather than a central propagator carries the burdens of risk, capital provision and decision-making responsibility. While the profitability associated with a particular urban center is important, this primarily operates as a threshold for agency establishment rather than as a basis for ranking alternative locations. Since the profitability threshold will be met by numerous urban areas, where and when agencies are established will depend upon the local entrepreneur learning about the innovation and about establishing an agency from which it may be propagated. Accordingly, characteristics of the local entrepreneur also are important. That person must, for example, have sufficient capital to establish an agency, be capable of seeing the potential of the innovation, be willing to take the required risks and to expend the required effort and possess certain promotion and management skills. Another factor is the congruence of the innovation with the ongoing activities of the entrepreneur. Thus, those places with human resources capable of being aware of and exploiting the innovation are more likely to receive diffusion agencies.

If there is a coordinating propagator in decentralized diffusion, some aspects of the situation, such as information flows or incentives for agency establishment, are controlled and orchestrated by that entity. Thus, in contrast to the centralized case, the diffusion pattern is influenced but not determined by the coordinating propagator. One thing in particular that cannot be controlled is the decision to establish an agency in the first place since, by definition, this must be done by the local entrepreneur. With regard to spatial patterns, the arguments once again fall on the side of expecting neighborhood effects or no marked spatial bias.

The various case studies illustrate the major types of diffusion agency establishment structures. The spatial pattern of Friendly Ice Cream stores evolved under a highly centralized structure. This diffusion was characterized by marked neighborhood or wave-like patterns, reflecting the importance of the logistics of service, supply and control and the ability of Friendly stores to be profitable in relatively small cities (that is, they had a low elasticity of profitability with respect to urban size). Capital availability also played a role in controlling the rate of diffusion agency establishment and the relative roles of each of the factors underlying this.

The diffusion of cable television systems in Ohio illustrates a decentralized structure without a coordinating propagator. Market potential (defined in terms of the number of households with poor television reception) acted as a threshold condition defining a gross area where agency establishment might occur. Within this constraint, a neighborhood wave pattern of diffusion from town to town was observed, reflecting the characteristics of information or exposure to the innovation in the form of a grass roots system of interpersonal contact and local spatial interaction among towns. The presence of human resources capable of being aware of and exploiting the innovation also was important. Finally, institutional factors played a role by creating external conditions which channeled the spatial and temporal patterns of diffusion.

Two case studies were used to illustrate diffusion in a decentralized structure with a coordinating propagator. The diffusion of the bank credit card in Ohio and West Virginia represents a profit-motivated situation, whereas the diffusion of Planned Parenthood affiliates represents a non-profit-motivated situation. The coordinating

propagators in both situations operated under an explicit strategy
that favored diffusion agency establishment in selected areas. A key
element in this strategy was the orchestration of information flows
whereby potential diffusion agents were exposed to the innovation
and made aware of the gain to be realized by establishing an agency.
Market potential or need for the innovation was one factor guiding
the meting out of information and related incentives for adoption.
Institutional and firm characteristics pertaining to management
aggressiveness and innovativeness also played a role. The former is
particularly interesting. In the case of the bank credit card, important
institutional factors include the different organizational structures of
the BankAmericard and Master Charge systems, City National
Bank's correspondent banking network which was a critical element
of its diffusion strategy, City National Bank's relatively lesser stature
as compared to the big city banks it initially courted, and the disparity
between the concept of credit embodied in the bank credit card and
that of traditional banking. In the diffusion of the Planned Parenthood affiliate, important institutional factors included local organizational capability, sympathy with women's reform projects and a
connection with the national network of such reformers. Finally, the
spatial patterns of these diffusions are quite different. The bank
credit card exhibited an almost random pattern whereas the Planned
Parenthood diffusion exhibited a pattern composed of hierarchy and
neighborhood effects. Yet, both cases indicate that it would be
unwarranted to expect patterns of diffusion to exhibit regularities
such as hierarchy and neighborhood effects, and that the simplistic
population and distance notions of traditional diffusion models
grossly underestimate and generally misstate the complexities and
vagaries of the innovation diffusion process.

One general point remains. The orientation of research on
diffusion has been towards adoption behavior, but, as indicated here,
the diffusion strategies actually used have been quite different. In the
case of any diffusion involving a coordinating propagator, for
example, it appears that the effort is likely to utilize existing societal
levers, organizations and networks from the top down, instead of
from the bottom up as the demand-based adoption paradigm would
suggest. That this pattern has been practiced in profit-motivated
settings may not be surprising, but it also has been practiced in
pragmatically oriented non-profit settings, as indicated by the
diffusion of Planned Parenthood and of Montessori education
(Meyer, 1975). As academics, however, we are only beginning to
examine this phenomenon, and we know relatively little about the

organizational structure and other aspects of diffusion by which innovations are made available to potential adopters, particularly in non-profit-motivated settings (Kotler, 1975; Lovelock and Weinberg, 1978). Clearly, then, our research priorities must be broadened and policy-relevant findings will be more likely. This question is addressed more directly in Chapter 9.

Attention now turns to the second part of the market and infrastructure perspective, the strategies employed by diffusion agencies to promote adoption among individuals or households in their market or service areas.

NOTES

1 For a review of this literature, see E.M. Rogers and Shoemaker (1971), Robertson (1971), Midgley (1977), L.A. Brown and Moore (1969) and Chapters 1 and 2 of this book.

2 For a broad review of these and related decisions, Kotler (1971, 1972) is exceptionally useful, although he gives little explicit attention to the situation of innovation or new product diffusion. The decisions of particular concern in this chapter pertain to what Kotler terms *distribution location* (Kotler, 1971: 302–23). Kotler (1971: 312–20) also provides a very good summary of materials pertaining to the selection of a specific site within the designated market area. This topic is of great importance in diffusion, but it is neglected in this chapter because it represents a different geographical scale from that being considered.

3 In earlier papers developing the diffusion agency establishment framework (L.A. Brown, 1975) the terminology used was, respectively, *diffusion in a mononuclear propagation structure, diffusion in a polynuclear propagation structure (without central propagator support),* and *diffusion in a polynuclear propagation structure with central propagator support.* Irrespective of the terminology, however, whether there is or is not a coordinating propagator, establishment of the agency is itself an adoption process in a decentralized setting whereas this is not so in a centralized setting. Finally, the ensuing discussion on these organizational structures is concerned with their relevance for diffusion to entities *outside of* the organization itself. A related literature that might provide some guidelines for further development of this topic deals with the effects of organizational structure on adoption *within* the organization. For an introduction to this literature, see Zaltman, Duncan and Holbeck (1973), E.M. Rogers and Agarwala-Rogers (1976) and Havelock (1969).

4 Griliches (1957) also makes this point with regard to rural settings. Other objectives may guide the propagator such as cost minimization or sales maximization, but these appear to operate on a short-term basis. This is discussed further above, beginning on page 59. For a discussion of firm objectives in general see Baumol (1972: 310–34).

5 Accessibility generally varies inversely with distance, but not always. For example, air service renders many distant locations more accessible than nearby ones, and the locational patterns of some agency systems reflect this.

6 The model is described in terms of establishing a single diffusion agency, but this is not a limiting assumption since the agency could be of any size and/or represent several agencies.

7 This could be estimated in several ways. Very common is to derive a sales potential index on the basis of the population of place i relative to all other places being

considered. The *Sales Management Magazine's: 1974 Survey of Buying Power* recommends deriving such an index on the basis of place i's per cent of buying power, retail sales and population, weighted at 0.5, 0.3 and 0.2, respectively. This index then would be applied to an estimate of unit sales potential overall to derive the unit sales potential for place i. One is still faced with the problem of estimating overall sales potential. In a locational context, however, this is of minimal significance because the major concern is the potential return of each place i relative to others.

8 At initiation of the diffusion there will be no competitive activity, and w_{ik} would be estimated as in equation (3.3). As the diffusion continues, however, competition may enter, and in locations where this occurs the market share of the initial propagator will be eroded. The single firm, then, would be concerned with its market share as well as the market potential and market penetration of the innovation. This could be incorporated into the model by

$$w_{ik} = (1 - v_{ik})w_{ik}$$

where v_{ik} is the degree of competition in location i at time k, $0 \leqslant v_{ik} \leqslant 1$.

9 An important aspect of demand not explicitly considered in equation (3.3) is the frequency of repurchase of the innovation. If repurchase occurs in each time period after initial adoption, for example, w_{ik} would never be less than the cumulative first time sales of the innovation, whereas this is unlikely if repurchase is less frequent. Incidently, the estimation equation for market share suggested in note 8 implies that competition takes away existing customers of a firm in the same proportion as it takes new customers. A formulation that applied full competitive effects only to new customers and lesser effects to old customers would be more realistic. For a review of the state of the art in models portraying the market response or growth in demand for the innovation, see Mahajan and Peterson (1978, 1979).

10 Equation (3.4) is stated generally because no single way of stating it explicitly is clearly preferable to alternatives. Craig and Brown (1974) employ a multiplicative format in which the variables p, a, h and e are indices, each taking on the value of one if price, advertising and outlet decisions, respectively, are optimal. Thus, the net effect under optimal decision making by the propagator would be sales (q_{ik}) equivalent to expectations on the basis of market potential, market penetration, market share (w_{ik}) and general economic conditions (g_{ik}); but if propagator decisions are otherwise, sales less than or greater than $w_{ik}g_{ik}$ are possible.

11 This model has been operationalized in a game simulation mode as PROMAR, the New Product Marketing Game. See L.A. Brown, Craig and Zeller (1977) and Craig and Brown (1978, 1980).

12 As noted in Chapter 2, a pattern exhibiting a hierarchy effect in combination with a neighborhood effect generally is associated with diffusion in an urban system (L.A. Brown and Cox, 1971; Hagerstrand, 1952; Hudson, 1969b), although sometimes the hierarchy effect has been treated as more important in this setting (Boon, 1967; Berry, 1972).

13 The following argument with regard to strategy was suggested by Jeffrey Osleeb of the Boston University Department of Geography.

14 Although expansion capital may be generated internally, say by retained earnings, financial institutions are a more important source. Thus, the credibility of the propagator and the innovation are critical, and the demonstration of credibility should be a goal of the initial efforts of the propagator. An important aspect in this is the market response with regard to the innovation.

15 There is a correspondence between the order of a good and the more common marketing scale of convenience, shopping and specialty goods. Specifically, higher-order goods correspond with specialty goods, and lower-order goods with convenience goods.

16 This is a synopsis of research reported more fully in Meyer, Brown and Camarco (1977) and Meyer and Brown (1979). Most of this material is based upon

information and data provided by the advertising and real estate divisions of Friendly Ice Cream.

17 This can be rationalized as follows. In the centralized case all aspects of the agency system affect propagator profit, so the propagator will want to maximize each agency's profit (one factor of which will be its location). In the decentralized case where there is a coordinating propagator, its profit will be related only to some aspects of agency experience, such as sales volume. Any intervention with regard to this aspect would depend upon the required commitment of resources compared to the potential gain. In general, however, there would be little incentive for intervention, particularly since adequate agency performance may consist only of meeting some threshold level. Likewise, an agency has little incentive to intervene in the affairs of another agency since the profits of each generally would be viewed as independent of one another. Thus, the failure or marginal success of a small number of agencies in a decentralized setting should not significantly affect the overall diffusion of the innovation, and only when the experience is pervasive will the diffusion be in jeopardy.

18 There is a correspondence between these characteristics and those noted as important in firm adoption behavior where the innovation is for the firm's own use. The diffusion problem treated in this section, that is of consumer innovations in a decentralized setting, also involves adoption by firms, but as an intermediary rather than as a final user. These similarities provide a link between the diffusion of consumer good and service innovations and the diffusion of organizational and technological innovations, which for the most part have been studied as distinct and unrelated phenomena. These points are elaborated in Chapter 5.

19 Pred's examples are from the United States in 1790–1840: banking, horse-drawn omnibuses and intraurban street railways, the suspension of specie payments during the panic of 1837, daily newspapers and the penny press, and steam-engine usage. Pedersen's are from Chile in the nineteenth and twentieth century: newspapers, fire brigades, Rotary clubs, radio stations and supermarkets. Support also can be found in Hagerstrand's (1952) study of the motor car and radio in southern Sweden. Related material also appears in Robson (1973: 131–85).

20 This is a synopsis of work reported more fully in L.A. Brown and Malecki (1977). Most of this material is based upon information and data provided by City National Bank, BancSystems Association, and the Delaware County Bank, all of Ohio.

21 CNB had no formal links with other banks through a bank holding company, but did have a state-wide network of correspondent banks. In correspondent banking a larger bank provides services for smaller banks such as holding deposits, clearing checks and foreign exchange, participating in loans, and providing management advice, personnel training and, more recently, data processing. In exchange, the correspondent bank pays a fee for the service and keeps some minimum balance on deposit in the central bank. Normally, there is a hierarchy of correspondent banks. The small town bank may, for example, employ the services of one or more large city banks, which in turn would employ the services of one or more banks in a regional or national banking center. Locationally, a large city bank would have correspondents throughout its state, although their prevalence would be somewhat greater nearby. For further information, see Fischer (1968: 110–21) and Borchert (1972).

22 The aggressiveness criterion involved a difficult and subjective assessment for the CNB directors, particularly since the more aggressive banks were not necessarily the largest or most prominent in an area.

23 In addition to the bank recruiting strategy, CNB developed a method of local marketing assistance. This involved a standardized advertising and merchants recruitment scheme that could be customized for each town. The mass media advertising portions of the package were directed simultaneously to both the merchants and the public.

24 The philosophy toward consumer credit embodied in the bank credit card conflicted with traditional practices. In credit card plans the qualifications for being a card-holder are minimal, and the card-holder is given a credit limit within which he controls the amount, use and timing of loans. Traditionally, though, bankers had been accustomed to maintaining complete control over credit. The additional risk of credit card plans presumably is compensated for by relatively high interest rates and fees charged to merchants who honor the card. Nevertheless, large city banks were more staunch in maintaining *conservative* practices, perhaps because the individual or household consumer was considered a less important part of their overall business.

25 For a critique of the innovativeness concept in light of the market and infrastructure perspective presented in this book, see L.A. Brown, Malecki and Spector (1976).

26 This is a synopsis of work reported more fully in L.A. Brown, Malecki, Gross, Shrestha and Semple (1974). General references on cable television include Phillips (1972), Steiner (1973), Tate (1971), Sloan Commission on Cable Communications (1971), Code of Federal Regulations (1973, Title 47, Part 76) and Seiden (1972). Instead of cable television, one frequently finds the terms 'cablevision,' 'community antenna television,' 'CATV,' 'CTV,' or simply 'cable.'

27 The advantages of the cable system in this use were better equipment, better location for signal reception and the sharing of a single antenna by many users via cable. Such master antenna systems had been in operation in New York City hotels and apartment buildings, for example, as early as 1947 (Stone, 1967: 1).

28 In the Lansford system, for example, a demonstration set in an appliance store was connected by cable to the master antenna, and hook-ups to the antenna were sold along with television receivers (Phillips, 1972: 35–9).

29 Market rankings are based on the total number of television homes within a thirty-five mile radius of a central reference point in each market. For further details and a list of the market rankings, see Code of Federal Regulations (1973, Title 47, Section 76.51).

30 A broadcast signal is defined as significantly viewed if it is from a full or partial network station and viewed by at least 25 per cent of the television households in a given community, or if it is from an independent station and viewed by at least 5 per cent of the television households in a given community. See Code of Federal Regulations (1973, Title 47, Section 76.5). Minimum service required of cable systems is specified in Code of Federal Regulations (1973, Title 47, Sections 76.61, 76.63).

31 The latter results from an increase both in the spatial extent of urban areas and in the number of signal blockings buildings and various generators of electrical noise.

32 J. Foley of the Ohio State University Department of Speech Communications points out that another factor is the regulatory climate of a state. Such regulation greatly influences the ease with which cable systems may be started. Connecticut, for instance, has the strictest laws and, consequently, no cable television systems at all. For an elaboration of these issues, see Seiden (1972:79–84).

33 A further discussion of the role of such condition creating institutional factors in innovation diffusion can be found in Rosenburg (1976a, 1976b), Sagers and Brown (1977) and Chapter 6 of this book.

34 Another instance of non-profit-motivated diffusion involves the community as either a final or intermediary adopter. Examples include fluoridation (Crain, 1966; Crain, Katz and Rosenthal, 1969), public housing (Aiken and Alford, 1970), city manager form of government (McVoy, 1940), model cities and urban renewal (Hawley, 1963). A framework for community adoption that is comparable to the one presented here is described in Agnew, Brown and Herr (1978).

35 Roessner (1977) makes such a finding for innovation within public organizations,

based upon an application of research and findings from economic theory, organization theory, public administration and political science.

36 An example receiving recent attention is the practice of *triage* whereby locations are divided into those which will improve without assistance, those which require assistance for improvement and those which would not be significantly improved were any amount of assistance given. For a discussion of this applied to the hunger problem, see Knight and Wilcox (1975) and the *New York Times Magazine*, January 5 1975.

37 This is a synopsis of work reported more fully in L.A. Brown and Philliber (1977).

38 A number of organizations preceded the American Birth Control League, but their lineage is difficult to follow. Notable is the National Birth Control League, the New York Birth Control League and the Voluntary Parenthood League (Kennedy, 1970 : 94). Further, during the American Birth Control League's existence, the National Committee on Federal Legislation for Birth Control was a legislative force which also had significant impact upon birth control awareness in the population at large (Kennedy, 1970: 105).

39 The various issues of the *Birth Control Review* also provide ample evidence of the use of the centralized propagation strategies, including details on matters such as conferences organized, persons dispatched to various locales, the infiltration of existing organizations and procedures for establishing a family planning program.

40 The Catholic issue was apparently aggravated beyond what it might have been by Margaret Sanger's actions, so that rapprochement was difficult if not impossible (Kennedy, 1970: 97–8).

41 Personal conversation with Miriam Garwood, a Planned Parenthood Federation field consultant from 1951 through 1963, supports this contention.

4

THE MARKET AND INFRASTRUCTURE
PERSPECTIVE II: DIFFUSION AGENCY
STRATEGY ASPECTS OF INNOVATION
DIFFUSION

Once the diffusion agency is established, whether through centralized or decentralized decision making, it becomes a vehicle for establishing the innovation in the surrounding area. To accomplish this, each agency implements a strategy designed to induce adoption. This strategy may originate with the diffusion agency itself, in which case it probably would differ from agency to agency. Alternatively, all or part of the strategy may be product or service wide and, thus, more or less similar among diffusion agencies. The latter is most common if there is a coordinating or centralized propagator. Whether the diffusion strategy is different or similar from agency to agency, however, its general dimensions remain the same.

These dimensions constitute another portion of the market and infrastructure perspective, which is elaborated in the present chapter. The first section presents a conceptualization that encompasses the various elements of diffusion agency strategy and discusses those elements in detail. The second section presents a more systematic theoretical perspective which provides additional insight into the spatial patterns of diffusion under different agency strategies. The third section reports four case studies which give particular attention to the strategies actually employed and the resulting spatial and temporal patterns of diffusion.

While diffusion agency strategy involves a variety of activities, (Kotler, 1971, 1972; Roberto, 1975), four are particularly relevant to the spatial pattern of diffusion. One of these is the *development of infrastructure and organizational capabilities*. This permits the diffusion process to be implemented, maintained and expanded and often channels its spatial form. A second element of strategy is the *price*

THE MARKET AND INFRASTRUCTURE PERSPECTIVE II 101

charged for the innovation, which is likely to change over time and to vary over space according to the location of the potential adopter. As such, price affects the density of adoption in a given population at a given time and may influence its spatial variation. Third, *promotional communications* are employed to provide individuals with information about the innovation and to persuade them to adopt. The fourth element of diffusion agency strategy is *market selection and segmentation,* that is, identification of the clientele for the innovation and targeting in differential ways upon segments of that clientele. In many instances, both promotional communications and market segmentation procedures have explicit effects upon the spatial pattern of diffusion.

Another consideration is how these elements *interact* with each other in the articulation of diffusion agency strategy, that is, the way the strategy elements are orchestrated to bring about an efficient manipulation of the diffusion process. One aspect of this is the affect of the details of one element of diffusion strategy upon other elements. The placing of infrastructure in certain locales and not others, for example, also would influence the spatial placement and effects of promotional communications. Second, there will be joint effects from various combinations of the strategy elements that will exceed the effects of each considered singly, as in a diffusion strategy involving both infrastructure development and associated promotional communications. A third aspect is that one or more of the strategy elements might originate from entities other than the diffusion agency, and this would affect the latter's strategy. For example, a new energy-efficient electrical appliance would employ an infrastructure provided by public utility companies. Further, while promotion of the appliance would be handled directly by the firm propagating it, that firm also would benefit from promotion by the utilities and by environmental agencies of the government stressing energy conservation. Finally, the actions of the potential adopter's social network also will have a direct impact on the temporal and spatial patterns of diffusion, and this is sometimes taken account of in designing diffusion agency strategy.

In order to understand better the influence of diffusion agency activities upon adoption, it is useful to consider separately the objective and subjective attributes of an innovation (M.A. Brown, 1977). In particular, infrastructure provision and pricing affect the objective attributes of the innovation, while market selection and segmentation and promotional communications primarily affect the potential adopter's beliefs about and evaluation of these attributes,

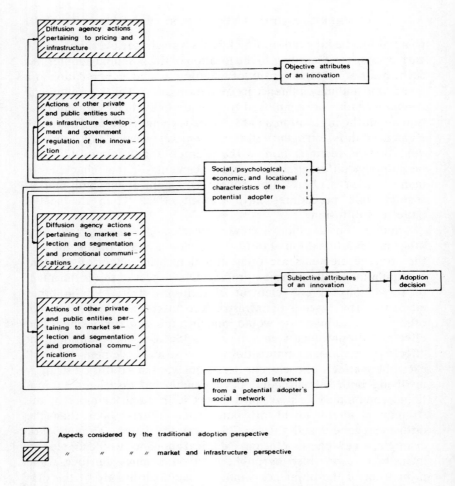

Figure 4.1   A Portrayal of the Interface between Diffusion Agency Actions
and Adoption Behavior

or the subjective attributes of the innovation. Figure 4.1 illustrates this
as well as the manner in which the diffusion agency strategy interfaces
with adoption behavior. Thus, one point incorporated in Figure 4.1 is
that each element of diffusion agency strategy and the activities of
related entities affects different aspects of the adoption decision.

It also is useful to consider Figure 4.1 in light of previous studies of
innovation diffusion. In particular, the traditional *adoption-* or
consumer behavior-oriented perspective concentrates almost exclusively upon the right, unshaded side of the diagram and neglects the
actions of diffusion agencies and their effects, represented by the left,

shaded side. Thus, there are many studies which examine the relationship between adoption and the social, psychological, economic and locational characteristics of the potential adopter as well as the role of information and influence from a potential adopter's social network (E.M. Rogers and Shoemaker, 1971). In general, the only diffusion agency actions given attention under the traditional perspective are extension agent influences, examined by rural sociologists for agricultural settings, and promotional communications influences, particularly advertising, examined by marketing professionals (E.M. Rogers and Shoemaker, 1971; Robertson, 1971; Midgley, 1977). Even when these elements are examined, however, they tend to be treated as exogenous, or given conditions, and evaluated in terms of their influence upon adoption relative to personal, *innovativeness*-related characteristics; that is, they are not treated as a manipulable variable with differential effects resulting from alternative strategies.[1]

One proviso is necessary before going on. For the practitioner the diffusion agency strategy portion of the market and infrastructure framework may seem elementary. Surely, for example, the entrepreneur already knows about the role of pricing in new product diffusion, and marketing texts recount a variety of options in pricing policies, when each ought to be used, and anticipated effects. Nevertheless, this knowledge has *not* been incorporated into the academic study of innovation diffusion, not even in marketing, and even less attention has been given to the spatial dimensions of these actions. Further, government or public programs seldom utilize the sophisticated and more effective strategies developed and employed in entrepreneurial settings, a point elaborated further in Chapter 9. A contention in developing this framework, then, is that we must formulate paradigms to reflect reality and, in doing this, that we have a great deal to learn from the practicing entrepreneur. In return, however, it is anticipated that our work eventually will lead to significantly increased capabilities for the community of practitioners.

Having set the stage, attention now turns to elaborating each of the elements of diffusion agency strategy. This is followed by a consideration of factors which affect the orchestration of these elements into an integrated package.

The Development of Infrastructure and Organizational Capabilities

This diffusion agency strategy element is one means of enabling or enhancing the use or adoption of an innovation. In the diffusion of BankAmericard among households in the United States, for instance, the utility of adoption depends upon the infrastructure of merchants willing to accept the card (M.A. Brown and Brown, 1976b; L.A. Brown and Malecki, 1977). Likewise, Nestlé's promotion of commercial dairying in Mexico was enhanced by its provision of a collection system whereby the farmer's milk product was shipped to the market (Nestlé's warehouse) (L.A. Brown and Lentnek, 1973).

The diffusion agency may develop its own infrastructure and organizational capabilities or it may utilize the existing capabilities of other public and private entities (Drucker, 1958; Glade, Strang, Udell and Littlefield, 1970; Garst, 1974b; Semple, Brown and Brown, 1975, 1977). Such existing or *generally available* infrastructure may have been created (1) in conjunction with the diffusion of a specific innovation and later made available to others; (2) as an innovation in its own right; or (3) as a generally available good intended to improve the overall conditions for economic and social development, one aspect of which is innovation diffusion. Examples include, respectively, service and repair stations, electricity infrastructure and transportation infrastructure.

Use of such generally available infrastructure is a necessity for some infrastructure needs, such as adequate rural roads, a rural public water system or a rural electrification system. If these are not present, then, the agency might have to await their development in order for innovation diffusion to be feasible. However, for other organizational or infrastructure needs the agency will have a choice, at least in part, of developing its own or utilizing existing capabilities. Examples include collection or distribution services; processing, marketing, warehouse, inventory and retail facilities; sales, market research, management and control systems; and personnel training and development programs.

In some situations, potential adopters are able to utilize an innovation only in proximity to the infrastructure, as in the case of cable television (Sieling, Malecki and Brown, 1975). In other situations, an innovation may be used anywhere, but must be serviced frequently, as in the adoption of computer equipment where access to maintenance and repair services is critical. Both these situations would be *infrastructure constrained* in that adoption will in general occur only *where* there is the required infrastructure and not elsewhere. Where access to such infrastructures does not play an important role, a diffusion process is *infrastructure independent* (L.A. Brown, 1975).

That there is some infrastructure which increases the utility of an innovation is not in itself a sufficient condition for classifying a given diffusion situation as infrastructure constrained, however. Other critical elements include the degree to which the innovation's utility increases as a result of access to the infrastructure, the relative cost to the potential adopter of providing the infrastructure him/herself and the spatial distribution or ubiquity of the infrastructure.

To illustrate, the operation of innovations such as electric light, telephone or television require an energy infrastructure that had to be developed as these innovations were being introduced, so that the locations of adopters were dependent upon the location of the infrastructure. While this continues to be the case today in Third World nations, it is not so in the United States where the relevant energy infrastructure is for the most part ubiquitous. Yet, the diffusion of computer innovations in the United States in the 1970s is constrained by the required service infrastructure; the diffusion of liquid propane gas and oil heating in rural areas is constrained by the required delivery infrastructure; and the diffusion of water-using appliances is constrained by the lack of public water systems in rural areas. Similarly, there is infrastructure constraint in the diffusion of many agricultural innovations that are enhanced by special marketing facilities and collection systems permitting cheap movement to market.

In terms of spatial patterns, we have already noted that adoption will in general occur where the infrastructure is and not elsewhere if the diffusion is infrastructure constrained. Further, there is generally a spatial order in the development of infrastructure which is mirrored in the diffusion of related innovations. More specifically, the economics associated with management, control, promotional and service infrastructures often militate towards a spatially restricted pattern, and the expansion of such infrastructures tends to be in a nearest neighbor fashion leading to wave-like or contagion patterns of diffusion.

Pricing

The monetary value associated with an innovation is to some degree intrinsic. The color television, for example, is moderately expensive, whereas the electric toothbrush is inexpensive. Within the range of feasible prices, however, the diffusion agency retains considerable discretion over the actual price charged. In general, higher prices within the range will result in a lower density of adoption among the target population and vice versa (Kotler, 1971: 334–9; 1972: 515–16).

Accordingly, the actual price charged ought to reflect the objective(s) of the diffusion agency. Over the long run, for example, the entrepreneurial agency probably would seek to maximize profits, while the public agency might seek to minimize costs or maximize the number of clients served. The more immediate pricing objective(s), however, may be different.

To illustrate, Kotler (1971: 336–7; 1972: 519–21) suggests the following range of possibilities, drawing upon actual practices in entrepreneurial settings. For purposes of *market penetration* a relatively low price is established in order to stimulate growth of the market and to capture a large share of it. Under *market skimming* the initial price is high in order to gain a premium from buyers with relatively inelastic demand, whereupon it is then gradually reduced to draw in the more price-elastic segments of the market. A third short-run pricing objective is *early cash recover*. With *satisficing*, the price achieves a less than maximum rate of return, but one that is satisfactory or conventional given a particular level of investment and risk. Finally, *product line promotion* pricing is designed to enhance the sales of an entire line rather than of the product itself.

Whatever the price charged by the agency, the total cost to the potential adopter generally will vary according to his/her location. For example, if the agency provides no delivery, service or other infrastructure and charges a *uniform price at the outlet,* the potential adopter will incur a transportation cost in getting to the outlet. Traditional spatial economic theory states that such transportation costs would vary directly with the buyer's distance from the diffusion agency, that the buyer would add these costs to the price of the innovation and that the level of demand for the innovation would decrease accordingly. This, then, would affect the spatial extent of the market area for the innovation and lead to a distance decay distribution of adoption within it (Beckmann, 1968: 29–58).

Alternatively, the diffusion agency or some other entity may provide some relevant infrastructure and charge either a *uniform price at the outlet,* a *uniform delivered price* or a *distance-related price.*[2] Whatever the pricing policy, the significance of the infrastructure would itself render the situation infrastructure constrained since adoption will in general be limited to the area served by the infrastructure. Applying traditional economic theory leads to the further conclusion that uniform-delivered pricing produces a tendency towards a uniform density of adopters *within* the area served by the infrastructure since access costs are equal across adopters. By similar reasoning, distance-related pricing or a uniform price at the outlet produces a tendency towards a distance decay pattern of adoption *within* the area served by the infrastructure.

It is questionable, however, whether distance decay diffusion patterns would in fact occur under the conditions specified above, even if pricing is explicitly distance related. One reason is that the demand for most modern products appears to be relatively inelastic with regard to price (Kotler, 1972: 515–16). Second, when the buyer incurs the transportation costs by traveling to the diffusion agency, as is most commonly the case, it is doubtful whether he/she directly associates those costs with those of the innovation, either because the trip is multiple purpose or because it is commonplace.[3] Finally, Getis (1969) provides evidence that one's own transportation costs are perceived as a stepped function of distance instead of a linear function and are not markedly differentiated except at extreme distances.

To sum up, when the diffusion agency provides *no* delivery, service or other infrastructure and charges a uniform price at the outlet, the spatial pattern of adoption will depend upon the price elasticity of demand for the innovation and the degree to which potential adopters perceive accessibility to the diffusion agency as a significant cost. If price elasticity and access costs are significant, a distance decay pattern of adoption would occur and the situation would be infrastructure constrained; otherwise, a uniform density of adopters would be expected, *ceteris paribus,* and the situation would be infrastructure independent. Alternatively, while the diffusion pattern would be infrastructure constrained if the agency *did* provide delivery, service or other infrastructure, the spatial pattern within that constraint— whether the pricing policy is uniform at the outlet, uniform delivered or distance related—also would depend upon the price elasticity of demand for the innovation and the degree to which potential adopters perceive accessibility to the diffusion agency as a significant cost. Thus, we see that pricing policy is one of the determinants of infrastructure effects upon adoption and the pattern of diffusion.

Promotional Communications

The diffusion agency generates information of various sorts, or utilizes information from other sources, in order to create awareness of the innovation and its characteristics. The impact of this information on the adoption decision and the resulting patterns of diffusion varies, however, according to its *channel, source, content* and *motivation* (Figure 4.2). Each of these dimensions is briefly discussed.

The *channel* or the medium conveying the information may be personal or impersonal. The former involves a one-to-one correspon-

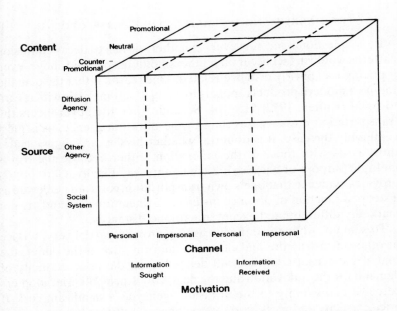

Figure 4.2 Classification of Information by Source, Channel, Content and Motivation

dence between sender and receiver and enables the sender to custom tailor the message and react to sender feedback. Thus, personal communications channels tend to be more effective than impersonal ones in transmitting a complexity of information and thereby altering attitudes (Coleman, Katz and Menzel, 1957, 1959, 1966; Arndt, 1967; Howard and Sheth, 1969: 368–70). However, impersonal communications, which include mass media, reach a larger number of people per message over a greater spatial range than personal channels (Hagerstrand, 1967a: 138–9).

Thus, when deciding upon a mixture of personal and impersonal information channels, diffusion agencies must trade-off effectiveness with spatial range and number of recipients. If, for example, the agency wishes to maintain a spatial facet in the diffusion, such as confining adoption to the vicinity of a service or delivery infrastructure in order to minimize the cost of maintaining the infrastructure, channels with a small, controllable spatial range and high effectiveness, such as personal selling, might be favored.

In general, channels vary greatly in terms of spatial characteristics. For example, impersonal channels usually reach a more spatially dispersed audience than personal ones; however, audiences may range from a neighborhood for a local newspaper to a nation for a metropolitan daily. Furthermore, within that audience radius, rates of contact may vary considerably. Subscriber and viewer ratios, for example, show much local variation both among neighborhoods within an urban area and among rural areas and small towns surrounding the origin of the newspaper or television station (the latter often in a distance decay fashion). A great deal of variation also occurs with personal promotional communications. The door-to-door salesperson, such as the Avon, Fuller Brush or encyclopedia representative, would utilize a definite spatial strategy with high focus upon certain areas that may be widely dispersed from one another. The market area of a store salesperson, on the other hand, would depend upon whether the store was neighborhood or city wide in its orientation. Finally, social channels are highly local in their focus, often involving a distance decay pattern of contacts (Marble and Nystuen, 1963; Moore, 1970; Moore and Brown, 1970; L.A. Brown and Moore, 1969, 1970; Morrill and Pitts, 1967).

The *source* of information may be a diffusion agency, another type of agency (for instance, an agency marketing competing or complementary goods, a government agency or a consumer interest group), or a member of the potential adopter's social system. The first two of these three categories can be further classified as either private or public (the latter including governmental and non-profit organizations).[4]

These various sources differ in their impact upon attitudes (E.M. Rogers and Shoemaker, 1971: 250–66). For instance, diffusion agencies tend to be most important in exposing individuals to an innovation and in providing them with information about its attributes (Howard and Sheth, 1969: 294–321). Information about the innovation is also obtained from an individual's social system, once news of the innovation has spread. In evaluating the innovation in terms of adoption, however, individuals tend to rely less upon diffusion or other agencies, and more upon information from their social system (Engel, Blackwell and Kollat, 1978: 412–21; Howard and Sheth, 1969: 294–321).[5]

The role of information sources also differs across adopter subgroups. E.M. Rogers and Shoemaker (1971: 250–66) conclude that innovators and early adopters have more diffusion agency and social system interaction than later adopters, and tend to use a greater variety of information sources. Later adopters, on the other hand, use fewer sources—relying, in particular, upon social interaction and adopting primarily as the result of favorable information from one or more existing adopters.

In terms of the spatial patterns of diffusion, communication levels are greater between individuals who are both geographically and socially proximate to one another (Hagerstrand, 1965, 1967a, 1967b; Karlsson, 1958: 32–6). Thus, because of the distance-constrained nature of social networks, diffusion processes which are highly influenced by social system interaction will tend to exhibit a neighborhood effect and a clustering of adopters. This pattern would not, however, characterize innovators and early adopters, who would instead be randomly located because of their greater reliance upon impersonal information sources. Later adopters, on the other hand, should be located in physical proximity to previous adopters because of their dependence on social interaction.

Information also varies in *content* and may be promotional, neutral or counter-promotional. Typically, there is a mixture of these although the existence of counter-promotional information might depend upon the structure of the market. Too often, the impact of the communications process upon spatial diffusion patterns is described only in terms of sources providing favorable information. Obviously, the location of other sources providing unfavorable information will have an analogous, but deterring impact on diffusion, and the location of neutral sources may also have spatial implications.

Finally, one can distinguish between types of information according to the *motivation* which initiates its transmission. In general, potential adopters may obtain information by seeking it or by merely receiving it without solicitation. This rarely made distinction is useful in comparing the relative importance of competing explanations of adoption behavior (M.A. Brown, 1977). For example, are innovators and early adopters particularly motivated to seek information about innovations, or are these market segments simply the targets of effective marketing campaigns? Addressing such questions should provide insight into the various ways that diffusion agencies manipulate diffusion patterns through promotional communications.[6]

Market Selection and Segmentation

This involves identification of the characteristics of potential adopters and division into *homogeneous* subgroups on the basis of those characteristics. The result is a partitioning that permits the diffusion agency to focus upon particular submarkets in preference to others and to customize its infrastructure development, pricing and promotional communications.

In general, three segmentation strategies may be followed (Kotler, 1972: 182–7).[7] In *undifferentiated marketing* the same strategy is employed for the whole market, focusing on what is common in the needs of the potential adopters instead of what is different. In *differentiated marketing* the firm operates in several or all segments of the market, but designs separate marketing programs for each. In *concentrated marketing* the firm only goes after a large share of one or a few submarkets instead of the total market. In general, the larger the number of segments and associated tailored strategies, the more effective and the more expensive the promotional effort (Roberto, 1975). Thus, diffusion agencies on limited budgets (and perhaps for this reason, public sector agencies) tend not to develop or institute elaborate segmentation policies.

Segmentation strategies are frequently based on socio-economic or demographic characteristics (Table 4.1).[8] Examples of such submarkets include senior citizens, black youths, young married couples or housewives.

Alternatively, a segmentation policy may be explicitly locational. This is reflected in the existence of sales territories and regional development strategies or segments such as urbanites, suburbanites or New Englanders. An example at a local scale is the service station, hardware or drug store manager who differentiates the service provided to regular neighborhood customers from the service provided to transients, and who accordingly beams promotional efforts to nearby households rather than to the urban area as a whole. In part, such strategies related to spatial scale occur because the market is spatially limited in accordance with the order of the good, that is, lower-order innovations have smaller market areas than do higher-order ones (Berry and Horton, 1970: 169–249; Yeates and Garner, 1976: 124–52, 274–301). However, such strategies also occur because distribution and client-oriented service costs are important factors in any marketing strategy (Stewart, 1965).

Even if a market segmentation strategy is not explicitly locational, however, it often is implicitly so. Socio-economic segments such as upwardly mobile middle-class households, for example, frequently are associated with distinct spatial patterns as evidenced by urban neighborhood typologies (Berry and Horton, 1970: 306–94; Timms, 1971; J.R. Johnston, 1972). New product promotional efforts based on such segments, then, would render distinct spatial patterns of innovation diffusion.

There also are other kinds of *implicit market segmentation strategies* that are important to consider. A diffusion agency, for example, may

Table 4.1 Major Segmentation Variables and Their Typical Breakdowns (after Kotler, 1972:170)

Variables	*Typical breakdowns*
Geographic	
Region	Pacific Mountain; West North Central; West South Central; South Atlantic; Middle Atlantic; New England
County size	A; B; C; D
City or SMSA size	Under 5000; 5000–19,999; 20,000–49,999; 50,000–99,999; 100,000–249,999; 250,000–499,999; 500,000–999,999; 1,000,000–3,999,999; 4,000,000 or over
Density	Urban; suburban; rural
Climate	Northern; southern
Demographic	
Age	Under 6; 6–11; 12–17; 18–34; 35–49; 50–64; 65+
Sex	Male; female
Family size	1–2; 3–4; 5+
Family life cycle	Young single; young married, no children; young married, youngest child under six; young married, youngest child six or over; older married with children; older married no children under 18; older single; other
Income	Under $5000; $5000–$7999; $8000–$9999; over $10,000
Occupation	Professional and technical; managers, officials, and proprietors; clerical, sales; craftsmen, foremen; operatives; farmers; retired; students; housewives; unemployed
Education	Grade school or less; some high school; graduated high school; some college; graduated college
Religion	Catholic; Protestant; Jewish; other

Race	White; Negro; Oriental
Nationality	American; British; French; German; Eastern European; Scandinavian; Italian; Spanish; Latin American; Middle Eastern; Japanese; and so on
Social class	Lower-lower; upper-lower; lower-middle; middle-middle; upper-middle; lower-upper; upper-upper
Psychographic	
Compulsiveness	Compulsive; non-compulsive
Gregariousness	Extrovert; introvert
Autonomy	Dependent; independent
Conservatism	Conservative; liberal; radical
Authoritarianism	Authoritarian; democratic
Leadership	Leader; follower
Ambitiousness	High achiever; low achiever
Buyer behavior	
Usage rate	Non-user; light user; medium user; heavy user
Readiness stage	Unaware; aware; interested; intending to try; trier; regular buyer
Benefits sought	Economy; status; dependability
End use	(Varies with product)
Brand loyalty	None; light; strong
Marketing-factor sensitivity	Quality; price; service; advertising; sales promotion

not consciously attempt to reach potential adopters differentially but may none the less do so by employing information channels used by subsets of the market, as discussed above under promotional communications. Implicit segmentation policies are particularly typical of government agency change efforts which rarely use sophisticated marketing techniques (Zaltman, Kotler and Kaufman, 1972; M.A. Brown, Maxson and Brown, 1977).

An example of implicit market segmentation is the use of the *two-step flow model of communications* in conjunction with measures of *innovativeness*, which is particularly prevalent in the diffusion efforts of government agencies. This is a *least-resistance-ordered* communications strategy in which the more motivated segment(s) of the market receive(s) information first and the less motivated later (Roberto, 1975: 22–3). The initial segment is contacted directly by the diffusion agency and is expected to provide opinion leadership by transmitting the information via interpersonal communications to the lesser-motivated segments (Copeland, 1966: 378; Pesson, 1966: 102–5; Sanders, 1966: 118; Rogers and Shoemaker, 1971: 198–225). Measures of innovativeness are used with this strategy to identify the more motivated, progressive elements of the potential adopter pool. This is generally done on the basis of socio-economic characteristics (such as income and education) and/or the amount and timing of adoption of other innovations. There is implicit segmentation in this strategy for two reasons. First, there is considerable evidence that the second step of the communications chain, involving interpersonal communications from opinion leaders to others, does not consistently occur (M.A. Brown, Maxson and Brown, 1977). Second, differences in adoption time, the traditional measure of innovativeness (Midgley, 1977), may be the result of the marketing strategy of public or private propagators of innovations rather than the result of actual innovativeness differences (L.A. Brown, Malecki and Spector, 1976). Thus, a focus upon one particular segment of the market is reinforced.

Note, however, that this policy, which is largely carried on by public sector diffusion agencies, is not inconsistent with the stated practices of private sector agencies which attempt to reach the most profitable segments first. Such a *market skimming* strategy is rationalized by Dhalla and Mahattoo (1976: 39) in terms of micro-economic theory:

One of the cardinal axioms of micro-economics is that profits are maximized when a firm allocates its expenditures in such a way that the incremental returns are equal for all subsets of markets. More money is spent on segments with greater potential until diminishing returns bring the incremental response down to the level for the less desirable segments. In actual practice, budget constraint stops the process before equality can be achieved, and the less desirable segments are almost always ignored.

In terms of the mandate to public sector diffusion agencies, however, an implicit market segmentation strategy that rarely goes beyond the market skimming stage (such as the two-step flow strategy) may not be socially acceptable (Meyerhoff, 1980). This topic is discussed further in Chapters 8 and 9.

The Orchestration of Diffusion Agency Strategies

Utilization of the diffusion agency strategy elements discussed above generally involves integrating them into an effective package. There is little choice in some aspects of this because of the interdependence among the individual elements of the strategy. For example, infrastructure development involves an implicit segmentation of the market by increasing the utility of adoption for those reached by the infrastructure. It therefore may affect both where promotional communications are directed and the types of channels employed. Conversely, if a particular market segment, as identified by some characteristic such as income, has distinct locational characteristics, infrastructure provision and promotional communications ought to reflect that. Similarly, since pricing policies affect the spatial distribution of adoption costs, they embody an implicit market selection and segmentation policy which may be reflected in the promotional communications strategy.

In addition, diffusion agency strategy will be interdependent with other characteristics such as (1) the nature and technical complexity of the innovation; (2) the type of agency and its relationship to corporate or institutional propagators; (3) the extent of market penetration and competitor imitation, reflections of the progress of the innovation's life cycle; and (4) the spatial extent of diffusion. Each of these factors in strategy formulation is now considered.

Innovation Characteristics. Goods and services for individual and household consumption, including innovations, may be categorized as being either *convenience, shopping,* or *specialty* goods (Kotler, 1972: 95–8). This scale is comparable to the low–medium–high order of good scales developed by geographers (Berry and Horton, 1970: 169–249; 440–511; Yeates and Garner, 1976: 124–52, 274–301).

Convenience goods are highly standardized and homogeneous in both form and price, low in unit price, distributed by agencies that

are locationally ubiquitous and purchased frequently with a minimum
of effort. Examples are sundries, groceries, hardware, gasoline,
patent medicines, and items of personal hygiene. Shopping goods, in
contrast, are less standardized and homogeneous in both form and
price, higher in price, distributed by markedly fewer agencies and
purchased less frequently. Further, the purchase of shopping goods
involves more comparison with other available offerings and their
market is more readily segmented than the market for convenience
goods. Examples of shopping goods include household furnishings,
clothing, automobiles and recreational equipment. Specialty goods
are further along the continuum. Buyers characteristically go to
considerably more length to seek out and purchase them, but almost
without exception, price is not a principal factor in their decision.
Examples include harpsichords, sports cars, rare books and specialized physicians' and lawyers' services.

Some significant characteristics of each of these types of goods and
services are technical complexity, homogeneity, price, degree of
availability or size of market area, and frequency of purchase. Table
4.2 presents approximate ratings for each type of innovation for each
of these characteristics.

We know from central place theory (Berry and Horton, 1970: 169–
249; Yeates and Garner, 1976: 124–52) that the order of the
innovation should affect the strategy of diffusion agency establishment, resulting, for example, in a more dense network for lower-order
innovations and a more spread-out network for higher-order ones.
However, diffusion agency strategy also should vary in accordance
with the order of the innovation. Thus, an innovation that is more a
specialty than a convenience good likely would be propagated (1) by a
careful segmentation of the market; (2) through agencies that are
designed to appeal to the market segment of interest and located
accordingly; (3) by means of promotional communications that carry a
customized message with a relatively high information content; (4) by
establishing an extensive service and information-providing infrastructure; and (5) by a price reflecting market skimming or satisficing
objectives (Kotler, 1971: 336–7; 1972: 519–21).

Agency Characteristics. The agency form itself may be an innovation.
Examples are the fast food outlet, the planned regional shopping
center (Y.S. Cohen, 1972; Sheppard, 1976), or the department store
in Japan (Tanaka, 1971). In general, however, it is most convenient
to consider these as service innovations, although their characteristics
would be somewhat at variance with those in Table 4.2.

Table 4.2   Innovation Type and Characteristics

Characteristics	Innovation type		
	Convenience	Shopping	Specialty
Corresponding order of good	low	medium	high
Technical complexity	low	moderate	high
Degree of homogeneity	high	moderate	low
Price	low	moderate	high
Frequency of purchase	high	moderate	low
Market size	small	medium	large
Degree of availability	high	moderate	low

This points up the fact that agencies, like innovations, may be seen as convenience, shopping or specialty stores in accordance with the types of goods they handle and the related spatial range of their clientele (Bucklin, 1967). Diffusion agencies also may be seen as low-, medium- or high-order function outlets without reference to the type of goods they handle since a high-order outlet such as a department store might be the distribution point for a low-order or convenience good innovation. In any case, diffusion agency strategy would vary accordingly. Thus, the convenience or low-order function diffusion agency might employ neighborhood-focused newspapers and handbills, whereas the specialty or high-order function outlet might employ a newspaper with regional readership and topically focused journals. Similarly, creation and maintenance of a delivery infrastructure is a more likely strategy for high-order function agencies than for lower-order ones, and the order of outlet chosen as a distribution point for an innovation carries with it an implicit spatial segmentation of the market.

A second characteristic of agencies is the nature of their linkage with the innovation propagator (Rachman, 1969; Murphy, 1948; Zeller, 1978; Zeller, Achabal and Brown, 1980). Recall that the agency may be agent owned and almost completely independent of the propagator's influence; it may be propagator owned and managed by persons that are designated and trained by the propagator; or, in between these two extremes, it may involve propagator support in a decentralized decision-making structure (Figure 3.1).[9] The implications of these various arrangements were examined in Chapter 3 in terms of the establishment of diffusion agencies. However, diffusion agency strategy also is affected. Specifically, a strong linkage to a propagator introduces the possibility of strategies that are more

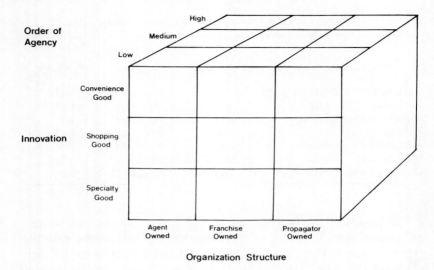

Figure 4.3   Diffusion Agency Typology

uniform among agencies, propagator-provided strategies designed by persons more expert than those the single agency can afford, and economies of scale in the overall innovation diffusion strategy.

Thus, agencies may be categorized both according to the type of innovation they distribute, the functional order of the agency, and the nature of their linkage with the innovation propagator (Figure 4.3).[10] This provides a complex array of possibilities with implications for the locational pattern of the agencies, the spatial range of the market area of each and the diffusion agency strategy.

The Innovation Life Cycle. A new product or innovation may be seen to pass through four stages: introduction, growth, maturity and decline (Figure 4.4) (Kotler, 1972: 429–31; Wasson, 1974; Rink and Swan, 1979). Throughout this life cycle diffusion strategies are continually modified regardless of the character of the innovation or of the diffusion agency.

The introduction stage usually involves only one product version, even if the propagator is large. Monopoly conditions with regard to the new product will prevail, but competition will exist in the form of other (substitutable) products on which the consumer may spend his/her disposable income. Accordingly, the initial strategy is to develop primary demand for the innovation (Kotler, 1972: 462–513). Test marketing may be the first step in this endeavor. Whether or not

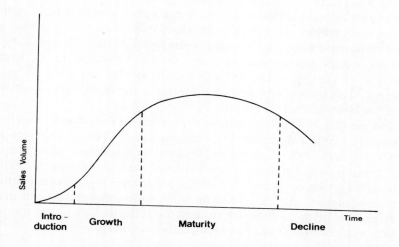

Figure 4.4   Stages in the Product Life Cycle
After Kotler, 1972: 430

this occurs, however, marketing in the introductory stage probably will concentrate upon a particular market segment(s) owing to the limits of capital resources. The selection criteria may be only geographic (for example, a particular region of the nation), and within the chosen market area promotion may be undifferentiated with regard to different types of persons. Alternatively, the market may be segmented on the basis of demographic and other characteristics as well as locational characteristics, and the propagator may concentrate upon a particular segment(s) or employ differentiated marketing within the geographic area of concentration.

As the product or service life cycle advances, demand grows and more diffusion agencies are established, both within already served and new market areas. This increase in market penetration and realization of sales potential are likely to lead to direct competition. The response to this may be the identification of new and unexploited needs, product or service modification, increased advertising and promotion, more extensive segmentation schemes or simply increased price competition. These trends are accentuated in the later stages of the life cycle, when typically, the innovation is either modified beyond recognition from the original or becomes obsolete and is discontinued.

The Spatial Extent of Diffusion. In the early stages of the product or service life cycle diffusion generally is concentrated in certain areas and non-existent in others. At that time, then, both diffusion agency establishment and diffusion agency strategy are critical factors in the form, extent and expansion of the diffusion pattern. In the later stages of the life cycle, extensive diffusion has occurred so that agency actions are a more primary factor in the further proliferation of the innovation.

In general, the homogeneity of the market varies inversely with the spatial extent of diffusion. As a consequence, when the diffusion is more spatially extended, market segmentation and the congruent use of promotional communications becomes a more important element of diffusion agency strategy. Further, geographic regions often differ extensively in market characteristics, and this, along with the exigencies of organizational control, is likely to lead to the use of sales territories and local market customization.

The spatial extent of diffusion, of course, varies directly with the degree of product acceptance and market penetration. These two factors vary from minimal at the introductory stage of product promotion to almost complete at the closing stage when the novelty wears off, product modifications have been made and use of the product is regarded as necessary (Pessemier, 1968). As adoption expands into more peripheral areas, then, the agency may employ price discrimination and allocate resources for infrastructure development and product promotion in a manner such that the core provides support while the innovation gains a foothold in the periphery. The ability to do this would depend upon the resource capabilities of the propagator and his level of success in core areas. Small companies with limited financial resources, for example, would only be able to concentrate their innovation establishment in core geographic areas rather than aim at complete market coverage.

A THEORETICAL PERSPECTIVE ON DIFFUSION AGENCY STRATEGY AND SPATIAL PATTERNS OF DIFFUSION

The preceding paragraphs provide a number of observations about the spatial patterns of diffusion that result from the various elements of diffusion agency strategy. Further insight is provided by systematically considering the topic for two prototype situations, utilizing the infrastructure-constrained/infrastructure-independent dichotomy.

Infrastructure-Constrained Diffusion

As noted above, the diffusion agency will implement a strategy designed to induce adoption within its market area and *infrastructure development* might be an element in this. An example is the delivery and service routes maintained by liquid propane fuel dealers (L.A. Brown, 1963). Alternatively, the diffusion agency might utilize existing infrastructure that is *generally available*. This subsection examines the case in which either diffusion agency developed or generally available infrastructure is an element of diffusion agency strategy.

Consider the following situation. First, there is a single urban center. Second, the innovation is dependent upon some service, such as electricity or repair. Third, the infrastructure carrying the service is not ubiquitous, but in the process of being developed outward from the urban center.[11] Fourth, all potential adopters are uniformly distributed throughout the hinterland of the urban center and are identical in characteristics pertinent to the utility of the innovation. Fifth, the response of the potential adopter depends upon the infrastructure-related costs associated with acquiring and operating the innovation, the price of the innovation itself, opportunity costs of the innovation relative to those associated with alternatives and the level of information about the innovation.

If the infrastructure is generally available, a uniform price at the outlet may be assumed. If the infrastructure is developed and maintained by the diffusion agency, the price of the innovation may be uniform at the outlet, uniform delivered or distance related. Under any of these uniform pricing policies the price itself would not affect the spatial pattern of diffusion, but the potential adopter's cost of utilizing the infrastructure would. Alternatively, if the price is distance related, both the price and the cost of utilizing the infrastructure would affect the spatial pattern of diffusion, *ceteris paribus*.

In the discussion of pricing policies in the previous subsection, it was argued that the real world costs of infrastructure utilization are likely to be stepwise. One basis of this argument was Getis' (1969) observation that one's own transportation costs are perceived as a stepped function of distance rather than as a linear function and are not markedly differentiated except at extreme distances.[12] Another basis of this argument was Kotler's (1972: 515–16) observation that the demand for most modern and particularly new products is relatively inelastic. A third point, not noted above, is that the direct costs of utilizing the infrastructure also tend to be stepped, as for telephone, bus and delivery services.

Accordingly, infrastructure-related costs in the areas penetrated by infrastructure will be uniform or mildly stepped and relatively low, whereas infrastructure-related costs in other areas of the urban hinterland, those not penetrated by infrastructure, will be significantly higher (Figures 4.5A and 4.5B). Assume that this cost differential together with the price of the innovation is such that demand for the innovation only exists within the infrastructure penetration boundary (Figures 4.5A and 4.5B). Also assume a uniform price throughout the urban hinterland, information levels and opportunity costs that are everywhere equal, and a demand function for the innovation that is price elastic. The density of adopters then would be represented either by a horizontal or a mildly stepped line, depending upon the character of infrastructure-related costs, that drops to zero at the penetration boundary, as in Figures 4.6A and 4.6B respectively.

If pricing is distance related, on the other hand, the total costs of the innovation will increase with distance from the market, either monotonically or in a quasi-step function, depending upon the nature of infrastructure-related costs (Figures 4.5C and 4.5D). Assume again that the cost differential on either side of the infrastructure penetration boundary is such that demand for the innovation only exists within the areas served by infrastructure and that information levels and opportunity costs are everywhere equal. Given also that demand for the innovation is price elastic, the density of adopters would be represented by a distance decay or stepped distance decay graph, depending upon the nature of infrastructure-related costs, that drops to zero at the penetration boundary, as in Figures 4.6C and 4.6D respectively.

Note, however, the effect of a demand function for the innovation that is (relatively) inelastic with regard to price, which Kotler (1972: 515–16) suggests may be common. Then, whether the pricing policy is uniform or distance related and whether infrastructure-related costs are uniform or mildly stepped, the density of adopters would be represented by a horizontal line that drops to zero at the infrastructure penetration boundary, as in Figure 4.6A!

Now consider the effects of relaxing the assumption that the level of information about the innovation is everywhere equal. Diffusion agencies will employ promotional communications and related endeavors to place information with those most likely to adopt, particularly in the early phases of diffusion when opinion leader

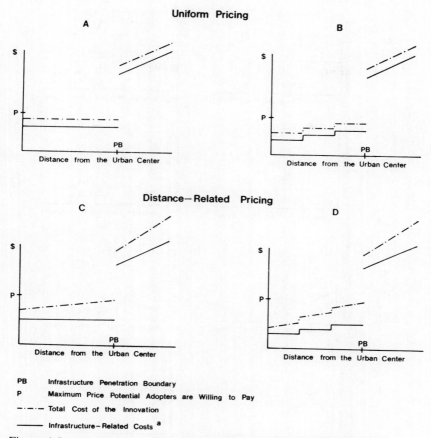

Figure 4.5   Alternative Profiles of Infrastructure-Related Costs and Price of the Innovation

[a]Infrastructure-related costs are assumed to increase monotonically with distance outside of the infrastructure penetration boundary reflecting the effort of gaining access to the infrastructure.

support is desirable (E.M. Rogers and Shoemaker, 1971: 200–27). Accordingly, if the locational density of persons most likely to adopt varies inversely with distance from the urban center, the level of information also should vary in this way. However, that distribution of potential adopters is likely only for the case of distance-related pricing and price-elastic demand for the innovation. Much more common, judging by the above discussion, are situations in which demand for the innovation within the infrastructure penetration boundary is not distance related, as with uniform pricing or price

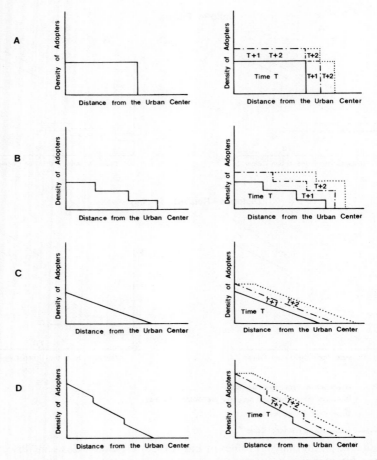

Figure 4.6   Alternative Profiles of the Density of Adopters under Infrastructure-Constrained Diffusion

inelastic demand. Then, the likelihood of adoption within the infrastructure penetration boundary is related to personal or site characteristics for which there is no inherent spatial distribution, and diffusion agency information should be distributed accordingly.

Considering infrastructure-related operating and acquisition costs, the price of the innovation itself, and information levels, then, lead in general to the expectation that initial adopters will be located randomly in the area circumscribed by the infrastructure penetration boundary, comprising an adoption surface as in Figure 4.6A. These adopters are the source of interpersonal communications which exhibit distance decay characteristics and lead to adoption by neighbors. The outcome is a pattern comprised of randomly distributed clusters of adopters that is constrained by the infrastructure penetration boundary.

Over time, the infrastructure penetration boundary moves outward and so does adoption (Figure 4.7). Initially, adopter density will be greater in the area(s) receiving the infrastructure earlier. Eventually, however, saturation levels will be reached and a uniform distribution of adopters will occur, whatever the characteristics of the diffusion situation (Figures 4.6A, 4.6B, 4.6C, 4.6D).

Finally, the discussion above has implicitly incorporated the notion of an infrastructure surface that is distance but not directionally biased (Figure 4.7A). It is more realistic, however, to recognize that infrastructure generally extends linearly, with an attendant effect upon the distribution of infrastructure-related costs and the infrastructure penetration boundary. The result will be a pattern of diffusion that is directionally as well as distance biased, perhaps in a cobweb form (Figure 4.7B) or skewed to one side of the urban area (Figure 4.7C).

A number of examples illustrate infrastructure-constrained diffusion, although they generally have not been examined in this context: the automobile in southern Sweden (Hagerstrand, 1952) involving transportation infrastructure; artificial insemination in southern Sweden (Hanham, 1973; L.A. Brown, Malecki and Spector, 1976) involving a technical service infrastructure maintained by a government diffusion agency; liquid propane gas in Grant County, Wisconsin (L.A. Brown, 1963) which involves a service and delivery infrastructure maintained by entrepreneurial diffusion agencies; credit card services in eastern Ohio (M.A. Brown and Brown, 1976b) involving an infrastructure of businesses that accept the card for purchases; cable television in Bowling Green, Ohio (Sieling, Malecki and Brown, (1975) involving signal supplying infrastructure maintained by an entrepreneurial diffusion agency; ammonia fertilizer in the corn belt (Erickson, 1973) involving a storage and distribution infrastructure maintained by private enterprise; broadcast television in Sweden (Tornqvist, 1967); a number of agricultural innovations in Kenya (Garst, 1974a, 1974b) which involve an infrastructure of marketing sites, collection systems and price and production controls maintained by both entrepreneurial diffusion agencies and government institutions; and hybrid grain corn in Quebec (W. Smith, 1974) involving an infrastructure of marketing and processing sites. Visual analysis of maps of these diffusions indicates patterns of adoption consistent with those postulated.

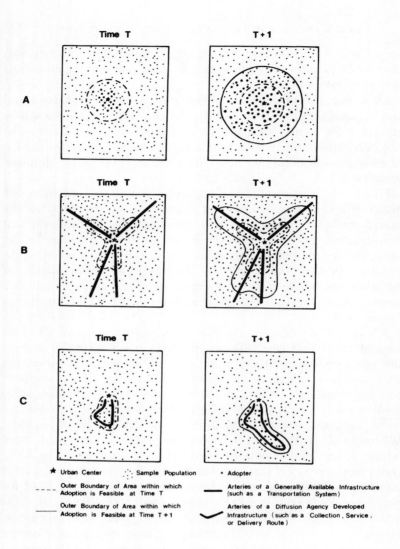

Time T   T + 1

A

Time T   T + 1

B

Time T   T + 1

C

★ Urban Center   ⠂ Sample Population   • Adopter

---- Outer Boundary of Area within which
     Adoption is Feasible at Time T

——— Outer Boundary of Area within which
     Adoption is Feasible at Time T + 1

——— Arteries of a Generally Available Infrastructure
     (such as a Transportation System)

⌒ Arteries of a Diffusion Agency Developed
   Infrastructure (such as a Collection, Service,
   or Delivery Route)

Figure 4.7   Directional Bias Effects in Infrastructure-Constrained
Diffusion

Infrastructure-Independent Diffusion

The rationale underlying the anticipated pattern of infrastructure-independent diffusion is similar to the rationale for the infrastructure-constrained case. The major difference is that infrastructure development pertaining to the innovation is not a factor in generating infrastructure-independent diffusion patterns. Thus, by reasoning otherwise similar to that in the previous section, it is expected that the pattern of adoption will be bounded only by the limit of the diffusion agency's service area and will in general be uniform but comprised of randomly distributed clusters of adopters reflecting interpersonal information flows.

A number of examples illustrate infrastructure-independent diffusion, although they generally have not been examined in this context. There is DeTemple (1971) on 2,4D weed spray around Collins, Iowa and Harvestore feed systems in north-east Iowa; M.A. Brown, Maxson and Brown (1977) on no-till farming, winter pasturing, round baling of hay, soil testing and the keeping of expense records on farm operations in south-eastern Ohio; Shannon (1970) on the utilization of the Community Health Association of Detroit, Michigan; Keger-reis, Engel and Blackwell (1970) on an automobile diagnostic center in Columbus, Ohio; and Hagerstrand (1967a) on postal-checking services in south-central Sweden. Visual analysis of maps from these various studies indicates patterns of adoption consistent with those postulated.

EMPIRICAL EXAMPLES OF THE DIFFUSION AGENCY/POTENTIAL ADOPTER INTERFACE

The previous two sections examined the various elements of diffusion agency strategy and provided a theoretical perspective pertaining to the spatial patterns of diffusion. Attention now turns to four empirical examples which illustrate the operation of the strategy portion of the market and infrastructure framework in a real world setting. Two or these examples are infrastructure-constrained diffusions which illustrate the effects of infrastructure and pricing elements of strategy, those affecting the objective attributes of the innovation. The other two examples are infrastructure-independent diffusions which illustrate the effects of promotional communications and market selection and segmentation, elements affecting the subjective attributes of the innovation. The interaction among these elements in formulating a diffusion strategy also is given attention.

In all four examples the innovations are agricultural in nature and the study area is a four-county portion of eastern Ohio (Figure 4.8), rendering an important comparability among the diffusions. Further, diffusion agency actions are examined jointly with potential adopter response. This is critical to elaborating the theoretical framework pertaining to the diffusion agency/potential adopter interface (Figure 4.1), and also unique. Many empirical studies have examined adoption behavior, but few if any consider diffusion agency actions, their interface with adoption and the resulting spatial patterns of diffusion.[13]

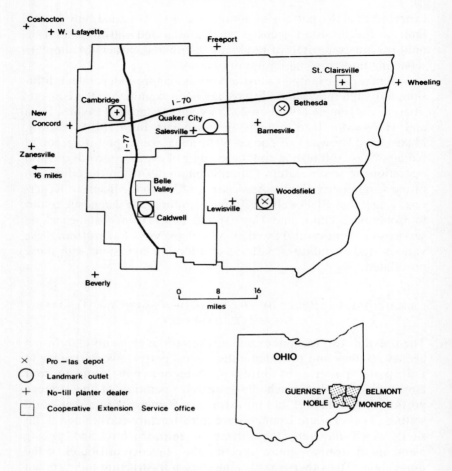

Figure 4.8   The Four-County Study Area

Infrastructure and Pricing Effects: The Diffusion of Pro-Las and Custom-Blended Fertilizer

The introductions of the cattle feed supplement pro-las and of custom-blended fertilizer into four counties of eastern Ohio provide an example of two infrastructure-constrained diffusions with contrasting pricing policies. This case study first describes the innovations; their propagation structure; and the infrastructure, pricing, promotional communications and market segmentation strategies undertaken to market them. These factors then are related to the temporal and spatial diffusion patterns of the two innovations.

Pro-las and custom-blended fertilizer were introduced into four counties of eastern Ohio in 1971 by the Belmont County Farm Bureau. This diffusion agency is a product distribution franchise of Landmark, Inc., the state-wide umbrella organization for Ohio's farm cooperatives. The two innovations were distributed under monopoly conditions, in part because Ohio farm bureaus honor each other's trade areas.

Pro-las is a liquified feed supplement containing protein, minerals, vitamins and molasses which involves the creation of a new consumption pattern in the use of liquid as well as dry cattle feed. Custom-blended fertilizer is fertilizer mixed individually to match the soil characteristics of each farm. This is a modification of a well-established product, prepackaged fertilizer, and involves only a slight alteration to the established consumption pattern. Accordingly, both innovations may be viewed as dynamically continuous, with pro-las being closer to discontinuous.

Both pro-las and custom-blended fertilizer are dependent upon a transportation infrastructure. Pro-las is stored in a tank in the farmer's pasture and filled periodically at a frequency dependent upon the tank's size and the number of cattle using it. Four delivery routes were developed to provide this service. Each serves one of the four counties in the Farm Bureau's market area and originates at a pro-las storage depot, two from Woodsfield and two from Bethesda (Figure 4.8). A uniform delivered price was established, thereby distributing transportation costs equally among all customers.

Custom-blended fertilizer is distributed from the Farm Bureau's blend plant in Quaker City, a location central to its market area (Figure 4.8). The farmer takes one or more soil samples to this plant, where fertilizer is mixed from bulk supplies. The fertilizer is then either transported by the purchaser or delivered by the Farm Bureau at a fee per ton mile. Thus, the total cost of the custom-blended fertilizer varies according to the location of the farmer.

The different pricing policies associated with the pro-las and custom-blended fertilizer infrastructures appear to account for different market segmentation and promotional communication policies. Pro-las, with a uniform delivered price, employed personal contact between Farm Bureau employees and potential adopters located in proximity to the delivery routes or to the storage depots at Woodsfield and Bethesda.[14] Further, the spatial segmentation of the market shifted over time since the Farm Bureau sequentially developed its delivery routes as each reached a threshold level of customers. Monroe County (Figure 4.8) was the first area developed.

This county contains its own depot, thereby allowing for initially minimal delivery costs. It was also where the employee in charge of the pro-las program lived, where he consequently knew many farmers and where promotional activities were therefore more economical and effective. In 1972 and 1973 the promotional campaign was extended to Belmont County where the second depot is located. More recently Guernsey and Noble Counties have been developed, but not as fully as the first two.

In contrast, the Farm Bureau had little incentive to spatially segment its market for custom-blended fertilizer. With a uniform price at the outlet and a distance-related delivered price, the spatial distribution of adopters did not affect profits associated with the innovation. Thus, the Farm Bureau vigorously promoted its product throughout the four-county market area, with no spatial bias and predominantly relying upon mass media. Ads were placed in one or more newspapers in each county, mailers were enclosed with bills to all Farm Bureau credit customers, radio advertising was undertaken and some farmers were visited by Farm Bureau employees.

Figure 4.9A illustrates the temporal trend of pro-las adoption from January 1971, when it was first made available. Most striking are the two periods of rapid growth in usage: first during the spring and summer of 1971 and again in the autumn, winter and spring of 1973–4. These spurts coincide with the Farm Bureaus's most active months of promotional activity and demonstrate the dramatic effect of agency efforts upon the temporal pattern of adoption.[15]

Custom-blended fertilizer presents a different temporal trend (Figure 4.9B). Starting in March 1971, the date of the blend plant's completion, this is approximately lincar with periodic fluctuations corresponding to the seasonal need for fertilizer. The extent of diffusion exceeds that for pro-las until July 1973, at least in part because custom-blended fertilizer is more of a continuous innovation and was more widely promoted.

Figure 4.9A also illustrates the spatial pattern of pro-las adoption, which decreases in density with distance from Bethesda and Woodsfield, the locations of the two pro-las depots. Over time, however, the pattern expands outward in a wave-like fashion, mirroring the Farm Bureau's intention to promote the new cattle feed first in Monroe County, next in Belmont County, and finally, in Guernsey and Noble Counties. This interpretation of the map portion of Figure 4.9A is supported by a quadrat analysis of the distribution of adopters in the years 1971 through 1974. The R-statistics of 0.252, 0.273, 0.385 and 0.405, respectively, indicate a

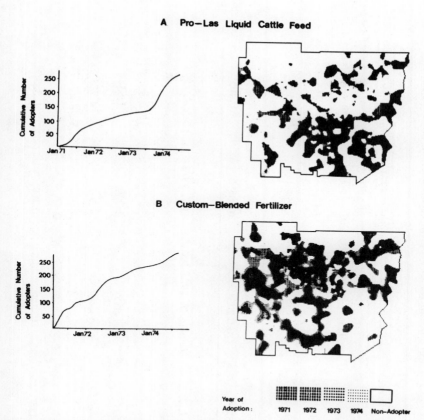

Figure 4.9 Temporal Trends of Adoption and Spatial Diffusion Patterns for Two Agricultural Innovations illustrating Infrastructure and Pricing Effects

markedly clustered distribution overall, but one which becomes less so over time (Table 4.3A).[16]

The spatial distribution of custom-blended fertilizer adopters also is clustered, but around the Quaker City blend plant (Figure 4.9B). Further, there is a scattering of adopters in peripheral areas. Since the cost to the adopter of obtaining the fertilizer increases with distance from the blend plant, and assuming the demand for custom-blended fertilizer is price elastic, such a decay in adoption with distance from Quaker City is predictable. Over time, however, it appears that earlier adopters were more scattered throughout the study area and that the clustering noted above occurred later. This observation is supported by a quadrat analysis of the distribution of adopters in the years 1971 through 1974. These R-statistics of 0.455,

Table 4.3 Quadrat Analysis of the Distribution of Pro-Las and Custom-Blended Fertilizer Adopters at Selected Times

A. Pro-Las

	January 1, 1972	January 1, 1973	January 1, 1974	July 1, 1974
Cumulative number of adopters (n)	81	121	207	256
Mean number of adopters per quadrat ($\bar{x} = n/176$)	0.460	0.688	1.176	1.455
Variance in the number of adopters per quadrat $\left(s^2 = \sum_{i=1}^{176} (x_i - \bar{x})^2/176\right)$	1.828	2.522	3.054	3.589
R-statistic ($\bar{x}/s^2$)	0.252[a]	0.273[a]	0.385[a]	0.405[a]

B. Custom-blended fertilizer

	January 1, 1972	January 1, 1973	January 1, 1974	July 1, 1974
Cumulative number of adopters (n)	104	191	234	270
Mean number of adopters per quadrat ($\bar{x} = n/176$)	0.591	1.085	1.330	1.534
Variance in the number of adopters per quadrat $\left(s^2 = \sum_{i=1}^{176} (x_i - \bar{x})^2/176\right)$	1.299	2.658	3.607	4.715
R-statistic ($\bar{x}/s^2$)	0.455[a]	0.408[a]	0.369[a]	0.325[a]

[a]The R-statistic for a random sample of potential adopters in the study area is 0.741

0.408, 0.369 and 0.325, respectively, indicate a trend towards greater clustering, a marked contrast from the pro-las diffusion patterns (Table 4.3B).

This difference in the evolution of the spatial pattern of diffusion for pro-las and custom-blended fertilizer provides an interesting observation about the consequences of diffusion agency strategy. The pricing policy for pro-las provided an incentive to develop the required delivery and service infrastructure in a spatially sequential and distance decay fashion and to undertake highly personalized promotional communications utilizing a parallel spatial segmentation of the market. The resulting gradual expansion of delivery and service routes accounts for the outward spread of pro-las adopters over time.

Alternatively, the pricing policy for custom-blended fertilizer provided little incentive to spatially segment the market or personalize promotional communications. Instead, the potential adopter bore the greater concern for discerning the real costs of adoption, and the contraction of the diffusion pattern over time would seem to reflect increased awareness of these costs, leading to a more *rational* distribution of adopters. For these reasons, then, the distribution of adopters for pro-las and custom-blended fertilizers are similar by 1974, but the evolution of the patterns over time follows opposite courses.

Promotional Communications and Market Segmentation Effects: The Diffusion of No-Till Farming and the Ohio Production Testing Program

The diffusions of no-till farming and the Ohio Production Testing Program in the four-county study area are independent of major infrastructure and pricing effects, so that the impact of diffusion agencies upon diffusion patterns occurs largely through promotional communications and market segmentation policies. Consequently, these innovations provide examples which contrast markedly from the previous ones in which both infrastructure and pricing were controlling factors.

This case study first describes the innovations; their propagation structure; and the infrastructure, pricing, promotional communications and market segmentation strategies undertaken to market them. Then, it describes the pattern of diffusion and interprets these in terms of diffusion agency actions.

No-till farming is a method of planting corn and forage crops without plowing. This was developed in the late 1960s and concurrently introduced into Ohio. By using herbicides (paraquot and/or atrozine) rather than tillage, labor is saved and a weed mulch is created which reduces soil erosion and conserves water.[17]

The Ohio Production Testing Program, which began in 1958, is a service developed by the Cooperative Extension Service to provide Ohio farmers with a method of improving their livestock through selective breeding. The Cooperative Extension Service analyzes the weight, size and other characteristics of an individual beef cow or sheep and calculates various evaluative indices for the animal such as its *most probable producing ability*. This information can then be used to cull herds and flocks.

The diffusion of no-till farming involved numerous private and public agencies. These include no-till planter dealers, the Chevron Chemical and Geigy Companies who supply the herbicides, farm supply dealers who sell the herbicides locally, the Cooperative Extension Service, the Soil Conservation Service and other government agencies. Thus, the diffusion agency system is complex and locationally pervasive.

The Ohio Production Testing Program only involved the Cooperative Extension Service. Nevertheless, its diffusion agency system also is locationally pervasive in that there is an extension office in each county seat (Cambridge, Woodsfield, Caldwell and St Clairsville) and an additional regional office in Belle Valley (Figure 4.8). Furthermore, agents from the state extension service, located in Columbus, Ohio, also actively promoted the Ohio Production Testing Program throughout the state and including the four-county study area.

Both innovations require a technological capability which may be considered as infrastructure. No-till farming employs a no-till planter and herbicides. The latter is widely available through the many farm supply dealers in the area. No-till planters were first manufactured by Allis Chalmers in 1968 and were almost immediately made available to the study area through a farm equipment dealer in Cambridge (Figure 4.8). Soon after, Ford, Massey-Ferguson and John Deere began manufacturing no-till planters, which were distributed through dealers in Lewisville, St Clairsville, Freeport, Barnesville and Salesville (Figure 4.8). However, purchasing a no-till planter is not always necessary. A farmer may borrow or rent one, pay a nearby farmer to custom no-till plant the land or convert a traditional planter into a no-till planter.

The technological capabilities for production testing include scales for weighing animals, livestock grading technicians and Extension Service agents for interpreting production testing results and recommending a course of action. As noted, the availability of these capabilities is widespread.

That these technological capabilities or infrastructures do not control the diffusion of either no-till farming or production testing is largely because of their locational pervasiveness. Further, and in part because of this pervasiveness, the price associated with both innovations is for all practical purposes uniform across the study area. One important difference, however, is the price magnitudes. When production testing began in 1958, the service was provided free of charge by the Cooperative Extension Service, and the current charge is only an annual $5.00 service fee and no more than $.50 per head for grading. By contrast, the cost of purchasing a new no-till planter ranges from $4000 upwards, and the cost of purchasing and applying the necessary herbicides is significant, particularly in that application is usually done by helicopter or airplane. These costs are now lower due to borrowing, renting, custom planting or converting traditional planters, but they remain considerably higher than those for production testing.

Promotional communications for no-till farming were undertaken by each of the numerous diffusion agents. The Cooperative Extension Service, Soil Conservation Service and other government agencies promoted no-till practices through personal contact with farmers, newsletters, local field demonstrations and talks at various local farm meetings. The chemical companies manufacturing no-till herbicides employed media advertising and field demonstrations in order to encourage no-till farming and thus promote the use of their herbicides which are a part of the *adoption package*. Finally, farm equipment manufacturers and dealers also were involved. Allis Chalmers pursued a national promotional campaign relying heavily upon farm journal advertisement, and the Cambridge dealer supplemented this exposure with local newspaper advertisements and personal contact with farm operators. Ford, Massey-Ferguson and John Deere undertook similar efforts.

Promotional efforts for the Ohio Production Testing Program were initiated in the late 1950s and early 1960s by state extension service agents who demonstrated the program's merits to both county agents and farmers. This was in part accomplished by mailing literature to local agents and to farm operators associated with breeding organizations. Articles on the program also were written for farm magazines and journals, and presentations were made at farm meetings.

Presently, county agents play the dominant role, employing similar promotional methods. However, these agents vary considerably in their promotional effectiveness, in part because of their varied interests and capabilities and the many other tasks for which they are responsible.

Because of the infrastructure and pricing characteristics noted above, the diffusion agents for both no-till farming and production testing had little incentive to tailor promotional communications to spatial segments of the market. However, for no-till farming there was an incentive, owing to the magnitude of costs, to beam promotional efforts towards those farmers financially most able to purchase a new, expensive piece of machinery and towards those likely to benefit most from adoption such as farmers with the larger corn acreages.

Further, the operating tradition of the Cooperative Extension Services is to employ the two-step flow of communications strategy by which promotional communications are relayed directly to *opinion leaders* who in turn *presumably* transmit them to the population at large. These opinion leaders tend to be the wealthier, better-educated farmers with larger operations (DeFleur, 1970: 124–9; E.M. Rogers and Shoemaker, 1971: 198–225; M.A. Brown, Maxson and Brown, 1977).

Thus, segmentation policies employing socio-economic criteria were used for both innovations. However, since eastern Ohio, like most rural areas, has no particular spatial clustering of wealthy or educated farmers or of large farm operations, the segmentation policy based on socio-economic variables did not incorporate an implicit spatial segmentation. Accordingly, one would not anticipate spatial clustering of no-till or production testing adopters, such as was observed for pro-las and custom-blended fertilizer.

The temporal trend of no-till farming usage is one of seasonal spurts at the time of corn planting with little growth in usage in between (Figure 4.10A). The overall trend, however, is linear with a relatively constant yearly growth. This trend is similar to that of custom-blended fertilizer, but the level of no-till adoption over approximately the same period is less. This slow diffusion is in part related to the discontinuous and costly nature of the innovation.

The temporal trend of adoption of the Ohio Production Testing Program indicates an initially slow rate of growth, an acceleration in this rate beginning in 1965, and a fairly constant rate of growth since then (Figure 4.10B). Thus, the curve resembles the first portion of the S-shaped curve traditionally associated with innovation diffusion.

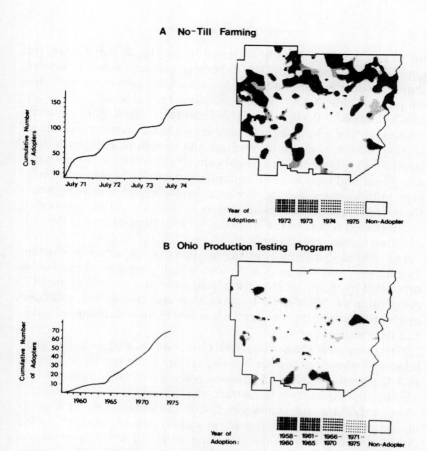

A   No-Till Farming

Cumulative Number of Adopters

150
100
50
10

July 71   July 72   July 73   July 74

Year of
Adoption: 1972   1973   1974   1975   Non-Adopter

B   Ohio Production Testing Program

Cumulative Number of Adopters

70
60
50
40
30
20
10

1960   1965   1970   1975

Year of
Adoption: 1958–   1961–   1966–   1971–
             1960   1965   1970   1975   Non-Adopter

Figure 4.10 Temporal Trends of Adoption and Spatial Diffusion
Patterns for Two Agricultural Innovations illustrating Promotional
Communications and Market Segmentation Effects

This is consistent with the fact that the promotional campaign for
production testing was not particularly vigorous, as is typical of many
non-profit innovation diffusions (Kotler, 1975; Kaufman, 1972: 11).[18]
The contrast extends not only to no-till farming but as well to pro-las
and custom-blended fertilizer (Figure 4.9) which also were promoted
largely through private sector efforts.

Figure 4.10A portrays the spatial distribution of no-till adopters.
This appears as small localized clusters spread throughout the
four-county study area, except in Monroe County which is characterized by cattle more than corn operations. This visual observation is
confirmed by the results of quadrat analysis.[19] The R-statistic for 1971

(0.761) is not significantly different from the R-statistic for the population as a whole (0.741), indicating a correspondence between those two distributions and a random locational pattern for the initial adopters (Table 4.4A). The R-statistics for succeeding years are smaller (0.557, 0.518, 0.515) indicating a slight shift towards clustering. The emergence of these local clusters reflects the role of renting or borrowing no-till planters and custom planting by nearby farmers, which operate in a neighborhood effect fashion. *Demonstration effects* and interpersonal communications also may have contributed to this patterning. More relevant to the theme of this chapter is the overall scattering of (these clusters of) adoption. This is related to the dispersed nature of the diffusion agencies themselves and the lack of infrastructure constraint.

The spatial distribution of the adopters of the Ohio Production Testing Program (Figure 4.10B) also is highly random, a conclusion supported by the 0.690 R-statistic from a quadrat analysis of the 1975 distribution (Table 4.4B).[20] Local clusters also are evident, reflecting neighborhood effect processes such as interpersonal communications and demonstration effects.

To summarize these empirical observations and evaluate them relative to those for custom-blended fertilizer and pro-las, it appears that the *temporal* trend of diffusion is not predictably influenced by whether the diffusion is infrastructure constrained or independent.[21] More important are characteristics of the innovation, such as its degree of continuity with ongoing practices, and characteristics of the diffusion agency such as the vigor and skill with which promotion is pursued.

However, the infrastructure constrained/independent distinction is an important influence on the *spatial* pattern of diffusion. Both custom-blended fertilizer and pro-las showed marked clustering overall, centering on the focal points of the infrastructure, and shifting over time in a manner coincident with the development of the infrastructure. By contrast, the spatial patterns of diffusion for no-till farming and the Ohio Production Testing Program, from their inception, were spread throughout the study area in random fashion.

Infrastructure effects, then, are amply demonstrated by these case studies. The no-till and production testing examples also provide evidence of how an area-wide diffusion process related to diffusion agency actions may operate jointly with a highly localized diffusion process to produce neighborhood effects and clusters of adoption. One thing not demonstrated by these examples, however, is the effects of promotional communications and market selection and

Table 4.4 Quadrat Analysis of the Distribution of No-Till Farming and the Ohio Production Testing Program Adopters at Selected Times

A. No-till farming

	January 1, 1972	January 1, 1973	January 1, 1974	January 1, 1975
Cumulative number of adopters (n)	43	74	101	141
Mean number of adopters per quadrat ($\bar{x} = n/176$)	0.244	0.420	0.574	0.801
Variance in the number of adopters per quadrat $\left(s^2 = \sum_{i=1}^{176} (x_i - \bar{x})^2/176\right)$	0.321	0.755	1.108	1.557
R-statistic ($\bar{x}/s^2$)	0.761[a]	0.557[a]	0.518[a]	0.515[a]

B. The Ohio Production Testing Program

	January 1, 1975
Cumulative number of adopters (n)	64
Mean number of adopters per quadrat ($\bar{x} = n/176$)	0.364
Variance in the number of adopters per quadrat $\left(s^2 = \sum_{i=1}^{176} (x_i - \bar{x})^2/176\right)$	0.527
R-statistic ($\bar{x}/s^2$)	0.690[a]

[a]The R-statistic for a random sample of potential adopters in the study area is 0.741

segmentation based upon socio-economic characteristics, when those strategies are not accompanied by an implicit locational component. Attention now turns to this problem.

Table 4.5 describes the socio-economic characteristics of those farmers who did and did not receive promotional communications pertaining to no-till farming and production testing.[22] Receivers of information about no-till farming, from both public and private agents, had significantly larger farms, farm incomes, family incomes and acres in corn. Receivers of promotional communications about production testing, which only came from public agents, were statistically indistinguishable from non-receivers, but there is a consistent trend indicating a favoring of the more successful and better educated. In general, then, there appears to have been a systematic segmentation of the market on the basis of socio-economic characteristics, although this is more marked for no-till farming.

That this segmentation strategy covaries with adoption behavior is indicated by comparing the socio-economic characteristics of those favored by the strategy with the same characteristics of earlier adopters and of adopters as a class. For no-till farming (Table 4.6A) these characteristics are exactly coincident. Earlier adopters, like the receivers of agency communications, had significantly larger farms, farm incomes, family incomes and acres in corn. This is also true for adopters versus non-adopters of no-till farming. For the Ohio Production Testing Program (Table 4.6B) earlier adopters and adopters as a class were in general more successful and better educated (although the time of adoption differences were not statistically significant), which is consistent with the characteristics of the Extension Service's segmentation strategy.

This is, however, a circumstantial argument for the effects of diffusion agency actions pertaining to promotional communications and market selection and segmentation, so that one could not insist that those actions are responsible for the observed patterns of diffusion. The conclusion becomes more obvious, however, by considering the opposite argument, namely that innovativeness differences are responsible. In making such an argument, one would assume similar levels of innovativeness for a given sample of farmers (E.M. Rogers and Shoemaker, 1971: 191–2; Midgley, 1977: 43–77), and therefore, the adopters of one innovation should be similar in socio-economic characteristics to the adopters of another innovation, particularly when the innovations are of a similar product category as in the present case. Such consistency, however, is not in evidence, as indicated by comparing Tables 4.6A and 4.6B. This—together with

Table 4.3 Mean Characteristics of Receivers and Non-receivers of Promotional Communications for No-Till Farming and the Ohio Production Testing Program

	Promotional communications about no-till farming through visits from public agents		Promotional communications about no-till farming through visits from no-till planter dealers		Promotional communications about the Ohio Production Testing Program through visits from cooperative extention service agents	
	Receivers $n = 134$	Non-receivers $n = 204$	Receivers $n = 75$	Non-receivers $n = 263$	Receivers $n = 103$	Non-receivers $n = 67$
Age	48.0	50.1	47.9	49.7	47.7	48.3
Years of college	0.910	0.686	0.627	0.818	1.282	0.836
Years of school	11.63	11.30	11.32	11.47	11.88	11.52
Agricultural training[a]	0.179	0.147	0.147	0.164	0.185	0.090
Full-time farmer[b]	0.448	0.373	0.493*	0.376*	0.282*	0.433*
Acres farmed	371.7***	261.3***	391.7*	280.4*	301.1	320.1
Farm income[c]	4.01***	3.12***	4.04*	3.32**	3.30	3.18
Family income[c]	5.07***	4.39***	4.80	4.62	4.74	4.49
Acres of corn	42.3***	20.9***	51.4***	23.1***		
Number of beef cattle					49.7	38.4
Number of sheep					25.1	25.7
Miles to nearest public agent[d]	7.21	7.71				
Miles to nearest extension service office					7.41	7.70

*, **, and *** Indicate that the difference between the group means for receivers and non-receivers is significant at 0.05, 0.01 and 0.001 levels of confidence, respectively.

[a] The values for this variable are: 1 = some agricultural training, 0 = no agricultural training.

[b] The values for this variable are: 1 = full-time farmer, 0 = not a full-time farmer.

[c] The values for this variable are: 1 = less than $2500; 2 = $2500–4999; 3 = $5000–9999; 4 = $10,000–14,999; 5 = $15,000–24,999; and 6 = $25,000 or more.

[d] Public agents include the Cooperative Extension Service, Soil Conservation Service and Agricultural Stabilization and Conservation Service.

Table 4.6 Mean Characteristics of Early, Middle and Late Adopters; All Adopters; and Non-Adopters of No-Till Farming and the Ohio Production Testing Program

A. No-till farming

	Early adopters (1965–70) n = 63	Middle adopters (1971–2) n = 56	Late adopters (1973–5) n = 49	All adopters n =168	Non-adopters n = 397
Age	51.1	48.7	48.3	49.9	51.4
Years of college	0.689	0.875	0.587	0.827	0.602
Years of school	11.59	11.50	11.04	11.49	11.15
Agricultural training[a]	0.180	0.143	0.196	0.167	0.139
Full-time farming[b]	0.590	0.464	0.478	0.506***	0.317***
Acres farmed	467.3*	348.1*	299.8*	375.6***	216.5***
Farm income[c]	4.64**	3.73**	3.74**	3.99***	2.64***
Family income[c]	5.08*	4.57*	4.91*	4.85***	4.27***
Acres of corn	63.4***	34.0***	24.0***	41.9***	13.4***
Miles to nearest public agency[d]	7.95	6.86	8.50	7.79	7.79

B. The Ohio Production Testing Program

	Early adopters (1958–65) n = 17	Middle adopters (1966–9) n = 16	Late adopters (1970–5) n = 30	All adopters n = 69	Non-adopters n = 495
Age	45.7	44.8	43.7	46.3***	51.7***
Years of college	1.41	1.73	1.57	1.657***	0.529***
Years of school	12.18	12.33	12.29	12.31***	11.10***
Agricultural training[a]	0.294	0.067	0.179	0.200	0.139
Full-time farming[b]	0.294	0.133	0.286	0.271*	0.388*
Acres farmed	327.2	308.7	292.6	328.1*	254.7*
Farm income[c]	3.65	2.93	2.82	3.10	3.03
Family income[c]	4.76	4.80	5.03	4.90***	4.38***
Number of sheep	21.8	7.3	12.1	22.1	15.4
Number of beef cattle	73.9	51.5	51.3	57.5***	27.2***
Miles to nearest extension service agency	7.18	7.81	7.29	7.43	7.84

*, **, and *** indicate that the difference between the group means of adopters and non-adopters is significant at 0.05, 0.01 and 0.001 levels of confidence, respectively, or that an analysis of variance of early, middle, and late adopter traits is similarly significant.

[a] The values for this variable are: 1=some agricultural training, 0=no agricultural training.

[b] The values for this variable are: 1=full-time farmer, 0=not a full-time farmer.

[c] The values for this variable are: 1=less than $2500; 2=$2500–4999; 3=$5000–9999; 4=$10,000–14,999; 5=$15,000–24,999; and 6=$25,000 or more.

[d] Public agents include the Cooperative Extension Service, Soil Conservation Service and Agricultural

the similarity between the characteristics of adopters of each innovation and the characteristics of those focused upon by the respective diffusion agency strategies—strongly supports the conclusion that diffusion agency actions pertaining to subjective attributes of the innovation, such as promotional communications and market selection and segmentation, are in general as, if not more, influential in determining adoption behavior than are innovativeness differences among potential adopters!

OVERVIEW

This chapter completes the delineation of the market and infrastructure perspective on innovation diffusion (Figure 4.11) by examining the strategies employed by diffusion agencies to induce adoption in their service or market areas. These strategies create differing levels of access to the innovation depending upon a potential adopter's economic, social and locational characteristics, and thus add to the constraints within which adoption occurs. Accordingly, while the where and when of *diffusion agency establishment* provides the general outlines of the innovation diffusion pattern, *diffusion agency strategies* add considerable detail by shaping the pattern at the more local market area level of aggregation.

The actions of other entities in both the public and private sectors also interact with and affect both diffusion agency establishment and diffusion agency strategy. Among other things, these actions provide various publicly available infrastructures such as service, delivery, information, transportation and water systems, as well as other incentives and disincentives for adoption. These *enabling actions* of public and private entities other than the diffusion agency will be returned to for a more detailed treatment in Chapters 7 and 8 on the development perspective.

The diffusion agency strategy portion of the market and infrastructure framework was examined in three ways. *First,* a conceptualization of innovation establishment that encompasses the various elements of diffusion agency strategy was presented. This considers the actions of both diffusion agencies and other public and private entities in terms of their *interface* with potential adopters and, ultimately, the adoption decision (Figure 4.1). Four elements of diffusion agency strategy deemed particularly relevant to the spatial pattern of diffusion are considered in this conceptualization: *the development of infrastructure and organizational capabilities, pricing policy, promotional communications* and *market selection and segmentation.*

One important observation derived from this conceptualization is that the first two of these elements primarily affect the *objective*

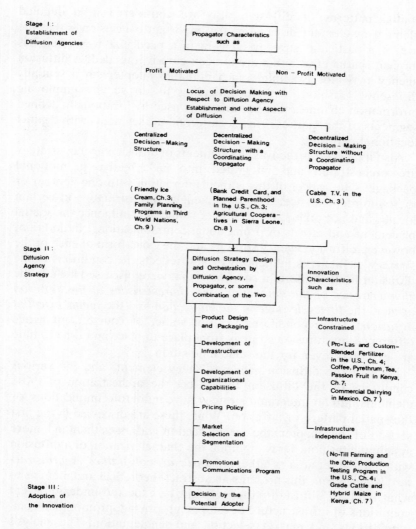

Figure 4.11 Overview of the Market and Infrastructure Perspective on Innovation Diffusion, showing Case Studies presented in this Book

attributes of the innovation, whereas the latter two primarily affect its *subjective attributes,* that is, the beliefs of potential adopters about the objective attributes and/or the potential adopter's evaluation of them. The conceptualization also indicates the domain of traditional innovation diffusion studies from the adoption perspective and how that concatenates with the diffusion agency strategy portion of the market and infrastructure perspective.

The possible effects of each of the strategy elements in terms of spatial patterns of diffusion also are considered in a detailed element-by-element discussion. An important conclusion is that the use of a particular strategy element in a particular way often has implicit spatial effects that are not consciously intended. A diffusion agency may, for example, reach potential adopters in a spatially differential fashion, without intending to do so, by employing information channels that are primarily used by locationally defined segments of the market or by socio-economic segments with distinct locational patterns.

Also important is the way the elements of diffusion agency strategy are orchestrated and integrated into an effective promotional package. One aspect of this is their interaction with one another or their interdependence. The placement of infrastructure in certain locales and not others, for example, would also influence the spatial placement and effects of promotional communications. In addition, however, diffusion agency strategy and the exact form of each of the strategy elements is influenced by and reflects the conditions of the diffusion itself. Important conditions that were discussed include the *characteristics of the innovation,* the *characteristics of the diffusion agency,* the *life cycle stage of the innovation* and the *spatial extent of diffusion.* These conditions are not static, of course, and hence differences in diffusion strategy from place to place and time to time are expected, even for the same innovation.

Each of the diffusion agency strategy elements and the various conditions of the diffusion that affect the orchestration of those elements into an integrated strategy have numerous implications for the spatial pattern of diffusion. While these are discussed in the first section of this chapter, the *second* section addresses them in a more systematic fashion. Drawing upon the characterization of a diffusion within a market area as either *infrastructure constrained* or *infrastructure independent,* this presents an abstract theoretical argument as to what kinds of diffusion patterns might be expected under different conditions of infrastructure development, pricing, promotional communications and market selection and segmentation. The analysis also extends to considering temporal changes in the pattern and the effects of real world infrastructure systems that induce directional biases in the diffusion.

While traditional models of diffusion primarily would predict distance decay patterns outwards from the urban center, the argument here only finds this for a limited set of circumstances. More common is a uniform distribution of adoption (Figure 4.6). In the case of infrastructure-independent diffusion, the spatial extent of this is in general unlimited, but from the perspective of the individual diffusion agency it is bounded by the limit of the agency's service area. In the case of infrastructure-constrained diffusion, a uniform distribution of adoption is expected only within the area served by the infrastructure, and no adoption is expected outside of the infrastructure penetration boundary.

The *third* section of this chapter is comprised of studies of actual diffusions which illustrate the operation of diffusion agency strategies in a real world setting. Four agricultural innovations in an identical four-county area of eastern Ohio (Figure 4.8) were examined: pro-las, a cattle feed supplement; custom-blended fertilizer; no-till farming; and production testing of beef cattle and sheep. The first two of these are infrastructure constrained and illustrate the effects of infrastructure and pricing elements of strategy, those which affect the objective attributes of the innovation. No-till farming and production testing are exemplary of infrastructure-independent innovations and illustrate the effects of promotional communications and market selection and segmentation, elements which affect the subjective attributes of the innovation. The interaction among these elements in formulating a diffusion strategy also is given attention.

These four examples provide ample support for the expectations generated by the preceding discussion of diffusion agency strategy. The spatial patterns of diffusion for pro-las and custom-blended fertilizer showed marked clustering overall, centering on the focal points of the infrastructure, and a shifting over time in a manner coincident with the development of the infrastructure, thus demonstrating the effects of the infrastructure constraint. By contrast, the spatial patterns of diffusion for no-till farming and the Ohio Production Testing Program, from their inception, were spread throughout the study area in random fashion. Further, socio-economic status statistics pertaining to adopters and non-adopters of no-till farming and production testing indicate that diffusion agency actions pertaining to subjective attributes of the innovation are as, if not more, influential in determining adoption behavior than are innovativeness differences.

In addition to these general findings, two other sets of findings are of particular interest. The first of these concerns the joint operation of elements of the market and infrastructure perspective and elements of the adoption perspective. In particular, the diffusions of no-till farming and production testing were characterized by an area-wide diffusion process related to diffusion agency actions operating jointly with a localized process based upon interpersonal communications emanating from adopters. The result is a spatial pattern of diffusion comprised of clusters of adoption within an overall random pattern.

The second set of findings concerns the evolution of diffusion patterns and the differential use of promotional communications and market selection and segmentation under different pricing and infrastructure policies. In particular, the diffusion agency developed and maintained the delivery and service infrastructure for pro-las under a uniform delivered pricing scheme, whereas the diffusion of custom-blended fertilizer employed a distance-related price if the agency delivered and a uniform price at the outlet otherwise. Thus, the infrastructure and pricing policy for pro-las provided an incentive to develop infrastructure in a spatially sequential fashion and to undertake highly personalized promotional communications utilizing a parallel spatial segmentation of the market. Alternatively, the infrastructure and pricing policy for custom-blended fertilizer provided little incentive to spatially segment the market or personalize promotional communications, leading to more media usage and market area-wide coverage. In terms of spatial patterns, the result for pro-las was a gradual outward expansion of the diffusion pattern over time, whereas the diffusion pattern of custom-blended fertilizer actually contracted over time in reflection of the potential adopter's increasing awareness of the real costs of adoption. By 1974, however, the patterns were similar and represented a *rational* distribution of adopters.

One general point remains. The market and infrastructure framework indicates an number of close ties between urban system processes, which have been extensively studied, and diffusion. The diffusion agency establishment portion of the framework, for example, employs location-allocation modeling principles and central place concepts related to the characteristics of individual urban areas and their interrelationships with one another. Similarly, the diffusion agency strategy portion of the framework employs a number of central place ideas pertaining to urban hinterlands, urban functions and the order and range of goods. However, this concatenation is only barely developed in the present work, leaving as a future task the development of an extensive theory that would fully integrate diffusion and urban system processes, to the benefit of both topics of study.

Another application of the market and infrastructure framework is to the diffusion of technological or firm innovations, which generally has been studied as a phenomenon distinctly different from the diffusion of consumer or household innovations. This link is explored in the following chapter.

NOTES

1 An exception to this observation is the product management literature of marketing (Pessemier, 1977), but this generally has not been directly associated with innovation diffusion, even by members of the marketing discipline. Further, most of that work tends to be primarily concerned with continuous innovations, and the effects of price and advertising, a narrower focus than the framework developed here. The congruence between product management models and the market and infrastructure framework is given further attention in Chapter 9, pages 298–9.

2 Some combination of these also may be charged. For example, an agency may charge a uniform-delivered price for the purchase of an innovation, but a uniform price at its outlet for service and repairs.

3 Note, however, that even if travel costs are not directly associated with acquisition of the innovation they may be a significant consideration. An example is when the innovation requires frequent service which must take place at the agency.

4 Little research has examined differences in the impact of information as a result of the public or private nature of the agency providing it. One would expect, however, that these sources might differ in their credibility—that is, in their *expertness* or perceived ability to communicate valid assertions and their *trustworthiness* or perceived intent to communicate valid information (Hovland, Janis and Kelley, 1953: 21). The trustworthiness of an agency probably depends upon the potential adopter's perception of the type of interest it has in persuading her or him, which may be different for public versus private entities. As Karlsson (1958:43) has noted, however

   the degree to which the message fits into earlier attitudes seems to be dominant over the credibility of the source. If a message is contrary to firmly held beliefs and values it will not be accepted even if the source has high credibility. Either the message will be dissociated from the source or the credibility of the source will diminish.

5 Accordingly, the use of communication from a potential adopter's social system can be an explicit part of the diffusion strategy. This is termed *indirect marketing* (Howard and Sheth, 1969). The importance of communication from a potential adopter's social system in part derives from the greater number of regular interactions with one's immediate acquaintances than with other sources of information. The effectiveness of social interaction also is enhanced by tendencies such as *compliance* and *identification*. Compliance is when a potential adopter accepts the communicator's opinion in order to induce a favorable reaction from him or her. *Identification* is when a potential adopter accepts the communicator's opinion as a part of remaining consistent with the potential adopter's image of their relationship (Howard and Sheth, 1969: 296–9).

6 Of all the tools available to the diffusion agency, communications has received the most attention by social scientists modeling social processes. For reviews of the multitude of efforts in this area, see Karlsson (1958), Hudson (1972), Coleman (1964), L.A. Brown (1968b), Bartholomew (1973) and Bartos (1967).

7 For a more complete discussion of market selection and segmentation and related strategies, see Kotler (1972: 165–91), Roberto (1975), and R.E. Frank, Massy and Wind (1972).

8 A more behavioralistic approach has been advocated (Yankelovich, 1964) in which markets are scrutinized for important differences in potential adopter attitudes,

motivations, values, usage patterns, aesthetic preferences or degree of susceptibility, but it has not been widely employed.

9 Illustrative of this is the franchise form of agency of which there are three basic types, each characterized by a different level of agency independence (Thompson, 1968; McGuire, 1971; Zeller, 1978). In the *product-distribution franchise* the agency is an exclusive conduit through which the innovation is distributed, but it may handle other products and for the most part determines its own marketing policies. Examples would include SCM typewriters. In the *trade-name franchise* the agency primarily obtains a licensed trade name such as Mayflower Moving and Storage or Martinizing Dry Cleaning, but propagator involvement with the agency is minimal. Finally, there is the *product-license franchise* whereby the propagator provides a complete package of brand name product, outlet design and image, methods of production and marketing, and training for organizational and technical manpower. This franchise type is characterized by near uniformity in most aspects of agency activities. Examples are Howard Johnsons, McDonald Hamburgers, Pier I Imports, Volkswagen of America, and automobile rental agencies.

10 An alternative not noted in Figure 4.3 is that propagator control may vary throughout an agency network. For example, the propagator may directly control a sufficient number of agencies to provide basic distribution and rely on agency-owned outlets to complete the market coverage (Evans, 1959). An example is Coca Cola of Ontario (Osleeb, 1973).

11 This assumption should not be taken to imply that infrastructure-constrained diffusion situations are restricted to developing areas in the world. In many parts of the rural United States, for example, public water supply is an infrastructure currently being developed that should give rise to extensive diffusion guided by infrastructure utilization costs that vary stepwise with distance. Other recent examples include broadcast television (Berry, 1972, 1973), cable television (Sieling, Malecki and Brown, 1975) and direct dial telephone service (Clark, 1974).

12 Trip frequency generally is inversely related to the distance of the potential adopter from the urban center, but from a research perspective its effects are neutralized by the fact that potential adopters generally would have sufficient opportunity to acquire the innovation in the time frame of reference usually employed in diffusion studies (one year or one month, for example).

13 The material reported here is a synopis of work reported more fully in M.A. Brown and Brown (1976) and M.A. Brown (1977). Data sources for this material include a comprehensive survey of 597 farm operators and 26 public and private diffusion agents in the four-county area, related diffusion records, and informal interviews with diffusion agents associated with the Belmont County Farm Bureau Cooperative and the county offices of the Cooperative Extension Service. For another dimension of these materials, see M.A. Brown's (1980) study of the role of personal attitudes as compared to social categories in adoption behavior.

14 A variety of personal contact strategies were used to develop each route. The employee in charge of the promotional program spoke about pro-las at farm meetings and followed through with visits to interested persons located near developed or developing delivery routes. Brochures were also sent to a sample of farmers who raised cattle and were good Farm Bureau customers; many of these farmers were subsequently visited by salesmen. Newspaper advertisements with testimonials from satisfied customers were placed in several newspapers, but there was no radio or television advertising.

15 In this context one could well argue that the rapid growth traditionally associated with the middle phase of diffusion has less to do with the innovativeness characteristics of adopters or their level of interpersonal interaction than with the extent and timing of diffusion agency promotional efforts. For an elaboration of this point with regard to innovativeness, see L.A. Brown, Malecki and Spector (1976). This observation also has relevance to S-curve models such as the logistic,

which often are formulated on the assumption that interpersonal communications are the critical factor in innovation diffusion (L.A. Brown, 1968b; Casetti, 1969).

16 The study area was divided into 176 cells for the quadrat analyses, and the number of adopters per quadrat was determined. From this data an R-statistic was calculated as the ratio of the mean number of adopters per quadrat to the variance. In general, an R value of 1 indicates a random distribution, values higher than 1 indicate a tendency toward uniformity, and values less than 1 indicate a tendency toward clustering (A. Rogers, 1969a, 1969b, 1974). These inferences are based upon the assumption that the population of potential adopters is randomly distributed. However, a randomly selected sample of 345 farm operators from the four-county area yields an R value of 0.741 indicating that the distribution of the base population of potential adopters is more clustered than random. Therefore, the R-statistics pertaining to adoption patterns are evaluated by comparison to the R-statistic for the base population rather than the value of 1.0.

17 No-till farming has the potential to markedly increase the productivity of hilly farmland which cannot be farmed using traditional tillage techniques. For a discussion of this see the *New York Times, News of the Week in Review*, February 15, 1976.

18 This is evidenced by the fact that only 97 of a sample of 345 farmers had information about the Ohio Production Testing Program, while 135, 176 and 196 had information about pro-las, custom-blended fertilizer and no-till farming, respectively.

19 See note 16 of this chapter for an explanation of the quadrat analysis.

20 Quadrat analyses were not done for earlier years, as with custom-blended fertilizer, pro-las and no-till farming. This is because there were only seventy-one adopters in 1975 and the sample sizes for preceding years were too small to provide R-statistics which are comparable with those for the other innovations. For a discussion of the impact of sample size upon R-statistics, see the references cited in note 16 of this chapter.

21 In the infrastructure-constrained situation, the rate at which relevant infrastructure is developed would affect the temporal trend of diffusion, but the exact nature of this is not predictable within the framework articulated in this paper. In infrastructure-independent diffusion, however, this influence would not be an issue.

22 Promotional communications are gauged by whether or not a respondent received a visit pertaining to the innovation. This index is taken as representative of the overall promotional effort because diffusion agents for both no-till and production testing judged it as moderately to very important in their strategy, and as considerably more important than other methods of disseminating information (M.A. Brown, 1977: 179–205).

5

A NOTE ON THE DIFFUSION OF INNOVATION AMONG FIRMS

The market and infrastructure perspective on innovation diffusion, presented in Chapters 3 and 4, is primarily concerned with innovations adopted by households or individuals, termed *consumer innovations,* and the ways in which entrepreneurial, government, or non-profit-motivated entities make these available to the population at large. In this chapter attention turns to innovations adopted by entrepreneurial entities for their own use, termed *technological* or *firm innovations.* These include innovations adopted by firms engaged in both manufacturing and tertiary activity, although the research literature is primarily in terms of the former.

The first section of this chapter is a brief review of research on the diffusion of technological innovations. One conclusion of this review is that research on the diffusion of innovations among firms has largely employed the adoption perspective also prevalent in work on consumer innovations. This provides the starting point for the second section of this chapter, which demonstrates a congruency between the adoption perspecive on technological innovations and aspects of the market and infrastructure perspective on consumer innovations, drawing upon the work of Malecki (1975, 1977). Articulating this congruency is significant because research endeavors on firm and consumer innovations have for the most part been seen as separate and unrelated. The third and final section of this chapter addresses the supply side of the firm innovation problem, examining some actual strategies used by the propagators of technological innovations in diffusing their product. This concludes that a perspective such as the market and infrastructure one also is applicable to technological innovations.

THE RESEARCH FRAMEWORK PERTAINING TO THE DIFFUSION OF TECHNOLOGICAL INNOVATIONS[1]

Research on the diffusion of innovation among firms has developed separately from that on household innovations. Until recently, in fact, there was little crossreferencing between the two traditions of study. This is quite curious, perhaps anomalous, since both share a preoccupation with adoption behavior and innovativeness and both traditions have received considerable attention over the past twenty years. Further, both have given a great deal of attention to mathematical models of the diffusion process, particularly those pertaining to the S-curve of diffusion over time.[2,3]

There are, however, some important differences in the factors which are emphasized by each tradition. Specifically, research on the diffusion of technological innovations has tended to give more attention to the characteristics of the innovation itself and of the adopting firm, whereas the consumer innovation tradition has tended to give relatively more emphasis to the communications or information flow process. Within these broad outlines, another important difference between the two traditions is that the diffusion of technological innovations is explicitly characterized as involving the replacement of an old technology with a new one, perhaps reflecting the dominance of economic approaches to the problem at hand. Thus, diffusion rates are often measured in terms of the proportion of firms using the new technology as compared to those using the old. Likewise, the diffusion itself is often explained in terms of the comparative characteristics of both the old and new technology, rather than focusing only upon the characteristics of the new.

In general, the *characteristics of technological innovations* identified as being most important in implementing this *substitution* are its *relative profitability* and the *required investment*. Linstone and Sahal (1976:59) note, for example,

ceteris paribus, the more profitable the innovation and smaller the required investment, the greater the rate of imitation [diffusion].

In the task of understanding and forecasting the rate and pattern of real world substitutions, however, there are a number of problems in implementing the concept of profitability, even though it is generally thought of in terms of *relative advantage* (of the new over the old technology) or *cost savings*.

First, the new technology may do the same task at a lesser cost, more tasks at the same or proportionately the same costs, and/or tasks that are essentially new. In this connection, Stern, Ayres and Shapanka (1976:123–4) note

When one material or technology competes with and gradually replaces another, the new material or technology is never an exact equivalent of the old; hence, the unit prices of the two are not directly comparable . . .

alternate technologies do not compete on the basis of price alone, but rather on the basis of maximum 'utility' provided per dollar of cost. Or, looked at the other way around, cost-effectiveness implies minimum cost per unit of 'utility.'

It is clear, however, that the latter point of this argument only shifts the focus to *utility* which, like profitability, is difficult if not impossible to measure.

A second problem in understanding and predicting the rate and pattern of real world substitutions has to do with identifying the applications or markets of the new technology. These are generally somewhat if not substantially different from those of the old technology (Stern, Ayres and Shapanka, 1976). And as Nabseth and Ray (1974: 302) note

it is the very essence of new technical processes, especially in the early stages, that the outcome of their introduction is uncertain.

A third problem with simply conceptualizing technological diffusion as a function of profitability is that this changes over time for a new process and for a given firm (Nabseth and Ray, 1974: 301–6). This occurs because the innovation is improved, both in general and differentially with respect to certain markets. It also occurs because factor input prices change, often in favor of the new technology. This uncertainty of outcome is endemic to technological innovation so that accurately anticipating the future on the basis of present evidence is always difficult and sometimes impossible. The following example illustrates this point.

it could be argued that even the most farsighted management could not have forseen, in the early 1960s when many oxygen steel decisions were being made, the drastic changes and improvements in continuous casting that were to occur in the late 1960s. (Nabseth and Ray, 1974: 303)

These aspects of technological diffusion pertain to the fact that innovation is a *continuous* process, in contrast to the assumption implicit in most diffusion research on both firms and household innovations that the innovation is a set, non-changing phenomenon. Chapter 6 reviews work on the continuity of innovation carried out by economic historians, almost the only group of researchers consistently concerned with the question.[4]

There also is a factor influencing the profitability and hence the rate of diffusion of a given technology which might derive from the innovation itself, as the factors discussed above, but also might derive from the adopting firm or the industry of the adopting firm. This factor pertains to whether the innovation constitutes an *addition* to employed technology or ongoing capacity, a *replacement* of technology or capacity being phased out anyway, or a *displacement* of functioning facilities (Gold, Peirce and Rosseger, 1975; Nabseth and Ray, 1974: 304–5). Following conventional investment theory, the rate of diffusion ought to be greater for additions and slower for replacements since in the latter case industry already has a *sunk* cost to be amortized or written off. In this context, the age of existing facilities also is important, older facilities being more readily displaced than newer ones. Looked at another way, the innovation constituting a *displacement* of functioning facilities, and particularly of less old functioning facilities, would have to be more profitable than the innovation constituting an addition to functioning facilities. Most commonly, this factor is a characteristic of the entire industry of which the potential adopter firm is a member. To illustrate,

The slow diffusion of the open hearth [even] in the face of sharply growing output was clearly attributable to the industry's heavy financial and technical commitments only a few years earlier to the Bessemer process. (Gold, Peirce and Rosegger, 1975: 139)

Another *industry characteristic* is *competition among firms*, the level of which varies from industry to industry. In part, early adoption takes place because certain firms wish to gain an advantage over their competitors. Later adopters, then, are either forced to adopt to remain competitive or do so to take advantage of the innovation's success (Parker, 1974: 99–117). Further, intraindustry competition is one of the causes of the *bandwagon* effect associated with the sharply rising middle portion of the S-curve of diffusion and frequently found in empirical studies.

A set of factors which affect both the innovation and the adopting firm but which are not intrinsic to either are *institutional effects*. A class of these are *societal concerns* which give added importance to some innovations that otherwise might have sat on the shelf, and reduce the importance of other innovations. Current examples falling in this category include the concern over environmental impact, which has dramatically increased the importance of pollution control innovations and decreased the importance of innovations involving high levels of pollutant emission, and the space race which has led to a variety of high technology innovations. Institutional occurrences also affect *relative factor prices* which in turn favors certain innovations over others. A recent example of this is the actions of the Organization of Petroleum Exporting Countries (OPEC) leading to greater use of and enhanced prospects for a number of petroleum substitute innovations. Gold, Peirce and Rosegger (1975: 139) provide two other examples. One concerns the diffusion of by-product coking.

the plentiful supply of excellent Pennsylvania coking coal and the availability of organic chemicals from foreign suppliers clearly retarded adoption of the new technology during the early period of its availability. Not until World War I did shortages of both lead to a rapidly growing interest in the by product process.

And, with regard to the slow diffusion of the open hearth process for steel,

the open hearth's ability to absorb considerable proportions of scrap did not turn into a major economic advantage until the expanded output of the industry generated sufficient quantities of home scrap.

Firm characteristics also affect the time and place of adoption of technological innovations. The characteristic which most comple-ments the profitability factor is that of *firm size*. In general, large firms have several advantages over smaller firms in the adoption of technological innovations (Nabseth and Ray, 1974: 306–8; Malecki, 1975: 9–11; 1977: 1292–3). One of these is their greater ability to raise capital, to bear the costs of the innovation and to bear the risk of failure. Larger firms also can better afford the managerial and technical specialists often needed to evaluate the innovation and implement it within the firm. The relative economic advantage to be gained from the innovation also might be related to firm size in that this quality is frequently a direct function of the scale of operations.

On the basis of this, one would expect an adoption sequence from larger to smaller firms. While this might be true for higher-cost innovations, there is evidence that the size sequence might not hold for lower-cost innovations (Myers and Marquis, 1969). In fact, after making a case for large firm adoption Nabseth and Ray (1974: 308) note

It is by no means inevitable that large firms should be the first to introduce a new process; on the contrary, there are many examples in our material of smaller firms taking the lead, for instance, in oxygen steel and continuous casting, also in shuttleless looms.

This finding leads to the suggestion that firm size might operate more as a threshold than as a scale, and that the threshold size of firm seems to vary for different technologies (Nabseth and Ray, 1974: 307).

A second firm characteristic of importance is the *aggressiveness and innovativeness* of its management. This may be more prevalent in medium- than in large-size firms since it is the former who have an incentive to grow and improve their competitive position (Malecki, 1975, 1977; Waite, 1973).[5] Such receptivity to innovation might well offset the many advantages that vary directly with firm size, particularly for lower cost and risk innovations which have a lower firm size threshold for adoption and are therefore as readily accessible to small firms as to large ones. However, testing the relationship between adoption behavior and management aggressiveness and innovativeness is a problem because

The concept . . . has not been easy to operationalize in empirical research and has therefore remained largely a qualitative explanation of residuals from adoption patterns. (Malecki, 1977: 1292)[6]

In spite of this operationalization problem, there is evidence that some firms are in general more innovative than others. Nabseth and Ray (1974: 310), for example, note

it is shown that the same firms tend to be early or late in the introduction of new processes, not just the one studied, and that this applies to most countries.

Blackman, Seligman and Sogliero (1976) reach a similar conclusion through a factor-analytic approach applied to variables that are manifestations of management innovativeness, such as research and development expenditures and new product sales.

A third important firm chracteristic is its *level of information about the innovation*. This information is often highly technical in nature, originating in trade or professional journals or from sales technicians, and is essential to each firm's appraisal of the costs and relative advantage of the innovation. Information also functions generally to create awareness of the innovation and reduce uncertainty, particularly as adopting firms provide a demonstration effect and evidence of the innovation's utility and solutions to attendant problems.

Unlike consumer innovations, however, the adoption of technological innovations often lags years behind the initial receipt of information, so that information itself, while essential, can not be used to account for the diffusion pattern. One reason for this lag is the need for information of a highly specialized nature. Also, cost and technical personnel factors are much more important aspects of adopting technological innovations. Accordingly, many firms quite willing to adopt simply do not have the resources to do so (Nabseth and Ray, 1974: 299–310). Finally, deliberation and slowness in the

adoption decision is encouraged by the *continuity* of the innovation
process which results in many improvements during the course of
diffusion. Thus,

There are many examples . . . of the difficulties encountered in using a new
technology, especially by the first firms. They may be 'leaders' in introducing
the process but 'followers' when it comes to its profitability. (Nabseth and
Ray, 1974: 303)

Whether there is opinion leadership or any kind of two-step flow
process in the spread of information about technological innovations
also has received attention, but the findings are ambiguous (Lancaster and White, 1976; Webster, 1972). The spatial sturcture of
information flows among firms also is relatively unknown. Earlier
ideas that the patterns of information transmission follow the urban
hierarchy or some kind of neighborhood effect pattern are no longer
considered valid, primarily due to recent work by Pred (1973a,
1973b, 1974a, 1974b, 1975a, 1976, 1977) which demonstrates that
there are no systematic regularities in the spatial structure of firm
linkages. Accordingly, Malecki (1977: 1293) notes

Any simplistic model of hierarchical or distance dependent information flows
among firms fails to take into account the specialized relationships and
institutional arrangements that operate in a given [technological] diffusion
situation.

To sum up, the diffusion of technological innovation is largely
viewed in terms of the adoption behavior of the firms using the innovation. Their decision is seen to be a function of the *characteristics of
the innovation* itself, such as its profitability or cost savings and required investment; *industry characteristics* such as the intraindustry
competitive structure and the nature of previous technological investment; *institutional effects* such as societal concerns and political actions; and *firm characteristics* such as its size, the aggressiveness and
innovativeness of management, and the level of information about
the innovation.

One other point should be made before we leave this literature.
One can readily see from the examples above that the reference point
for research on the diffusion of innovations among firms generally
has been technological innovations adopted by manufacturing entities. However, firms engaged in tertiary activities also adopt
inovations for their own use. Examples include the adoption of
computer-based accounting and data processing systems by banks
(Malecki, 1975, 1977; Berg, 1973), the adoption of electronic cash
register and inventory systems by discount stores and supermarkets

(Berg, 1973) and the adoption of microwave ovens by restaurants. The findings noted above also apply in this arena. Thus, the model(s) developed by those studying the diffusion of technological innovations among firms is actually much broader in its applicability than is indicated by the examples reported in the research literatu: ?.

Another set of pertinent observations comes by considering the intersection of the firm adoption model, pertaining to technological innovations, and the market and infrastructure perspective pertaining to consumer innovations. Recall from the latter that diffusion agency establishment under a decentralized decision-making structure, which covers the majority of occurrences, is essentially a situation in which establishment represents an adoption by the local entrepreneur. This is parallel to the firm's decision to adopt a technological innovation. Accordingly, it is possible to construct a model which covers both situations and integrates two bodies of thought that heretofore had been considered (and treated) as distinct. Such a task has been initiated by Malecki (1975, 1977). His work is presented in the following section.

A MODEL OF INNOVATION DIFFUSION AMONG FIRMS[7]

This section presents two models. One accounts for the diffusion of technological and consumer innovation among firms; the second, which is derived from the first, accounts for the diffusion of technological and consumer innovations in an urban system. For ease of exposition, however, the models are developed initially only with reference to technological innovations, drawing upon the above review.

The first step is to model the time of adoption as a function of firm size, where size is simultaneously a surrogate for cost and risk constraints and for management aggressiveness and innovativeness. Through the relationship between firm size and city size, the firm adoption model is then related to city-size diffusion patterns. Third, by integrating urban area characteristics with regard to the distribution of firm sizes and those pertaining to competition, information and market potential, a more general model for diffusion among urban areas is developed. Finally, the applicability of these models to both technological and consumer innovations is demonstrated.

The Firm Adoption Model

In modeling the diffusion of technological innovation, an important relationship is that between firm size and time of adoption. A common assumption is that, because large firms are more able to afford the risk and cost associated with innovations, the time order of adoption will vary inversely with firm size, larger firms adopting earlier and smaller firms later (Hakanson, 1974; Mansfield, 1968a, 1968b; Nabseth, 1973; R.J. Smith, 1974). This relationship can be readily depicted in mathematical terms by drawing on the fact that the size distribution of firms follows a regular and monotonic trend.[8] In this task, one may employ the Pareto distribution,

$$y = gx^{-q} \tag{5.1}$$

where y is the number of firms greater than or equal to size x, and g and q are parameters. The intercept, g, indicates the number of firms in the set, and q, the slope, measures the range of firm sizes. In its logarithmic form

$$\log_e y = \log_e g - q \log_e x \tag{5.2}$$

the distribution is a straight line sloping downward to the right from the intercept value, $\log_e g$.

Given the strong relationship between firm size and adoption time, the Pareto distribution also may serve to express the latter. Thus,

$$A = dx^{-k} \tag{5.3}$$

and

$$\log_e A = \log_e d - k \log_e x \tag{5.4}$$

By direct analogy to equations (5.1) and (5.2), A is the date by which firms of x or larger will adopt or the date of adoption by a firm of size x, and d is the date of adoption by the smallest firm or the latest adoption date. Likewise, k indicates the range of adoption times among the set of firms (Figure 5.1). Thus, if the value of k is small, the adoption times for firms of all sizes are similar, and diffusion through the set of firms is rapid. Alternatively, in a slow diffusion process, k is larger, indicating a greater range in adoption times.

In addition to considering the greater ability of large firms to bear the cost and risk associated with adoption, the model also must consider management qualities such as their aggressiveness and innovativeness. As noted in the review above, these qualities tend to be more prevalent among small firms which are anxious to grow and increase their industry share (Mueller, 1972; Waite, 1973). However, the resulting propensity toward early adoption by small firms is constrained and mitigated by their lesser ability to absorb the cost and risk aspects of adoption.

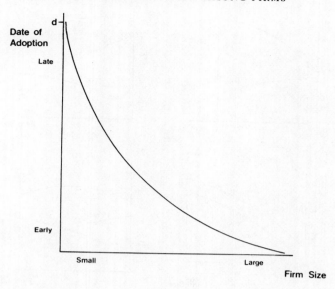

d: Date of adoption of the smallest firm or the latest adoption date

Figure 5.1 Pareto Function Relationship Between Date of Adoption and Firm Size under the Assumption that Larger Firms have a Higher Adoption Propensity
After equations (5.3) and (5.4)

Thus, we have a diffusion situation in which two factors are critical but each works in opposite directions. Accordingly, whether the early adopters are large, medium or small firms depends both upon the importance of cost/risk considerations relative to aggressiveness/innovativeness considerations and upon the way in which these qualities vary with firm size (Figure 5.2).[9] The likelihood of early adoption is greatest among large (but not the largest) firms if the cost/risk constraint, varying so as to favor early adoption by larger firms, is more important to adoption propensity than is the effect of management aggressiveness and innovativeness, varying so as to favor adoption by smaller firms (Figure 5.2A). If the situation is altered only in that mangement qualities are more important to adoption propensity than is the constraint of innovation cost and risk (Figure 5.2B), overall adoption propensity is greatest among smaller firms. Alternatively, if the effect of management qualities is the same for all firms sizes but the effect of cost and risk considerations favors

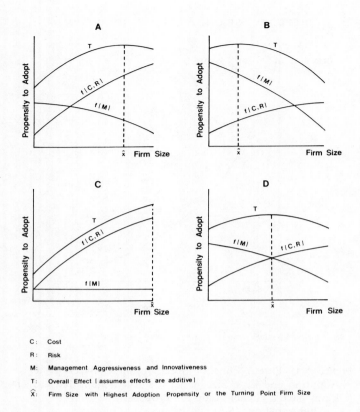

C : Cost

R : Risk

M: Management Aggressiveness and Innovativeness

T: Overall Effect (assumes effects are additive)

$\hat{X}$: Firm Size with Highest Adoption Propensity or the Turning Point Firm Size

Figure 5.2   Conceptual Representations of Firm Size Effects
on Propensity to Adopt Innovations

the larger firms, then the largest firms have the highest adoption
propensities (Figure 5.2C). Finally, if the effect of the two sets of
factors are balanced in that each varies in the same way with firm size
except in the opposite direction, then medium-size firms have the
highest propensities to adopt (Figure 5.2D). Several empirical studies
(Hakanson, 1974; Maddala and Knight, 1967; Mansfield, 1968a,
1968b; Myers and Marquis, 1969; Nabseth, 1973; Ray, 1969) indicate
that the outcomes portrayed in Figures 5.2A and 5.2D are extremely
common.

The greater likelihood that the early adopters will be medium-size
firms can be incorporated into a formal model by an expansion of the
linear Pareto model of equation (5.4). As stated, the date of adoption
varies inversely with firm size at a constant rate, k, that is, the date of
adoption associated with a small firm is later than that associated with

a large firm all the way up the firm size hierarchy to the very largest firm. To change this to account for later adoption by large firms, k is set equal to $(a - b \log_e x)$, that is,

$$\begin{aligned} \log_e A &= \log_e d - ((a - b \log_e x) \log_e x) \\ &= \log_e d - a \log_e x + b (\log_e x)^2 \end{aligned} \qquad (5.5)$$

Then, the date of adoption associated with a small firm will be later than that associated with a larger firm, but only up to a firm size $\hat{x}$, whereupon the relationship is reversed. Thus, there is a firm size beyond which larger size is associated with later, rather than earlier, adoption (Figure 5.3).[10]

In fitting the quadratic function model depicted by equation (5.5) to actual data, the following outcomes are possible. If its parameters are estimated on the basis of a diffusion in which the first adoptions are *not* by the largest firms, the value of a will be negative and the value of b will be positive. Alternatively, if the first adoptions are by the largest firms, the value of b will be zero, leaving the linear relationship of equation (5.4). Thus, the b value in equation (5.5) indicates whether the quadratic or linear relationship is more appropriate in a given diffusion.

The size of firm which adopts earliest, $\hat{x}$ or the *turning-point firm size,* may be estimated by differentiating equation (5.5) with respect to $\log_e x$, that is,

$$\begin{aligned} (\log_e A)' &= -a/x + (2b \log_e x)/x \\ &= (-a + 2b \log_e x)/x \end{aligned} \qquad (5.6)$$

Setting $(\log_e A)'$ equal to zero and solving for $\log_e \hat{x}$ yields

$$\log_e \hat{x} = a/2b \qquad (5.7)$$

and

$$\hat{x} = e^{(a/2b)} \qquad (5.8)$$

where $\hat{x}$ is the turning-point firm size.

Firm Adoption in an Urban Area Context

A spatial component to the diffusion of innovation among firms is provided by the fact that, in general, the number of firms, the range of firm sizes and the size of the largest firm all will be greater in larger as compared to smaller urban areas (Figure 5.4). A similar variation might be expected of the level of interfirm competition and amount of information about the innovation. One might conclude

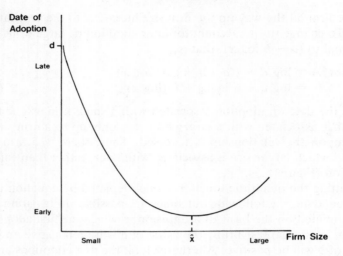

x̂: Firm size with highest adoption propensity or the turning point firm size

d: Date of adoption by the smallest firm or the latest adoption date

Figure 5.3   Quadratic Relationship between Date of Adop-
tion and Firm Size to Take Account of the Higher
Adoption Propensity of medium-size Firms
After equation (5.5)

from this that, whether the earlier adopters are large or medium-size
firms, large cities are most likely to contain the earlier adopters since
they will have more firms of every size, as well as higher levels of
information and interfirm competiton.

Given this, the Pareto distribution again is appropriate, but now
expressed as

$$T = mp^{-s} \qquad (5.9)$$

By direct analogy to equation (5.4), T is the date of *first adoption* in
an urban area of population size P, or the date by which urban areas
of size P or larger each will have experienced an initial adoption
(Figure 5.5). Likewise, the parameter m in equation (5.9) represents
the latest date of initial adoption among all urban areas, or that date
at which initial adoption occurs in the smallest town. Finally, the
parameter s represents the rate of progression to earlier adoption as a
function of population, which in turn is representative of the number
of firms, the range of firm sizes and the size of the largest firm. Thus,
if the value of s is small, the initial adoption times for all urban areas

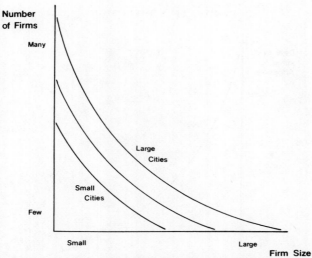

Figure 5.4   General Relationship between Firm Sizes and
Number of Firms as it Varies with City Size

are similar and diffusion through the urban system is rapid.
Alternatively, in a slow diffusion process, s is larger indicating a
greater range in the times of initial adoption among urban areas.

The expectaton embodied in equation (5.9) is contradicted,
however, by empirical evidence indicating that the earliest adopters
for many innovations are often found in medium rather than
large-size cities (Pred, 1973b, 1976, 1977). Several innovations in the
United States iron and steel industry, for example, began among
medium-size firms located in medium-size cities (Mansfield, 1968a:
86–7). Similar examples of technological innovations adopted by
firms engaged in tertiary activities include computer-based accounting and data processing systems in banks (Malecki, 1975, 1977),
automatic banking machines and electronic cash register and point of
sale inventory systems for supermarkets and discount stores.

Just as this regularity was built into the firm adoption model, the
linear form of equation (5.9),

$$\log_e T = \log_e m - s \log_e p \qquad (5.10)$$

may be expanded to

$$\log_e T = \log_e m - c \log_e p + r (\log_e p)^2 \qquad (5.11)$$

by setting s equal to $(c - r \log_e p)$. In equation (5.11), then, the date of
first adoption in the urban area will be later for smaller cities than for
larger cities, that is it will vary inversely with city population, but only

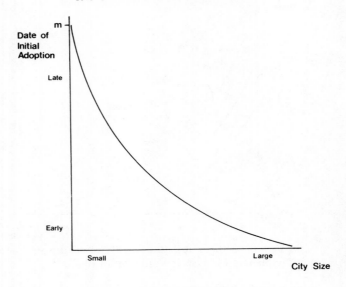

m: Latest date of initial adoption among all urban areas or that date at which initial
   adoption occurs in the smallest town

Figure 5.5 Pareto Function Relationship between Date of
   Adoption and City Size under the Assumption that Higher
   Adoption Propensities are Found in Larger Cities
   After equation (5.9)

up to the turning-point city size $\hat{p}$, whereupon the relationship is
reversed. Beyond $\hat{p}$, therefore, larger city size is associated with later
rather than earlier adoption (Figure 5.6).

If the parameters of the *city size diffusion model* (equation 5.11) are
estimated with data from a diffusion in which the early adoptions take
place in medium- rather than large-size cities, the value of c will be
negative and the value of r will be positive. Alternatively, if the first
adoptions are in the largest cities, the value of r will be zero, leaving the
linear relationship of equation (5.10). Thus, the r value in equation
(5.11) indicates whether the quadratic or the linear relationship is
more appropriate in a given diffusion through an urban system.

The size of city in which the first adoption occurs, $\hat{p}$ or the
turning-point city size, may be estimated in a manner similar to that of
equation (5.8). Thus, using the parameter values derived from fitting
equation (5.11) to actual data,

$$\hat{p} = e^{(c/2r)} \tag{5.12}$$

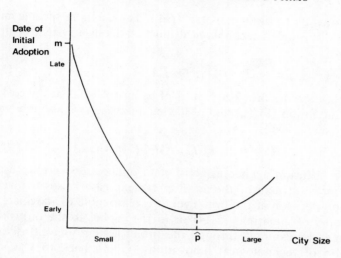

$\hat{p}$:   City size with highest adoption propensity or the turning point city size

m: Latest date of initial adoption across all urban areas or that date at
     which initial adoption occurs in the smallest town

Figure 5.6   Quadratic Relationship between Date of Adoption and City Size under the Assumption that Higher Adoption Propensities are Found in medium-size Cities After equation (5.11)

A General Urban Area Model of Innovation Diffusion

Attention now turns to demonstrating the congruence between the model for the diffusion of technological innovations among urban areas and processes pertaining to the diffusion of consumer innovations. In doing this, only functional forms are used.

The basic urban system diffusion model of equation (5.11), in functional form, is

$$T_j = f(p_j, p_j^2) \tag{5.13}$$

where T_j is the date of first adoption in urban area j and p_j is its population. This model was derived under the assumption that population could be a surrogate for firm size (F_j), competition (C_j) and information effects (I_j). There also is an implicit factor pertaining to the activities of the firm and the relevance or relative advantage of the innovation to those activities (FA_j). Thus, a more specific model for the diffusion of technological innovations in a system of urban areas is

$$T_j = f(P_j,\ F_j,\ FA_j,\ C_j,\ I_j) \qquad (5.14)$$

or, separating the firm-size factors of being able to bear the cost and risk of adoption (FCR_j) and of having an aggressive and innovative management (FM_j)

$$T_j = f(P_j,\ FCR_j,\ FM_j,\ FA_j,\ C_j,\ I_j) \qquad (5.15)$$

Since diffusion agency establishment under a decentralized decision-making structure, the most prevalent case, also involves an adoption decision at the firm level, it is reasonable to anticipate that the model of equations (5.14) or (5.15) applies to the diffusion of consumer innovations through the urban system as well as to the diffusion of technological innovations. Going back to Chapter 3 indicates that this is indeed the case. Thus, using symbols in parentheses to indicate the concordance between the consumer and technological innovation situations

where and when agencies are established (T_j) will depend upon the local entrepreneur learning about the innovation and about establishing an agency from which it may be propagated (I_j). Accordingly, characteristics of the local entrepreneur also are important (F_j). That person must, for example, have sufficient capital to establish an agency (FCR_j), be capable of seeing the potential of the innovation (FM_j), be willing to take the required risks and to expend the required effort (FM_j), and possess certain promotion and management skills $(FCR_j,\ FM_j)$. Another factor is the congruence of the innovation with the ongoing activities of the entrepreneur (FA_j). Thus, those places with human resources capable of being aware of and exploiting the innovation are more likely to receive diffusion agencies (P_j). (Chapter 3, pages 92–3, symbols in parentheses added.)

The only factor in equations (5.14) and (5.15) not accounted for by the above summary is interfirm competition effects, C_j, but that also is applicable to the consumer innovation situation. In the diffusion of the bank credit card, for example, the adoption of the service by banks in a given town after the initial adoption was a clear response to local competition effects (Malecki and Brown, 1975).

One factor, however, must be added to the consumer innovation model, market potential (M_j). While the population variable might be seen as a surrogate for this, it alone is not likely to indicate the probable retail success of a new good or service. Further, market potential is of such singular importance in the diffusion of consumer innovations that it should be expressed separately. Accordingly, the consumer innovation equivalent of equations (5.14) and (5.15) is

$$T_j = f(P_j, F_j, FA_j, C_j, I_j, M_j) \tag{5.16}$$

or

$$T_j = f(P_j, FCR_j, FM_j, FA_j, C_j, I_j, M_j) \tag{5.17}$$

Thus, the same set of factors is expected to operate in the diffusion of technological and consumer innovations, with the exception that market potential also is important for the latter.

One implication of the market and infrastructure perspective, then, is its provision of a conceptual and operational link between research on consumer innovations and (the adoption perspective of) research on technological innovations, which hitherto have been seen as separate and unrelated endeavors. There also is a second implication of the market and infrastructure perspective in the context of technological innovations. If it has proven fruitful to examine the supply side of consumer innovation diffusions, would not a similar exercise be useful for the supply side of technological innovation diffusions, which also has been neglected? Attention now turns to this theme.

THE AVAILABILITY OF TECHNOLOGICAL INNOVATIONS AND RELATED DIFFUSION PATTERNS

Technological innovations, like consumer innovations, are promoted by entrepreneurial and government entities with the objective of maximizing the extent of diffusion. To accomplish this, each propagator designs strategies which affect how the innovations are marketed and where and when they are made available to potential adopters. Accordingly, a framework such as the market and infrastructure perspective ought to be applicable to technological as well as consumer innovations.

This section summarizes evidence supporting the view that there is a distinct supply side to the diffusion of technological innovations. Hopefully, this will serve as a starting point for future research on the topic, leading ultimately to the articulation of a suitable conceptual framework.

The main body of literature pertaining to the differential availability of technological innovation appears to be in *industrial marketing*. Much of this work takes on an adoption perspective, but a direct concern with the propagation of technological innovations is occasionally in evidence. An example is Wasson (1974, 1976). This examines changes in the strategy of the firm over the life cycle of its products. Particular elements of strategy considered include its overall objective, the characteristics and level of competition, product design, pricing, promotional communications, product distribution and market development. Examples used to elaborate elements of this framework include rayon, nylon, the electric typewriter, the desk top calculator, hybrid corn and DDT.

A broader treatment of the differential availability of technological innovations is presented by Briscoe, Cannon and Lewis (1972). They carried out nine case studies pertaining to the initial market development for new industrial products. These case studies focus upon new materials which must be fabricated into a finished product and then transmitted to an *end user* or consumer firm. Thus, the initial propagator may either focus upon the fabricator market, the consumer market or both. Of the nine case studies, two were from the aluminum industry, three from plastics and four from steel. The innovations represent either a new material or an attempt to introduce an old material into a new market. The authors tender a number of suggestions with regard to marketing new industrial products. These include clearly defining objectives so the marketing program can be well designed before being employed, realistically appraising the propagator's strengths and weaknesses which should affect both the design of strategy and the choice of markets, insuring a high quality product so as to overcome the anticipated skepticism of the fabricator and end user, and choosing a fabricator (the middle man in this particular set of cases) with great care. Other aspects of strategy considerations, which fit more within the concerns of the market and infrastructure perspective, include providing technical service and information for both fabricators and end users, choosing product markets with great care, developing market segments and specifying pricing policies.

Another study of interest is Feller, Menzel and Kozak (1976) on the diffusion of innovations to muncipal governments. While this situation is not completely coincident with the other situations addressed in this chapter, it is sufficiently close to warrant attention. More important, however, this is the only work which explicitly examines the role of the propagators of technological innovations (or innovations akin to technological ones).

Three innovations were studied: optically programmed signals for traffic control, elevated platform fire trucks, and SHU-PAK, a one-man solid waste collection vehicle. The interviewed firms propagating these innovations all felt that their efforts influenced the pattern of diffusion, and several used the word *determined* (Feller, Menzel and Kozak, 1976: 234). More generally,

it is inconsistent with almost any variant of a profit seeking theory of the firm to assume that firms have no marketing strategy or that the marketing strategy has no effect upon adopters. The fact that a manufacturer may sell to the public sector rather than or in addition to the private sector does not vitiate its pursuit of profit. Municipal agencies differ in their size, their potential influence on non-adopters, and in their distance from points of production. It seems reasonable to assume [therefore] that manufacturers do in some manner seek to relate their marketing efforts to these differences. (Feller, Menzel and Kozak, 1976: 234)

One point brought out in this study is the unique role of the salesperson of technological innovations. This person is not only a provider of general information about the innovation but also a technical expert. In some sense, then, the salesperson plays a technical infrastructure role as well as a promotional communications role, a point also noted by Webster (1972).

Second, all three case studies showed evidence of market selection and segmentation. The propagation of optically programmed traffic-controlled signals employed a two-step flow of communications strategy in which initial contact was with a small group of known leaders or innovators in the traffic engineering field. Another market selection strategy for optically controlled traffic signals was to focus on regions with high levels of new highway construction. In the propagation of elevated platform fire trucks, promotional efforts were directed towards the fire chief under either of two market selection strategies. One was to focus on larger or key cities in a given region and depend upon imitation and demonstration effects to bring about spread to lesser members of the urban hierarchy. An alternative strategy was to concentrate on suburban or middle-size cities under the assumption that their adoption would lead to eventual imitation by nearby larger cities. In the propagation of SHU-PAK, this latter strategy was followed exclusively. The rationale for doing so was that suburban or middle-size cities are more innovative than larger cities and that larger cities have more institutional barriers to adoption such as entrenched unions which are threatened by a labor-saving innovation such as SHU-PAK.

Another aspect of market selection that emerged was a pronounced neighborhood effect relative to the manufacturing plant of the propagator. This was rationalized both in terms of minimizing propagation costs and of having, or being able to create more easily, a higher level of credibility with nearby municipalities, particularly the suburban ones where personal contact was readily initiated.

Two relevant observations about pricing policies emerged. One pertained to the propagation of elevated platform fire trucks. This is a highly fragmented and competitive industry, and low bidding or price cutting was often employed to gain a foothold in new markets as a basis for further sales at a higher price. Second, in the propagation of SHU-PAK, municipalities were allowed to field-test a vehicle with their own personnel on a short-term basis or to lease SHU-PAK for several months. This was necessary because the properties and relative advantages of the innovation were not readily apparent to the market.

It is clear, then, that the diffusion of technological innovations also involves a conscious strategy on the part of the propagators that affects both the spatial and temporal patterns of diffusion. Further, there is at least some similarity between the components comprising the propagation strategy in this setting and those in the setting of consumer innovations for which the market and infrastructure perspective was developed. More specifically, it appears that considerations pertaining to industry or organizational structure, market penetration, infrastructure and organizational development, pricing, promotional communications and market selection and segmentation also are relevant in the diffusion of technological innovations. Thus, as Feller, Menzel and Kozak (1976: 252) note

our observations indicate the presence of an entire category of marketing influences on the diffusion process, and suggest the likelihood that . . . at the very least . . . there are dangers in attempting to explain such [diffusion] patterns . . . solely in terms of the characteristics of adopters.

Accordingly, it is hoped that the evidence reported in this section will provide an incentive for future research endeavors pointed towards developing a model of the diffusion of technological innovation which is parallel to the market and infrastructure perspective for consumer innovations.

OVERVIEW

This chapter focuses on innovations adopted by entrepreneurial entities for their own use, which are referred to as technological or firm innovations. These include innovations adopted by firms engaged in both manufacturing and tertiary activity.

The first section of this chapter presents a brief review of research on the diffusion of technological innovations. In general, the firm adoption decision has been seen as a function of the characteristics of the innovation, such as its profitability or cost savings and required investment; industry characteristics such as the intraindustry competitive structure and the nature of previous technological investment; institutional effects, such as societal concerns and political actions; and firm characteristics such as their size, the aggressiveness and innovativeness of management and the level of information about the innovation.

The literature on the diffusion of technological or firm innovations almost exclusively focuses upon innovations adopted for use in secondary, rather than tertiary activity, and almost exclusively employs the adoption perspective also prevalent in work on consumer innovations. Despite this latter communality, however, there is little crossreferencing between research on the diffusion of technological innovations and that on consumer innovations, and each has emerged as a relatively distinct line of endeavor.

One of the differences between the two traditions is that research on the diffusion of technological innovations has tended to give more attention to the characteristics of the innovation itself and of the adopting firm, whereas the consumer innovation tradition has tended to give relatively more emphasis to the communications or information flow process. Within these broad outlines, another important difference is that the diffusion of technological innovations is explicitly characterized as involving the replacement of an old technology with a new one. Thus, diffusion rates are often measured in terms of the proportion of firms using the new technology as compared to those using the old, and the diffusion itself is often explained in terms of the comparative characteristics of the old versus the new technology, rather than focusing only on the characteristics of the new.

In order to provide a bridge between these research traditions, the second section of this chapter demonstrates a congruency between the adoption perspective of work on firm innovations and aspects of the market and infrastructure perspective. The basis of this is that diffusion agency establishment under a decentralized decision-making structure, the most prevalent situation for consumer innovations, actually represents adoption by a local entrepreneur, which renders it comparable to the firm's decision to adopt a technological innovation. This parallelism provides the basis for a mathematical model that accounts for diffusion among firms and urban areas of both technological and consumer innovations.

One implication of the market and infrastructure perspective, therefore, is its provision of a conceptual and operational link between research on consumer innovations and (the adoption perspective) of research on technological innovations, which hitherto have been seen as relatively distinct endeavors. There also is a second implication of the market and infrastructure perspective in the context of technological innovations. If it has proven useful to examine the supply side of consumer innovation diffusions, would not a similar exercise be useful for the supply side of technological innovation diffusions, which also has been neglected?

This theme is elaborated in the third section of this chapter by summarizing evidence that there is a distinct supply side to the diffusion of technological innovations which affects both the spatial and temporal patterns of diffusion. That section also demonstrates that there is at least some similarity between the components comprising the propagation strategy in this setting and those utilized in the diffusion of consumer innovations for which the market and infrastructure perspective was developed. More specifically, it appears that considerations pertaining to industry or organizational structure, market penetration, infrastructure and organizational development, pricing, promotional communications and market selection and segmentation also are relevant in the diffusion of technological innovations. Accordingly, a framework such as the market and infrastructure perspective ought to be applicable to technological as well as consumer innovations, and it is hoped that this theme will be pursued and developed in future research.

At points in the review section of this chapter, reference was made to the continuity of innovation. This refers to the continual modification and improvement of the innovation throughout the diffusion process. Such continuity is itself an important aspect of the diffusion, both in encouraging and impeding the process. Chapter 6 examines this in detail.

NOTES

1 This review is designed only to provide the flavor of research on the diffusion of innovation among firms, and hence, it should not be taken as comprehensive. For further detail, there are a number of broadly focused papers on the topic that should be consulted by the interested reader: Gold (1975, 1977), Hurter and Rubenstein (1978), Lancaster and White (1976), Linstone and Sahal (1976), Nabseth and Ray (1974) and Webster (1972, 1978). Assistance in preparing this chapter was provided by Edward J. Malecki of the University of Oklahoma Department of Geography; this is appreciated.

2 Perhaps the paucity of interaction between these two traditions is because research

on firm innovations has been carried on largely within economics whereas that on household innovations has been carried on largely within sociology. However, the separation of the two traditions appears to be breaking down as evidenced by recent articles on firm innovations, such as Rosegger (1977), Sahal (1976) and Nabseth and Ray (1974), that reference the extensive work on household innovations.

3 For an indication of the extensive scope of mathematical modeling of the diffusion of technological innovations, see Hurter and Rubenstein (1978) and Linstone and Sahal (1976). The roots of this concern appear to begin with the work of Griliches (1957) and Mansfield (1961, 1968a, 1968b).

4 In looking at the product life cycle and its characteristics, marketing research also has considered the continuity of innovation. However, their work is not systematic or comprehensive in the same way as that of the economic historians, nor has it been incorporated into the marketing model of innovation diffusion. For an example of marketing research on the product life cycle, see Wasson (1974, 1976).

5 The advertisements for the Avis automobile rental company are relevant to this point. These proclaim 'We Try Harder' because of their number two position behind Hertz in the car rental business.

6 For a description of the several methods employed to operationalize management aggressiveness and innovativeness, see Nabseth and Ray (1974) and Mansfield (1968a, 1968b).

7 The essence of this section is taken from Malecki (1975: 17–30).

8 There is a sizable literature on the topic of firm size distributions. For examples, see Collins (1973), Engwall (1973), Hjalmarsson (1974), Ijiri and Simon (1971, 1974), Simon and Bonini (1958), Steindl (1965) and Wedervang (1965).

9 Both the relative importance of each of these factors and the way they vary with firm size would depend upon the type of innovation being diffused and upon the firms themselves. To illustrate, if the innovation is an inexpensive one, the ability to bear its cost and risk would be almost the same for a small firm as for a large firm, whereas this would not be so if the innovation is very expensive. Similarly, evidence such as P.S. Johnson (1975: 54–8) indicates that firm size differences in the level of management innovativeness are minimal in newer technology oriented industries but significant in older durable goods industries.

10 If Figure 5.3 were reversed by plotting adoption time on the horizontal axis and firm size on the vertical axis, the resulting graph would be similar in functional form and appearance to the *crater* function employed by Newling (1969) in his examination of urban population density gradients.

6

A NOTE ON THE CONTINUITY OF INNOVATION: THE ECONOMIC HISTORY PERSPECTIVE[1]

The adoption and market and infrastructure perspectives, as well as much of the research on the diffusion of technological innovations, embodies the assumption that the innovation is essentially the same throughout the diffusion process, even though this is contradicted by our own experience. As noted in Chapter 1, for example, the computer has gone through almost yearly changes since becoming commercially available, so that today's models, while still called a computer, are hardly recognizable as the offspring of the UNIVAC of thirty years ago. In the consumer innovation area, color television now costs less, and has better color and better programming than its initial counterpart. It is reasonable to conclude, therefore, that a critical component of successful innovation is its continual technological improvement and *adaptation* to the market, leading to *adoption* by an increasingly wider range of persons or organizations.

One important aspect of this *continuity* of innovation is that it, as much as any other element, can directly affect the temporal and spatial patterns of diffusion.[2] As an illustration of this, consider the alternative explanations put forth for the diffusion of hybrid corn. The sociologists, in accord with the adoption perspective, attribute this to individual innovativeness and personal interaction or communications effects (Ryan and Gross, 1943), whereas the economist Griliches (1957), in accord with the market and infrastructure perspective, attributes this to profitability. Yet, Griliches (1957: 502) himself notes

Hybrid corn . . . was not a single invention immediately adaptable everywhere. The actual breeding of adaptable hybrids had to be done separately for each area. Hence . . . we have . . . to explain the lag in the development of adaptable hybrids for specific areas

raising the possibility, in accord with the economic history perspective, that the organizations responsible for adapting hybrid corn to various locales thereby determined the spatial and temporal sequencing of its availability and the resulting patterns of diffusion.[3]

A second important aspect of this *continuity* of innovation, not unrelated to the first, is that it enters directly into the adoption decision. More specifically, there is often a delay in adoption (solely) because of the expectation of further improvements in the innovation (Rosenberg, 1976a). Note that this delay is not because the potential adopter is overly resistant, nor because that person is less innovative, nor because that person has not been targeted by diffusion agency strategy—the explanations provided by the perspectives examined thus far in this book. Rather, the delay is the outcome of a *rational* decision-making process based upon the knowledge that tomorrow's innovation is likely to be considerably different and better than today's! Thus, the early adopting firms

may be 'leaders' in introducing the process but 'followers' when it comes to . . . profitability. (Nabseth and Ray, 1974: 303)

Rosenberg (1976a: 527–8) discusses the introduction of commercial jet airplanes as an illustration of this. The British de Havilland company introduced the Comet I two years before the Americans began developing a jet airliner. Yet, the delay actually helped the American Douglas and Boeing companies eventually to win out over the British. In part, this occurred because the American's offering was designed around later and more powerful engines and therefore could carry significantly more passengers (180 versus 100) at faster speeds (550 mph versus 480 mph). Another aspect of the American's success was their acquisition of knowledge about metal fatigue, derived from Britain's efforts to make the Comet safe after its then mysterious accidents, without suffering the negative image of the British plane.

Similar illustrations can be found for consumer innovations. Many persons, for example, delayed the buying of color television or home electronic calculators in anticipation of lower prices and technological imporovements in the innovation.

In general, then,

Expectations of continued improvement in a new technology may therefore lead to postponement of an innovation, to a slowing down in the rate of its diffusion, or to an adoption in a modified form to permit greater future flexibility. (Rosenberg, 1976a: 531)

The process of change in the innovation itself, while neglected by others, has been a primary concern of one school of economic history. In their perspective, innovation is seen as a *continual* rather than as a *discrete* process whereby the form and function of an innovation and the environment into which it might be adopted are modified throughout the life of the innovation. More generally, the market or economy is perceived to be in a long-run competitive equilibrium (or a series of such) between the old and the new technology. The proportion of each technology represented at any particular time reflects the costs of each relative to the other, and the old technology is replaced gradually as the cost ratio (of the new to the old) decreases. These costs are both *endogenous* to the technology, as represented by its productivity, and *exogenous,* as represented by the price of required inputs or the relative factor costs. Further, although this perspective has been developed with regard to technological innovations, it has a considerable amount of transferability to consumer innovations, as indicated by the examples above.

These ideas about the continuity of the innovation and the effect of that upon the diffusion process are aspects of economic history which are of primary relevance to the themes developed in this book. For purposes of perspective, however, this chapter also presents a brief synopsis of other economic history work pertaining to diffusion, but which views innovation as a discontinuous, rather than continuous, phenomena. The chapter is divided into two sections. The first outlines the economic history perspective on innovation diffusion; the second considers the concatenation of the economic history perspective with other paradigms of innovation diffusion.

THE ECONOMIC HISTORY PERSPECTIVE ON INNOVATION DIFFUSION[4]

The economic historian's concern with innovation diffusion is related to their broader interest in economic growth and development. As stated by Rosenberg,

the rate at which new techniques are adopted and incorporated into the productive process is, without doubt, one of the central questions of economic growth. (Rosenberg, 1972: 1)

Accordingly, economic history research almost exclusively examines technological rather than consumer innovations. This focus does, however, include agricultural innovations (Griliches, 1957; Hayami, 1974; Evanson, 1974), taking their role in economic production as the critical factor. It is interesting to compare this view with that of the rural sociologists who treat agricultural innovations as consumer innovations, taking their adoption by households as the critical factor (E. M. Rogers and Shoemaker, 1971).

Another characteristic of the economic history literature is that innovation diffusion *per se* is a rather recent concern, dating perhaps from no more than twenty years ago. Prior studies were largely concerned with technological history and viewed the onset of rapid economic growth in terms of major inventions relevant to the industry being studied (Rosenberg, 1972a: 3). This *traditional* interpretation thus highlights the inventions and neglects the diffusion process (Fogel and Engerman, 1971b: 206). By contrast, the *reinterpretation* of economic history notes: (1) that rapid advances in technological efficiency do not coincide with the dates of major new inventions; (2) that the interval between inventions and their commercial application is usually quite protracted and (3) that there is a further lapse of time from the commercial application to general adoption by the firms that make up an industry or geographic region (Fogel and Engerman, 1971b: 206).

Finally, both the *traditional* interpretation of economic history and the *reinterpretation* have a concern with *institutional* factors. Consistent with their broader concerns, however, the traditionalist tends to stress the influence of institutional factors upon economic growth in the aggregate, while the reinterpretation tends to stress their influence upon the diffusion of particular technologies.

These points are elaborated in the remainder of this review of the work in economic history relevant to diffusion. Focus turns first to the traditional interpretation, then to the reinterpretation and, finally, to the institutional context of diffusion.

The Traditional Interpretation of Economic History

Early studies of economic history focused upon three aspects of technological change. One approach, that of the *technology historians,* focused upon the *invention* associated with growth in a particular industry and dated the start of growth from the date of invention (Dickinson, 1939; Lilley, 1948; Forbes, 1958). This approach generally was not concerned with economic consequences of the invention and took as a given that the invention would find its way into the economy due to its superiority over the old technology. Thus, the diffusion question was neglected.

A second approach, attributed to Schumpeter (Harley, 1971, 1973), distinguished *invention* from *innovation,* where the latter generally included both the commercial application of the invention and its diffusion to users. More specifically, Schumpeter posited that there would be intermittent spurts of inventive activity; that the resulting invention(s) would create stress, discontinuities or disequilibria in the economy; and that these imbalances would eventually be eliminated by the commercial application of the invention and its diffusion, that is, by *innovation*. Entrepreneurs were seen to provide the mechanism(s) by which the latter is accomplished in that they perceive potential profit or opportunity in the invention and therefore seek to exploit it in their own activities.

The distinction between invention and innovation implies a time lag between them, but determining the dates of each presented a problem. Enos (1962) studied this lag for thirty-five important inventions, defining the date of invention as

the earliest conception of the product in substantially its commercial form

and the date of innovation as

the first commercial application or sale.[5]

However, such a view leaves unresolved the question of subsequent improvements in the technique. For instance, did Newcomen invent the steam engine in 1712 or did Watt in the 1760s?[6] Likewise is it reasonable to date the invention of the cotton picker at 1889 and its innovation at 1942 (Enos, 1962: 307)?

Another problem with the Schumpeterian approach is the assumption that once commercial application is achieved, diffusion readily follows. In this spirit, Enos' method of dating innovation, cited immediately above, only looks at the initial commercial application or sale. This ignores subsequent improvements in the innovation that may affect its diffusion and embodies the implicit view that diffusion is merely a process of *imitation* wherein firms or entrepreneurs copy those first making the commercial application (Mansfield, 1961: 1). Accordingly, the diffusion problem itself is never really addressed.

A third approach of the traditional interpretation was to view (anomalous) lags in the use of innovation (both its commercial application and diffusion to users) as being related to lack of information and resistance to change, rather than to economic considerations such as profitability. This conclusion derives from the assumption that the new technology is *ipso facto* superior, originally posited by the technology historians and never challenged by the Schumpeterians, and the further assumption of rationality on the part of the entrepreneur.

The Reinterprentation of Economic History

The reinterpretation of economic history also consists of several diverse strands. In contrast to the traditional interpretation, however, technological change and its diffusion are viewed as an economic phenomenon. Further, the occurrence and pace of technological change is explained largely in terms of profitability, and there is no assumption that the new technology is *ipso facto* superior.

The explicit attention given profitability coincides with the largely economic orientation of the *new economic historians* and the concomitant dissatisfaction with the *non-economic* bases of the traditional interpretations.[7] The central tenet of their conceptual framework is that technological change and its diffusion occurs as a *single continuous process*, rather than the series of disjointed events (invention and innovation) posited by the Schumpeterians (Harley, 1971). Consequently, the Schumpeterian ideas on discontinuity and market disequilibria also are rejected.[8]

Instead, the new economic historians perceive the market or economy to be in a long-run competitive equilibrium (or a series of such) between the old and new technology. The proportion of each technology represented at any particular time reflects the costs of each relative to the other, and the old technology is replaced gradually as the cost ratio (of new to old) decreases.[9] These costs are both endogenous to the technology, as represented by its productivity, and exogenous, as represented by the price of required inputs or the *relative factor costs*.

To illustrate, consider the replacement of sailing vessels by steamships in the nineteenth century. Harley (1971: 216) says that the sailing ship competed with steam from 1850 to 1890, not

as Schumpeter suggests, because of *extrarational preference or habit*, but because of the nature of the costs of steam transportation.

The critical variable affected by *endogenous* factors was the length of voyage for which either the steamship or sailing vessel was more economical. As ongoing technological change improved the fuel consumption of the marine engine, the steamship replaced the sailing vessel on increasingly longer routes. This occurred because each ship could carry only so much coal, imposing an outer limit on voyage length, but also because improved fuel consuption reduced the amount of the ship and crew employed in fuel-related activities and the voyage costs per mile.

The increase in the ratio of steamships to sailing vessels in the economy as a whole also was related to a decrease in the price of iron from which steamships were built, a factor *exogenous* to the steamship technology. This occurred because of the development of a process that utilized hot instead of cold air in the blast for furnaces, which enabled Scotland's deposits of blackband ironstone to be used and halved iron production costs (Campbell, 1955: 209).[10]

Critical to this entire process of diffusion is the pace of technological change through which the costs associated with the new technology are lowered as its efficiency or productivity is increased. This also affects the impact of exogenous factors, such as the price of inputs or the relative factor costs. Because of occurrences such as these, the *reinterpretation of economic history* sees the events associated with technological change *per se* as the important determinants of the diffusion of a given innovation. These would be events such as those that led to the increased fuel efficiency of the marine engines used in steamships, discussed above. This argument also extends to the many other non-economic and non-technical variables which may affect diffusion (Rosenberg, 1972a: 29). Accordingly, the new economic historians focus upon technical considerations which affect the *supply* of innovations, that is, the nature of the technology being developed and when it is provided for users (Rosenberg, 1972a: 5). This orientation may be looked upon as a reaction to the traditional interpretation, considered *demand* oriented, wherein the new technology was assumed to be superior and the only factors hindering diffusion were information and resistance to change.

Attention will now be focused upon each of the technical considerations thought to be especially important by the new economic historians: (1) the continuity of inventive activity, (2) the development of technical skills among users, (3) the development of skills in machine making, (4) complementarities and (5) improvements in old technologies (Rosenberg, 1972a: 6–28, 1976b: 189–210).

The Continuity of Inventive Activity. When a new technique is first developed it is generally crude and inefficient, offering few or no advantages over the established technology. Thus, improvements in the innovation prior to and during diffusion are important determinants of the rate and extent of diffusion, and this is related to continuing inventive activity.

To illustrate, consider the steam engine. Newcomen's atmospheric engine of 1712 was technically workable, but it experienced great heat loss in its operation and was a voracious consumer of fuel (Rosenberg, 1972a: 6). Its use was primarily limited to pumping out coal mines. In the 1760s Watt transformed the steam engine from an instrument of limited applicability at locations peculiarly favored by access to cheap fuel, to a generalized power source of much wider significance. (Rosenberg, 1971a: 7).

Watt's work has so much significance in an economic sense that he is commonly credited with inventing the steam engine, but from another perspective

one might almost be tempted to say of James Watt that he was *just an improver*. (Rosenberg, 1972a: 7)

This latter argument is even more persuasive when one considers that it took yet another century of further improvement before the steam engine replaced waterpower in manufacturing or the sail on ocean-going vessels (Rosenberg, 1972a: 7).

Similarly, Mak and Walton (1972) found that although the introduction of the steamboat provided an increase in the productivity of river transportation, subsequent improvements led to an even greater increase. The early steamboats resembled sea-going vessels of the time; they were long and thin, with heavily built hulls, and sat low in the water. To better suit the vessels to river navigation, they were subsequently made wider, more lightly constructed and equipped, and built with a higher mounted superstructure. These physical changes provided the ability to navigate in shallower water, permitted operations through a greater portion of the year, made loading and unloading easier, created shorter passage times by requiring less time in port and, most importantly, increased the ratio of carrying capacity to the measured tonnage of the boat.

Besides improving the efficiency and performance of the new technology, continuing inventive activity also results in modification to satisfy the needs of specialized users, thus broadening the set of potential adopters. To illustrate, the diffusion of the Draper Loom, an automatic shuttle-changing loom developed in the late nineteenth century, was initially limited by its inability to handle fancy goods and ginghams, *high count* fabrics using mule top spun yarns which comprised 60 per cent of the output of the New England textile industry (Feller, 1966: 331). Subsequent improvements in the technical capabilities of the loom enabled it to handle these types of fabrics and yarn, and it then was more widely adopted (Feller, 1966).[11]

The Development of Technical Skills Among Users. In addition to the gradual improvement of the new technique through continuing inventive activity, it is also necessary that prospective users learn and develop skills to exploit the innovation's potential. The time this involves depends upon the nature of the new technology itself, such as its complexity or the extent to which it is novel, and the degree to which the required skills are similar to those already available or transferable from other activities (Rosenberg, 1972a: 15).

An illustration of this is the puddling process of producing high quality bar iron. Hyde (1971: 112–13) notes

One of the most important problems associated with puddling in its early years was that of training a labor force that could produce high quality bar iron with the process. The ironmasters who initially adopted puddling had to train workers in the use of a process that was not only new, but was also somewhat of a *mystery* to everyone, including Cort (its inventor). An efficient puddler was a workman who could not only do the strenuous labor of moving masses of iron in and out of the puddling furnaces, but could also develop a *feel* for the process itself. He had to learn to determine from the color of the flames in the puddling furnace and the texture of the molten metal when the pig iron was fully decarburized or had *come to nature,* i.e., when the carbon and other impurities had been sufficiently removed. Puddling was a backbreaking job that also required a great deal of judgement, and experience was probably the best teacher. The development of a highly skilled labor force was probably the greatest single impediment to its rapid adoption.

One of the important factors in the development of such technical skills among users is the migration of labor already trained in these skills and capable of passing them on to others (Rosenberg, 1972a: 18). The early diffusion of the steam engine to continental Europe, for example, was limited by the movement of skilled British engineers. Throughout Europe it was these persons who set up all the successful installations, and thus, their presence seems to have been a prerequisite despite the many technical publications, writings and letters on the topic (Robinson, 1974: 97).

The Development of Skills in Machine Making. The translation of a new technology into applicability generally requires that the capital goods sector develop the ability to devise, adapt, produce and make available machinery relevant to the new technology at a low cost. This affects the relative costs associated with the new technology, but more generally the emergence of a capital goods sector may be thought of as a *routinization* or an *institutionalization* of the accomplished inventive activity.

Another dimension of the development of skills in machine making is the capital goods sector's role in an economy's transition to economic growth as it internally adapts to the continually altering technological requirements of an industrializing economy (Rosenberg, 1963: 417). This is accomplished by the improvement of production techniques by the capital goods sector, which reduces the price of its machinery and thus affects investment activity throughout the economy. This increases the rate of diffusion of new technologies by altering the speed at which the economy installs and applies new techniques of production (Rosenberg, 1963: 416).

The critical importance of machine-making skills can be illustrated by the steam engine, the commercial practicability of which depended upon the perfection of Wilkinson's boring mill. This machine provided accurate and uniform cylinders whereas previously it was necessary to stuff rags between the pistons and cylinders to prevent the loss of steam (Rosenberg, 1972a: 19).

Complementarities. Generally, a new technology cannot fulfill its potential without complementary technologies which relax or bypass constraints that develop. Exemplary of this is the steam engine and Wilkinson's boring mill, discussed in the previous section, or in the case of the steamship, the blast furnace technology that lowered the price of iron. Sometimes the complementarities are such that knowledge and/or skills can be transferred or adapted from other activities. For instance, Wilkinson relied upon technology developed for the boring of cannons, and in turn, the technology for manufacturing cannons drew upon the skills originally developed for bell casting (Rosnberg, 1972a: 19).

Sometimes this phenomenon is a broadly based *technological convergence* wherein skills, techniques and facilities of production are employed in producing a wide variety of final products (Rosenberg, 1963: 423). This occurred in the American economy of the nineteenth century where the machine tools industry served as the focal point of change and the skills acquired in one type of machine production were rapidly transmitted to other sectors of the economy (Rosenberg, 1963).

More often, however, the diffusion of a new technology is held in check, awaiting the development of a complementary technology(ies). Thus, inventive activity is required to overcome the constraint and a single invention seldom constitutes a *complete* technology (Rosenberg, 1972a: 21).

For example, Fishlow (1966) found that the increased productivity of American railroads from 1840 to 1910 was the result of the accumulation of small innovations and relatively modest design changes which brought about improved rolling stock and more powerful locomotives. Further, the utilization of the greater loads and speeds made possible by these improvements depended upon developments in technologies such as the control of train movements through the telegraph and block signalling, air brakes, automatic couplers and the substitution of steel for iron rails. These innovations were not adopted with the same speed, since they were not equal in reducing costs. At one extreme were air brakes and automatic couplers, which required the passage of national legislation. At the other extreme, steel rails were adopted rapidly in spite of their considerable costs, first being used in the 1860s but constituting 80 per cent of total trackage by 1890. These were more durable than iron rails, lasting ten times longer, could bear heavier loads and were the only kind that could have supported the modern locomotives that were in existence by 1910.

Improvements in Old Technologies. In general, evidence indicates that the appearance of a new technology induces improvements in the technology(ies) it is replacing as an entrepreneurial response to altered prospects in regard to profit (Rosenberg, 1972a: 26). This postpones the time when the new technology will be clearly superior and *smooths* the transition from one technology to another, that is, it retards the diffusion of the new technology.

The nineteenth century American iron industry provides an illustration (Fogel and Engerman, 1971a). The late introduction and slow diffusion of the *modern* British technology employing coal was partly due to the location of resource inputs and their chemical properties, but mostly due to improvements in the efficiency of the established charcoal-using technology. Thus, almost 100 per cent of all pig iron was produced by charcoal in 1840 (Temin, 1964: 82) even though initial successes with the coal technology had been achieved in Britain as early as 1709 (Rosenberg, 1972a: 10). Although this proportion dropped subsequently, the tonnage of charcoal-produced pig iron continued to rise, reaching an all-time high in 1890 (Temin, 1964: 82). Further, Fogel and Engerman calculate that between 1842 and 1858 the growth in total factor productivity in the *backward* charcoal sector exceeded that in the *modern* coal sector (Fogel and Engerman, 1971a: 159–62).

Two factors in addition to increased efficiency are important in prolonging the old technology. One of these is the resources available at any given location. A second is externality effects of the new technology.

An example of locational influences is the use of steam engines as stationary power sources *circa* 1840 (Temin, 1966a). Water power, the old technology, had higher capital costs, and required physical accouterments such as channelized, steadily flowing water and a gradient. These accouterments were already present in the north-eastern United States, whereas coal, the major input for steam power, had to be imported. Accordingly, water power was not replaced by steam power in the north-eastern United States, but prevailed almost until the onset of electrification. In contrast, steam power was more advantageous west of the Appalachians where there was coal and capital and suitable water power sites were lacking.

Europe provides similar examples. Robinson (1974) notes that regions rich in coal, such as Liège and Silesia, developed steam power early, as did the town of St Petersburg which had access to the coal that was used as ballast in British ships. Areas with water-power resources on the other hand, such as Germany and the rest of Russia, did not develop steam power as rapidly.

Another example of locational effects is the persistence of wooden shipbuilding in Maine and British North America through the end of the nineteenth century, long after metal ships had usurped almost all ocean trade (Harley, 1973). The wooden shipbuilding centers had included Britain, Boston, New York, Maine and British North America (now the Maritime Provinces of Canada). When one of the British centers, Glascow and the Clyde region, came to produce metal ships for which it had a world-wide competitive advantage as the result of resource conditions, it set the price for ships in general. All other centers, then, had to adjust their product to sell at this price or go out of the shipbuilding business. The response of each area was conditioned by the degree to which the factors employed in shipbuilding could be reallocated to other endeavors, which at least in part reflected the degree of diversification of the local economy of each. Thus, British wooden shipbuilding ceased by the early 1870s and that in Boston and New York ceased by the end of the 1860s. In Maine and British North America, however, alternative employment for the factors of production was negligible, so there was a strong impetus to continue building wooden ships. To do this and meet the going world price, adjustments such as the lowering of wages and raw material prices were made.

Externality effects of the new technology, leading to improvements in the old technology, are illustrated by the increased productivity of flat-boating in western rivers after the steamboat technology was introduced (Mak and Walton, 1973). Because flat-boats float downriver without power and were disassembled at the destination,

other modes of transportation had to be used for flat-boatmen to
return upriver and man another flat-boat. Prior to the steamboat, this
return was a long, arduous journey, most often undertaken by land.
With the advent of the steamboat, this trip was shortened from
several months to a week. This raised flat-boat productivity by
facilitating the repetition of flat-boat voyages, and led to more
specialized and skilled flat-boatmen. Another externality that increased the productivity of flat-boating was the removal of snags from
the rivers to make them safe for steamboats. This, together with the
increased skills among flat-boatmen, led to the use of larger flat-boats
and to the passage of flat-boats by night, further shortening the
voyage time and raising productivity.

The Institutional Context of Diffusion

The five previously discussed technological factors—the continuity of
inventive activity, the development of technical skills among users,
the development of skills in machine making, complementarities and
improvements in old technologies—help to explain the pace of
diffusion. However, *institutional* factors also influence the diffusion
process by affecting the context within which the technological
factors operate.

The concern with institutional factors as they pertain to diffusion is
primarily a facet of the reinterpretation of economic history. Within
this group, however, there is a division of opinion as to the relative
importance of technological versus institutional factors in the
diffusion process. The conflict can be illustrated by considering an
increase in productivity occurring after the introduction of new
technology. This is generally calibrated as the residual output after
accounting for changes in the amount of input. This increase may be
interpreted as the result of the technological change, institutional
effects or both, and available methodology is not able to sort out the
issue.

Consider, for instance, the 50 per cent increase in output per milk
animal per year in American dairying from 1850 to 1910 (Bateman,
1968). On the one hand this increase resulted from the post-1850
diffusion of the then modern techniques and practices to areas that
had not utilized them in 1850, a technological factor. However,
institutional changes also played a role. Between 1850 and 1910 there
was substantial urban growth in the United States which drastically
changed the market for dairy products and enabled more dairy farms
to engage in commerical operations, an incentive which increased the

farmers' demand for the then modern techniques and led to their adoption.

Similarly, consider the improvement in productivity of ocean-going shipping from 1600 to 1850. North (1971), taking an institutional approach, attributes this to improvements in economic organization and to a decline in piracy. Organizational improvements made it easier and quicker to obtain a cargo, which reduced the amount of time spent in port and increased the number of voyages made by a given ship per year. The decline in piracy decreased manning requirements. This argument is supported by the fact that the Dutch had developed a ship in 1600 with a similar tons per man ratio as the sailing ships of the nineteenth century. It is thus concluded that changes in institutional conditions and not improvements in technology caused the productivity changes.

In institutional change situations such as this, however, it is often the case that the change is itself an innovation, although not a technological one (L. E. Davis and North, 1970, 1971; North and Thomas, 1970). Developing this perspective in the context of economic history involves the premise that an individual or group will innovate a new organizational form or other institutional arrangement when it becomes profitable to do so, that is when the costs of innovation are exceeded by the potential stream of benefits that it will yield.[12]

This suggests a symbiotic relationship between technological change and its institutional context, and the need for considering both together (Rosenberg, 1972a: 33). Thus, while the Dutch ship was a superior technology, being lightly built and utilizing a simple rigging that needed fewer sailors, it was not conducive to carrying armaments. Accordingly, its advantages in large-volume bulk trade could not be exploited until piracy was reduced and organizational improvements were effected (Walton, 1970, 1971). Alternatively, however, the superior Dutch ship technology provided an incentive to force the decline of piracy and to create a new economic organization.

Thus, a change in institutional conditions may be necessary for realizing the benefits of a technological change, but at the same time the technological change, providing an opportunity to increase profits, may be the impetus to innovate a new institutional arrangement (Davis and North, 1971: 3–25). Interestingly, there is a similarity between this observation and the Schumpeterian perspective in that the new technology becomes a source of disequilibrium in the economy. It also becomes clear that information and resistance to change are important in perceiving the costs and benefits of a new institutional arrangment and that in any situation there are specific, already existing institutions which facilitate or retard such perception.

The institution of slavery provides an example of this latter point (Aufhaser, 1974). Common opinion associates slavery with backwardness and assumes that it would retard the adoption of new techniques. However, Aufhaser finds that the slave status of workers did not interfere with the adoption of labor-saving or other input-saving techniques, and he even implies that slavery might have been a facilitator in certain ways. His argument on this point is that historically it has been groups whose services have been jeopardized that have fought the spread of new technologies, and slaves, being at the bottom of the social ladder, would have no reason to resist.

Another interesting example in this context is in the Japanese cotton textile industry of the Meiji Period wherein an institutional arrangement lowered the costs associated with acquiring information and facilitated its unobstructed flow (Saxonhouse, 1974). All firms had to join the *Boren Geppo* (the All Japan Cotton Spinners' Association) and in turn received a trade journal that contained *unusually* careful, explicit discussions of practices within the industry. In addition to this firm-to-firm cooperation on technical matters, one British company provided 90 per cent of the machinery so that nearly the entire industry was serviced by the same personnel. Thus, the spread of ideas was facilitated, the cost of obtaining information was very low and diffusion was very rapid. Most important in creating this situation was a specific institution, the *Boren Geppo*.

THE ECONOMIC HISTORY PERSPECTIVE AND OTHER INNOVATION DIFFUSION PARADIGMS

It is difficult in some ways to relate the economic history perspective on innovation diffusion to the other perspectives discussed in this book. In part this is because the innovations studied by economic historians are from a different time era, often having occurred more than a hundred years ago. Another inhibiting factor is the extensive focus on technological innovations and, particularly, technological aspects of those innovations. A third inhibiting factor is the degree to which economic history concerns are removed from the diffusion process itself, focusing more upon aspects that constitute preconditions for diffusion (Figure 1.3). Finally, the lack of an abstract, simplified model makes it difficult to perceive the extensive complementarity between the economic history perspective and others on innovation diffusion.

Perhaps a way to overcome these obstacles is to return to the observations in the introduction of this chapter and consider the S-curve portraying diffusion over time. There are several alternative explanations for the flatness of the S-curve's left tail representing the period prior to the onset of some sort of *bandwagon* effect. The adoption perspective would attribute this to innovativeness characteristics or resistance to adoption. The market and infrastructure perspective would attribute this to propagator and diffusion agency strategies. Researchers on the diffusion of technological innovations among firms would employ profitability conditions as an explanation. Finally, the economic historian would argue that the slow initial rate of diffusion reflects the time needed to improve the innovation and adapt it to a variety of potential markets or uses, as well as delays and caution in adoption in expectation of such improvements.

A similar set of explanations might be employed to account for the bandwagon effect itself, or differences in the rates of diffusion of different innovations. That is, the adoption perspective might attribute the bandwagon effect to a lowering of resistance to adoption through demonstration effects, social interaction and other communications; and the variance in diffusion rates to different resistance levels for each innovation. By contrast, the market and infrastructure perspective might attribute these same occurrences to a broad range of propagator and diffusion agency actions, and the economic history perspective might attribute them to the development of technical skills among users, the routinization of skills in machine making, the development of complementarities and the completion of the bulk of ongoing inventive or adaptive activity with regard to the innovation.

These comparisons, then, indicate that the economic history perspective offers unique insights into the innovation diffusion process of today, as do the other perspectives. Let us, then, go on with the task of exploring the *complementarities between paradigms* and working towards including all in a comprehensive model, a theme of this book, rather than arguing which is best.

In the comparisons above, the expectation of further improvements in the innovation, leading to a delay in the decision to adopt, was cited as one of the economic historian's explanations of retardation effects in the S-curve of diffusion. This explanation complements the *adoption perspective* in two ways. In the context of adoption by firms, such expectations may be seen as a critical element in the potential adopter's calculation of profitability or economic advantage related to the innovation. In the context of adoption by households, the expectation of further improvements in the innovation is an alternative to the traditional explanation that lags reflect innovativeness or resistance differences among households. An interesting observation in this regard is that the economic history explanation also does not have the pejorative overtones of the adoption perspective explanation, a topic to be given more attention in Chapters 8 and 9.

The second economic history explanation for the flatness of the S-curve's left tail is that improving the innovation and adapting it to a variety of potential markets and uses takes time and often is, furthermore, a location-specific process. This explanation pertains to the availability of the innovation and thus complements the *market and infrastructure perspective.*

To illustrate, consider agricultural technology. This generally is location and ecology specific so that one technique or set of techniques is economically superior to an alternative *only* over a range of climate, soil, economic and social conditions. Initially, then, there may be many techniques to produce the same crop, and the diffusion of any one outside of its locational domain is unlikely (Hayami, 1974; Evanson, 1974: 52). One way that this locational constraint has been overcome is through agricultural research, or *continuing inventive activity,* by which new technologies are adapted to different local environments (Hayami, 1974: 131). Hybrid corn, for example, was differentially bred to suit different environments (Griliches, 1957: 502). Another way of overcoming the initial locational constraints on a given technology is to adapt local environments to suit the innovation (Hayami, 1974: 131). This might involve the use of fertilizers or the construction of infrastructure such as irrigation, transportation or processing facilities, endeavors which either create important *complementarities* to the innovation or represent *institutional* activities that improve the context within which diffusion takes place.[13]

Thus, adaptive agricultural research and efforts to adapt the local environment to a given innovation affect the availability of the innovation to particular locales and potential adopters. Accordingly, in order to understand diffusion patterns, it is important to examine the factors guiding the efforts of adaptive research organizations and institutional actions pertaining to adapting the local environment, just as we examined the factors guiding diffusion agency establishment and diffusion agency strategy.

OVERVIEW

This chapter focuses upon the continual technological improvement and adaptation of the innovation to the market, which leads to adoption by an increasingly wider range of persons or organizations. This *continuity of innovation* directly affects the temporal and spatial patterns of diffusion in two ways. First, on the supply side, the time at which a particular innovation is adapted or improved for a given use, market or set of potential adopters has a direct bearing on where and when the innovation will be (made) available and hence adopted. Second, on the demand side, even after the innovation is made available, potential adopter individuals or firms will often delay their decision on the basis of expecting further improvements in the innovation.

Thus, the economic history perspective complements both the market and infrastructure and adoption perspectives. With regard to the former, the time needed to improve the innovation and adapt it to a variety of potential markets retards the diffusion wave in its initial stages, and the order by which markets are developed channels the wave by a means other than diffusion agency-related actions. With regard to the adoption perspective, the expectation of further improvements in the innovation is an alternative to the traditional explanation that lags in adoption reflect innovativeness or resistance differences among individuals or firms.

The economic history material pertaining to the diffusion of innovation is divided into two schools. The *traditional interpretation of economic history* is largely historical in its focus and more concerned with the invention than with the diffusion process. Further, like the perspectives examined thus far in this book, it embodies the assumption that the innovation is essentially the same throughout the diffusion process. While this work is briefly reviewed, greater attention is given to the *reinterpretation of economic history*. It is this focus which takes the view that innovation is continuous and examines various aspects of that continuity in a largely economic frame of reference. Both schools of thought are developed in terms of technological innovations that generally diffused some time ago, particularly during the industrialization of the late nineteenth and early twentieth century.

With regard to the continuity of innovation, six factors are discussed. The first five of these are endogenous in that they relate directly to the innovation's production process or to the technology it is replacing. One such factor is the continuity of inventive activity. A second factor is the development of technical skills among users of the innovation which enable exploitation of its potential. The third factor is the development or routinization of skills in machine making so that the innovation can be made widely available to potential users at a relatively low cost. In effect, this represents institutionalization of the new technology. The fourth factor is complementarities which relax or enable the bypassing of constraints that develop in the course of applying the new technology. Finally, improvements in the technology being replaced by the innovation will often retard the diffusion of the latter. These improvements often are related to the innovation and represent an entrepreneurial response to the competitive technology.

The sixth factor examined by the economic historian in the context of the continuity of innovation is the institutional. Unlike the five endogenous factors listed above, institutional occurrences are exogenous in that they are outside of the innovation's production process or the technology it is replacing, although either might be affected by these occurrences. Examples of institutional occurrences include political moves or technological changes which affect resource scarcity or abundance and relative factor prices, broad-scale processes such as urbanization which significantly alter market potentials either in favor of or against the innovation, and various sorts of arrangements that provide and channel production related or specialized information.

Referring back to Figure 1.3, we see that this treatment of the economic history perspective completes the picture of the diffusion process itself. Specifically, three complementary perspectives have been examined: the economic history perspective, a supply side concern dealing with the preconditions for diffusion; the market and infrastructure perspective, a supply side concern dealing with the way innovations are made available to potential adopters; and the adoption perspective, a demand side concern dealing with adoption of the innovation. Further, these perspectives have been considered both with regard to consumer and technological innovations. Attention now turns to the development perspective, the last to be considered. This is addressed in Chapters 7 and 8.

NOTES

1 Although this chapter primarily considers economic history research on the continuity of innovation, it should be noted that marketing management reearch also has contributed to this topic. The general concept they have worked with is

that of *product* or *market adaptation*. One way this occurs is through the *technological improvement* of an existing product. Examples include the various IBM main frame computers (e.g. the 709, 7090, 360, 370 series) or color television receivers, wherein later models have had more extensive capabilities than earlier ones. Alternatively, product or market adaptation may occur through *market stretching* whereby new uses or markets are found for an existing product. An example is the use of computer technology in point of sale inventory control, cash register or twenty-four hour banking machine systems. Another example is the adaptation of transistor or micro circuit technologies to such diverse uses as computers, hand-held calculators, television receivers and automobile control systems. For a more extensive discussion of this marketing work, see Levitt (1965) and Wind (1980). Another relevant body of literature addresses the ways in which adopters modify innovations to satisfy their own needs; see E.M. Rogers (1978) and Yin (1978; Yin, Quick, Bateman, and Marks, 1978).

2 To avoid confusion, it should be noted that the term *continuity* is employed in two different ways in this book. Whereas the economic historians have used it as above, marketing has used it as in Chapter 1 (page 2) to refer to the degree of congruence between a new product/innovation and existing products or practices, particularly as that affects the disruption (or *continuity*) of previous consumption patterns.

3 Whether innovativeness, interaction effects, profitability, or technological improvement and adaptation to different markets account for the diffusion of hybrid corn provides a classic example of the difficulty in social science of determining which of several competing explanations is most appropriate. For an elaboration in terms of profitability versus interaction effects, as they affect adoption patterns, see E.M. Rogers and Havens (1961, 1962), Griliches (1962) and Babcock (1962). Webber and Joseph (1977) address a similar issue in terms of the role of market size versus information availability as they affect diffusion agency establishment.

4 This review is designed only to provide the flavor of economic history work pertaining to innovation diffusion, and hence, it should not be taken as comprehensive. The review and the following section of this chapter were prepared jointly by the author of this book and Matthew J. Sagers of the Ohio State University Department of Geography. An earlier version of these sections comprises a portion of Sagers and Brown (1977).

5 Fogel and Engerman (1971b: 206) would probably consider Enos to be part of the reinterpretation because of his concern with the temporal protraction between invention and commercial application, a basic tenet of the reinterpretation. Others, however, do not appear to agree (Rosenberg, 1972a: 9).

6 Newcomen worked out the basic principles of the steam engine, but the excessive fuel requirements of his engine limited its applicability primarily to pumping out coal mines. Watt's engine was economically more feasible.

7 The *new economic historians,* or those reinterpreting economic history, are characterized by a greater reliance upon quantitative techniques and economic theory, whereas the earlier economic historians had a stronger historical orientation, used qualitative analysis, and tended to treat each study in terms of a unique, rather than a generalized occurrence.

8 This view of technological change and its diffusion leads the *new economic historians* to use terminology that calls attention to the idea of a single continuous process, such as the *displacement of one technique by another,* or *technological change and its diffusion* rather than the invention-innovation dichotomy terminology of the traditional interpretation.

9 Details on the nature of such cost ratios are outside the scope of this chapter. However, two basic situations might be noted. One is when the new technology replaces existing productive capacity; the other is when the new technology is adding productive capacity in response to an increase in the demand for the output of the technology. For *new capacity* the relevant cost ratio is the total cost of the

new technology versus the total cost of the old technology since one or the other must be installed. For *replacement capacity,* however, the relevant cost ratio is the total cost of the new technology versus *only* the variable cost of the old technology. This reflects the fact that the fixed or *sunk* costs of the old technology will already have been expended at the time the entrepreneur is making a decision about the new technology. Obviously, then, adoption is in general more likely in the *new capacity* situation. For an elaboration see Sandberg (1969, 1974) and Temin (1966b).

10 For an example of the role of relative factor prices in the textile industry, see Sandberg (1969, 1974).

11 It is instructive to contrast this explanation with earlier traditional accounts of the Draper Loom which concluded that slow and incomplete adoption was due to the conservative management of the New England textile industry (Harris, 1952; Wolfbein, 1944). See also, Sandberg's (1969, 1974) argument on the importance of relative factor costs.

12 Typically, institutional innovations of this sort have been created to realize economies of scale, reduce information costs, spread risk and internalize externalities (L.E. Davis and North, 1971: 3–25).

13 Environment-adapting activities such as these also must be considered as an aspect of, or complementary to, the development perspective. This is discussed further in Chapter 8.

7

THE DEVELOPMENT PERSPECTIVE I: THE APPLICABILITY OF THE MARKET AND INFRASTRUCTURE FRAMEWORK IN THIRD WORLD SETTINGS

Previous chapters have examined the preconditions and mechanisms of diffusion, focusing upon the adoption, market and infrastructure, and economic history perspectives. Attention now turns to the development perspective which concerns both the ways in which the level of development affects the diffusion process and the outcomes or impacts of that process. The first step in elaborating this perspective, and the focus of this chapter, is to demonstrate the applicability of the market and infrastructure framework in Third World settings. Apart from being an important topic in its own right, this provides the basis for employing the market and infrastructure perspective to examine the mechanisms by which diffusion and development interrelate, the topic of Chapter 8.

Previous research has given a good deal of attention to the diffusion of innovations in Third World settings. This follows from the fact that innovation diffusion has been an integral aspect of efforts to promote economic development—whether the effort is aimed at duplicating the experience of Europe and North America by encouraging urbanization and industrial development; or whether the effort focuses on rural areas and small towns with the goal of improving agricultural production, improving living conditions and generating rural or small town enterprise and related employment.[1]

The innovation diffusion research that has been carried out, however, is largely in terms of the adoption perspective. Examples include Deutschmann and Fals Borda (1962), E.M. Rogers (1969), and Hanneman, Carroll, Rogers, Stanfield and Lin (1969) on agricultural innovations in Colombia; Menanteau-Horta (1967) on agricultural innovations in Chile; Lin and Burt (1975) and Lin, Hingson and Allwood-Paredes (1971) on mass immunization in El Salvador; Lin (1971) on mass immunization in Honduras; Sujono (1974) on family planning in Indonesia; Deutschmann, Mendez and Herzog (1967) and Woods and Graves (1973) on medical practices, drugs and food in Guatemalan towns; Sexton (1972) on the adoption of Hispanic culture in a Guatemalan town; Mayfield and Yapa (1974) and Wilbanks (1972) on innovations in rural India; Fuller (1974) on family planning in Chile; and Garst (1972, 1973) on agricultural innovations in Kenya. Furthermore, the adoption perspective is the mainstay of family planning programs in Third World nations (E.M. Rogers, 1973; Blaikie, 1975) and development programs such as those of the United States Agency for International Development.

By contrast, the market and infrastructure perspective has been applied in Third World settings in only a few instances, two of which are reported in this chapter. A study of the diffusion of several agricultural innovations in a region of Kenya illustrates the role of a variety of market and infrastructure factors, while a study of the diffusion of commercial dairying in a region of Mexico provides a theoretical perspective and also indicates the interrelationship between the market and infrastructure and adoption perspectives. Both of these studies pertain to diffusion agency strategy or innovation establishment. A study of the rural cooperative movement in Sierra Leone, presented in Chapter 8, provides an illustration of diffusion agency establishment in a Third World setting.

SPATIAL DIFFUSION IN RURAL KENYA: THE IMPACT OF INFRASTRUCTURE AND CENTRALIZED DECISION MAKING[2]

This is a study of the diffusion of six agricultural innovations in Kisii District, Kenya (Figure 7.1), situated about 400 kilometers west of the capital, Nairobi, and less than one degree south of the equator. The study area covers 2217 square kilometers and ranges from 1500 to 2100 meters above sea level. The rainfall, temperature and soil are favorable to agriculture throughout the district.

The semisubsistence agricultural landscape of Kisii is dotted with approximately ninety periodic markets (Figure 7.1). As a result, 91 per cent of a sample of Kisii farmers reported their normal market trip to be at a distance of 4 kilometers or less, and in more densely populated parts of the district, where the markets are even closer together, the distance drops to only 2 kilometers or less (Garst, 1973). Population density in the area also is very high, averaging 350 persons per square kilometer. Finally, Kisii District is remarkably homogeneous in ethnicity, with 97.98 per cent of the population being Gusii. As a result of these characteristics, the potential for interpersonal contact is very high. Employing the mean population density and assuming no barriers due to cultural differences, there are nearly 18,000 possible contacts within a radius of 4 kilometers, and even if this maximum level were halved, it would be far more potential contacts than a rural setting in the United States.

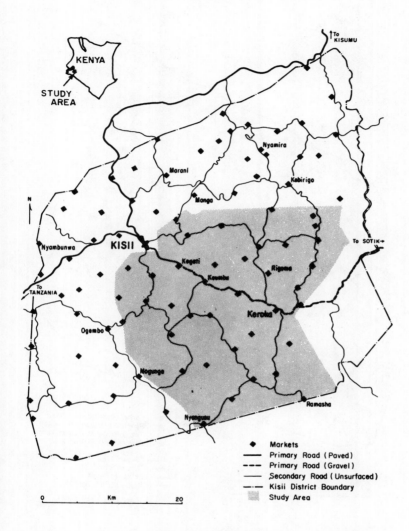

Figure 7.1   Kisii District, Kenya and the Study Area
Source: Survey of Kenya, 1:250,000 topographic (Kisumu), 1969

Accordingly, information flows and access to periodic markets ought
not to be a barrier to innovation diffusion.

Access to the more specialized facilities related to commercial
agricultural production is another matter. Kisii is laced with an
omnidirectional maze of pathways that connect nearby locations by
fairly direct routes and thus allow easy movement within that range.

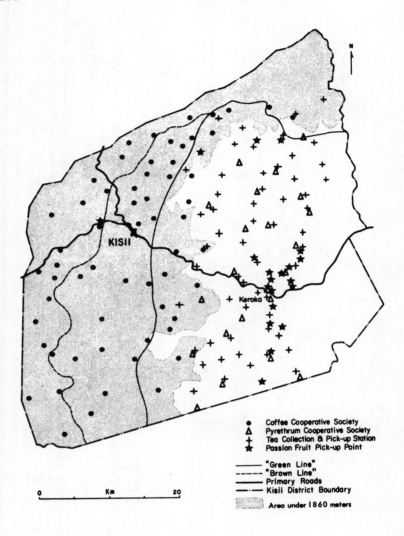

Figure 7.2 Cash-Crop Marketing Locations in
Kisii District

Transportation is a problem, however, when farmers are traveling
longer distances since this involves a system of largely unimproved
roads that are difficult to traverse and not usable for all-weather
travel (Figure 7.1). Accordingly, the human portage from the
farmstead to the nearest motorable road plus the subsequent motor
transport over poor quality roads to the market are excessively costly.
Also, the farmer generally is dependent upon bus transportation

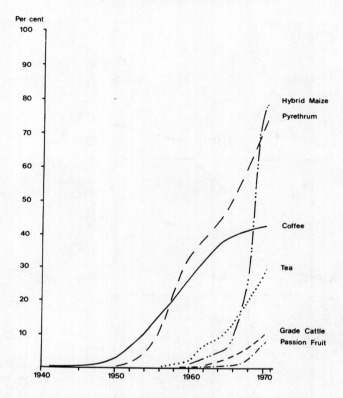

Figure 7.3   Adoption Trends Over Time for Six Agricultural Innovations in the Kisii District Study Area

since only a small number of local households own motor vehicles.
Thus, transportation has been and is a principal impediment to the
development of cash-crop agriculture in Kisii.

To examine this situation further, six commercial agricultural
innovations are considered: coffee, pyrethrum, tea, passion fruit,
grade cattle and hybrid maize. Although decisions affecting the
diffusion of these innovations were made in Kisii, the only town of
consequence in the area, it has not functioned as a diffusion node
since none of these innovations uses Kisii as either a source of inputs
or as a marketing site. Instead, these functions are dispersed
throughout the rural countryside (Figure 7.2).

Growth curves for each of the six innovations are presented in
Figure 7.3. Coffee's is the classic S-shape. The growth curve for
passion fruit and grade cattle also may be S-shaped, but both are
recent innovations so the upward inflection is not yet in evidence.
Pyrethrum, tea and hybrid maize have more of an exponential-type

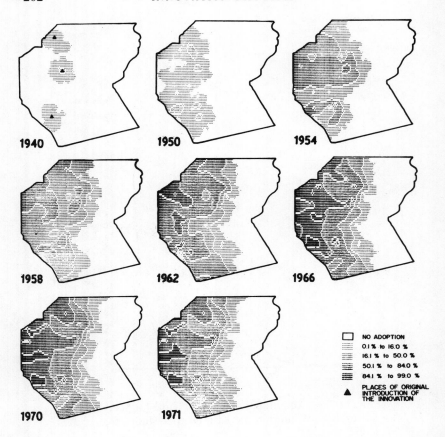

Figure 7.4   The Diffusion of Coffee in the Kisii District
        Study Area

growth curve, with the latter showing the highest adoption level of the six innovations.

An account of the diffusion of each innovation is now presented. This is followed by a section summarizing the market and infrastructure aspects of these diffusions.

Coffee

Coffee was first grown in Kisii District by a European resident in 1921. Due to the British colonial administration's unjustified fears that low-quality coffee would be marketed by African farmers, however, it was not until the late 1930s that Africans were finally

Table 7.1   Relationship of Time and Level of Adoption for Six Commercial Agricultural Innovations in Kisii District, Kenya[a]

	Correlation between	
	Mean year of adoption and mean hectares planted	Mean year of adoption and % of farmers adopting
Coffee	0.91*	0.86*
Pyrethrum	0.39*	0.61*
Tea	0.54*	0.51*
Passion fruit	0.79*	0.68*
Grade cattle	0.74*	0.67*
Hybrid maize	0.08	0.23**

[a]Units of observation are sampling areas as described in Garst (1972, 1974).
*Significant at 0.01 level.
**Significant at 0.05 level.

allowed to plant coffee with no restrictions. Initially adoption was slow, but after ten years the forward edge of diffusion wave began to move beyond the western edge of the study area and gradually eastward (Figure 7.4). By 1956 coffee adoption had advanced to its maximum eastern position and subsequent adoption occurred in areas that already raised coffee. The principal deterrent to the eastward spread of coffee was the westward spread of pyrethrum adoption. The latter was introduced in the higher elevation, eastern part of the study area, spread westward, and competed economically with coffee. There are no major environmental constraints, but coffee does do better at the lower elevations while pyrethrum thrives at higher elevations.

Even after thirty years of adoption, the areas of initial introduction are easily detectable. This is illustrated in Table 7.1 which shows that earlier adopting areas have the highest percentage of coffee farmers and plant the most area in coffee.

Another factor in the spread of coffee, due to its considerable weight, is transport to the coffee factory. Some sixty-five factories owned by the Kisii Farmers Cooperative Union (Figure 7.2) clean, dry, grade and package the coffee for shipment. To build a factory, sufficient production to warrant the expenditure must be present at greater than head portage distance. The construction of a coffee-processing factory is therefore a response to previous adoption. Yet, this also leads to subsequent adoption as a response to market site convenience. Indicative of this is the fact that ten of thirteen sampling areas with 100 per cent coffee adoption were less than 2.5 kilometers from a factory. More generally, with every kilometer increase in distance from the coffee factory, there is a decline of 9.2 per cent in the number of farmers growing coffee, with a correlation coefficient of −0.698.

Pyrethrum

Pyrethrum was first introduced in the eastern part of the study area (Figure 7.5) where the highest elevations are found (pyrethrum content increases with high elevation).[3] From there it spread rapidly in a north-western direction at a low level of adoption. By 1954 several areas had surpassed 50 per cent adoption and by 1958 nearly all of the study area evidenced some adoption. Since then a number of areas have obtained total acceptance, particularly in the eastern part of the study area. The pattern of diffusion has been influenced by three factors that impinge on the farmer's adoption decision: (1) the price and penalty policy of the Pyrethrum Marketing Board, (2) the acquisition of specific information about pyrethrum and (3) the location of marketing sites.

One act of the Pyrethrum Marketing Board was to prohibit planting below the 1860-meter contour line (Figure 7.2). Initially, this led to a restriction of the outward expansion of pyrethrum adoption and to intensified growth within such areas (Kisii, 1970). To prevent overproduction, they also instituted a system of quotas, or production ceilings, for each marketing society. In 1960, for example, Gusii farmers exceeded the quota by 60 per cent. The marketing board paid the full price for all production up to one-and-one-third times the quota, but only 38 per cent of the established price for additional production. As an initial response to the financial penalty much of the pyrethrum was uprooted, although few farmers disadopted completely (Kisii, 1962). Since then, however, the price and penalty system has stabilized income from pyrethrum, thus increasing the perceived advantages of pyrethrum as a cash crop and leading to adoption over a wider area.

Related to the actions of the Pyrethrum Marketing Board, the local marketing society pays lower prices to farmers who raise pyrethrum of low pyrethrins content. Without adequate horticultural knowledge concerning the planting, weeding, fertilizing, harvesting and drying of the crop, therefore, a farmer's profit level will be low. As a result, the pace of the diffusion wave is highly influenced by the rate of spread of specific, rather than general, knowledge. While awareness of pyrethrum has been nearly universal since a few years after its initial introduction, specific agronomic knowledge generally is acquired from an experienced previous adopter, leading to a steep gradient from high to low adoption and a slowing of the diffusion wave.

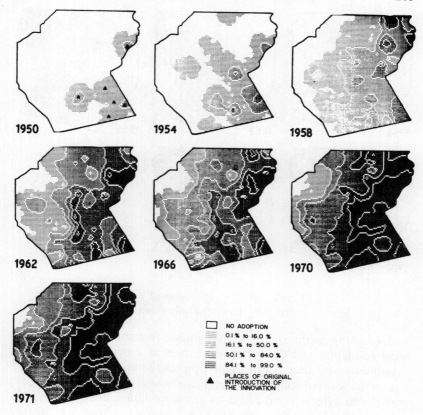

Figure 7.5 The Diffusion of Pyrethrum in the Kisii
District Study Area

A third factor influencing the diffusion pattern is the location of pyrethrum cooperative societies, which were established in 1959 and 1960 (Figure 7.2). Previously, all cooperative marketing activities centered on Keroka, at the east central edge of the study area (Figure 7.1). Pyrethrum flowers were transported there through a system of designated pick-up points to which the farmer had to deliver his crop and meet collection trucks at specified times.[4] The attenuated transport system that resulted was expensive to operate, inconvenient for the farmer and a drain on the farmer's potential profit. Nevertheless, adoption was rather widespread, though at low levels, and approximately the first 35 per cent of the farmers to adopt pyrethrum did so under this system.

The new cooperative society sites, by contrast, contain office facilities for the local society, local records and pyrethrum storage

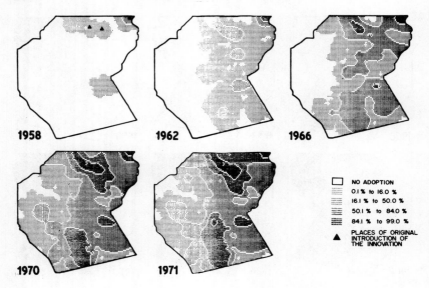

Figure 7.6   The Diffusion of Tea in
the Kisii District Study Area

and weighing facilities; the society manager and board members are
local residents; and the office site serves as a minor focal point for
community activities. Accordingly, these created an important incentive in the form of convenience and ease of marketing as well as lower
costs. The effect is indicated by the correlation coefficient of the
percentage of adoption in 1971 and distance from the nearest
cooperative, −0.662. The associated regression equation also indicates a similar distance decay effect to that for coffee; a 7.9 per cent
decrease in adoption with every kilometer increase in distance from
the nearest cooperative society.

The importance of the location of original introduction is indicated
in Table 7.1. Earlier adopting areas have a larger percentage of
pyrethrum farmers than do later adopting areas. However, the
correlation between the time of adoption and area planted is lower
than for most of the other innovations, probably because of the
pyrethrum uprooting described above.

Tea

Tea was first grown in Kisii upon the prompting of the Kenya
Ministry of Agriculture through its subsidiary, the Kenya Tea
Development Authority (KTDA). The north-east was selected
(Figure 7.6) for ecological and communications reasons. Most adults

in that area had experience working with tea on the tea estates of the nearby European settlement area (which today is African owned), and its higher elevations are ecologically suitable. Initial adoption was confined to this northern border area. In the period 1956 to 1958 a node appeared along the east central border near Keroka (Figure 7.1), followed in 1958 by another small node in the south-east corner of the study area. The three areas of adoption quickly expanded, and coalesced by 1962. After that time, diffusion consisted of a rapid westward expansion at low intensities of adoption. By 1971 the greatest intensity of adoption was in the north, along the edge of the study area, and in a north–south trending band in the south-central portion of the study area. Only one small area had achieved 100 per cent acceptance of tea raising, but 50 per cent adoption was widespread.

To market tea the individual farmer must transport it on his own to the nearest tea collection pick-up station. These are simple structures, made of wood with corregated metal roofs. While the tea may be stored at these stations for a short time after picking, spoilage will occur if the collection trucks are significantly delayed. Thus, they must be able to get through in all weather conditions. The collection trucks take the tea to the KTDA processing plant in the central part of the study area for cutting, drying, grading and packaging. The processing plant is not an influence on diffusion, however, because farmers are not allowed to bring their tea directly there. Also, processing plant employees generally do not know about tea planting and harvesting.

The relationship between distance to the nearest tea pick-up station and the percentage of farmers raising tea in 1971 is indicated by the correlation coefficient of -0.416, and a decline in adoption of 7.2 per cent for every kilometer increase in distance from a tea collection station. Difficulty in transporting the harvested tea by human portage is, of course, a prime cause of this relationship, reflecting once again the extreme friction of distance operating in a peasant society and the significance of the tea collection infrastructure.

Another influence on the diffusion pattern was a *tea line* established around the original diffusion node (Figure 7.2). This actually consists of two parts, an inner *green line* inside of which anyone may plant tea, and an outer *brown line*. In the area between the two lines planting is rigidly controlled by the KTDA.

The *tea line* represented an effort to concentrate the area of adoption in order to minimize transport costs and investment in road improvements without giving way on production levels. However, the normal diffusion process was not spatially constricted by the approximately 5 kilometers annual outward movement of the *tea line*.

Farmers also realized that the KTDA would establish a collection station when and where needed, thus reducing the effectiveness of KTDA decisions. Nevertheless, earlier adopting areas did have both a higher percentage of farmers adopting and more land planted in tea than later adopting areas, although this relationship is not as strong as it is for some other innovations (Table 7.1).

Passion Fruit

Passion fruit was first grown in western Kenya on European-owned farms near Sotik, to the east of Kisii District and some 25 kilometers outside the study area (Figure 7.1).[5] Prior to 1959 production was exclusively from these farms and was processed through a privately owned plant in Sotik. To expand production, the plant manager then directed some African employees to plant passion fruit and to encourage acquaintances to do likewise. Most of the employees were Gusii living in the Keroka area, and the initial diffusion node was located slightly to the north of that village (Figure 7.7).

Over the next seven years, the adoption rate was steady but very low. This was in part due to the lack of encouragement (interspersed with active and open discouragement) by the Ministry of Agriculture. In addition, because a hectare could potentially produce over 10,000 kilograms of passion fruit, and the Sotik plant had no collection system, the farmer was required to hire a truck to transport his crop. Production was expanding nevertheless until 1966 (Figure 7.7) when three events occurred simultaneously that nearly destroyed the fledgling passion fruit industry in Kisii.

First, the crop was almost wiped out by brown-spot disease. Any vine attacked by the disease had to be immediately uprooted and burned to prevent its spread.

Second, in fear of massive overproduction the price of passion fruit was decreased by 50 per cent, a reduction that was more than needed and overly harsh. This was possible because the Ministry of Agriculture, through its subsidiary, the Horticultural Crops Development Authority, purchased the processed passion fruit juice and thus indirectly controlled the prices paid to farmers.

Third, the manager of the passion fruit factory instituted extremely rigid quality controls. He personally inspected every truckload of fruit and often threw out approximately half of the crop, claiming it was of inferior quality. The road near by was said to have been covered with rejected passion fruit. As a result the farmer lost twice: for the discarded fruit and for the cost of transporting that which was rejected.

As a result of these three factors, most farmers uprooted a majority

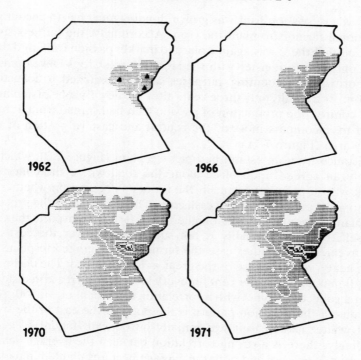

1962   1966

1970   1971

NO ADOPTION
0.1 % to 16.0 %
16.1 % to 50.0 %
50.1 % to 84.0 %
84.1 % to 99.0 %

▲ PLACES OF ORIGINAL
INTRODUCTION OF
THE INNOVATION

Figure 7.7   The Diffusion of Passion Fruit
in the Kisii District Study Area

of their passion fruit vines, keeping only a few for personal use. Thus, only about 12 hectares of Kisii were still in production by August 1967.

A new European manager took control in that year. To increase production and encourage new adoptions, a collection truck was dispatched daily on a designated route, and pick-ups were made any place along the way. An insufficient amount of passion fruit was collected to justify the cost, but the company's interest was communicated to the farmer. Also, the manager personally visited all areas where passion fruit was grown, holding meetings to encourage additional farmers to plant the crop. Accordingly, the farmers soon realized that there was again a place to market passion fruit, and they then only had to register with the Horticultural Crops Development Authority for accounting purposes and be assigned a collection station. As a result, only three years after the new European manager took control, the production of passion fruit had spread from a small node to encompass most of the central and eastern portion of the study area (Figure 7.7).

Distance from an established pick-up point (Figure 7.2), which is simply an agreed upon place along the road where the collection truck will stop, is important in the farmer's decision on whether or not to grow passion fruit as a cash crop. The price paid at the processing plant is about 16 per cent higher if the farmer transports the crop himself, but that probably is not sufficient to cover the cost and inconvenience. In either case the farmer is encouraged to plant the crop near a road because of the great weight involved. The decline in adoption is about 6.3 per cent for every kilometer increase in distance from a collection point, with a correlation coefficient of −0.550. Also obvious in the diffusion pattern is the point in the east of the study area where passion fruit was initially introduced (Figure 7.7). Accordingly, there is a strong correlation between the average year of adoption in an area and both the average hectares planted in passion fruit (0.79) and the per cent of farmers adopting (0.68) (Table 7.1).

Grade Cattle

Grade cattle were initially introduced in three widely separated parts of the study area but new adoptions immediately occurred at scattered locations between (Figure 7.8). Thus, the diffusion was not characterized by a wave, so much as by differential intensification wherein some areas experienced intense adoption, while others nearby experienced no adoption.

Grade cattle diffused in a different manner from the previously discussed innovations for a number of reasons. First, the set of potential adopters was initially very small because of the high cost of grade cattle and because owners had to meet several requirements set by the Gusii County Council, including registration. A related factor restricting the set of potential adopters is that a loan generally is needed to purchase grade cattle. This entails information about how to initiate a loan, a formidable amount of paper work (at least for a peasant farmer) and personal characteristics acceptable to the loaning agency.

A second difference in the diffusion of grade cattle, compared to

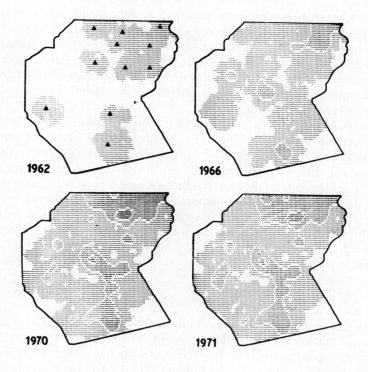

1962   1966

1970   1971

NO ADOPTION
0.1 % to 16.0 %
16.1 % to 50.0 %
50.1 % to 84.0 %
84.1 % to 99.0 %

▲   PLACES OF ORIGINAL
    INTRODUCTION OF
    THE INNOVATION

Figure 7.8   The Diffusion of Grade
Cattle in the Kisii District
Study Area

other innovations examined in this section, is that these high-quality
cattle were by design introduced simultaneously in a number of
locations, and the German Agricultural Team, which provided most
of the loan money, spread its activities over the district to avoid
charges of favoritism. Further, sale of the milk product is conducted
door to door by the farmer, so market sites and proximity to a good
road are not important. These factors, then, account for the lack of a
wave-like pattern in the diffusion of grade cattle.

There are, however, more localized neighborhood effects (Figure 7.8). One factor contributing to this is the need for information about the intricacies of caring for grade cattle, which is transferred most effectively from an owner to a potential owner. Also, there is considerable prestige associated with ownership, leading to significant imitation effects once adoption in a locale reaches approximately 20 per cent.

In the case of grade cattle, then, the diffusion pattern largely reflects the decisions of the Gusii County Council and the German Agricultural Team to spread their activities throughout the study area, and the insignificant role of infrastructure or environmental variables. In spite of the fact that there is no diffusion wave, however, the locations of initial introduction remain important determinants of the diffusion pattern (Table 7.1 and Figure 7.8). One reason for this is the role of the local social environment through which peer group prestige and information about the raising of grade cattle are communicated.

Hybrid Maize

Maize, when dried and ground into a flour and boiled with water to form a thick porridge called *poshe*, is the staple of the Gusii diet. Market or infrastructure characteristics do not affect its diffusion since hybrid maize is a food product raised for home consumption. This is further enhanced by the government policy of restricting transport across district borders in order to encourage local self-sufficiency (Kenya, 1969).

Further, hybrid maize is a continuous innovation, representing only a change in the type of seed used, and a farmer can plant a small quantity for trial while retaining nearly the same production level of local maize. Thus, the crop has all the desirable features for a rapid rate of adoption (E.M. Rogers and Shoemaker, 1971: 134–72), and this is what occurred (Figure 7.3). While the level of adoption was quite low initially, because the hybrid seed was not widely available, it jumped to 78 per cent in the five years following the removal of that problem.

The introduction of hybrid maize occurred in 1959 at twelve different locations within the study area (Figure 7.9). These soon coalesced into an eastern and western cluster of adoption, both at low intensity, separated by a central belt of non-adoption. By 1968 the innovation had spread over the entire study area, and by 1971 twelve separate areas, some of them quite large, had achieved total acceptance. Finally, following the initial, widespread, low-level

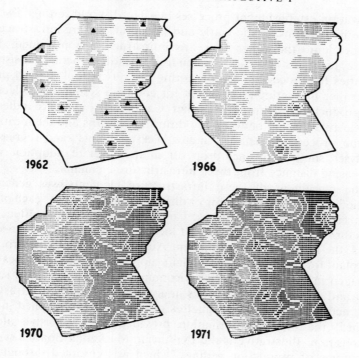

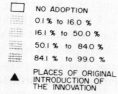

NO ADOPTION
0.1 % to 16.0 %
16.1 % to 50.0 %
50.1 % to 84.0 %
84.1 % to 99.0 %
▲ PLACES OF ORIGINAL
  INTRODUCTION OF
  THE INNOVATION

Figure 7.9   The Diffusion of Hybrid
Maize in the Kisii District
Study Area

diffusion, a wave of higher adoption is moving from east to west. In contrast to the other innovations discussed here, however, the locations of the original adopters are not evident in the current pattern of diffusion (Table 7.1), nor are infrastructure effects.

The Diffusion of Agricultural Innovations in Rural Kenya and the Market and Infrastructure Framework

This section has presented vignettes of the diffusion of six cash crop innovations in a rural area of Kenya, which are illustrative of innovation establishment processes in a Third World setting. Two of these innovations, grade cattle and hybrid maize, are infrastructure independent; the other four are infrastructure constrained. For coffee, tea, pyrethrum and passion fruit, the infrastructure consists of facilities for processing and/or storing the agricultural product prior to further marketing and, except for coffee, a system for collecting the product directly from the farmer. Cartographic evidence indicates a clear relationship between the diffusion patterns and the locations of the processing facilities and/or pick-up points, and regression analyses show a distinct drop off in the level of adoption with increasing distance from these infrastructure elements.

The placement of these infrastructure elements was generally carried out by the propagator or diffusion agency(ies) for each of the cash crops: the Kisii Farmers' Cooperative Union for coffee, the Pyrethrum Marketing Board and local pyrethrum cooperative societies, the Kenya Tea Development Authority and the Sotik processing plant for passion fruit. We might suppose that these agencies also engaged in pricing, promotional communications and market selection and segmentation activities in accordance with their infrastructure activities. While the vignettes generally are not explicit in this regard, the bits of information provided are supportive of the supposition. Illustrative is the Pyrethrum Marketing Board's system of quotas or production ceilings, which was enforced through the price paid for pyrethrum. For the purpose of obtaining crops with high pyrethrins content, the Pyrethrum Marketing Board and the related local cooperative society also provided technical agronomic information, and the price paid to the farmer is pegged to the pyrethrin level. Likewise, the Horticulture Crops Development Authority altered the price paid for passion fruit in accordance with its production goals, and the manager of the Sotik passion fruit-processing plant engaged in promotional communications at a personal level to persuade farmers to raise the crop. Among the infrastructure-independent innovations, the Gusii County Council and the German Agricultural Team simultaneously introduced grade cattle at several locations throughout the study area in an effort to eliminate locational favoritism, and followed the same strategy in dispersing loans for obtaining the cattle and technical information on raising them.

A set of broad institutional actions also affected the diffusion. Mentioned above are the Pyrethrum Marketing Board's system of production ceilings and related price controls, and the price controls of the Horticulture Crops Development Authority for passion fruit. There also is the Pyrethrum Marketing Board's prohibition on planting below the 1860-meter contour line, and the Kenya Tea Development Authority's *green* and *brown* lines controlling the planting of tea. The transportation system represents yet another manifestation of broadly focused institutional policy that affected the diffusion of all six innovations.

In summary, these six vignettes provide strong evidence that government, propagator and diffusion agency actions affect diffusion patterns in Third World settings. Their supply side activities include infrastructure and organizational development, pricing, promotional communications and market selection and segmentation. However, broad policies, manifest for example in the form of price controls or transportation system development strategies, also have an effect. Finally, in all six cases the crop was initially introduced into consciously selected areas that conformed to the strategy of the propagator and/or diffusion agency, and many years later the diffusion pattern still reflects that decision.

This raises the question of exactly how, and by what criteria, the diffusion strategies and the array of related actions are decided upon. Since accessibility to the innovation and its eventual adoption is likely to enhance the economic well-being of the farmer, or of the area in which the farmer resides, this question is one with equity overtones and relevance to the extensive economic disparities among individuals and regions that characterize Third World settings. The passion fruit example is interesting in this regard by its demonstration that a change in attitude and related actions by the processing plant manager had a dramatic effect on the potential adopter's accessibility to the innovation. However, such accessibility also is affected by broadly focused institutional actions, such as transportation system development, which in turn is related to the overall level of regional or national prosperity. Further consideration of these dimensions of diffusion will be taken up in Chapter 8. Before that, attention turns to examining the establishment of cash crop agricultural innovations from a theoretical perspective.

COMMERCIAL DAIRYING IN AGUASCALIENTES, MEXICO: A THEORETICAL PERSPECTIVE ON INFRASTRUCTURE-CONSTRAINED DIFFUSION IN DEVELOPING WORLD SETTINGS[6]

This section focuses upon the spatial diffusion of commercial dairying in the state of Aguascalientes, Mexico (Figure 7.10) from 1942 through 1968. The dominant propagator of this innovation in the study area is the Nestlé Company, which primarily produces powdered milk from that supplied by the farmers.

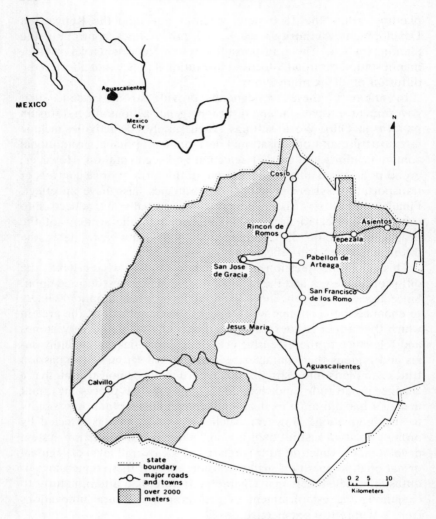

Figure 7.10   The State of Aguascalientes, Mexico

The market for powdered milk in Mexican rural areas has been rapidly expanding over the past three decades due to changing dietary patterns among the population, the encouragement of milk consumption in school lunch programs and the widespread absence of refrigeration facilities. In 1942, Nestlé established a powdered-milk plant in Lagos de Moreno, Jalisco, to the south of Aguascalientes. Finding its supply shed encroached upon from the south by the rapidly expanding demand for fluid milk and cheese in the industrial core of Mexico, and hampered by government restrictions upon the maximum purchase price that Nestlé was allowed to pay, Nestlé expanded its supply region to the north during the decades of the fifties and sixties. In 1958, a collection depot was established in the town in Pabellon de Arteaga, just north of the city of Aguascalientes (Figure 7.10). Thereafter, being anxious to purchase as much milk as possible, Nestlé continuously opened new milk-collection routes out of Pabellon.

The resulting diffusion pattern reflects these activities (Figure 1.2). The earliest adopters are in the south of the study area, mirroring the orientation to the Lagos de Moreno market. The pattern then expands northward, in neighborhood effect fashion, but largely along the major transportation artery (Figure 7.10). In 1958, with the opening of the Pabellon depot, the focal point of the diffusion pattern shifts to that locale. Neighborhood effects continue, but primarily in the north while filling in occurs elsewhere. However, the correlation between the transportation system and the pattern of diffusion is maintained.

As a part of its diffusion strategy, Nestlé provided much support for the dairy farmers. Specifically, Nestlé bore all transport costs, provided necessary inputs such as feed supplements at company cost and technical advice free of charge, assured farmers of a long-term stable market and provided a demand for fluid milk from individual suppliers that was infinitely elastic at a fixed price. Further, dairy production yields in this area are less sensitive to weather fluctuations than other viable production alternatives; dairy production results in a weekly cash flow, thus minimizing problems related to capitalization of a beginning enterprise; most farmers in the region possess range cattle for domestic milk consumption which can be used to begin commercial sale to Nestlé; and land tenure is secure throughout most of the study area. Finally, the return to investment in commercial dairying was more than four times the return to investment in subsistence production of corn and beans, the major alternatives.

Clearly, then, the economic environment is and has been extremely favorable to the adoption of the practice of commercial dairying. Nevertheless, by 1968 it had reached only a small proportion of the farmers in the study area. Certainly, factors other than the purely economic must be considered. The following model is proposed.

A Model of the Diffusion of Cash-Crop Innovations

Certain innovations result in or constitute a product that must be transported some distance, and this transportation cost may be a significant consideration in the adoption decision. This is generally the case in Third World settings where transportation networks are not well developed and the associated costs are therefore high. It is more specifically so in the change-over from subsistence to commercial agriculture; in the diffusions of coffee, tea, passion fruit and pyrethrum production among the Gusii of Kenya, described above; and in the diffusion of commercial dairying in Aguascalientes, Mexico.

These examples involve both a diffusion agency that promotes the innovation and an entity which purchases (or receives) the product of the innovation. These functions may be performed by separate entities or by a single organization. The latter arrangement increases the options in diffusion agency strategy, as will be shown below.

To explore this further, consider the situation in which the innovation is an agricultural production process with an output that must be transported to a purchasing entity; there is a single market center with all potential adopters (farmers) located in its hinterland; and the price for the output is directly related to demand for it as either an intermediate or final good. The response of the potential adopter (farmer) depends upon the market price, the costs of producing and transporting the innovation, opportunity costs relative to those associated with alternative economic endeavors, and the level of information about the innovation.[7] Another factor is the market structure. If there are several entities to purchase the good, *perfect competition* prevails; if there is only one such entity, or if the several are organized to function as one, *monopsony* prevails.

Assume that: (1) Incentive to adopt is directly proportional to the marginal return from adoption. (2) Awareness of this marginal return is directly proportional to the amount of information held by a potential adopter. (3) All potential adopters (or their farmsteads) are uniformly distributed throughout the market center's hinterland and are identical in characteristics pertinent to the utility of the innovation, resulting in production and opportunity costs that are everywhere equal.[8] (4) Transportation costs vary continuously with distance from the market. (5) The density of adopters at a given distance from the market is proportional to the known adoption incentive at that distance.[9]

With these conditions and perfect competition, the spatial variation in marginal returns and incentive to adopt, or *the surface of adoption potential,* is represented by the variation in transportation costs, which are borne by the adopting farmer. Assuming information levels to be everywhere equal, the density of adopters will decrease with distance from the market center, reaching zero at the distance where market price is equal to the sum of production and transportation costs (Figure 7.11A). That distance defines a supply-shed boundary within which there will be sufficient production, as the result of adoption, to satisfy demand. Since all adopters receive the same price, whatever their location, those closer to the market center receive a greater marginal return which is, in effect, a *location rent*.

With monopsony, however, a rational pricing policy is one by which location rent accrues to the buyer, rather than to adopting farmers. This occurs if the buyer pays a base price that covers production costs, and adds on a varying amount for the adopter's transportation costs, a form of *spatial price discrimination*. A policy having the same effect is the operation of a collection system by which transportation costs are absorbed. This has the advantage of tendering to the buyer control over route selection and other aspects of collection, which is tantamount to control over the spatial configuration of the supply shed and related matters. The result, then, should be a more *rational* diffusion pattern than under either perfect competition or monopsony with spatial price discrimination.

By either approach, the cost of the product to the monopsonist buyer varies according to the adopting farmer's location, but the buyer receives the location rent that in perfect competition went to adopters.[10] Since the marginal return from adoption or adoption incentive will then be the same everywhere within the supply shed, the density of adopters is uniform to its boundary and then drops directly to zero (Figure 7.11B).

Pricing or *infrastructure development* of this sort is an option for innovation establishment strategy if the diffusion agency also functions as a monopsonist buyer, as is indicated to be common by the empirical examples in this chapter. Another option, open to any diffusion agency, is *promotional communications*. The expectation is that the diffusion agency will direct its information (and related efforts) to those locations nearest the market center where the marginal return from adoption and adoption incentive are greatest.[11] These locations also will contain earlier adopters who generate an interpersonal information field which reinforces that of the diffusion agency. Hence, the level of information should be greater the closer one is to the market center.

Considered together, then, the marginal return from adoption and information level lead to the expectation that the density of adopters would exhibit a downward-trending slope from the market center for both the perfect competition and monopsony market structures. However, the spatially invariant adoption incentive under monopsony will yield a slope that is less steep than that produced under perfectly competitive conditions (as in Figure 7.11C compared to

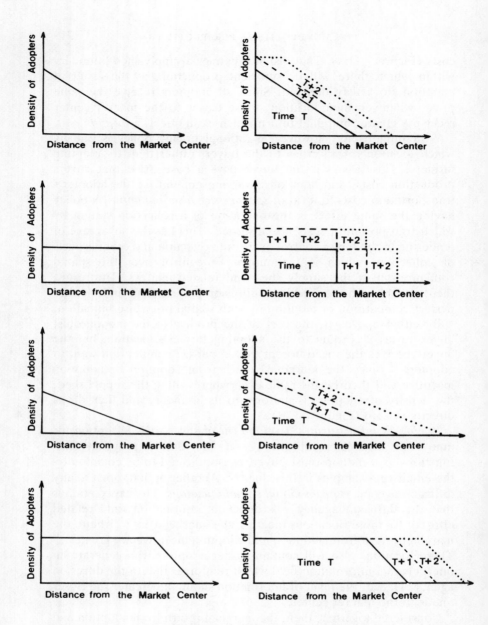

Figure 7.11 Alternative Profiles of the Density of Adopters for Infrastructure-Constrained Agriculture Production Process Innovations in a Third
World Setting
   Note: These profiles of the density of adopters over distance from an
urban center also portray the distribution of known adoption incentives
and the marginal returns from adoption (see text for explanation).

Figure 7.11A). Also, the monopsonist buyer theoretically will seek out potential adopter farmers near existing collection routes who possess more economic incentive for adoption, a strategy that minimizes information dissemination costs per new adopter as well as collection costs. The result will be a more compact diffusion pattern, closely clustered along collection routes, than either under perfect competition or under monopsony with spatial price discrimination.

An additional consideration is the likelihood that information has a saturation or redundancy level, beyond which additional information does not increase the probability of adoption. As this level is reached, spatial differentials resulting from information availability disappear. For monopsony the density of adopters then would be uniform to the outermost point of saturation, whereupon it drops diagonally towards the supply-shed boundary (Figure 7.11D). There is also an upper limit to adoption itself and reaching this would bring about a similar profile in the density of adopters (the time sequence profiles of Figures 7.11A, 7.11B, 7.11C, 7.11D) for both perfect competition and monopsony.

To meet an increasing derived demand in the short run, the monopsonist operating a collection system may either (1) extend transport routes to include previously untapped areas containing farmers with little resistance to adoption or (2) undertake to persuade non-adopters (who would be presumed to be of higher resistance) within the existing supply shed. Eventually, extension of the transportation system will be necessary, but the choice of a short-run strategy could be rationally resolved by comparing the increase in transport costs for collecting from an extended supply shed with the increase in information dissemination costs for attempting to persuade potential adopters of relatively high resistance.

The same choice may be relevant if the monopsonist desires to increase the degree to which his plant capacity is used. Many plants, particularly those processing agricultural goods, are subject to economies of scale in that average production costs fall rapidly as capacity levels of operation are approached. This provides an incentive to expand the supply shed as quickly as possible, a kind of market skimming strategy to bring in the most innovative farmers, until collection approaches capacity levels. In this situation, an optimal diffusion strategy would be based upon relative production costs as well as transportation and information dissemination costs.

Viewed over time, then, diffusion proceeds by stages (Figure 4.9A). (1) A given level of demand and related price result in the definition of a supply shed within which some farmers adopt and others do not. (2) If demand is not satisfied or if it increases, price increases and the supply-shed boundary shifts outward from the market; the result is additional adoption both within the initial supply shed and in the new supply area (except where adoption is at saturation level). The same effect may be brought about by *institutional actions* that lower costs (thus increasing marginal return and adoption incentive), such as improvements in the transportation system or government subsidies to adopters.

The discussion above has incorporated the assumption that transportation costs vary continuously with distance. It is more realistic, however, to recognize that transportation infrastructure extends linearly along an artery. Thus, a farmer located at a given distance from the market center on the artery can get to the center less expensively than a farmer at the same distance who is not on the artery. Likewise, a given transportation cost will permit a farmer to be located farther from the market center if he is on the artery, than if not. This would result in a cobweb-type pattern of diffusion that is directionally as well as distance biased (Figure 4.9B). Both directional and distance bias also might result from *infrastructure development* by the monopsonist buyer (Figure 4.9C), which thus takes on *market selection* implications.

Empirical Analyses Related to the Model of the Diffusion of Cash-Crop Innovations in Third World Settings

In order to test the above model, twenty *explanatory* variables were employed in a regression format. These were divided according to whether they pertained to the potential adopter's *site* or *situation,* and each of those sets were factor analyzed.[12] The result was five site components relating to the age of the farmer at the time of adoption, economic indices of the farm enterprise during 1967–8 (the only years for which data were available), the size of the farm enterprise during 1967–8, contact with United States agriculture and education of the farmer. Two situation components also were identified. These relate to the density of prior or contemporaneous adopters around the farmer at the time of adoption and the farmer's distance or accessibility to the market at Pabellon.

Three separate analyses were carried out, each employing the five site and two situation components as independent variables in a step-wise regression procedure. The first probe into the diffusion of commercial dairying in Aguascalientes identified the bases for statistically discriminating between adopters and non-adopters, using a 1/0 or dummy-dependent variable. Significant in this analysis was a site component pertaining to the *age of the potential adopter farmer*

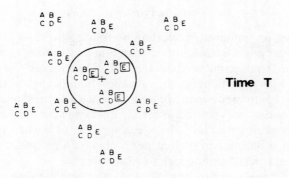

Time T

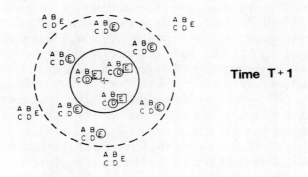

Time T+1

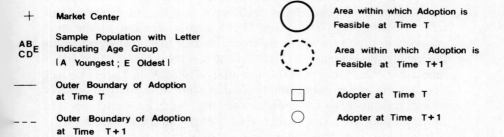

+   Market Center

AB
CD E   Sample Population with Letter Indicating Age Group [A Youngest ; E Oldest]

——   Outer Boundary of Adoption at Time T

- - -   Outer Boundary of Adoption at Time T+1

⬭   Area within which Adoption is Feasible at Time T

⬭   Area within which Adoption is Feasible at Time T+1

☐   Adopter at Time T

◯   Adopter at Time T+1

Figure 7.12   A Generalized Sequence of Diffusion Events for a Cash-Crop Innovation in a Third World Setting

and situation components pertaining to the *density of prior adoption* around the potential adopter farmer and *accessibility to the market* at Pabellon. The second analysis treated adopters only, with years since adoption as the dependent variable. Significant in this was the situation component *accessibility to market*. The third analysis treated both adopters and non-adopters, again using years since adoption as the dependent variable.[13] Being a composite of the first two analyses, both the situation component pertaining to *accessibility* and the site component pertaining to *age* were significant.

These three analyses together indicate the following (generalized) sequence of diffusion events, which are in accord with the theoretical model above. At time *t,* accessibility to market and information about the innovation—situation-related factors—act as a filter that partitions the hinterland population into farmers for whom adoption is feasible and farmers for whom adoption is not feasible. Because both accessibility and information vary with distance from market, this partition is manifested spatially as an outer boundary to adoption (Figure 7.12A). The exact distance of that boundary from the market, or the extent of the commercial dairying supply shed, will depend upon the level of demand for raw milk at the time. Among the farmers located within the time *t* supply shed, all of whom are potential adopters, site characteristics related to age of the farmer determine who will actually adopt (Figure 7.12A).[14]

In time *t*+1 the supply-shed boundary shifts further from the market, possibly because of an increase in demand for raw milk and related extension of the collection infrastructure, thus adding new farmers to the pool of potential adopters (Figure 7.12B). Assume that age groups are uniformly distributed in space so that a sample of the population in two equal-sized areas at different locations will have the same age structure. Then, a large portion of the new adopters in time *t*+1 will come from the area that is newly added to the supply shed (Figure 7.12B), since that is the location of the more *innovative* older farmers of the potential adopter pool. There also will be adoption in the initial supply shed by somewhat younger farmers whose resistance to commercial dairying has been overcome.[15] In time *t*+2 and later, this sequence of events would continue.

In general, then, the theoretical and empirical analyses pertaining to the infrastructure-constrained diffusion of cash-crop production indicate that: (1) the supply shed expands in a spatially sequential fashion such that accessibility to market and information is a major filter in defining potential adopter farmers; (2) within the supply shed, site factors such as those related to age or innovativeness are the major determinant of adoption; and (3) to meet increased demand for a cash crop such as raw milk, the diffusion agency extends collection routes to include areas previously untapped, as well as undertaking to persuade non-adopters within the existing supply shed. However, it appears that the former strategy is given more attention than the latter, at least in the initial stages of the diffusion.

OVERVIEW

The applicability of the market and infrastructure framework in Third World settings is the concern of this chapter. This is demonstrated through two case studies. One on the diffusion of several agricultural innovations in the Kisii District of Kenya illustrates the role of a variety of market and infrastructure factors, while a study of the diffusion of commercial dairying in the Aguascalientes region of Mexico provides a theoretical perspective.[16]

Both the study of the diffusion of agricultural innovations in Kenya and the study of the diffusion of commercial dairying in Mexico pertain to diffusion agency strategy or innovation establishment. An illustration of diffusion agency establishment in a Third World setting is presented in Chapter 8, which contains a study of the diffusion of the cooperative movement in Sierra Leone. More generally, that chapter considers the ways in which diffusion and development processes interrelate.

The first case study here consists of vignettes of the diffusion of six cash crop innovations in the Kisii District of Kenya. Two of these, grade cattle and hybrid maize, are infrastructure independent, while four—coffee, tea, pyrethrum and passion fruit—are infrastructure constrained. For the latter, the infrastructure consists of facilities for processing and/or storing the agricultural product prior to further marketing and, except for coffee, a system for collecting the product directly from the farmer. Cartographic evidence indicates a clear relationship between the diffusion patterns and the locations of the processing facilities and/or pick-up points, and regression analyses show a distinct drop off in the level of adoption with increasing distance from these infrastructure elements.

The placement of these infrastructure elements generally was carried out by the propagator or diffusion agency(ies) for each of the cash crops, and it appears that these entities also engaged in pricing, promotional communications and market selection and segmentation activities in accordance with their infrastructure activities. This also is evident among the infrastructure-independent innovations. The Gusii County Council and German Agricultural Team, for example,

simultaneously introduced grade cattle at several locations throughout the study area, in an effort to eliminate locational favortism, and
they followed the same strategy in dispersing loans for obtaining the
cattle and technical information on raising them.

A set of broad institutional actions also affected the diffusions.
These include production and related price controls, various lines
controlling where a crop could be planted and the transportation
system itself.

Thus, these six vignettes provide strong evidence that government,
propagator and diffusion agency actions affect diffusion patterns in
Third World settings. Their supply side activities include infrastructure and organizational development, pricing, promotional communications and market selection and segmentation. However, broad
policies, manifest for example in the form of price controls or
transportation system development strategies, also have an effect.
Finally, in all six cases the crop was initially introduced into
consciously selected areas that conformed to the strategy of the
propagator and/or diffusion agency, and many years later the
diffusion pattern still reflects that decision.

The second case study examined the diffusion of commercial
dairying in Aguascalientes, Mexico. The propagator in this instance
was the Nestlé company which established a collection depot in the
area and operated collection routes originating from that. It also
supported dairy farmers in other ways by bearing all transport costs,
providing necessary inputs such as feed supplements at company cost
and technical advice free of charge, assuring farmers a long-term
stable market and providing a demand for fluid milk that was
infinitely elastic at a fixed price.

The perspective in examining this diffusion was a theoretical one
which applies in general to the diffusion of infrastructure-constrained
diffusions of cash crops in Third World settings. One of the factors
demonstrated as important by this analysis is market structure, that
is, whether monopsony or perfect competition prevails among the
agencies diffusing the innovation. Pricing policy also is important,
particularly under monopsony where a rational behavior by the
diffusion agency consists either of operating a collection system by
which transportation costs are absorbed or of employing a spatially
discriminant pricing scheme by which a base price is paid to all
farmers plus a varying amount to cover the farmer's transportation
costs. The collection route option is particularly interesting in that it
tenders to the buyer control over route selection and other aspects of
collection, which is tantamount to control over the spatial configura-

tion of the supply shed and related matters. The result, then, should be a more rational diffusion pattern than under either perfect competition or monopsony with spatial price discrimination.

The establishment of a collection system represents a market selection decision, and the diffusion agency also employed promotional communications. Thus, all four of the elements of diffusion agency strategy discussed in Chapter 3—pricing, infrastructure development, promotional communications and market selection and segmentation—are represented in the commercial dairying case study. These were employed in projecting expected patterns of diffusion under different conditions. In general, these patterns tend to be uniform in adoption density out to some distance from the market center or collection depot. That distance represents the extent of the infrastructure penetration boundary, defined either by the extent of the collection infrastructure or by the spatially discriminant pricing scheme. Over time, the supply shed shifts outwards (or inwards) by stages as a function of demand for the cash crop. However, institutional actions that lower costs associated with the innovation, such as improvements in the transportation system or government subsidies to adopters, may have a similar effect. Finally, the analysis takes into account that the development of a collection infrastructure would be directionally as well as distance biased, affecting the diffusion pattern accordingly.

An empirical test of this model was carried out using variables representing five aspects of the potential adopter's site and two aspects of his situation or relative location. This indicates that the diffusion was molded and constrained by diffusion agency actions such as the establishment of a collection infrastructure. Within these constraints, however, adoption depended upon personal characteristics such as the age of the farmer, which may be related to innovativeness. Thus, the empirical analysis generally confirms the theoretical findings, and it also indicates how the market and infrastructure and adoption perspectives interrelate.

NOTES

1 Development programs are discussed in greater detail in Chapter 8.
2 The essence of this section is taken from Garst (1974b). The empirical material is based upon fieldwork reported in detail in Garst (1972, 1974a).
3 Pyrethrum flowers (*Chrysanthemum cinerariaefolium*) are used to produce pyrethrins, a bio-degradable, non-persistent, insecticide additive of low toxicity.
4 Unfortunately no records could be found indicating locations for pick-up points.
5 Passion fruit, the edible fruit of the plant of genus *Passiflora*, is used to make a fruit juice drink or natural flavoring concentrate for use in other food products.

6 This is a synopsis of research reported more fully in L.A. Brown and Lentnek (1973). The empirical material is based upon fieldwork by Lentnek, described in Lentnek (1969) and Lentnek, Charnews and Cotter (1978).

7 Production and transportation costs together are functionally similar to the operating costs associated with product types of innovations. Recognizing this enables one to relate this infrastructure-constrained diffusion to other innovation establishment situations, as discussed in Chapter 4, pages 121–6.

8 In the absence of further knowledge, characteristics pertinent to the utility of the innovation could be assumed to be distributed randomly, instead of assumption (3) that they are everywhere equal. This would introduce random variation in the distribution of adopter density, but that distribution would in general retain the properties resulting from other factors. Thus, whether the *random* or *everywhere equal* assumption is made, the general conclusions of this analysis would be the same.

9 An alternative assumption to (5) is that adoption occurs wherever the marginal return from adoption, or adoption incentive, is greater than zero, but (5) is more realistic.

10 This leads to the paradox that locational factors have relatively little effect on the adoption decision of the individual farmer, but have a significant effect on the overall distribution of adopters!

11 Note that this is a type of *market selection* strategy on the part of the diffusion agency.

12 Site variables are those pertaining directly to the farmer or the farm enterprise; situation variables are those pertaining to the relative location (of the farmer or the farm enterprise) *vis-à-vis,* for example, previous adopters, the transportation system or the market. Suitable testing of the theoretical model necessitated treating site and situation components separately. As a check, however, a single principal components analysis of all twenty variables also was executed, and this resulted in a components pattern that was similar to that produced by the separate analyses.

13 Non-adopters were assigned a value of zero for this analysis.

14 A number of studies of adoption in Third World settings, as well as the commercial dairying study summarized here, find a direct relationship between innovativeness and age or age-related characteristics (Foster, 1962, 1973; E.M. Rogers, 1969). However, as discussed in Chapter 8, pages 235–6 and 264, this occurrence is more prevalent in traditional societies, and as the society moves towards modernity, other characteristics should become pertinent to innovativeness. Also, as discussed in Chapter 8, the correlation between age and time of adoption could have more to do with diffusion agency strategy and/or access to resources than with innovativeness.

15 Although this observation is cast in terms of resistance to adoption and innovativeness, access to resources or diffusion agency actions could be the critical factor as well. See note 14 above and pages 230–51.

16 The applicability or relevance of the market and infrastructure framework in Third World settings also is indicated by the literature on marketing in that context. See, for example, Glade, Strang, Udell and Littlefield (1970), West and Pearson (1979) or Vertinsky and Barth (1972).

8

THE DEVELOPMENT PERSPECTIVE II: THE INTERRELATIONSHIP BETWEEN DEVELOPMENT PROCESSES AND DIFFUSION[1]

For many years it was widely assumed that innovation diffusion had a positive impact upon individual welfare and, collectively, economic development and social change. As E.M. Rogers (1976b: 7) notes

A decade or so ago, there was much optimism and high hopes for the role that mass communication [innovation diffusion under the adoption perspective] might play in fostering development in Latin America, Africa, and Asia. . . . Some authors even used such terms as . . . 'magic multipliers' in describing the media and what they could do in the development process.

Accordingly, development programs forged ahead, giving little if any attention to the assumed benefits of innovation. Thirty plus years after the initiation of the first of such programs, however, the picture is not encouraging. Within Third World nations élitist entrenchment prevails and there are still enormous disparities between social and economic classes, as well as among regions, in their level of social welfare and economic development. Further, some would argue that these characteristics have worsened over the period, often as a consequence of the innovation diffusion process itself (Roling, Ascroft and Chege, 1976; Havens and Flinn, 1970, 1975; Yapa, 1976, 1977, 1979, 1980). Thus, Rogers himself writes (1976b: 7)

Now in 1976, we look backward. The mass media have indeed penetrated much further than in 1965. New communication technology, such as broadcasting satellites, has come on the scene. Government officials in most developing countries have indeed heeded our advice and sought to utilize mass communication for development purposes. But little real development has occurred by just about any standard.

This awareness has led to a reexamination of development strategies in general and the development aspects of innovation diffusion in particular. The previous chapter contributed to this ongoing discussion by considering the applicability of the market and infrastructure framework in Third World settings. Two related, and more germane, questions are examined in this chapter.

First, what are the social and economic consequences of innovation diffusion? Second, what is the impact of the level of development, or the development process itself, upon innovation diffusion?

Background for the first question is provided in the opening paragraphs of this chapter. With regard to the second question, one way in which the level of development affects innovation diffusion is through infrastructure and other publicly available goods. This link is articulated by the market and infrastructure perspective, which indicates that these aspects of development have a significant influence on the extent of diffusion and the type of innovations diffused. Transportation, for example, is in effect a subsidy to the potential adopter that stimulates innovation diffusion.[2] Another way in which the level of development affects innovation diffusion is through societal norms, which influence an individual's response to innovation and, hence, his likelihood of adoption. Thus, acceptance of a contemporary technology is more likely in a modern society, whereas traditional societies would have greater orientation towards innovations more congruent with indigenous practices.

Attention now turns to these two questions. The social and economic consequences of innovation diffusion are addressed immediately. The discussion pertaining to the impact of the development process on innovation diffusion begins on page 263.

THE SOCIAL AND ECONOMIC CONSEQUENCES OF INNOVATION DIFFUSION

This section begins by considering the impact of innovation diffusion upon individuals or households. Of particular concern is the concept of *adoption rent*, which pertains to the gains that derive from innovation. This concept is elaborated both in a theoretical mode and by examining a number of common diffusion practices in terms of the way(s) they favor certain members of society, thus granting those persons a greater likelihood of gaining through adoption rent. Attention then turns to the impact of diffusion upon regional development, giving particular attention to the regional inequalities that have been inherent in that process.

Innovation Diffusion, Individual Welfare and Adoption Rent

As a simple means of understanding the impact of innovation diffusion upon individual welfare, consider an agricultural setting oriented towards commercial production. Assuming that the innovation constitutes an improvement to existing practices, a larger cash crop output would be derived from a given level of input and the production function of the adopter would shift upwards (Figure 8.1A). Although total supply is increased accordingly, a few adopters would not affect market price in a manner that offsets their related reduction in costs. This is expected because the market price must adequately compensate the more marginal, non-adopting farmers in order to meet total demand (Stevens, 1961) and because of the market's lag in adjusting to supply conditions.

Thus, the early adopter of this agricultural innovation related to cash crop production will experience excess or *windfall* profits which may be termed an *adoption rent*. Over time, however, as more farmers adopt, leading to supply increases, and as the market comes into accord with supply conditions, leading to price decreases, adoption rent related to the innovation will decrease to zero (Figure 8.1B).

There also will be a growing pressure upon non-adopting farmers since it will become increasingly difficult for them to compete in the market place.[3] This pressure might result in adoption, although adoption rent gains could be relatively little and perhaps zero, depending upon when adoption occurred (Figure 8.1B). Alternatively, however, farmers lagging in adoption could be forced out of production if the innovation is not cost effective at their scale of operations and/or if the supply after innovation comes to exceed what the market can absorb. One important characteristic in this regard would be the price elasticity of demand for the agricultural product. Irrespective of that, however, the market might not have the capacity in processing facilities to absorb agricultural output beyond a certain level.[4]

The concept of adoption rent is not only applicable in an agricultural setting; in general, there is a high probability that the early adopter of an innovation will enjoy a *windfall* gain or a competitive advantage. Comparing the Japanese and United States steel industries provides a current illustration, as do the extensive profits of early entrants to the fast food industry. Likewise, the individual local entrepreneur who is *in on the ground floor* is likely to prosper, as is the academic who employs the most current ideas, models and techniques in research. There also are social windfalls, as evidenced by the status or psychic income that accrues to the early adopter of a color television, a new model sports car or a modern appliance. These observations must be tempered, however, by the realization that there may be penalities for adopting *too* early due to the continuity of innovation, as discussed in Chapter 6.

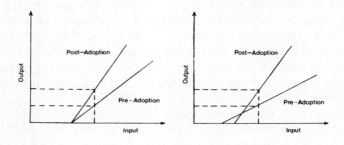

A   Possible Effects of Innovation Adoption
    upon Agricultural Production Functions

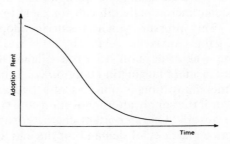

B   Shifts in Adoption Rent over Time

Figure 8.1   Windfall Gains Associated with Innovation
             Adoption ('Adoption Rent')

Adoption rent is a particularly critical issue, both in Developed and Developing World settings, in that diffusion programs generally incorporate systematic biases which enable some members of society to more readily adopt innovations and thus enjoy the attendant windfall gains on a continuing basis, resulting in maintenance and, often, exacerbation of the economic disparities between individuals or social classes. Many of these programatic biases may be traced to the prevalence of the adoption perspective. One reason for this is its emphasis of a communications strategy focused on potential adopters with an orientation towards progressiveness or modernity of the Developed World variety (Beltran, 1976; Bordenave, 1976; Roling, Ascroft and Chege, 1976). Further, the adoption perspective embodies the view that non-adoption is the result of insufficient individual innovativeness or entrepreneurship. Thus, the responsibility for non-adoption ultimately rests with the individual.

An alternative view, with which the market and infrastructure perspective is consistent, is that diffusion and entrepreneurship are affected by the availability and distribution of resources or individual access to the means of production and *public* goods (Yapa, 1976). Examples of resources in this context would include information; capital or access to capital through loans; skills or education; public infrastructure such as transportation, electricity or water systems; and public facilities providing service, collection, delivery or processing related to the innovation or its implementation. Such resources are provided by government, entrepreneurial or non-profit institutions, some entities of which would be diffusion agencies that serve as intermediaries between governmental strategies and individual adoption.

In support of the *resource availability* view, Weeks (1970) presents a general economic analysis drawing upon his experiences in south-east Asia and reports

it may not be 'apathy' that prevents poor farmers from availing themselves of innovative advantages, but . . . the lack of 'means . . . to avail themselves' . . . which limits innovative behavior. (Weeks, 1970: 32)

Similar conclusions are reported by Gotsch (1972), Yapa (1976, 1977) and Yapa and Mayfield (1978).[5]

With regard to the effects of systematic biases in diffusion strategies, Havens and Flinn (1975) studied the diffusion of green revolution technology in Tamesis, a community of the Colombian state of Antioquia. They note

It has been demonstrated that the distribution of income and land has become more concentrated in the community under study and that the adopters of the new coffee varieties began with more resources and have enjoyed the bulk of these gains in income and land from 1963 to 1971. (Havens and Flinn, 1975: 478)

However, the implications of these systematic biases go beyond the mere enjoyment of gains and increased concentration of wealth. Sixty-five families were sampled by Havens and Flinn, seventeen of which adopted and forty-eight not. Fourteen of the non-adopters (approximately 30 per cent) lost control of their land, and of these, eight immediately migrated to other areas and six became local day laborers, that is, ripe prospects for future migration (Guerrero, 1975). Thus, this innovation diffusion in rural Colombia directly contributed to a significant Third World problem, that of extensive rural-to-urban migration and overcrowding of urban areas.[6] More generally, Havens and Flinn (1975: 480) note

The Green Revolution technology may be exacerbating what is already a bad situation—increasing rural-to-urban migration, increasing the income gap between rich and poor, and trading underemployment for unemployment.

Similar conclusions are reached by Mitchelson, Brown and Osleeb (1977). They find that location *vis-à-vis* the market center and size of farm, interacting with the type of innovation diffused and market characteristics such as the elasticity of demand for agricultural products, strongly influence the timing of adoption, the ability to enjoy gains through adoption rent, and the likelihood of losing control of the land and becoming either a local laborer or migrant.[7] An analysis parallel to theirs is elaborated below, but, first, attention turns to a general consideration of *structural* characteristics affecting the likelihood of acquiring gains of the adoption rent type.

Structural Characteristics and Adoption Rent. In the discussion above, *economic wealth* and *farm size* or, more generally, *size of the economic enterprise* were cited as important structural characteristics affecting the timing of adoption (or whether adoption occurs at all) and the attendant gains through adoption rent. Under some conditions, *location* also might be a relevant structural characteristic. In infrastructure-constrained diffusions in an agricultural setting, for example, the prevalence of circumstances favoring adoption varies according to a household's location *vis-à-vis* the urban center from which the relevant infrastructure emanates. More specifically, households located closer to the urban center are likely to have access to the infrastructure earlier, and thus adopt earlier, than households located farther away. In this case, then, adoption rent should have an inherent spatial dimension.[8]

In infrastructure-independent diffusions, by contrast, adoption rent would have a spatial dimension only in so far as a household's location is *coincidently* near a previous adopter or a source of information about the innovation. Nevertheless, *coincidental proximity* is in general another important structural characteristic, particularly in social space. To illustrate, the acquisition of many innovations, or *opportunities* as they are commonly called, is related to social or economic contacts derived from *the old boy network,* the club, the business persons' luncheon group, the special interest group or the neighborhood acquaintance circle.

Propagator or diffusion agency actions constitute another structural element that may systematically favor a certain segment of society and thus increase the likelihood of that segment prospering through adoption rent. In an infrastructure-constrained diffusion in an agricultural setting, for example, a household's *natural* locational advantage might be offset by the agency developing infrastructure in a direction from the urban center other than that in which the household is located, as in Figure 4.9C. Propagator and diffusion agency actions such as this have been discussed in preceding chapters. These include actions pertaining to adapting an innovation to certain uses or locales (Chapter 6); diffusion agency location and time of establishment (Chapter 3); and diffusion agency strategies such as pricing, infrastructure and organizational development, market selection and segmentation, and promotional communications (Chapter 4).

Sometimes, propagator or diffusion agency actions are explicit in their bias, such as a market selection strategy which concentrates on upper middle-class households or large farms. While these may be worrisome in their own right, of greater concern here are those actions with implicit or indirect effects that are not so apparent.

An example is the *two-step flow of communications strategy* which is widely used by the Agricultural Extension Service of the United States and by many development programs in Third World countries. On the surface, this is an egalitarian strategy which employs media and change agents to feed information and assistance concerning the innovation to *opinion leader, innovator* or *progressive* members of the target population, who in turn communicate interpersonally with the *less innovative* individuals. In light of the adoption rent concept, however, this is a questionable strategy since it ensures that the opinion leaders will be able to adopt earlier and enjoy greater adoption rents, leading to increased élitist entrenchment!

But the practice is even more questionable in that individuals initially targeted may not be inherently more innovative. In E.M. Rogers' (1969) study of five rural villages in Colombia, for example, those identified as opinion leaders were better educated, of higher social status and income, older, more politically knowledgeable, more innovative and with larger farms. Yet, the achievement motivation scores of the opinion leaders were actually less than those of the *followers* (E.M. Rogers, 1969: 228)! Consider also that measures of opinion leadership, innovativeness and/or progressiveness, generally give considerable weight (directly or indirectly) to the number of innovations adopted or the time of adoption of prior innovations (E.M. Rogers and Shoemaker, 1971: 27 and 171–96;

Midgley, 1977: 43–77; E.M. Rogers, 1969: 290–315). These facts, then, suggest that the farmer may be *progressive* as a result of being the targets of prior diffusion efforts, rather than because of innate characteristics! That is, as L.A. Brown, Malecki and Spector (1976: 315) note,

differences in adoption time may be the result of the marketing strategies of public or private propagators of the innovation, rather than the result of innovativeness characteristics of potential adopters.

Even more to the point, Yapa (1976: 13–14) notes

A common premise is that underdevelopment is related to a lack of enterprise or entrepreneurship . . . . Yet, even the casual tourist has learned to come away with a healthy respect for merchant enterprise in the markets of Third World cities and towns, and the acquisitive skill of the ubiquitous money lender is only too well known.

The *type of innovation diffused* is another element that may systematically favor a certain segment of society and thus increase the likelihood of that segment prospering through adoption rent. If an innovation only is cost effective in economic operations of a given size, for example, entrepreneurs with either larger- or smaller-size operations will find themselves at a competitive disadvantage after innovation. Alternatively, if an innovation is cost effective at many scales of operation, but requires a considerable capital outlay and the ability to take a significant risk, the larger-scale entrepreneur will be more able and likely to adopt. In more general terms, specifically relevant is whether an innovation benefits workers or entrepreneurs or, if entrepreneurs, whether it benefits large- or small-scale operations. Those favoring entrepreneurs and particularly large-scale entrepreneurial operations tend to increase economic disparities among households (Yapa, 1976, 1977).

A theoretical framework relevant to these considerations in an agricultural setting has been elaborated by Yapa (1976, 1977), drawing on work by Griffin (1974). This argues that, since access to the factors of production varies by social class in the Third World, a factor bias in an innovation is simultaneously a social bias. Thus, the choice of innovation to diffuse has a social (or socio-economic) consequence as well as a production consequence. Accordingly, innovations may be viewed in terms of three types. *Labor-augmenting* or *peasant-biased innovations,* such as a metal hoe, increase the marginal productivity of labor and thereby favor small landholders. At the other extreme are *material-augmenting* or *landlord-biased innovations,* such as a tractor, which increase the marginal productivity of capital and thereby favor large landholders. In between are *neutral innovations* which are simultaneously advantageous to both large- and small-scale operations.

Classifying a given innovation as either peasant or landlord biased appears to be a straightforward task. Thus Fiorentino, Pineiro and Trigo (1978), drawing on their studies of the Colombian agricultural sector, discuss the characteristics of innovations that are

available, profitable and technically feasible for small farmers. (Fiorentino, Pineiro and Trigo, 1978: 17)

One such characteristic is that the technology should be neutral to the scale of operations in terms of its effectiveness. Second, it should be biased towards making use of labor factors of production and physical inputs that are readily available to small producers. Third, in order to bypass the farmer's aversion to risk, the yields related to the new technology should be consistent and fairly invariable with respect to climatic conditions.

However, evaluating a landlord or peasant bias is complicated by the need to consider the whole package of which the innovation is a part, not just the innovation alone. The innovations central to the Green Revolution, for example, are high-yielding varieties (HYV) of grain. Generally, though, fertilizers, herbicides, pesticides and irrigation also must be employed in order to realize the HYV's full potential, and it is these aspects of the *adoption package* that lends a material bias to the Green Revolution (Yapa, 1979: 372–4).

In considering the adoption package with regard to its landlord or peasant basis, *institutional aspects* also are important. Gotsch (1972), for example, shows that the *tubewell*, a labor-augmenting innovation, had dramatically different impacts on the income distribution and social organization of two agriculturally similar areas in different institutional settings, one in Bangladesh and one in Pakistan.[9] Specifically, the Bangladesh study area is characterized by smaller farms, a fairly equal distribution of land among the population and grass roots organizations that operate as coopera- tives in agricultural matters; while the Pakistan study area is characterized by larger landholdings on the average, an unequal distribution of land among the population so that there are some very large landholdings and many small ones and service organiza- tions that feature a *top down* mode of operation and favor the larger landholdings. Accordingly, in the Bangladesh study area the tubewell's income impacts were more evenly distributed and the egalitarian nature of social organizations was strengthened, whereas in the Pakistan study area social class disparities in terms of both income and power were aggravated.[10]

In a similar vein, Havens and Flinn (1975: 478) demonstrate the importance of a particular institutional arrangement in the diffusion of Green Revolution innovations in Colombia, arguing that

lack of adoption is partially due to perceived or real institutional blocks to credit availability.

More specifically, they found that lack of credit thwarted more than half the farmers from adopting and thus gaining through adoption rent. In some cases this occurred because the larger-scale farmers

[had] more land to use as collateral . . . [and therefore] greater access to credit than non-adopters. (Havens and Flinn, 1975: 478)

Also, however,

It seems that small scale farmers have 'learned' over a long period of time that credit can only be used by those with greater levels of income and larger acreages. Indeed, [on the basis of this expectation] the small-acreage farmers may not even ask for credit. (Havens and Flinn, 1975: 479)[11]

Institutional characteristics also affect the type of innovation diffused, and in this context, many would argue it is not coincidental that most innovations introduced into Third World settings have been materially biased (Yapa, 1980). One reason is the prevalence of development strategies based on the *dual economy model.* Basically, this involves creating a *modern sector* which is to serve as an agent or catalyst for eroding and transforming the *traditional sector,* and an important component of the modern sector is Developed World technology transplanted into a Third World setting.

Given this exhortation towards modernity defined in developed world terms, it is consistent to promote innovations that are similarly biased, whether they are introduced to the agricultural, commercial or manufacturing sectors of the Third World economy. This tendency is reinforced by the fact that the persons making decisions about which innovations to develop and introduce often are themselves most in tune with the modern sector, or with the social classes that primarily benefit from modern sector activities.[12] The Third World personnel in both national government and international agencies, for example, are generally from the middle- or upper-class stratum of their respective societies.[13]

Finally, there is considerable pressure upon the development missions of nations such as the United States to vigorously promote materially biased innovations among their Third World clientele.

This stems from the fact that materially biased innovations tend to increase or at least maintain the economic dependency of Third World nations on the developed world and its economic enterprises, which translates into profits for nations of the Developed World and positive contributions to their trade balance. To this point, Yapa (1980: 128) shows that developing country imports of manufactured fertilizer increased dramatically from 1971 through 1974, coincident with the propagation of Green Revolution technology.

The observations throughout this section underline the fact that a given innovation is not adopted in isolation of one's social, economic, locational and institutional context, or, said another way, that each innovation has associated with it a specific social, economic, locational and institutional *niche* within which diffusion is likely. In the case of an adoption package such as the Green Revolution, then, the diffusion of any one of its innovations generally will be limited to that niche of characteristics which is common to all elements of the package.[14] Accordingly, understanding the distribution of adoption rents might involve considering the diffusion of two or more innovations and their interrelationship(s). This is addressed in the following subsection.

Another consideration relevant to the *diffusion niche* is the distribution and/or ubiquity of infrastructures which affect the utility of innovations. It was shown in Chapter 7, for example, that the diffusion of commercial agriculture in Third World settings depends upon adequate transportation, marketing and warehousing infrastructures which are not everywhere available. Likewise, the diffusion of many consumer innovations in Third World settings is limited by the distribution of energy infrastructures. It is government or entrepreneurial agencies which generally provide these infrastructures and their actions reflect both the overall level of development and the prevailing development strategy.[15] Pages 266–70 of this chapter address this aspect of diffusion.

Innovation Diffusion in a Rural Hinterland and Its Consequences: A Theoretical Analysis. Attention now turns to three hypothetical situations which embody a number of the structural elements discussed above. One objective in examining these is to illustrate by some simple analyses the differential effects of structural elements on adoption rents and on other consequences of innovation diffusion. A second objective is to illustrate how the diffusion of one innovation interrelates with the diffusion of another.

To give these situations a real world reference, they are discussed in terms of actual cash crop innovations. One of these is the commercial cultivation of grains. The second innovation is Green Revolution technologies which pertain to the commercial raising of grains. Generally, some elements of the Green Revolution technology are infrastructure independent such as the high-yielding variety seeds, irrigation and fertilizers. However, pesticides and herbicides usually are delivered and applied by an agency, assumed here to be located in the nearby market center, which renders an infrastructure constraint to the total package.[16]

As a *first* situation, assume that farmers surrounding the market center have previously adopted and currently engage in the commercial cultivation of grains from O, the market center, outwards to E_1 in Figure 8.2A, where E_1 is beyond the infrastructure penetration boundary I. That is, the *production shed* for commercial grains extends from O to E_1, and $O-E_1 > O-I$. Prior to the Green Revolution innovation, the per unit costs of production are P_1, the per unit costs of producing and shipping the grain to the market are PT_1, and the market price is MP_1, yielding a conventional location rent MP_1-PT_1 that decreases with distance from the market center.[17]

With introduction of the Green Revolution technology, adoption occurs out to the infrastructure penetration boundary over the range $O-I$, resulting in a reduction of per unit production and production plus transport costs to P_2 and PT_2 respectively. The adoption of the Green Revolution technology also results in either an increase in total yield or, if yield remains the same, in unused factors of production. If there is additional yield and the market absorbs it at the current price, MP_1, then the farmers within the infrastructure penetration boundary enjoy an additional return of magnitude P_1-P_2 (or PT_1-PT_2) which constitutes an adoption rent! Alternatively, if there is additional yield and the market adjusts to supply conditions by lowering its price to MP_2, the farmers within the infrastructure penetration boundary will enjoy an adoption rent only until this adjustment occurs. However, farmers at the *production frontier* or the farthest edge of the original production shed, in the range E_2-E_1, will be forced out of the commercial raising of grains, that is, they will in effect disadopt (!), and the new production shed will extend only over the range O to E_2. Finally, if the farmers adopting the Green Revolution technology maintain preadoption yields by not fully employing their factors of production, they will still enjoy an adoption rent of magnitude P_1-P_2 since the market price would remain at MP_1. Further, however, those farmers might apply their unused factors of production to another, perhaps innovative activity

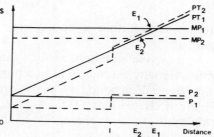

A Infrastructure-Constrained Diffusion: Economic Activity Extends Beyond an Infrastructure Penetration Boundary

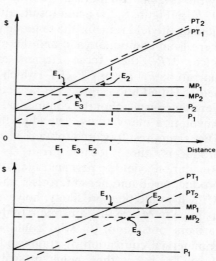

B Infrastructure-Constrained Diffusion: Economic Activity Does Not Extend to the Infrastructure Penetration Boundary

C Infrastructure-Independent Diffusion

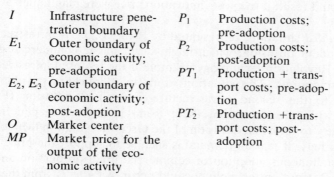

I	Infrastructure penetration boundary	P_1	Production costs; pre-adoption
E_1	Outer boundary of economic activity; pre-adoption	P_2	Production costs; post-adoption
E_2, E_3	Outer boundary of economic activity; post-adoption	PT_1	Production + transport costs; pre-adoption
O	Market center	PT_2	Production + transport costs; post-adoption
MP	Market price for the output of the economic activity		

Figure 8.2 The Effect of Innovation Diffusion upon the Spatial Extent of Ongoing Economic Activity and Associated Adoption Rents in a Rural Hinterland

from which further adoption rents or windfall profits might be gained!

As a *second* situation, assume that the commercial cultivation of grains initially extends only to a point which is inside the infrastructure penetration boundary, that is, from O, the market center, to E_1 in Figure 8.2B, so that $O-E_1 < O-I$. By arguments similar to those employed above, the adoption of the Green Revolution technology by the original commercial grain farmers (those located in the range $O-E_1$ in Figure 8.2B) again results either in an increase in their total yield or, if yield remains the same, in unused factors of production. If there is an additional yield and the market absorbs it at the current price, MP_1, then these farmers enjoy an additional return of magnitude P_1-P_2 (or PT_1-PT_2) which constitutes an adoption rent, as before. In addition, however, farmers within the range E_1-E_2 might simultaneously adopt the commercial raising of grains and the Green Revolution innovations, extending the grain production shed to E_2! The same result would obtain if the original commercial grain producers, those located from O to E_1, maintained pre-Green Revolution yields, perhaps employing their unused factors of production in another enterprise, and the market price remained at MP_1. It would be more likely, however, that the market would lower its price to MP_2 as an adjustment to the additional supply provided by farmers outside of E_1 who could now simultaneously adopt the commercial cultivation of grains and the Green Revolution innovations. The result, then, would be an extension of the grain production frontier only to E_3, yielding a production shed $(O-E_3)$ which is more extensive than the initial shed $(O-E_1)$ but less extensive than the shed that would result if the post-innovation price were maintained at MP_1 $(O-E_2)$.

The *third* situation, represented by Figure 8.2C, is infrastructure-independent diffusion, which might occur in the commercial grain/ Green Revolution technology example if the required infrastructure were ubiquitous. This situation would be identical in possible outcomes to the second infrastructure-constrained diffusion (Figure 8.2B) with one exception; there is no infrastructure penetration boundary to limit the diffusion of the Green Revolution technology. Accordingly, if market demand is such as to support the price MP_1, the simultaneous adoption of commercial grain production and the Green Revolution technology could occur as far as E_2 from the market center, whereas E_3 would be the limit if the price drops to MP_2. Both these points, however, are beyond the distance E_1, the location of the infrastructure penetration boundary in Figure 8.2A and 8.2B.

Taken together, these three hypothetical situations illustrate the effects of a number of structural characteristics upon innovation diffusion and its consequences. *First* consider distance from the market center. This can be seen as a surrogate for a variety of individual or place attributes that pertain to the expected time of adoption and the consequent enjoyment of adoption rent or windfall gains. Examples of such attributes include size of the economic enterprise, wealth, social connections, age or educational level. In all three of the hypothetical situations represented in Figure 8.2, no matter what the other structural characteristics, persons closest to the market center adopted earlier and enjoyed greater location and adoption rents! The generalization from this, supported by empirical evidence such as that discussed in the preceding sections of this chapter, is that real world diffusion systems consistently favor potential adopters with certain individual attributes, thus leading to the élitist entrenchment we so often see in Third World settings.

A *second* structural characteristic is the type of innovation diffused. In all three examples, the innovation of commercial grain production awarded greater returns, in the form of conventional location rents, to those with the individual attribute of being closer to the market center. Likewise, in all three examples the innovation of the Green Revolution technology was only adoptable by those within the reach of the infrastructure. Yet, if a farmer was within that reach but not located so as to economically produce and deliver grain to the market (for example, the farmers located between E_2 and I in Figure 8.2B), that farmer would not adopt the Green Revolution. Thus, both innovations are biased towards a certain diffusion niche.

A *third* structural characteristic pertains to the market, an institutional aspect which controls the expansion or contraction of the diffusion niche in the examples examined here. The market's price elasticity of demand determines how much grain can be produced, which in turn determines how many persons with which attributes can participate in that enterprise. Thus, in the situation portrayed in Figure 8.2A, a movement of price to MP_2, after the Green Revolution innovation, contracts the diffusion niche and thus forces some farmers out of grain production (those located between E_2 and E_1). Alternatively, in the situations portrayed in Figure 8.2B and 8.2C, if the price remains at MP_1 after the Green Revolution innovation, or even if it moves lower to MP_2, the diffusion niche is expanded and a wider variety of persons participate in commercial grain production. Whether the diffusion niche is contracted or expanded, however, the more privileged, those closest to the market in the present examples, continue to experience the greatest windfall gains, and it is the marginal members of society, those at or near the production frontier, that are affected by shifts in the diffusion niche!

Infrastructure is a *fourth* structural component of these examples. Its extent might reflect the actions of a diffusion agency in the market center or the level of development of the region. The effect of infrastructure in limiting the extent of diffusion is evident by comparing the infrastructure-constrained examples (Figures 8.2A and 8.2B) with the infrastructure-independent one (Figure 8.2C). Nevertheless, the situation portrayed in Figure 8.2A suggests that the infrastructure barrier can be bypassed if market demand is sufficient to support the costs of doing so.

These examples indicate that the rich get richer and the poor get poorer through innovation diffusion. While the popular notion has often been otherwise, research suggests that this is in large part the case in Third World settings. The diffusion of agricultural cooperatives in Sierra Leone provides further evidence to the point.

Structural Characteristics and Diffusion: Agricultural Cooperatives in Sierra Leone.[18] There are many different types of agricultural cooperatives in Sierra Leone, but two—thrift-credit and marketing societies—comprise about 95 per cent of the total number at the mid-1960s. The popularity of the thrift and credit cooperatives lay in the fact that they are relevant to a wide slice of the rural population, including a high proportion of women and less well-off people who sell privately grown crops in small quantities. The marketing cooperatives also are highly accessible, including many small-scale agriculturalists in their memberships (Riddell, 1970). These provide economies of scale for individual farmers which enable low-cost, high-yield produciton via mechanical cultivation; the marketing of products at substantially higher prices through bulk selling; and, in general, increased access to resources and the means of production. In a broader context, cooperatives acted as an important accelerator for economic development by supporting productive investment, eliminating some middleman functions and successfully abolishing the high rural indebtedness caused by the existing money-lending system (Karr and Bangura, 1968; Riddell, 1970).

Of concern here is the establishment and spread of the cooperatives, viewing them as diffusion agencies, rather than the processes by which individuals gained membership and participation. More specifically, this provides a Third World example of *diffusion agency establishment under a decentralized decision-making structure with a coordinating propagator*. This is so in that each cooperative generally was established by different sets of individuals independently of one another, but the government provided incentives and impulses to induce cooperative establishment in a systematic fashion which favored some areas more than others.

The Cooperative Movement was initiated in the 1930s when the Department of Agriculture organized a few societies in the Northern Province with the purpose of promoting rice cultivation and marketing. These cooperatives resulted in greater quantities of high-quality output which obtained up to 28 per cent higher prices in the export market than would have been achieved in local trade. Consequently, farmers in surrounding areas demanded the creation of cooperatives, resulting in a contagion-type diffusion. This was aborted by the Second World War when markets were cut off and even the existing cooperatives ceased functioning (R.E. Johnston, 1968: 114–15).

In 1946 a group of educated Africans formed the Sierra Leone Organization Society in an effort to revive the Cooperative Movement. Although this group both spread the concept of cooperative action and established cooperatives in remote districts, the cooperatives tended to exist as independent entities without affecting surrounding areas (R.E. Johnston, 1968:116–18).

Sustained growth of the Cooperative Movement began with the appointment of a Registrar of Cooperative Societies in 1948 and the creation of the Department of Cooperatives in 1949. Both had the function of actively promoting cooperative development and greatly accelerated cooperative establishment. An even greater increase occurred in 1952–5 with the government's policy of accelerated expansion that created training programs for cooperative personnel (R.E. Johnston, 1968: 171). Nevertheless, development was damp-ened by capital scarcity and a lack of qualified personnel to meet the demand for cooperatives (Bangura, 1965). For these reasons, only selected parts of the country were assisted in cooperative development, primarily where the authorities *believed* cooperatives had the best prospects of solving regional problems and where the demand was greatest. Also, the Department of Cooperatives preferred to promote cooperatives in areas adjacent to already established societies to make the most efficient use of the limited personnel. Thus, the areal expansion of cooperatives occurred only as fast as staff availability permitted (R.E. Johnston, 1968: 168), and that expansion which did occur tended to be focused on several core areas from which there was only a gradual spread outward.

These core areas of focus were dominated by the Mende people. This may be entirely fortuitous, owing to their location in the geographic areas that were environmentally suitable to the specific cash crops which the government propagators had decided to encourage. It also may represent favoritism, owing to the fact that the African positions in the colonial and post-colonial government were dominated by Mende. In any case, whether intrinsically correct or not, the Mende also were regarded as more receptive to modernization, or more *innovative*, than other ethnic groups. This quality has been attributed in part to their long contact with the commercial activities of Lebanese and Syrian traders in the cash crop regions, and it is supported by the observation that many Mende chiefs played a direct role in molding the population's receptivity to cocoa cultivation and the new cooperatives (Van der Laan, 1975: 58).[19] Also to this point, Van der Laan (1975: 58) notes

Many farmers had been away during the war, for instance soldiers in Burma, and they returned to their villages with new ideas and a new sense of their rights. Also, many farmers had observed the Lebanese for so long that they knew pretty well what mattered in the produce trade.

In terms of process, then, the Cooperative Department and other government entities served as coordinating propagators, encouraging cooperative establishment in selected areas where the utility and receptivity towards cooperatives was believed to be greatest. This led to an initial clustering of cooperatives in southern and south-eastern Sierra Leone, where the Mende people dominated and where climate, terrain and other ecological conditions were conducive to cash crop agriculture. Within this constraint, the spread of information about cooperatives through interpersonal communications also was important in molding the receptivity of the population.

The temporal trend in cooperative establishment for the whole of Sierra Leone may be interpreted either as conforming to the S-curve empirical regularity or as representing a more linear trend (Figure 8.3A). In viewing such graphs for the district level, however, the S-curve is more evident (Figure 8.3B).[20] There are two apparent inflection points—in the middle 1950s and in the early 1960s. These correspond with two government efforts to promote cooperative action and to train cooperative personnel, the first in 1950–5 and the second initiated in 1960 (R. E Johnston, 1968: 149).

These graphs also indicate a significant variation in the time order of adoption among districts and more particularly that the districts of south and south-east Sierra Leone, compared to other parts of the

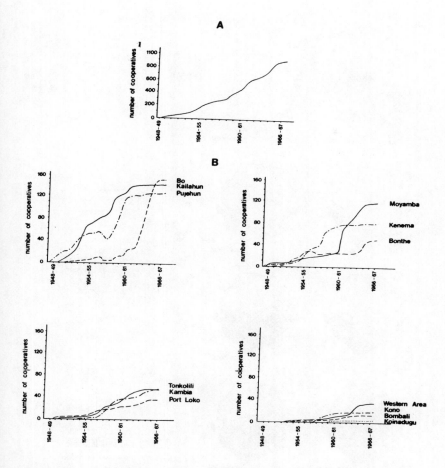

Figure 8.3 The Growth of the Cooperative Movement in Sierra Leone (A) and by District (B), 1948–67

country, established cooperatives earlier and had established more cooperatives by 1967. To gain further insight into the spatial pattern of diffusion, a series of maps for selected years was prepared (Figure 8.4). The early diffusion in the southern and south-eastern districts of Kailahun and Pujehun apparently occurred because of their favorable ecological conditions for cash crops and because they are areas where the Mende influence was extremely strong. The importance of both these factors is further illustrated by the fact that there is a significantly smaller number of cooperatives established once the diffusion wave moves beyond the borders of the areas of major Mende concentrations into areas dominated by the Temne and into

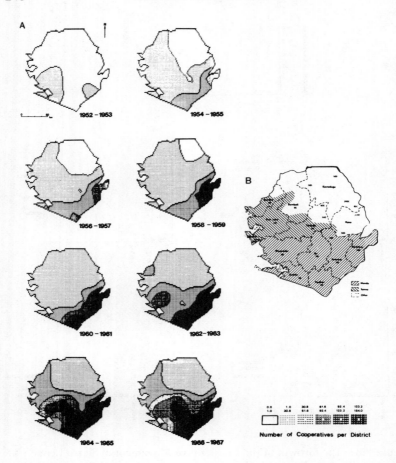

Figure 8.4A The Diffusion of the Cooperative Movement in
Sierra Leone at Selected Years
     B District Map of Sierra Leone showing the Major Ethnic
Groups and Average Geographical height (m above sea-level)

areas of higher elevation, a surrogate for ecological suitability for
cash crop agriculture.

More generally, there appear to be two diffusion nodes (Pujehun
and Kailahun) from which a wave-like or neighborhood-type
diffusion pattern emerges. A hierarchical pattern of diffusion is of
course not expected since we are dealing with an agricultural
innovation and areas with primarily lower-order centers. Yet it is
noteworthy that the origins of the Cooperative Movement are in

areas that are located rather far from Freetown, the capital city. It would not be unreasonable to hypothesize otherwise, that is, that even though the innovation is only relevant for rural areas it might be more likely to originate in the rural hinterland of Freetown or of another major urban center. Instead, if there is a hierarchy effect at all, it is a reverse one directed from more rural areas towards less rural areas in proximity to the major city.

The cartographical and historical analyses indicate that more agricultural cooperatives are found in areas with lower relief, a high percentage of Mende population and in proximity to the original diffusion nodes of Pujehun and Kailahun. To develop this lead in greater detail, statistical analyses were employed with independent variables representing three dimensions: information linkages and exposure to the innovation, the need for or relevance of agricultural cooperatives in a given locale and the entrepreneurship or innovativeness of the population in a given locale.

In distinguishing between chiefdoms with cooperatives and those without, it was found that relevant factors were the need for or relevance of the cooperative and the entrepreneurship or innovativeness of the population. These, then, appear to constitute threshold conditions for diffusion agency establishment. Among those chiefdoms that met these conditions and had cooperatives, the time order of establishment was related to the level of information and exposure to the cooperative idea and, again, the entrepreneurship or innovativeness of the population. These findings are in conformance with the conjectures of contemporary theory pertaining to diffusion agency establishment under a decentralized decision-making structure, as discussed in Chapter 3.

The problem becomes more interesting, however, when the role of the government is contemplated. It provided training programs for cooperative personnel, promotional stimuli and other incentives for establishing cooperatives. The effect of these programs is evident in the temporal trend of the diffusion wherein upward spurts in the establishment of cooperatives correspond with increased effort by the government.

As stated previously, however, incentives were not offered uniformly to all parts of the country. Because of capital scarcity and a shortage of qualified personnel, a spatial strategy was devised favoring areas located in proximity to already established cooperatives and areas where the utility of and receptivity towards the cooperative would be greatest. As implemented, this policy favored chiefdoms in south and south-eastern Sierra Leone where climate, terrain and other ecological conditions were seen as most conducive to cash crop agriculture and where the major ethnic group was the Mende who were regarded as more receptive to modernization (innovative) than other ethnic groups. The effects of this strategy are evident in the spatial pattern of diffusion which exhibits marked neighborhood effects, higher levels of cooperative establishment in Mende Country, and almost no cooperatives in the north of Sierra Leone.

Thus, considering the government's role together with the findings of the statistical analyses raises an important chicken-and-egg question. Entrepreneurship or innovativeness is an essential quality according to most theories of development and innovation adoption, and indeed, this factor was shown to be significant by our statistical analyses. *But,* is more education and the number of Mende people really representative of innovativeness, *or* do these kinds of people adopt earlier because the government used these characteristics as criteria for meting out incentives?[21] Similar questions have been raised above in this chapter (pages 234–6) and in other contexts. With regard to the two-step flow of communications model, for example, M.A. Brown, Maxson and Brown (1977: 23) note

[This] communications strategy implicitly segments its market in favor of the more progressive farmer, thereby reinforcing income differentials. This practice has traditionally been justified on the basis of the innovativeness of such persons, but this paper as well as other recent research has questioned this assumption, pointing out that diffusion agency strategies and differential access to institutional resources are often more important determinants of who adopts when.

Considering further that the early cooperatives in Sierra Leone were in the north and in remote scattered areas, instead of in the south, raises the possibility that the government played a distinct discriminating role, albeit inadvertently, by knighting some locales and some types of people as innovative or of high entrepreneurship!

In making this point it is recognized that a spatial allocation system is necessary, given scarce resources. Nevertheless, it remains important to examine critically the prevailing allocation systems employed in diffusion programs of the Third World, such as that controlling the establishment of cooperatives in Sierra Leone. This theme, or exhortation, underlies much of the discussion in this chapter, and will be returned to in Chapter 9 on the policy implications of the material in this book.

One important question not addressed by this study of agricultural cooperatives in Sierra Leone is the adoption of the cooperative by individual users and the innovation establishment strategies related thereto. On the basis of other studies and the observations of earlier sections of this chapter, it is anticipated that the differential treatment of chiefdoms noted in the present study also would be found among individuals. Accordingly, it is important to examine further the actions of diffusion agencies and governments in Third World settings in order to identify the ways in which potential adopters are differentially treated and the resulting effects.

Finally, the diffusion of agricultural cooperatives ought to affect the development paths of the various regions of Sierra Leone. A likely outcome, for example, would be an increase in the economic disparities among regions, particularly in comparing the favored south under Mende dominance with the north under Temne dominance. This and other considerations pertaining to the regional impact of diffusion processes are now given further attention.

The Regional Impact of Innovation Diffusion

That diffusion is an important aspect of the evolution of the human landscape has long been recognized, dating at least from the work of the cultural geographers of the earlier part of this century. More current attention has focused on the role of diffusion in the complex process of urban systems growth and regional development (J. C. Miller, 1974, 1979; Pred, 1966, 1977; DeSouza and Porter, 1974; Richardson, 1978; Stohr, 1974; Robson, 1973; Berry, 1972). Inherent in this process is the creation of social and economic inequalities among regions, such as those anticipated from the diffusion of agricultural cooperatives in Sierra Leone. Similarly, Friedmann (1975) observes that regions differ markedly in their economic power, and that innovation diffusion is a primary mechanism by which such differences are created, maintained and exacerbated. Some would say that this imbalance should be tolerated and even encouraged in that it provides the energy for the development process itself (Hirschman, 1958). Others, including this author, have been more concerned with the welfare side of the question.

The various impacts of innovation diffusion in a regional setting are addressed here in terms of three topics. The first is the spatial organization of regions as seen by models of the development process. Attention then turns to the process of development posited by these models and by other, more inductive studies, giving particular attention to the role of diffusion in that process. The final consideration is the spatial patterns associated with the regional impact of innovation diffusion.

Spatial Organization in a Regional Setting as Viewed by Models of the Development Process. The most prevalent paradigm pertaining to development processes in Third World settings has been that of the *dual economy* (Lewis, 1954; Ranis and Fei, 1961; E.A.J. Johnson, 1970). As previously noted, this views developing nations as consisting of a dynamic, growing entrepreneurial, innovative *modern sector* and a stagnant, declining, conservative *traditional sector.* Representative of the modern sector is economic activity characterized by high capital intensity and high productivity, such as modern industry, whereas economic activity characterized by high labor intensity and lower productivity, such as small-scale indigenous agriculture or the *penny capitalism* of periodic markets, is found in the traditional sector.

Although the dual economy model is itself primarily concerned with economic aspects, others, and particularly diffusion researchers, have noted that these sectors also differ in their social norms. Thus, the modern sector is characterized by consumption patterns oriented towards goods produced by contemporary technology and production behavior reflecting a high degree of *economic entrepreneurship, achievement motivation* or innovativeness. By contrast, the traditional sector is characterized by a *subculture of peasantry* or social norms oriented towards maintaining the status quo.[22] In general, then, the traditional sector is comprised of the indigenous culture, and the modern sector incorporates the influence of foreign, primarily Developed World economic practices and social norms.

Important to this discussion is how the dual economy would be manifest on the landscape, that is, how it would look on a map. This frame of reference is not articulated in the model, but it is readily derived in that the modern sector generally would be associated with urban agglomerations and the traditional sector with rural areas and small towns.

The implicit spatial dimension of the dual economy model has been captured at the regional level by Friedmann (1972, 1973; E.A.J. Johnson, 1970; Richardson, 1978; J.C. Miller, 1974, 1979) in his *core–periphery* paradigm.[23] In this, the core dominates the periphery in economic, political and innovative functions, but there also is a symbiotic relationship in that raw materials and staples flow from the periphery to the core, where they are transformed into manufactured goods, part of which are returned to satisfy the needs of the periphery.

However, the periphery is not a homogeneous entity in that parts of it differ in their potential for development. On the one hand, periphery areas may be upward transitional because of their mineral resource endownment, because they are located in proximity to development impulses emanating from the core, or because they are located between two core cities and thus constitute a development corridor. Alternatively, there are periphery areas that are downward transitional because they have a poor or depleted resource base, because they are located far from the centers of economic activity, or because their social norms are exceptionally traditional.

Another spatial expression of the dual economy is the *growth center model*. This is based upon *growth pole theory,* a non-spatial model which notes that industries differ in terms of their multiplier effects and consequent ability to stimulate or give rise to economic growth, and holds, therefore, that investment for development purposes should be directed towards *propulsive* activities (Hansen, 1971). The growth center model, on the other hand, addresses the spatial transmission of growth impulses from urban centers, in which propulsive industries and their related agglomerations generally are located, to the rural hinterlands of those urban centers (Hansen, 1971; Richardson, 1978; Thomas, 1972a, 1972b; E.A.J. Johnson, 1970; J.C. Miller, 1974, 1979).[24]

Thus, the core–periphery and growth center models differ in the level of spatial aggregation to which they apply, that is, the core–periphery model primarily pertains to an interregional setting, and the growth center model primarily pertains to the more local setting of an urban center and its hinterland. However, this same characteristic provides a complementarity. In Brazil, for example, the core is the São Paulo–Rio de Janeiro region, and the periphery is the remainder. However, we can also look at the São Paulo urban area as a growth center and the state of São Paulo as its hinterland (Gauthier, 1968). The concepts also are applicable to the developed world. In the United States, the core or heartland region, until recently, would be represented by the American Manufacturing Belt, which extends from the mid-Atlantic and southern New England states of the east across the expanse of the Great Lakes, and the periphery or hinterland region would be represented by the remaining southern and western portions of the nation. Finally, this latter example also indicates that the core–periphery distinction of Friedmann is parallel to the traditional *heartland–hinterland* distinction.

In addition to this complementarity between the core–periphery and growth center models, they also posit similar processes of growth impulse initiation and dissemination. Attention now turns to this topic.

Diffusion Processes and Regional Development. The models of the dual economy type posit a socio-economic process of development with a distinct spatial component. This process involves the gradual erosion of the traditional sector by expansion of the modern sector or, said another way, the conversion of the traditional sector by modernization impulses emanating from the modern sector. These impulses are sometimes viewed in terms of technological innovation (Pred, 1966); sometimes in terms of entrepreneurial, employment providing, or other organizational entities which are related to urban area growth and regional development (Pred, 1966, 1973a, 1973b, 1974a, 1974b, 1975a, 1975b, 1976, 1977; Robson, 1973; Pedersen, 1975; L.A. Brown, 1968b; Zelinski, 1962); and sometimes more generally as *growth impulses* (Jeffrey, 1970, 1974; King, Casetti and Jeffrey, 1969; Hanham and Brown, 1976).

Another set of impulses pertain to transforming individuals from their *subculture of peasantry* or traditional norms. This is seen to occur through the communication of modern norms, patterns of entrepreneurial behavior, achievement motivation, new ideas and new practices. These are transmitted through the media, through demonstration effects or through interpersonal communications from professional change agents, innovative individuals and opinion leaders.[25] It is in this respect that the diffusion model of the adoption perspective has been an important aspect, to some a cornerstone, of development theory and strategy.

The transmission of these various impulses, or the dynamics of core–periphery and growth center–hinterland relationships, generally involve two types of mechanisms. *Backwash or polarization effects* direct growth impulses to the core or growth center and drain the periphery or hinterland, thus exacerbating the disparity between them. Elements of polarization or backwash effects include movement from the periphery to the core of human capital through migration, physical capital through the trade of raw materials or staples, and monetary capital through the purchase of manufactured goods or investment in core area activities. This type of movement is countered by *spread or trickle-down effects* which direct growth impulses to the periphery or hinterland, thus reducing regional disparities. One element of spread or trickle-down effects is capital flows arising from the trade of raw materials and staples to the core. Also important are capital flows through the labor force, either in the form of wages paid to commuters residing in the periphery or remittances to family members in the periphery from workers residing in the core. Another element of spread or trickle-down effects is the diffusion of technical advancements and skills to the periphery. Finally, entrepreneurial activities which generate growth multipliers might be located in the periphery.

Evidence indicates that polarization effects have far outweighed trickle-down effects in growth pole or core–periphery situations, thus leading to the extreme regional disparities characterizing Third World nations today. This may not be surprising in view of the deteriorating terms of trade for the periphery as compared to the core and the marked agglomeration economies associated with the core or growth center. The low level of infrastructure development and the consequent lack of spatial integration of the Third World economy also is a contributing factor.[26]

With regard to growth impulse initiation, therefore, it is generally agreed that whenever the reason for the initial expansion of the core region or growth center,

thereafter cumulatively expanding internal and external economies would fortify its growth at the expense of other areas. (Hansen, 1971: 26)

This occurrence can be understood in terms of the market and infrastructure perspective on innovation diffusion (L.A. Brown, 1974). In using this approach, a growth-inducing (economic) activity would be seen as the equivalent of a diffusion agency. Accordingly, its ultimate location would be one of several alternatives representing peaks on a profitability surface. Considering the temporal as well as the spatial dimension, however, leads to the conclusion that core areas or growth centers would appear as *increasingly* attractive peaks on the profitability surface because the location there of some economic activities would lead to agglomeration economies and a build-up of infrastructure and other public goods, which would lead to more economic activity and so on. Another part of the attractiveness of the core area or growth center would be an associated increase in labor force skills and in the population's capability of becoming aware of and exploiting economic opportunities. This increase in innovativeness, entrepreneurial ability and achievement motivation would in turn lead to an increased likelihood for locally spawned economic entities and innovations. Thus, there is a *circular and cumulative* process by which the core area or growth center maintains and fortifies its position and generates growth impulses at increasing levels.[27]

Said another way, the regional impacts of diffusion processes operate in a manner such that (1) the growth-inducing mechanism is created or installed in a given region and not others; (2) that region

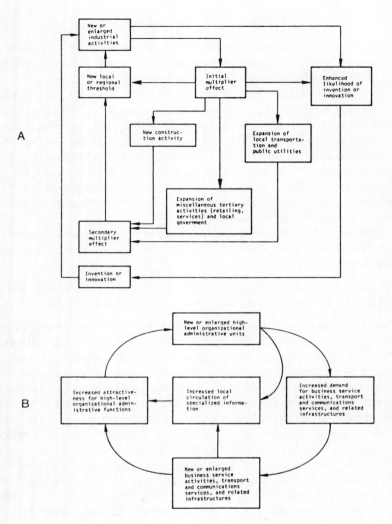

Figure 8.5 The Circular and Cumulative Effect in Regional Development for Industrial Activities and Innovations (A) and for Organizational Headquarters (B) After Pred, 1977: 90 and 117

then enjoys windfall gains or adoption rents which increase its level of economic well-being relative to other regions; (3) all of which leads to the attraction of other growth-inducing entities, additional invention or adoption of growth-inducing innovations, and, accordingly, further increases in regional disparities (Pedersen, 1975; Robson, 1973; Pred, 1966). Thus, consistent with the core–periphery and growth pole models, there is a circular and cumulative effect, as shown in Figure 8.5A for industrial activities and innovations and in Figure

8.5B for organizational headquarters (which are seen by Pred (1977) to be a major initiator of growth impulses).

Illustrative of this conceptual perspective is Friedmann's (1975: 278) observations relating spatial diffusion to the distribution of economic power among regions.

The adoption of innovations, and particularly of entrepreneurial innovations, *translates directly into an increase of effective power by the adopting unit over portions of its environment.* The firm adopting a corporate structure may push more traditionally organized competitors out of business; or the manufacturer introducing a piece of new machinery may improve the quality of his product (or lower his costs), capturing a larger share of the market. The cumulation of entrepreneurial innovations in a given city—the city being conceived as a spatially integrated subsystem of society—will therefore lead not only to its accelerated economic and demographic growth, but also to the consolidation of its hierarchical control over that portion of the urban system that has failed to adopt this particular set of innovations. Such a concentration of innovations in cities that have a high propensity for further innovation, produces the well known phenomenon of core regions that extend their control over the dependent peripheries of the country and, in some cases, abroad. The basic relations in the spatial distribution of economic power are thus seen to be an immediate outcome of the diffusion of innovations.

For an account of this process in a broader scale and an indication of how inequalities are inherently linked with the regional development process, consider the work of Pedersen (1975) on urban system and regional development in South America. He suggests a four-phase scheme, paraphrased below and summarized in Figure 8.6.

1 The first phase is a traditional society characterized by independent villages, little or no specialization, and poor transportation and communications. Little or no technological innovation occurs, but what does occur spreads in a neighborhood effect fashion from village to village. Throughout this phase, there is some specialization in traditional lines of production, and these lead to low-level multiplier effects, the dominant growth mechanism. Regional income differences are minor.

2 The second phase of Pedersen's conceptualization begins with the emergence of a dominant urban center which is of relatively high accessibility, the focal point of much trade and a locus of innovation. This leads into an urban system comprised of a few sizeable towns, where there is only one town in each size class, and many smaller towns of approximately the same size. There also is specialization of production among cities, and a more complex transportation and communications system focused upon the dominant urban centers. While multiplier effect growth still occurs, growth related to innovation diffusion dominates by the end of this phase. This spreads in a hierarchical fashion among the larger cities and in a neighborhood effect fashion among the smaller cities. Marked regional disparities appear, particularly in comparing the largely urban regions with those characterized by small towns and a rural economy.

PHASES

	I	II	III	IV
The innovation process	Little innovation and neighborhood effect diffusion	Significant innovation and both neighborhood effect and hierarchial diffusion	Significant innovation and hierarchial diffusion	Conscious research and development
Growth mechanisms	Multiplier effect	Innovation diffusion		Spill-over effects
The urban system	Independent villages	An emerging urban hierarchy	A mature urban system with a rank-size distribution of towns	A system of urban fields
Degree of specialization in economic activity	None	Specialization between cities of different size	Specialization between cities of same size	High level of specialization
Transport and communication network	Undeveloped network. Equally bad access in all directions	Multi-purpose network focussed on the dominant urban centers	Highly connected inter-urban network	Specialized transport and communication networks

Figure 8.6   Phases of Urban System and Regional Development in South
America
After Pederson, 1975: 108

3   The third phase features the emergence of a relatively mature urban
system with a continual distribution of town sizes and several towns in
each size class. Increased specialization in production and a highly
connected transportation and communications system also emerges.
Innovation diffusion, operating now in a completely hierarchical fashion,
remains a dominant growth mechanism, but of increasing importance is
the concentration of ongoing economic activites in growing regions, which
Pedersen terms spillover effects. Multiplier effect growth continues, but
constitutes a relatively minor element. Regional disparities also persist.
4   In the fourth phase of Pedersen's conceptualization, urban-related endeavors penetrate into nearby rural hinterlands to form sizeable fields of
integrated activity. In accordance with this, there is an increase in economic specialization and the emergence of specialized transportation and
communications networks. Spillover effects now dominate as a growth
mechanism, innovation diffusion is of second importance and multiplier
effects are least important. There also is a conscious effort in research and
development which thus becomes another growth mechanism.

Observations such as Pedersen's provide a general account of the
regional impacts of diffusion processes, but they do not address the
specific mechanisms which transmit and channel these impulses.
Efforts directed towards this concern generally focus on *spatial
economic structure,* holding that the spread of growth (or recession)

impulses depends upon the intra- and interlocational linkages within and between economic sectors.

One way to visualize the workings of these linkages is through an interregional input–output table (Richardson, 1972, 1978). According to this, (1) the growth or recession of an industry in region i will have direct and indirect effects upon that and other industries in the same and other regions, and (2) the nature of these effects will depend upon what industries in which locations provide inputs to each other's production process. Thus, if the cotton textile industry in São Paulo, Brazil (and its environs) is growing at a rapid rate, the larger São Paulo region is also likely to exhibit increased growth since its cotton farms provide an important input. Alternatively, little if any benefit would accrue to the largely mining region of Minas Gerais, which does not have a strong structural linkage to textile production, or to the north-east region of Brazil which primarily grows long-fibre cotton for export and is only weakly linked to the cotton textile industry of São Paulo. Accordingly, the regions of Minas Gerais and the north-east would lag, relatively, in economic development.

It is expected, of course, that the patterning of these interregional linkages would be congruent with the pattern of core–periphery or growth center–hinterland relationships. Nevertheless, it has been difficult to directly study the interrelationships between spatial economic structure, diffusion and regional development because suitable interregional input–output data is rarely available. To bypass this bottleneck, some researchers have taken a shift-share approach in which regional growth or decline is a function of three elements: a national growth factor which affects all regions equally; an industrial mix growth factor which affects regions differentially according to whether they have strong representation in growing or declining industries; and a local competition growth factor which affects regions differentially according to local qualities such as the innovativeness or resourcefulness of the population (Berry and Horton, 1970: 98–9; Paris, 1970; Berry, 1967). Representative of this approach is the study by Casetti, King and Jeffrey (1971) which examines the spread of economic cycle effects, measured by unemployment from 1960 through 1965, as a function of the industrial structure of 140 United States SMSAs or labor market areas.

Pred (1973a, 1974a, 1974b, 1975a, 1975b, 1976, 1977) has proposed another way of implementing the spatial economic structure perspective in examining the regional impacts of diffusion processes. This focuses on the spatial structure of multilocational organizations in both the public and private sectors, that is, organizations composed of a number of spatially separated and functionally differentiated units. As Pred states (1976: 153–54),

With flow-data and input-output options closed, probably the best means of gaining insight into the economic dependencies and channels of growth transmission operating within the city system . . . is through examining the spatial structure of multilocational organizations . . . [that is] insofar as multilocational organizations control the lion's share of any advanced economy, they are the overwhelmingly most important propagators of flows of goods, services, economic information, and capital; hence, the predominant source of interdependencies within the national city-system; and, hence, clearly the most important generators of interurban growth transmission.

One point remains to be considered under the topic of this subsection, 'Diffusion Processes and Regional Development'. In theory, core–periphery, heartland–hinterland, or growth center–hinterland differences should dissolve as development progresses. The evidence from the Third World, however, indicates that polarization effects have far outweighed trickle-down effects, resulting in marked concentrations of economic power in core regions and marked disparities between core regions and their respective peripheries. On what basis short of revolution, then, could one argue that this trend of the Third World will be reversed?

One approach is through the *product life cycle of industrial development,* which has contributed to the breakdown of the heartland–hinterland distinction in the United States over the past three decades.[28] Recalling the economic history perspective on diffusion (Chapter 6), a new process and invention initially requires relatively large numbers of engineers and skilled workers in the production process. In a second phase of the cycle, the manufacturing process becomes sufficiently routine that mass production techniques may be introduced and production can take place in locations other than the center of invention. Finally, as the industry becomes fully mature, much of the production is assigned to highly specialized machines primarily requiring unskilled labor. At this point, then, production is more economical in peripheral areas with a surplus of cheap labor, and a movement to such areas is to be expected.[29]

Factors other than the product life cycle also would be important in bringing about a spinoff or outward diffusion of growth-related activities to hinterland locations. These would include the existence of agglomeration diseconomies associated with overcrowded and congested conditions in the core cities, leading to increasing land, labor, production and living costs. Also important would be changes in the periphery brought about by the proliferation of communications and other infrastructure as development progresses, leading to a greater level of spatial and economic integration, expanding markets (both internal and external) and the diffusion of technical knowledge and skills. Eventually, then, imbalances brought about by conditions such as these would set off a circular and cumulative process of growth whereby certain periphery locations come to be characterized by their own agglomeration and other scale economies and, ultimately, core–periphery differences dissolve.[30]

Having examined spatial organization in a regional setting as viewed by models of development, and the processes related to growth impulse initiation and dissemination in a regional setting, attention now turns to the geographer's concern with the spatial patterns characterizing these phenomena.

Spatial Patterns and the Regional Impact of Innovation Diffusion. Whether regional development has been approached abstractly in terms of either a *core–periphery* or *growth center model;* or inductively in terms of the *invention or adoption of growth-inducing technological innovations,* the *establishment of growth-inducing entrepreneurial or other organizational entities,* the *spread of growth impulses* or *spatial economic structure*—there has been a good deal of concern with spatial patterns. Furthermore, this concern has been rather pervasive, including among its adherents economists, planners and persons actively implementing regional development policy in all parts of the world, as well as geographers.

Addressing the spatial patterning of innovation diffusion and its regional impacts generally has involved the assumption that diffusion into a rural hinterland (and related impacts) occurs in a neighborhood-effect or wave-like pattern and that diffusion through an urban system primarily exhibits a hierarchy effect pattern.[31] Illustrative in this regard is the conceptualization of Pedersen, outlined immediately above (pages 257–8). Likewise, Berry (1972: 136) states

Growth occurs as a consequence of the filtering of innovations downward through the urban hierarchy and the spread of use of the innovations among consumers residing within the urban fields of the adopting centers.

Operational expressions generally employ a gravity model type formulation in which population sizes guide the hierarchical movement, and distance between towns or regions guides the neighborhood effect flows. Examples include models by Berry (1972),

262 INNOVATION DIFFUSION

presented in Chapter 2 (pages 25–6); Pedersen (1970, 1975), presented in Chapter 3 (70–2); Hanham and Brown (1976) and Robson (1973). There also are studies which only examine the spread of growth impulses outward from an urban center into its hinterland, positing that the strength of the growth impulses declines with distance from the dominant urban center (Morrill, 1968, 1970, 1974). An example is the study of Casetti, King and Odland (1971) which examines employment changes for several urban centers in the hinterland of Los Angeles.

Recently, however, this practice of examining regional development in terms of supposed spatial patterns has been sharply criticized. Exemplary in this regard is the work of Pred (1973b, 1974a, 1974b, 1975a, 1975b, 1976, 1977). After examining intra-organizational interactions for multilocational businesses head-quartered in seven cities of the western United States, he concludes (Pred, 1977: 165–66)

[evidence] would seem to indicate that the hinterland-spread and hierarchical-diffusion assumptions . . . concerning the spatial transmission of growth are both over-simple and flagrantly incorrect . . . observed deviations are so great that it seems safe to suggest that *only under quite unusual conditions can there be a firm basis for the assumption that growth is transmitted solely via hierarchical diffusion from cities of a given size to less populous nearby centres.*[32]

A similar conclusion is reached by L.A. Brown and Malecki (1977), drawing upon the analyses of expected diffusion patterns presented in Chapters 3 and 4 above, the study of the diffusion of the bank credit card presented in Chapter 3 (pages 74–9), and Pred's empirical findings. They also chart a direction for future research on the spatial patterning of innovation diffusion and its regional impacts (1977: 222)

to account for the diffusion underpinnings of [human] landscape evolution, the simplistic population and distance notions of traditional diffusion models are not adequate. The goal we must aim for, instead, is a more comprehensive [and substantively specific] model. . . . However, in deriving this model it appears certain that we must look towards the organizational decision making process, which often involves turning to the unique institutional setting in which such decisions are made. This would seem to require more case studies [such as those by Pred, Robson, Pedersen and the ones presented in this book] . . . with an emphasis on qualitative as well as quantitative analysis.[33]

These conclusions by Pred, Brown and Malecki are based on evidence from advanced economies such as the Untied States, and it is conceivable that the emergence of hierarchical and neighborhood effect patterns would be more likely in Third World settings with less complex transmission structures. Even if this is the case, however, it remains essential to understand the substantive processes underlying diffusion aspects of regional development in the Third World. One reason is because the transmission structure will grow increasingly complex as development progresses, but, more importantly, the actual process might be quite different from what one might conclude from merely matching expected and observed patterns.

In the diffusion of agricultural cooperatives in Sierra Leone (pages 244–51 above), for example, the predisposition of the government, and related actions, arguably were responsible for the early adoption by the Mende, rather than their inherent innovativeness. Likewise, it is plausible that the neighborhood effect patterns of diffusion resulted from the scarcity of development resources and resulting government policies, rather than the interpersonal communications process posited by traditional models of diffusion. As a more general example, consider the finding that greater economic growth takes place in large urban centers. While this might pertain to some inherent qualities of urban centers, it also might be a reflection of government agencies acting in accord with the precepts of the dual economy model, which pervades the planning efforts of Third World nations. Thus, for the Third World as well as for advanced economies,

if we are dealing with the spatial manifestations of human events (which we are in all phases of human geography), then there is no way we can divorce these events from the processes that generate them and still hope to account for or explain them. (Amedeo and Golledge, 1975: 172)

DEVELOPMENT IMPACTS UPON INNOVATION DIFFUSION

Thus far, this chapter has been concerned with the ways in which diffusion processes affect development. It is now time to turn the table and enquire how the level of development and the development process itself influence innovation diffusion. Little attention has been given to this topic, and accordingly it is hoped that this section will be a prelude to future research. In setting the stage for that endeavor, the impact of development upon diffusion is first discussed in terms of the adoption perspective and then in terms of the market and infrastructure perspective.

The Adoption Perspective and the Impacts of Development upon Diffusion

Diffusion research primarily has focused upon innovations associated with the *modern sector*. Accordingly, many of the personal characteristics related to adoption also are associated with the modern sector such as literacy, cosmopoliteness, communication channel orientation, achievement motivation or entrepreneurship (E.M. Rogers, 1969). Recognizing this relationship suggests two important points. First, the *appropriateness* of an innovation, and the likelihood of extensive diffusion, is in part dependent upon its congruence with the level of development of the population to which it has been introduced. Thus, a *modern* innovation introduced into a *traditional* society may be inappropriate, just as may be a traditional innovation introduced into a modern society, and an extensive diffusion of either should not be expected. Second, personal characteristics related to innovativeness will vary according to the level of societal development. Thus, while literacy might be related to diffusion in a modern society, it may not be in a traditional society. Accordingly, E.M. Rogers (1969: 338–9) finds that age correlates negatively with change orientation in a modern village, but positively in a traditional village!

Generally, then, the ease with which a given innovation will diffuse through a population depends upon its congruence with the development level, personal characteristics and social norms associated with that population. However, since personal characteristics and social norms relevant to innovation diffusion are related to the level of development, the critical factor may be seen as the congruence between the innovation being diffused and the level of development.[34] Accordingly, this fit ought to be an important consideration, both in choosing an innovation to diffuse and in designing a diffusion strategy (Figure 8.7).

The observations of Lin and Melick (1977: 21–7) with regard to the diffusion of immunization and family planning in Haiti and Costa Rica illustrate this interrelationship between development level and diffusion, and how it might be reflected in diffusion strategy. If the fit between the social norm and the innovation is positive, the initial community view towards the innovation is likely to be favorable. Then, an *interpersonal communications strategy* wherein opinion leaders would perform a relaying function is suggested. If the fit between the social norm and the innovation is neutral, the initial community view towards the innovation is likely to be one of indifference, which would slow its spread. In this case, then, an

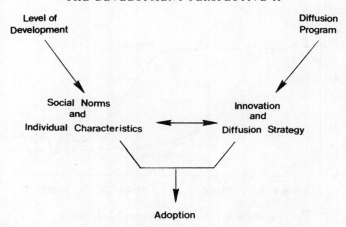

Figure 8.7   The Interrelationship between Innovation Adoption and the Level of Development

interventionist strategy which offered incentives for and pressures towards adoption would be more effective. Finally, if the fit between the social norm and the innovation were negative, the initial community view towards the innovation would be one of opposition. Under these circumstances, an interpersonal communications strategy would be immediately squashed, while an interventionist strategy would further enhance the resistance level. Accordingly, a *local media strategy* employing change agents, impersonal media and external sources of information would be more appropriate since it first identifies points of sympathy within the community, cultivates those points in order to generate favorable interpersonal communications and demonstration effects, and continuously monitors and addresses community reactions.

The social science literature is replete with many other examples of the influence of the level of development upon innovation diffusion, but they generally are not phrased or analyzed in terms of that concern. An illustration is found in statements of *demographic transition theory* (Pedersen, 1975; Nam and Gustavus, 1976; Chung, 1970), which is based upon the experiences of Western Europe and North America (Figure 8.8). This posits an initial phase in which both birth and death rates are high and population growth is nil. In phase two, there is a diffusion of health-related practices among the population as a corollary of incipient industrialization and modernization. Accordingly, the death rate begins to fall while the birth rate remains high and population rapidly expands. In phase three, social

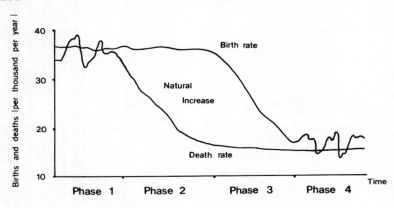

Figure 8.8   The Demographic Transition

practices limiting family size also begin to diffuse among the
population, as a corollary of increased levels of development,
urbanization and related changes in social norms. Thus, by the end of
phase three the birth rate has gradually fallen to a point of balance
with the death rate. In phase four, then, the development cycle is
complete and population growth is again nil, but now with a low birth
and death rate and a proliferation of family planning and health-
related innovations.[35]

The Market and Infrastructure Perspective and Development Impacts

The previous subsection discussed some ways in which development
affects innovation diffusion through its interrelationship with personal characteristics and social norms. Another set of influences
derives from the interrelationship of the level of development with
societal institutions, public policy objectives and *artifacts* of the
human landscape such as infrastructure.

The improvement and proliferation of infrastructure is a corollary
to development that is particularly critical to diffusion processes
because it enables more rapid and complex communications, bridges
core–periphery differences, increases the spatial integration of
national economies, acts as a stimulus to further development, and
increases the utility of many innovations. Accordingly, infrastructure
additions and improvements may be seen as *enabling innovations*
which generally increase the rate of diffusion agency establishment
and innovation diffusion.

One illustration of the interrelationship between infrastructure

THE DEVELOPMENT PERSPECTIVE II

characteristics and the level of development is the schema proposed by Pedersen for the articulation of Latin American urban systems, summarized above (pages 257–8). A more detailed illustration is Taaffe, Morrill and Gould's (1963) *ideal-typical sequence of transportation system growth*, which draws on the experience of several Third World nations (Figure 8.9). In the first phase of this sequence, several undifferentiated port towns are established, with a slight penetration of the transportation system into the hinterland of each (Figure 8.9A). In the second phase, activities are concentrated in a few port towns, which thus become larger and more important (Figure 8.9B). There also is a marked penetration into the hinterland of the major port towns, connecting to an inland city, but the systems emanating from each port remain separate. In the third phase, several intermediate cities are established along the main transportation arteries, and there is further penetration into the hinterlands of all towns (Figure 8.9C). In the fourth phase of the sequence, some intermediate cities become more important than others, both the port and inland cities grow in size, and the previously separate transportation systems become interconnected between both the port and inland cities (Figure 8.9D). Integration of the transportation system continues in phase five in that the major intermediate cities become connected to one another and to the inland and port cities of the other system (Figure 8.9E). Also, there is a further increase in the differentiation among town sizes as the intermediate, inland and port cities all spurt in growth (Figure 8.9E). Finally, certain transportation routes are upgraded into what Taaffe, Morrill and Gould term *high-priority main streets* to form something akin to the interstate freeway system of the United States (Figure 8.9F).

Given the role of logistics costs and infrastructure as set out by the market and infrastructure perspective and the sequence of transportation system growth just outlined, it is a simple matter to expand our understanding of the relationship between the level of development and infrastructure characteristics to also include the diffusion of innovations. Illustrative of this are the observations of Taaffe, Morrill and Gould (1963: 525–28) on the spread of commercialization in Ghana and Nigeria; the observations of Witthuhn (1968) on the establishment of postal agencies in Uganda; and the observations of Riddell (1970) on the spread in Sierra Leone of native administration, medical facilities, primary and secondary education faciliites, agricultural cooperatives, postal services and banking. More generally, Riddell (1970: 47–8) notes

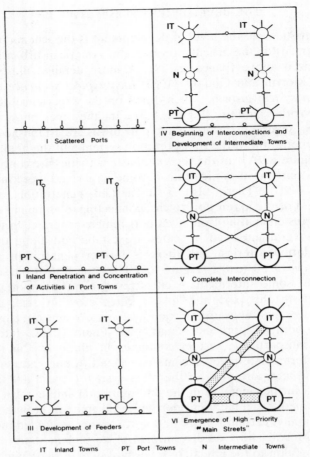

I Scattered Ports	IV Beginning of Interconnections and Development of Intermediate Towns
II Inland Penetration and Concentration of Activities in Port Towns	V Complete Interconnection
III Development of Feeders	VI Emergence of High – Priority "Main Streets"

IT Inland Towns   PT Port Towns   N Intermediate Towns

Figure 8.9   Ideal-Typical Sequence of Transport Development in a Developing Country
After Taaffe, Morrill and Gould, 1963: 504

While the growth of transport system [and other infrastructure] is part of the modernization process, it is also much more. The spreading network of rail and roads [and other infrastructure] continually redefines the spatial fabric of the country in which health services are located, schools are opened, communications are structured, ideas spread, and new ways of life emerge. The network acts . . . as the very framework within which . . . the process of change [occurs].[36]

In extending our understanding of the relationship between development and innovation diffusion, it is important to note that the *ideal-typical* sequence of transportation system growth (an artifact of development in the above examples) does not represent the manifestation of some *laws of nature,* nor is this sequence merely a matter of chance. Instead, it reflects the role of transportation as a policy instrument of European colonialism. Similarly, the infrastructure development of Latin America generally mirrors an orientation towards the export of minerals and plantation crops to the United States.

Infrastructure deployment also may be employed as a policy instrument for internal development. The first transcontinental railway line of the United States is an example. Another is the establishment of Brasilia and the infrastructure complementing that, which represents a conscious effort to move Brazil's focus westward and to exploit unused resources. Similarly, implementation of the dual economy model of development would lead to more infrastructure in core regions with a focus upon large, modern urban areas, whereas a dramatically different deployment of infrastructure would emerge from a national policy concerned with developing the small-scale enterprise, rural non-farm, or agricultural sectors of the economy (Miller, 1979; Rondinelli and Ruddle, 1976).[37] Illustrative of the latter is F. D. Roosevelt's focus on rural American in the 1930s leading to such programs as farm-to-market roads, rural electrification and the projects related to the Tennessee Valley Authority.

Development policies such as those mentioned above would be mirrored in the rate and spatial patterning of diffusion, as well as in the kinds of innovations diffused. In a development scheme such as that implied by the ideal-typical sequence of transportation growth, for example, modern sector innovations would not be available in inland towns until phase three or in intermediate towns until phase four, and they would not be found in abundance throughout the system until phase six (Figure 8.9). Likewise, as noted on pages 238–9, the introduction of materially and modern sector biased innovations is to be expected if the national development policy is of the dual economy variety. Alternatively, if the rural non-farm sector is an important component of national development policy, we might expect to find *village technology* innovations that are

at the current level of village technical competance . . . ; [that use] materials . . . available locally at relatively low cost . . . ; and [that are] . . . capable of local maintenance and repair. (Rondinelli and Ruddle, 1976: 134)

In general, then, important criteria for the *appropriateness* of a *technology* include its congruence with an ongoing development program and related objectives or, as discussed at the beginning of this section, with the overall level of development and societal norms. Thus, *appropriate* is a relative characteristic, rather than an inherent quality of a technology.[38] This theme will be elaborated further in Chapter 9.

OVERVIEW

This chapter is concerned with the interrelationships between innovation diffusion and development. This is addressed in terms of two questions: the social and economic consequences of innovation diffusion and the impact of the level of development, or the development process itself, upon innovation diffusion.

With regard to the first question, for many years it was widely assumed that innovation diffusion had a positive impact upon individual welfare and, collectively, economic development and social change. Accordingly, development programs forged ahead, giving little if any attention to the benefits of innovation. Thirty plus years after the initiation of such programs, however, élitist entrenchment still prevails in Third World nations and there are still enormous disparities between social classes, as well as among regions, in their level of economic development. Further, some would argue that these characteristics have worsened, often as a consequence of innovation diffusion itself. Accordingly, the development aspects of innovation diffusion have come under increasing scrutiny in recent years, and this chapter is a part of that ongoing discussion.

In examining the social and economic consequences of innovation diffusion, attention first turns to its impact upon individuals or households. Early adopters of an innovation related to an ongoing economic activity generally will obtain excess or windfall profits, which are termed *adoption rents*. These are likely to decrease to zero as the diffusion progresses, but the initial adopter will still have gained the excess profit for a time, which may be invested for further gain or otherwise used, while later adopters will not have this advantage. There also are other consequences to being a late or non-adopter. In a commercial agricultural setting, for example, persons or households lagging in adoption may well be forced out of production and become either local laborers or rural-to-urban migrants, thus exacerbating an already critical problem of the Third World.

The adoption rent concept is developed primarily with regard to agricultural activity. However, the chapter also demonstrates its applicability to other economic activity, carried out by either individuals or firms, and its applicability to the adoption of consumer innovations wherein early adopters experience a social windfall.

Adoption rent is a particularly critical issue, both in Developed and Developing world settings, in that diffusion programs generally incorporate systematic biases which enable some members of society to more readily adopt and thus enjoy the attendant windfall gains on a continuing basis. The result is maintenance and, often, exacerbation of the economic disparities between individuals and social classes. In part, these biases may be traced to the prevalence of the adoption perspective in diffusion programs, which emphasizes a communications strategy oriented towards potential adopters who are deemed progressive or modern. The adoption perspective also embodies the view that non-adoption is the result of insufficient innovativeness or entrepreneurship, so that responsibility is seen to rest with the individual potential adopter rather than the diffusion program itself or societal institutions.

An alternative view, consistent with the market and infrastructure perspective, is that diffusion and entrepreneurship are affected by the availability and distribution of resources or individual access to the means of production and public goods. Examples of resources in this context would include information; capital or access to capital through loans; skills or education; public infrastructure such as transportation, electricity or water systems; and public facilities providing service, collection, delivery or processing related to the innovation or its implementation. Such resources are provided by government, entrepreneurial or non-profit institutions, some entities of which would be diffusion agencies that serve as intermediaries between governmental strategies and individual adoption.

A number of *structural characteristics* have been seen as affecting the timing of adoption (or whether adoption occurs at all) and the attendant gains through adoption rent. These were first discussed in general and then examined through a theoretical analysis of innovation diffusion in a rural hinterland and through a case study of the diffusion of agricultural cooperatives in Sierra Leone. The conclusions of these three approaches to the adoption rent question are as follows.

One set of structural characteristics affecting adoption rent is comprised of individual or place attributes such as economic wealth or size of the economic enterprise, social connections, age, education level, and location in social, economic or geographic space. The favoring of potential adopters with certain individual attributes in part occurs through the many propagator and diffusion agency actions discussed in this book, that is, actions pertaining to adapting an innovation to certain uses or locales (Chapter 6); diffusion agency location and time of establishment (Chapter 3); and diffusion agency strategies such as pricing, infrastructure and organizational development, market selection and segmentation, and promotional communications (Chapter 4). Particular attention was given in this chapter to the two-step flow of communications strategy, which ensures that the opinion leaders will be able to adopt earlier and enjoy greater adoption rents, leading to increased élitist entrenchment. Locational attributes also were given attention. Infrastructure-constrained diffusions in an agricultural setting, for example, generally favor persons or households located closer to the urban center from which the relevant infrastructure emanates. Similarly, the strategy underlying the diffusion of agricultural cooperatives in Sierra Leone generally favored persons of the Mende culture located in the cash crop regions of the south-east.

A *second* structural characteristic affecting adoption rent is the type of innovation diffused. For an agricultural setting, a tripartite typology has been suggested. *Labor-augmenting* or *peasant-biased innovations* increase the marginal productivity of labor and thereby favor small landholders. At the other extreme are *material-augmenting* or *landlord-biased innovations* which increase the marginal productivity of capital and thereby favor large landholders. In between are *neutral innovations* which are simultaneously advantageous to both large- and small-scale operations. In general, innovations promoted through public or private programs of diffusion have tended to be landlord biased. A complicating factor in evaluating landlord or peasant bias, however, is the need to consider the whole package of which the innovation is a part, that is, the *adoption package*. This is comprised of other goods or services (some of which might be innovations in their own right) needed to realize the full potential of the innovation. Another factor of importance is the individual or place attributes favored by the diffusion strategy. Taken together, then, these factors define a specific social, economic, locational and institutional *niche* within which diffusion of a given innovation is likely. That is, the diffusion of any one innovation generally will be limited to places with all the characteristics comprising the *diffusion niche* and reflecting the elements of the innovation's adoption package and related diffusion strategies.

Institutional characteristics are a *third* influence on adoption rent. In the hypothetical example, this was manifest in the price offered by the market for commercial grains, which controlled the expansion or contraction of the *diffusion niche*. This example further noted, however, that only the marginal members of society were affected by shifts in the diffusion niche, whereas the more privileged continued to enjoy the greatest windfall gains under any circumstances. Generalizing from this example leads to the observation that the distribution of power within a local society is an important determinant of the consequences of a given innovation. The entrenchment of specific social classes or ethnic groups within the government also is important. This is exemplified by the favoring of Mende regions in the diffusion of agricultural cooperatives in Sierra Leone. Finally, such entrenchment, together with the prevalence of development strategies based on the dual economy model, partially explains the extensive fostering of materially biased innovations in both Developed and Developing world settings.

A *fourth* structural component affecting the distribution of adoption rents is infrastructure. It was shown in Chapter 7 that the diffusion of commercial agriculture in Third World settings depends upon adequate transportation, marketing and warehousing infrastructures which are not everywhere available. This also is illustrated by the diffusion of agricultural cooperatives in Sierra Leone, where the promotional and personnel training infrastructures were restricted to areas adjacent to already established cooperatives in order to make the most efficient use of limited government resources. Likewise, the hypothetical example of the diffusion of commercial grain production and Green Revolution technologies illustrates the interaction between infrastructure and the enjoyment of adoption rents. Thus, infrastructure, which is created by diffusion agencies or others of the public and private sectors and generally reflects the level of development, seems to be a singularly important factor in diffusion.

In addition to impacting upon individuals or households, innovation diffusion also impacts upon regional development processes. The diffusion of agricultural cooperatives in Sierra Leone, for example, ought to contribute to an increase in the economic disparities among regions, particularly in comparing the favored south under Mende dominance with the north under Temne dominance. More generally, diffusion has long been recognized as an important element of the complex process of urban systems growth and regional development, but also recognized is that the creation of social and economic inequalities among regions is inherent in this process. Thus, there is an equity dimension to both the individual and regional impacts of innovation diffusion.

In considering the diffusion aspects of regional development, a nation or region generally is conceived as consisting of a dominant *modern sector,* usually associated with urban agglomerations, and a dependent *traditional sector,* usually associated with rural areas and small towns. This conceptualization is parallel to the traditional *heartland–hinterland dichotomy,* and it is more formally expressed by the *core–periphery model* of Friedmann for interregional situations and by the *growth center model* for the situation of a single urban center and its surrounding hinterland. Another model of relevance is that of the *dual economy.* While this views the modern and traditional sectors only in economic and social terms, rather than spatial, it has been the most prevalent paradigm pertaining to development processes in Third World settings. The dual economy model also has provided the rationale for much of the diffusion work oriented towards development processes.

The process of development posited by these conceptualizations generally involves the gradual erosion of the traditional sector by expansion of the modern sector or, said another way, the conversion of the traditional sector by modernization impulses emanating from the modern sector. These impulses are sometimes viewed in terms of technological innovations; sometimes in terms of entrepreneurial, employment providing or other organizational entities which are related to urban area growth and regional development; or sometimes more generally as *growth impulses,* all of which spread from the core to the periphery or from the growth center to its hinterland. Another set of impulses pertain to transforming individuals from their traditional mentality, sometimes described as the *subculture of peasantry.* This is seen to occur through the *communication* of modern norms, patterns of entrepreneurial behavior, achievement motivation, new ideas and new practices from the modern to the traditional sector of the economy, and it is in this context that the diffusion model of the adoption perspective has been an important aspect of development theory and strategy.

The dynamics of core–periphery or growth center–hinterland relationships involve *backwash or polarization effects,* which direct growth impulses to the core or growth center and drain the periphery or hinterland, and *spread or trickle-down effects* which direct growth impulses in the opposite direction. Evidence indicates that polarization effects have far outweighed trickle-down effects, thus leading to the extreme regional disparities characterizing Third World nations today. One reason is that development is a *circular and cumulative* process whereby internal and external economies of the core or growth center are increased over time and generally fortify their growth at the expense of the peripheral or hinterland areas. In theory, however, spatial integration and agglomeration diseconomies should come about eventually, leading to a spinoff or outward diffusion of growth-related activities to hinterland locations. This view is supported by the occurrence of these spinoffs in advanced economies such as the United States, by extensions of *growth pole* and *core–periphery* theories, and by the *product life cycle of industrial development*. The latter notes that a new process or invention initially requires relatively large numbers or skilled workers in the production process and therefore is tied to core regions, whereas maturity of the industry leads to routinized production and location in peripheral areas with a less costly labor force.

In line with the above considerations, researchers also have examined the mechanisms by which spread and trickle-down effects and the regional impact of diffusion processes are transmitted and channeled. These efforts generally have focused upon *spatial economic structure* holding that the spread of growth (or recession) impulses depends upon the intra- and interlocational linkages within and between economic sectors. Since data availability makes the direct implementation of this approach difficult, however, these researchers sometimes have taken a shift-share approach in which regional growth or decline is seen as a function of three elements: a national growth factor which affects all regions equally; an industrial mix growth factor which affects regions differentially according to whether they have strong representation in growing or declining industries; and a local competition growth factor which affects regions differentially according to local qualities such as the innovativeness or resourcefulness of their population. Another approach, proposed by Pred, is to examine the spatial structure of multilocational organizations in both the public and private sectors, which are seen to comprise a predominant segment of the interdependencies within the national city system.

In all these endeavors concerning the role of diffusion in regional development processes, there has been a good deal of concern with spatial patterns. This generally has involved the assumption that diffusion into a rural hinterland occurs in a neighborhood effect or wave-like pattern, and that diffusion through an urban system exhibits a hierarchy effect pattern. The operational expressions of these effects generally employ a gravity model type of formulation in which population sizes guide the hierarchical movement and distance between towns guides the neighborhood effect flows. Recently, however, this practice has been sharply criticized, holding that it is more important directly to examine the substantive processes

underlying diffusion aspects of regional development and that these
processes rarely result in pattern regularities such as the hierarchy
and neighborhood effects.

The second major question addressed in this chapter is the impact
of the level of development, or the development process itself, upon
innovation diffusion. This is first discussed in terms of the adoption
perspective and then in terms of the market and infrastructure
perspective.

With respect to the adoption perspective, the ease with which a
given innovation will diffuse through a population generally depends
upon its congruence with the personal characteristics and social
norms of that population, which in turn are interrelated with the level
of development. Thus, the *appropriateness* of an innovation is not an
abstract quality so much as an indication of such congruence. To
illustrate this, two examples were discussed. One concerns the
introduction of family planning into a community wherein suggestions were made for altering the diffusion strategy according to
whether the fit between the social norm and the innovation is
positive, neutral or negative. The second example is demographic
transition theory. This was employed to demonstrate that there is
much in the social science literature which illustrates the influence of
the level of development upon diffusion but which generally has not
been phrased or analyzed in terms of that concern.

With respect to the market and infrastructure perspective, development also affects innovation diffusion through its interrelationship
with societal institutions, public policy objectives, and artifacts of the
human landscape such as intrastructure. Particular attention is given
to the improvement and proliferation of infrastructure that occurs as
a corollary of development. This enables more rapid and complex
communications, bridges core–periphery differences, increases the
spatial integration of national economies, acts as a stimulus to further
development and increases the utility of many innovations. Accordingly, infrastructure additions and improvements may be seen as
enabling innovations which generally increase the rate of diffusion
agency establishment and innovation diffusion. One illustration of
the interrelationship between infrastructure characteristics and the
level of development is the schema proposed by Pedersen for the
articulation of Latin American urban systems. Another is the
ideal-typical sequence of transportation development, which draws
upon the experience of several Third World nations.

It is also noted, however, that the ideal-typical sequence of
transportation system development reflects its role as a policy

instrument of European colonialism. The use of infrastructure development as a policy instrument also occurs in internal affairs, as illustrated by the first transcontinental railway line of the United States. Thus, implementation of the dual economy model of development would lead to more infrastructure in core regions with a focus upon large, modern urban areas whereas a dramatically different deployment of infrastructure would emerge from a national policy concerned with developing the small enterprise, rural non-farm or agricultural sectors of the economy. Such differences would be mirrored in the rate and spatial patterning of innovation diffusion, as well as in the types of innovations diffused.

With this lead-in, the book now turns to a more comprehensive discussion of innovation diffusion and public policy, the primary topic of Chapter 9.

NOTES

1 Assistance in preparing this chapter was provided by William L. Flinn of the Ohio State University Department of Rural Sociology and by Rickie Gilliard and Rita Schneider of the Ohio State University Department of Geography.
2 The importance of infrastructure and other publicly available goods to economic development has been acknowledged for some time (Hirschman, 1958; Wilson, Bergmann, Hirsch and Klein, 1966). It is the author's impression, however, that the ways in which infrastructures are linked in to the innovation diffusion process have not been explicitly articulated prior to the elaboration of the market and infrastructure perspective.
3 DeJanvry (1973: 422) terms this *economic coercion* in adoption.
4 Other discussions pertaining to adoption rents, their origins and their consequences in an agricultural setting can be found in E.M. Rogers and Shoemaker (1971: 331–2), who use the term *windfall profits,* and DeJanvry (1973) who uses the term *quasi rents.* The concept also is relevant to the development of power in urban systems. On this point, see Friedmann (1975) and the discussion above on the regional impact of innovation diffusion, especially pages 254–8.
5 To simply illustrate the basis of such conclusions, consider Yapa and Mayfield's (1978) analysis in which the adopters of Green Revolution technology in an area of India were statistically discriminated from non-adopters. They found that individual characteristics usually seen as related to innovativeness and communications behavior correctly classified only 60 per cent and 64 per cent, respectively, of the population, little better than a chance occurrence. By contrast, variables pertaining to access to resources correctly classified 74 per cent of the population. Further, many of the variables used as indices of innovativeness and communications behavior, such as educational attainment, reflect prior access to resources.
6 It seems that a similar process operated in the demise of the small farmer in the United States, resulting in extensive rural to urban migration in the 1930s and 1940s. Meyerhoff (1980), quoted on page 295 below, indicates this also is a matter of current concern.
7 Also see Gotsch (1972) who presents a conceptual framework and related empirical analyses linking technology characteristics, the distribution of productive assets, the distribution of services by local level institutions and organizations, social customs and traditions, innovation diffusion and out-migration.

8 It is interesting to note the parallel between this observation and that of D. Harvey (1971) relating social welfare in the city to locational characteristics.

9 As described by Gotsch (1972: 332) the *tubewell* is a water-producing technology consisting, in its simplest form, of a 6–8 inch tubular shaft sunk to a depth of 50–150 feet to which a small motor-driven pump is attached. This innovation resulted in a significant reduction in the ratio of capital to labor for farmers in Gotch's study areas.

10 A similar point is made by Yapa (1979: 373–4) in noting the effects of the Green Revolution in India as compared to other Asian countries, particularly China.

11 For a related study of the effects of credit in the proliferation of Green Revolution technologies in Mexico, see Burke (1979).

12 This also affects strategies for diffusing innovations. Gladwin (1979), for example, shows that a fertilizer-related innovation introduced in Mexico did *not* diffuse because the diffusion strategy was designed in terms of how the agents would make agricultural decisions, rather than taking account of the different decision-making calculus of the farmer. On this point, also see Foster (1962, 1973).

13 Relevant to this point is the induced innovation model of agricultural development posited by Hayami and Ruttan (1971) and DeJanvry (1973). This holds that the creation of an innovation and its availability through diffusion are the result of pressures—levied on agribusiness, agricultural experiment stations and R&D operations—from socially and politically dominant farm interests. For a more general examination of the development process, but from a similar perspective, also see Bodenheimer (1970) and Chilcote and Edelstein (1974).

14 The concept of a diffusion niche is more fully developed in Hudson (1969a), where it is applied to the study of frontier settlement.

15 Looking at the diffusion niche concept in this broader perspective allows us to see it as an expression of the more general time geography of Hagerstrand and his research associates, discussed in Chapter 2 (pages 29–30). That is, an innovation requires certain resources to be present, both at certain times and at the location of the potential adopter. An agricultural innovation, for example, might require seed, fertilizer, irrigation, credit, human resources, transportation and market facilities at a given place, but these also must be present at particular times in the production process. To the extent that this example is generalizable, then, the diffusion niche would have both a time and space dimension.

16 These observations as to the characteristics of Green Revolution technologies were derived from personal conversation with William L. Flinn of the Ohio State University Department of Rural Sociology. Also see Yapa (1979).

17 For a discussion of the conventional location rent concept, see Stevens (1961).

18 This is a synopsis of research reported more fully in L.A. Brown, Schneider, Harvey and Riddell (1979), which originated from an M.A. thesis by Rita Schneider of the Ohio State University Department of Geography.

19 Some like Paramont Chief Kai Samba I went as far as evicting several Lebanese from their chiefdoms so as to reduce competition for the new cooperatives (Van der Laan, 1975: 59).

20 The district is a regional subdivision of Sierra Leone which is comprised of several chiefdoms, the smallest non-urban administrative unit. Data are available for chiefdoms and were used in statistical analyses, but generally there are not enough cooperatives per chiefdom to discern temporal and spatial trends.

21 In the context of this question it is also noteworthy to recall the discussion above (page 246) pertaining to the ambiguity of the Mende's innovativeness.

22 E.M. Rogers (1969: 19–41) contains an extensive discussion of the social norms and related values characterizing the *subculture of peasantry*. These include a distrust of interpersonal relations, perception of a limited good, a high degree of familism and fatalism, a lack of innovativeness and achievement motivation, limited aspirations, a lack of a sense of deferred gratification and a limited view of the world.

23 It should be noted that Friedmann's orientation is towards showing that the development scenario of the dual economy paradigm is unlikely to occur and, therefore, towards putting forth alternative strategies that better take account of the political, social, and economic realities of core–periphery relationships. In this respect, while still maintaining a regional convergence posture, Friedmann could be considered as a part of the *dependency school* of development, which argues that spatial inequalities and the marginality of peripheral or poor regions *(internal colonies)* are the inevitable consequence of their position in the development process as presently constituted (Gonzalez, 1965; A.G. Frank, 1967; Gilbert and Goodman, 1976; Sunkel, 1969). This and other aspects of the regional development process are discussed in the section beginning on page 254.

24 In addition to the economic sector aspects of growth center theory, attention has also been given to the role of human resources or capital. This holds that growth results from organizational modes, ways of thinking, states of mind and skills among the population of the growth center and its hinterland. These relate to the ability to become aware of and exploit economic possibilities and innovation. Consequently, more important than investment in industry may be investment in skills, education, training, economic organization abilities and organizations themselves, particularly when the lack of these would result in an industry importing trained personnel and exporting profits with little effect upon the local population. This approach is more recent and therefore represented by less research than the approach focusing upon economic sectors, but Hansen (1971) believes it will ultimately be more useful. Note, however, the similarity between this approach and the concern with the entrepreneurship and achievement motivation usually associated with the dual economy paradigm. Note also the parallel role of entrepreneurship both in the diffusion model of Pedersen (1970, 1975) and in the case of diffusion agency establishment under a decentralized decision-making structure, outlined on pages 68–74.

25 For a comprehensive discussion of the role of cummunications and diffusion in bringing about modernization, see E.M. Rogers (1969). For a somewhat jaundiced perspective on this, see Grunig (1971).

26 For a recent discussion of spread/trickle-down and backwash/polarization effects and their role in the development process, see Gaile (1980).

27 Apparently, the term *circular and cumulative* was originally suggested by Myrdal (1957).

28 A comprehensive coverage of the product life cycle, regional diffusion processes, and the breakdown of the heartland–hinterland distinction in the United States can be found in Rees (1979) and Norton and Rees (1979). A parallel discussion for Europe can be found in Hall and Hay (1980).

29 Illustrative of this is the electronics and textile industries of the United States (Berry, Conkling and Ray, 1976: 170–6, 200). The manufacture of televisions first occurred in the Boston area where electronic applications were pioneered, later became established in medium-size towns of the Midwest, and more recently moved to areas in the south-west bordering on Mexico. Likewise, textile production initially was a largely New England enterprise which began its shift to the south in the early part of this century after extensive mechanization enabled the exploitation of regional differences in wage rates.

30 This argument is developed more fully by Richardson (1976, 1977, 1980; Richardson and Richardson, 1975). He uses the term *polarization reversal* to characterize the process.

31 In part, the concern with spatial patterns and its attendant assumptions derives from central place theory, which has strongly influenced geographic thinking. This holds that there is a hierarchy of urban centers, each dominating a specific hinterland, and a pattern of interaction which generally flows in its initial impetus from higher- to lower-order (or from larger to smaller) urban centers. Hager-

strand's (1952) model of urban system diffusion, discussed in Chapter 2 (pages 20–2) is another influence on the effort to discern the spatial patterning of growth-inducing elements in regional development.

32 Pred also cites a number of other studies that support his conclusions. These include a study by Gilmour (1974) on input–output linkages of manufacturing establishments located in the Montreal metropolitan complex, Earickson's (1975) study of interorganizational linkages of the Boeing Company of Seattle-Tacoma, Moseley's (1973a, 1973b) study of growth transmission impulses from growth centers in East Anglia and Brittany (England), Borchert's (1972) study of linkages in wholesaling and correspondent banking in the United States, and studies of manufacturing linkages in Britain by Salt (1967), Steele (1969) and Chisholm (1974).

33 The influence upon diffusion research of both the quantitative revolution and the more contemporary concern with substantive reality were discussed in Chapter 2 (pages 31–7). These influences also are evident in the concern with spatial pattern as compared with the more recent focus on substantive processes in studies of regional development.

34 This congruence has been examined, but usually in terms of cultural values (E.M. Rogers and Shoemaker, 1971: 134–72; Foster, 1962; 1973) rather than as a development question. Also relevant to this point is Gladwin (1979) who examines how differences between the cognitive processes of diffusion agents and farmers affect adoption behavior in a Third World setting.

35 It should be noted, however, that this view of the demographic transition has been a topic of debate. Rather than viewing this transition as an innovation diffusion process, others have interpreted it as a demographic response to altered conditions through an adjustment of ongoing practices (K. Davis, 1963; Carlsson, 1966).

36 Pertinent to the observations of this paragraph are a number of studies that examine modernization in general as it relates to transportation. These include Gauthier (1968), Kresge and Roberts (1971) and Wilson, Bergmann, Hirsch and Klein (1966). For an examination of several different types of infrastructure and their role in development and (by implication) innovation diffusion, see Rondinelli and Ruddle (1976). Finally, Weinand (1972; Knight and Newman, 1976: 390–1) presents a conceptual structure which merges perspectives on transportation spread, growth poles and economic development to portray the development process in a spatial context.

37 Generally, the implementation of the dual economy model in the Third World has involved the introduction of modern industry to core regions (or to regions with the relevant natural resources and/or particular locational advantages); a *top down* strategy that assumes growth will filter downwards through the economic system to less-developed regions. Recently, however, attention has turned to *bottom up* strategies which focus upon the small-scale enterprise and/or the rural non-farm sectors of the economy (Anderson and Leiserson, 1978, 1980; Gordon, 1978; Page, 1979; Liedholm and Chuta, 1976). These are comprised of small-scale, rural-based economic activities, located in intermediate and smaller-size towns and their hinterlands, which are characterized by high labor-to-capital ratios, and which utilize (and develop upon) indigenous activites, skills and resources. These bottom up strategies assume that growth will percolate upwards through the economic system, an assumption that is more consistent with the historical record of development in the North American and European economies.

38 The *small is beautiful* exhortations (Schumacher, 1973) provide a good example of the political dimension of appropriate technology (Buttell and Flinn, 1977).

9

CONCLUDING OBSERVATIONS, WITH SPECIAL EMPHASIS ON INNOVATION DIFFUSION IN A PUBLIC POLICY CONTEXT

This book has presented a comprehensive examination of the innovation diffusion process. Background is provided by a review of the various traditions of diffusion research in geography (Chapter 2), which traces the evolution of our thinking from a concern with the role of diffusion in the formation of the cultural landscape, dating from the earlier part of this century, to the more recent concern with entrepreneurial aspects of innovation diffusion. Most of this book, however, is directed towards developing a contemporary understanding of innovation diffusion. This is done in terms of four perspectives.

The first of these perspectives focuses on the processes by which *adoption* occurs or the *demand* aspect of diffusion. This views the spread of innovation across the landscape as the outcome of a learning or communications process. The *adoption perspective* also emphasizes the role of an individual's *innovativeness* or general propensity to adopt and the congruence of the innovation with a potential adopter's social and economic characteristics. The innovations most frequently considered by this framework are *consumer innovations* or those adopted by households.

The adoption perspective is the most completely developed area of diffusion research, representing an effort spanning about forty-five years, and it has dominated academic thinking on the subject. It is also that concern which has had the most direct input into policy and is best represented in diffusion programs. However, there are many good reviews of the adoption perspective, such as E.M. Rogers and Shoemaker (1971), and for that reason, it is given relatively little attention in this book outside of Chapter 1.

A second view of the innovation diffusion process is the *market and infrastructure perspective,* presented in Chapters 3 and 4. This considers the ways by which innovations and the conditions for adoption are made available to individuals or households, aspects of the *supply* side of diffusion. Two stages are involved: the establishment of diffusion agencies (or outlets) through which the innovation is distributed to the population at large; and the implementation of a strategy by each agency to induce adoption among the population in its service area. It is only after these events that adoption would occur, although expectations with regard to adoption behavior would enter into both agency establishment and agency strategy decisions. In examining the market and infrastructure perspective several case studies of consumer innovations were presented: Friendly Ice Cream shops, the bank credit card, cable television, Planned Parenthood affiliates and four agricultural innovations.

Conceptually recognizing the supply side of diffusion, as in the market and infrastructure perspective, shifts attention to the diffusion agency instead of the adopter. The locations of these agencies and the temporal sequencing of their establishment determine where and when the innovation will be available. This provides the general outline of the spatial pattern of diffusion. Further detail is contributed by the operating procedures of each agency. These create differing levels of access to the innovation depending upon a potential adopter's economic, locational, social and demographic characteristics. The establishment of diffusion agencies and the operating procedures of each agency are, more generally, aspects of marketing the innovation. This marketing involves both the creation of infrastructure and its utilization. Thus, the characteristics of the relevant public and private infrastructure, such as service, delivery, information, transportation, electricity or water systems, also have an important effect upon the rate and spatial patterning of diffusion. Accordingly, both within the immediate agency service area and the larger region of which it is a part, the diffusion is shaped by the market and infrastructure context of innovation adoption and diffusion. This perspective is grahically summarized in Figure 4.11.

The application of the market and infrastructure perspective to the diffusion of *technological innovations,* those adopted by firms for their own use, is demonstrated in Chapter 5, the first part of which reviews previous work on the subject. One conclusion is that research on the diffusion of innovations among firms has largely employed the adoption perspective, also prevalent in work on consumer innovations. This provides the starting point for the second part of the chapter, which demonstrates a congruency between the adoption perspective on technological innovations and the market and infrastructure perspective on consumer innovations. Articulating this congruency is significant because research endeavors on the two types of innovations have for the most part been seen as separate and unrelated. Finally, Chapter 5 examines some actual strategies used by the propagators of technological innovations in diffusing their product. In doing so, it raises a new set of questions pertaining to the ways in which these innovations are made available to potential adopter firms, and suggests that a framework such as the market and infrastructure perspective is applicable to technological as well as consumer innovations.

The adoption and market and infrastructure perspectives, as well as much of the research on the diffusion of technological innovations, embodies the assumption that the innovation is essentially the same throughout the diffusion process. In fact, however, a critical component of successful innovation is its continual technological improvement and *adaptation* to an increasing variety of uses, leading to *adoption* by an increasingly wider range of places, persons or organizations. This *continuity of innovation* is addressed by the *economic history perspective* reviewed in Chapter 6.

In the context of the themes developed in this book, an important aspect of adaptation efforts is their role in controlling where, when and for whom the innovation will be available, thus contributing, along with market and infrastructure-related actions, towards channeling the diffusion wave. Another effect of economic history considerations is that adoption often is delayed (solely) in anticipation of further improvements in the innovation. In terms of the overall diffusion paradigm (Figure 1.4), however, adaptation efforts are viewed as a portion of the *preconditions for diffusion* because they directly affect the development of the innovation, whereas market and infrastructure and adoption considerations are treated as primarily pertaining to *diffusion*.

The fourth view of the innovation diffusion process is the *development perspective*. One part of this concerns the *impact* of diffusion, dealing among other things with its effects upon individual welfare and its role in the process of regional development, often leading to economic disparities among regions and social classes. However, the reverse question also is of concern, that is, the way in which diffusion is affected by the overall level of development. Illustrative of this is the proliferation and change in infrastructure, an important component of the diffusion process, as an artifact of increasing development. In this latter sense, then, the development perspective pertains to another set of *preconditions for diffusion*.

Two chapters are devoted to the development perspective. Chapter 7 demonstrates the applicability of the market and infrastructure perspective in a Third World setting, providing the basis for Chapter

8, which examines the interrelationships between diffusion and development. The case studies in these chapters concern the diffusion of six agricultural innovations in a region of Kenya; the diffusion of commercial dairying in the state of Aguascalientes, Mexico; and the spread of agricultural cooperatives in Sierra Leone.

The above discussion, as well as the entire book, generally gives separate treatment to each of the four perspectives—the adoption perspective, the market and infrastructure perspective, the economic history perspective and the development perspective. This reflects the way these perspectives have been viewed by their various social science proponents.

Unlike the social science literature at large, however, the discussion here underemphasizes the adoption perspective. One reason for this is the author's own view that individual behavior, adoption in the present context, does not represent free will so much as a choice within a constraint set, and that the constraints are established and controlled by government and private institutions. A research corollary of this view is that we can account for a great deal of variance in the spatial patterns and temporal rates of diffusion by looking at institutional, rather than individual, behavior, and the relevant institutional behavior, in this instance, pertains to the supply side of diffusion and its impacts.

A second reason for the approach taken in this book is the need to balance our awareness of the various perspectives on innovation diffusion. Specifically, with so much attention and acceptance having been given to the demand or adoption side of diffusion, we may well be in a situation of diminishing returns to research effort on that topic, whereas the supply side and the consideration of diffusion impacts is virtually virgin territory for both academic and applied endeavors.

However, having made an argument for the importance of perspectives other than the adoption perspective, it is now time to more evenly address their complementarity. This is depicted in Figure 1.4 which indicates how the four perspectives together provide a comprehensive view of the innovation diffusion process. Another medium for demonstrating their complementarity is the S-curve protraying diffusion over time.

In accounting for the flatness of the S-curve's left tail, representing the period prior to the onset of a *bandwagon* effect, the adoption perspective would cite innovativeness characteristics or resistance to adoption. The market and infrastructure perspective, on the other hand, would attribute this to propagator and diffusion agency strategies pertaining to the establishment of diffusion agencies, pricing, infrastructure and organizational development, promotional communications, and market selection and segmentation. Researchers on the diffusion of technological innovation among firms would employ profitability conditions as an explanation. Finally, the economic historian would argue that the slow initial rate of diffusion reflects the time needed to improve the innovation and adapt it to a variety of potential markets and uses, as well as delays and caution in adoption because such improvements are anticipated.

A similar set of explanations might be employed to account for the bandwagon effect itself, or differences in the rates of diffusion of different innovations. That is, the adoption perspective would attribute the bandwagon effect to a lowering of resistance to adoption through demonstration effects, social interaction and other communications; and variances in diffusion rates to different resistance levels for each innovation. By contrast, the market and infrastructure perspective would attribute these same occurences to a broad range of propagator and diffusion agency actions, and the economic history perspective would attribute them to the development of technical skills among users, the routinization of skills in manufacturing the innovation, the development of complementarities, and the completion of the bulk of ongoing inventive or adaptive activity with regard to the innovation.

One conclusion that might be drawn from the above demonstration of complementarity among diffusion perspectives is that all four must be considered in coming to understand and use the innovation diffusion process. This point is especially relevant for policy applications, a theme elaborated in the remainder of this chapter. The first step in this endeavor is to address the implications of the material in this book for *public* programs of innovation diffusion. This is followed by a section which provides a detailed account of family planning programs in Third World settings as an illustration of these policy implications. A brief set of concluding remarks constitutes the final section. Before beginning this discourse on policy, however, it should be noted that the task is undertaken only with the intent of providing suggestive observations, rather than a thorough examination, since the latter would constitute a book in itself.

SOCIAL SCIENCE RESEARCH, PUBLIC POLICY FORMULATION AND PROGRAMS OF INNOVATION DIFFUSION[1]

In addressing the implications of the material presented in this book for public sector organizations engaged in innovation diffusion, it is useful to begin by considering the general relevance of social science research to public policy formulation. This is of widespread concern, but the question frequently generates more skepticism than confidence. Rein and White (1977: 120), for example, state

in all the large domestic agencies there are now centers for policy planning, management, and evaluation . . . [but] . . . along with the growth of research, which is often mandated by the legislation that institutes new social policies, there has grown a chronic sense of frustration, among both those who carry out the research and those who commission it. The feeling is that research does not really serve to guide policy, or is misused, or lies on a shelf unused. Has the contribution of research to action been oversold?

Harvey (1973: 128–9) elaborates on another side of the problem, which perhaps explains its existence:

There is a clear disparity between the sophisticated theoretical and methodological framework which we are using and our ability to say anything really meaningful about events as they unfold around us. There are too many anomalies between what we purport to explain and manipulate and what actually happens. There is an ecological problem, an urban problem, an international trade problem, and yet we seem incapable of saying anything of depth or profundity about any of them. When we do say anything it appears trite and rather ludicrous. In short our paradigm is not coping well.

It is not surprising, then, that the marriage between social science research and public policy is one frequently proposed but seldom consumated.[2]

Given this context, innovation diffusion research is particularly interesting since it has been directly employed in strategy formulation by public agencies such as the Agricultural Extension Service of the United States and family planning programs in the Developing or Third World. Yet, consistent with the above observation of Harvey, the efficacy of the extension model has been questioned (M.A. Brown, Maxson and Brown, 1977; Hightower, 1973), as have the contributions to fertility decline of government- or foundation-operated family planning programs (Demerath, 1976; Stycos, 1977; E.M. Rogers, 1973).[3]

In contrast to the preceding observations, however, the marriage between social science research and public policy in innovation diffusion is viewed by this author with excitement and optimism rather than dismay. One reason is because of the open dialogue between research and application, which is essential yet rare. More important, however, there has been a distinct evolution in diffusion theory in a manner that is congruent with the expressed concerns of the practitioners and the recognition of shortcomings in programs of innovation diffusion. Thus, the applicability and effectiveness of diffusion theory has increased at the same time that practitioners have recognized the need for reviewing and reformulating programs of innovation diffusion. The result should be a change in these programs, with a concomitant opportunity to test our new thinking about innovation diffusion in a real world *laboratory* that social scientists rarely have access to.

This section is seen as a contribution to the ongoing dialogue between theory and practice in innovation diffusion. Three topics are treated. The *first* is the strategy of innovation diffusion programs which deals with the means of bringing about adoption. The *second* topic is the impacts of innovation diffusion programs. *Finally,* attention is given to research methodology in a policy context.

Before continuing, it is useful to briefly consider a related issue, the social context of innovation diffusion. Innovation, or new products, are generally seen as inherently good and as a panacea for many of our major problems. This is probably a legacy of the industrial revolution, the mechanical wizardry of the Thomas Edison/Alexander Graham Bell variety, and the electronic spinoffs of the space age, all of which have affected our lives dramatically. A side effect of this, however, is that the innovation process has become institutionalized in society as witnessed by the many R&D labs, the overwhelming presence of Madison Avenue hype leading even to advertising as entertainment, and a societal imperative to innovate and diffuse (Rich, 1979; Gregg, Preston, Geist and Caplan, 1979). Even when questions are raised about the implementation of this imperative and its effects upon society, as in the debate over small versus large technology (Buttell and Flinn, 1977; Schumacher, 1973) or development policies (Chapter 8), the inquiry generally does not extend to the desirability of the imperative itself or to the way in which innovation and diffusion have become institutionalized and seen as inherently good.[4] While this issue also is not addressed here, it should be kept in mind as a backdrop to the ensuing discussion.

The Strategy of Innovation Diffusion Programs

Public programs concerned with the diffusion of innovations have largely employed the *adoption perspective*. This is most evident in the programs of the Cooperative Extension Service of the United States (Sanders, 1966) and in family planning programs of Third World nations (E.M. Rogers, 1973; Watson, 1977). However, reliance upon the adoption perspective also is indicated by the emphasis on *communications* in the diffusion strategies of most public programs (Hough, 1975).

The type of innovation that is most congruent with the adoption perspective is one that does not change over the term of the diffusion and is adopted by households or individuals, and generally, the innovations dealt with by the programs referred to above can be characterized in this manner. The basic tenet of the diffusion strategy is that individuals may be persuaded to adopt through communications. The primary mode of communications is often through *change* (or *extension*) *agents* who represent the innovation in direct contact with potential adopters, but media communications also are used extensively. Whatever the mode(s) or mix of communications, the *two-step flow model* is given a great deal of credence (Copeland, 1966; Warner, 1966; E.M. Rogers, 1973). Accordingly, communications efforts are directed to the *influentials, progressives, achievement motivateds, innovators* or *opinion leaders* in the target population. The identification of such persons is generally based on the criteria that they are better educated, more wealthy, etc. and have been early adopters of previous innovations. An extension of this overall (communications) approach to diffusion is the broader strategy of altering the innovativeness or achievement motivation of potential adopters (E.M. Rogers, 1969).

Despite, or perhaps because of, its prevalence, the adoption perspective has been *questioned as a cornerstone* for the design of public programs of diffusion. *One* criticism is that this perspective, and (by implication) diffusion policy formulated on the basis of it, places the responsibility for non-adoption upon the potential adopter(s) who is thereby deemed to be not sufficiently innovative or achievement motivated. An alternative view, advanced in this book (especially in Chapters 1 and 8), is that a shift in responsibility towards society, government policy, the propagator or the diffusion agency would be more realistic and perhaps lead to better results (Yapa, 1976; L.A. Brown, 1975, 1978, 1980; L.A. Brown, Schneider, Harvey and Riddell, 1979). A *second* criticism is that the implementation of the adoption perspective requires focusing a good number of monetary and personnel resources upon a comparably small number of persons, such as a single community, and as implemented, usually involves establishing new distribution, personnel and communication systems. Thus, this strategy may be characterized as *person intensive* and, accordingly, involves an allocation of resources in a manner that may provide only a minimum amount of leverage or return per dollar invested (Roberto, 1975, 1977; L.A. Brown, 1975, 1978). *Finally,* the adoption perspective is viewed by some as naive, or at least limited in applicability, because it recognizes or incorporates few of the commonly used business strategies for diffusing innovations (L.A. Brown, 1975, 1978; Roberto, 1975).

Serious consideration of these criticisms seems especially important in light of the questionable effectiveness of diffusion programs employing the adoption perspective. With regard to the Eastern Ohio Resource Development Center (EORDC), a research farm that is a part of the United States Cooperative Extension Service, M.A. Brown, Maxson and Brown (1977: 22–3) note

nearly 20 percent of the sample had adopted none of the six EORDC practices studied . . . the average person had adopted less than one-half of those practices applicable to his or her farming activities, and . . . only 18 percent had adopted more than two-thirds of the applicable recommended practices.

Likewise, in discussing family planning efforts, Stycos (1977: 19) observes

Perhaps one of the major impediments . . . has been the model lifted from communications research in agriculture. However useful this simple-minded view of diffusion has been for extension agents, it has probably done more harm than good for family planners.[5]

One possible response to criticisms and failures such as these is outlined by the *market and infrastructure perspective* (Chapters 3 and 4). This alters the way in which innovation diffusion is perceived by emphasizing the role of its social, economic, political and psychological contexts, rather than the role of individual adopters. Thus, innovation diffusion becomes a problem in *logistics, distribution* and *promotion* instead of *consumer behavior,* and the operational emphasis shifts to *stimulating demand* for the innovation and making it *available* and *accessible* to the potential adopter. Accordingly, accepting this perspective ought to lead to a broadening of the perceived role of the public diffusion agency (agent) and to a decrease in its passivity.

In the more specific terms of diffusion strategy, the market and infrastructure perspective suggests a broadly based marketing approach that utilizes several levers in addition to those contained in strategies based on the adoption perspective, which tend to be communications oriented. One set of these levers pertain to *market penetration* or *diffusion agency establishment*. These involve considerations such as the locales in which diffusion agencies should be located, diffusion agency siting within those locales selected and diffusion agency design.[6] Another set of levers pertain to *diffusion agency strategy*. Elements of this include the price of the innovation, infrastructure and organization development, product packaging, promotional communications, and market selection and segmentation wherein diffusion strategies are differentiated and tailored to particular groups of potential adopters. Finally, the overall strategy emerging from these various alternatives would reflect an orchestration in response to each diffusion situation.

It is probably not an insignificant consideration that the market and infrastructure perspective is consistent with the practices of private enterprise, whether profit or non-profit motivated (L.A. Brown and Philliber, 1977; L.A. Brown and Malecki, 1977; Meyer and Brown, 1979; M.A. Brown, 1977; Semple, Brown and Brown, 1975, 1977). To the degree, therefore, that we believe that the *best* practices are more likely to evolve in a competitive milieu, why not also employ the market and infrastructure perspective in the formulation of diffusion strategy in the public sector?

In the area of family planning it appears that such a change is occurring, particularly as the shortcomings of previous programs become evident (Demerath, 1976; E.M. Rogers, 1973; Stycos, 1977; Weinstein, 1976). A largely marketing-based strategy for that situation has been detailed by Roberto (1975) and partially implemented in his own Commercial Contraceptive Marketing Program in the Philippines (Roberto, 1976, 1977). Commercial programs, often of long standing, also are found in most other nations with a public family planning program, and their performance is at least comparable and often better than that of the public programs (E.M. Rogers, 1973: 352–4). As Rogers (1973: 354) notes, however,

Unfortunately, government family planning programs usually act as though the commercial systems were not there.[7]

A similar observation has been made by M.A. Brown, Maxson and Brown (1977: 23) regarding the lack of coordination between the programs of the United States Cooperative Extension Service and the efforts of farm implement dealers and other private sector diffusion agents.

One general advantage accruing to public sector diffusion strategies formulated in accordance with the market and infrastructure perspective is that they generally tap into the existing market system in a given situation and utilize its *natural* structure. In the Commercial Contraceptive Marketing Program of the Philippines, for example, we defined the long term objective as that of harnessing the widespread participation of the appropriate commercial resources towards the creation and servicing of a mass market demand for nonclinical contraceptives starting with condoms. We stressed the commercial sector because of its unmatched capability for maximizing the availability of nonclinical contraceptives. The vast commercial distribution network reaches out to some 200,000 small retail outlets all over the country—the so called *sari-sari* stores which not only supply the daily needs of a neighborhood or community but also serve as meeting places for information and social activities. In addition, the commercial network includes groceries, supermarkets, drug stores, and bazaars which service a large volume of buyers daily. Compared with the approximately 2400 clinics that constitute the national [family planning] program's distribution structure, the commercial network is clearly superior in both intensity of reach and efficiency. Even in the area of demand creation, the commercial sector has tremendous capability. Consider the sales forces of its distributor organizations—a trained and experienced cadre of personal communications medium—and the advertising agencies which make up a mass persuader group of unequalled expertise and experience. (Roberto, 1977: 3)

Thus, compared to the adoption perspective, the market and infrastructure approach tends to be *person extensive* so that a greater leverage or return per dollar invested in diffusion ought to be obtained. The approach is to splice into the existing systems of interaction, trust and distribution relationships, rather than creating new organizational entities, new distribution systems, new patterns of interaction, etc. Said another way, resources are utilized to enter the existing market system, not to establish a new one, and existing societal levers and institutions are employed.

A second general point of policy relevance deriving from the market and infrastructure perspective is that the measurement of innovativeness usually employed in public programs (by the number of innovations adopted or the time of adoption) reflects diffusion agency behavior, government policies and social conditions; not necessarily the real innovativeness of potential or actual adopters (L.A. Brown, Malecki and Spector, 1976). Thus, the responsibility for non-adoption or lesser levels of diffusion than are desired, is shifted to the diffusion agency or the government, and this will hopefully lead to beneficial changes in diffusion programs.

Third, the market and infrastructure perspective suggests the use of several planning tools that have not been associated with innovation diffusion but which have proven extremely useful in other contexts. Exemplary of this are the standard marketing strategies referred to above and related analytical and modeling procedures. Possible, however, is an even greater expansion in the range of techniques employed with innovation diffusion, including those of operations research and management analysis (H. M. Wagner, 1975a, 1975b).[8] Illustrative of this potential is the model proposed in Chapter 3 (pages 57–9) which uses location-allocation principles from geography and operations research (Lea, 1973a, 1973b; Hodgart, 1978) and marketing models pertaining to market penetration (Kotler, 1971) to design an algorithm for determining the optimal locations of diffusion agencies and the time at which each should be established. Other examples include the work on new product management, discussed below on pages 297–300, and Roberto's (1975) application of marketing principles to the diffusion of family planning practices. Extensions of efforts such as these and a more explicit consideration of the market and infrastructure perspective in an applied context ought to greatly enhance our abilities in the task of innovation and new product diffusion.

Finally, the market and infrastructure perspective recognizes and rationalizes the role of public and private infrastructure and other aspects of the general level of development, as discussed in Chapter 8 (pages 263–70). One implication of this is that diffusion strategy ought to be formulated in cognizance of development realities (Rossini and Bozeman, 1977; Glade, Strang, Udell and Littlefield, 1970). Exemplary of this is Lin and Melick's (1977) proposal, summarized in Chapter 8 (pages 264–5), to tailor communications strategies according to a community's *social readiness* for family planning. Likewise, the innovation chosen for propagation also should be *appropriate* in terms of its congruency with a community's level of development (Figure 8.7). A broader implication lies in the provision of a rationale for actions that improve the well-being and skill levels of the populace, and for the creation of infrastructure such as transportation systems, storage depots, credit availability, collection and delivery systems, public processing plants for agricultural products, electricity and water systems. In this context one might even argue that if the proper conditions are created, diffusion, change and growth will soon follow (Rondinelli and Ruddle, 1976; J. C. Miller, 1979: 40–55).

The *economic history perspective* (Chapter 6) provides another set of diffusion strategy options for public programs. Whereas the adoption and market and infrastructure perspectives assume an innovation that does not change over the diffusion period, the economic history perspective explicitly introduces the notion that innovations evolve and are *continually* being perfected and adapted to new uses and new markets. The effect of this is to link research and development endeavors to the diffusion process itself, as well as to acknowledge that diffusion is periodically renewed. Although this perspective has been developed with regard to firm innovations, it is readily applied to innovations adopted by households.

Griliches' (1957: 502) classic study of the diffusion of hybrid corn, for example, noted in Chapter 6, observes

Hybrid corn . . . was not a single invention immediately adaptable everywhere. The actual breeding of adaptable hybrids had to be done separately for each area. Hence . . . we have . . . to explain the lag in the development of adaptable hybrids for specific areas.

In doing this, however, Griliches only cites the fact of

seed producers ranking different areas according to the expected profitability of entry and deciding their actions on this basis. (Griliches, 1957: 507)

An additional, and perhaps more poignant question is the systematic biases of R&D efforts which favor certain classes of markets, activities or uses.[9] Given such knowledge, adaptive or developmental activities could be explicitly directed towards the inadequately served market or those for which a given innovation is not effectively packaged. The question thus becomes not only one of inventing a better mousetrap, but also for whom and for where.[10] Alternatively, the diffusion strategist might well seek an explanation for non-adoption, or for lesser levels of diffusion than are desired, by considering the R&D lab or the manufacturer, as well as in the potential adopter or the practices of the propagator and diffusion agencies.

In short, the full range of policy questions associated with the economic history perspective have hardly been addressed. Once assimilated, however, the concept of continuity in the diffusion process should modify the perspective of most researchers and their programatic counterparts and should lead to important changes in the set of policy alternatives.

Most of the above observations also apply to public programs dealing with *technological innovations*.[11] For example, the diffusion strategies of these programs usually assume an unchanging innovation and are based upon the adoption perspective. One step forward, then, would be to incorporate the notion of continuity and its technological counterpart. However, as discussed in Chapter 5 (pages 169–72), it is also important to recognize that firms supplying innovations to other firms have a market penetration strategy and

carry out practices with regard to price, infrastructure and organization development, promotional communications, packaging, and
market selection and segmentation. As with consumer innovations,
therefore, technological innovations are more readily available (or
more accessible) to some firms than to others. Clearly, then, the
market and infrastructure perspective also should be considered in
formulating policy for the diffusion of innovations among firms.

In summary, in order to be more effective in bringing about
innovation diffusion and adoption, the orientation of present-day
diffusion programs could draw upon the precepts of the market and
infrastructure (Chapters 3 and 4) and economic history (Chapter 6)
perspectives. This does not reflect a preference for strategies derived
from these perspectives so much as the fact that ongoing programs in
the public sector are already designed around the adoption perspective and generally neglect actions consistent with the other perspectives. What is intended, then, is to broaden the public practitioner's
awareness of diffusion strategy options, so that resort may be made to
elements of any of the three diffusion related perspectives, depending
on the situation at hand.[12]

Policy Considerations Pertaining to the Impacts of Innovation Diffusion Programs

A dimension of innovation diffusion that has been given little
attention (or perhaps naive attention) in policy formulation is its
effects upon collective and individual welfare. It is apparently
common to assume that innovation is *ipso facto* good or to only take
immediate effects into account in articulating diffusion policy,
ignoring the second-order or indirect effects. The *development
perspective,* presented in Chapter 8, addresses the consequences of
this orthodox approach and puts forth some new concepts that are
relevant to practitioners. This latter theme is given more attention
here.

One important consideration in a policy context is the choice of
innovation to develop, adapt and diffuse. In a rural developing
economy, for example, it might be a labor-augmenting, peasant-
biased innovation, a neutral innovation, or a material-augmenting,
landlord-biased innovation. A widely held opinion in this regard is
that public programs have leaned towards landlord-biased innovations such as the Green Revolution technology (Yapa, 1977, 1979,
1980; Havens and Flinn, 1970, 1975; DeSouza and Porter, 1974;
Griffin, 1974; Hayami and Ruttan, 1971). Similarly, the Cooperative

Extension Service of the United States has been criticized for its promotion of material-intensive technologies such as no-till farming which implicitly favor the large, well-to-do farmer (Buttel and Flinn, 1977; Hightower, 1973; Goss, 1976; Chapter 4, pages 127–44). Illustrative of this are the observations of Meyerhoff (1980: 11):

Available statistics on the impact of farm mechanization are startling. According to a study done for the U.S. Department of Labor, harvest mechanization in thirteen California crops alone could result in the loss of as many as 128,000 jobs during the next ten years. In the South, the mechanization of tobacco harvesting has already resulted in the loss of nearly 200,000 harvest-time jobs between 1964 and 1972. And in the Midwest, tomato mechanization is displacing thousands of farm workers while small family farmers are going under in disturbing numbers.

Consider the case of the tomato. In the mid-1960s, when the tomato harvester developed by UC was introduced in California, that industry was entirely labor-intensive. In less than ten years, the number of harvest-time jobs declined from more than 50,000 to less than 18,000. The number of tomato farmers dropped from more than 4,000 in 1963 to only 597 in 1973. The average tomato plot grew from 32 acres to 363 acres. Only the most affluent growers had access to the capital needed to purchase these harvesters (at as much as $150,000 each); the companies used the machines and their financial clout to take over the tomato industry. This change has hardly been a boon to consumers, however. During the same time, this now highly concentrated industry increased the price of tomatoes by 111 percent, substantially more than the increase in price for any other fruit or vegetable.

A second important consideration is the design of the diffusion strategy itself. There is considerable evidence that the strategies of traditional diffusion programs tend to favor the better-off in society and thus increase *élitist entrenchment*. Exemplary of this is the two-step flow of communications strategy, which uses socio-economic characteristics and past adoption behavior to identify potential adopters of high innovativeness, achievement motivation or entrepreneurship. Similarly, there are often biases in supporting services and infrastructure. Access to technical or financial resources and loans, for example, typically is differentiated by socioeconomic, ethnic and racial characteristics in a manner that favors the more advantaged in society (Bordenave, 1976, 1977; Havens and Flinn, 1970, 1975; Roling, Ascroft and Chege, 1976). Thus,

Government policies which identify the poorer cultivators as 'tradition-bound', 'conservative' and 'change-resistant', and therefore direct agricultural improvement programmes at the 'kulak' or middle-level peasant because he is more 'rational', 'innovative' and less 'tradition-bound', may be based on a false view of the motivation to innovate. The difference between poor cultivators and wealthier cultivators which is important for innovative behaviour may not be the degree of 'conservatism', but the difference between the poor and the rich pointed out by Ernest Hemingway to F. Scott Fitzgerald. In response to Fitzgerald's comment that 'the rich are different from us', Hemingway replied, 'Yes, they have more money'. (Weeks, 1970: 32)

Less obvious but nevertheless important are a number of biases that derive from the locational dimension of diffusion strategy (Chapters 3 and 4). One instance of this is the choice of where to establish diffusion agencies and when. Cable television in Ohio, for example, was available in small towns in the eastern and south-eastern portions of the state beginning in 1950; in 1965 it first became available in the small towns of the north-west portion of the state; and it did not become available in Columbus, the capital city of approximately 1,000,000 population, until 1970 (pages 79–86). Similarly, public infrastructure or that provided by the diffusion agency itself is rarely ubiquitous, but in any case is established by stages such that some locations receive the infrastructure before others. Thus, within Columbus cable service was first made available in 1970 to portions of the city comprised largely of middle- and upper middle-class white households, and the portions of the city largely comprised of black households did not have access to cable service until January 1979 (Sieling, Malecki and Brown, 1975).[13] Finally, many communications strategies also contain spatial biases by targeting on selected areas or by utilizing media with particular spatial coverage characteristics (L.A. Brown and Moore, 1977: 6–7).

Biases such as those referred to above, whether explicit or implicit, create a distinction between people in terms of when they can adopt a given innovation (or whether they can adopt at all). Further, if it is an innovation related to an economic endeavor, such biases may create or enhance inequities between individuals or groups because of differential gains in adoption rent, which varies according to the time of adoption. That such differences exist is not a problem in itself since the chronic scarcity of resources leaves no other alternative. But a problem *might* arise in so far as people with certain social, economic, demographic and locational characteristics *continually* and *consistently* benefit from the various diffusion programs.

Whether there is or is not a problem in who benefits from diffusion programs depends upon the congruency of that outcome with broad policy objectives. In order to address this, policy makers utilizing diffusion strategies must first be *sensitive* to the explicit and implicit, direct and indirect effects of their actions, and programs must be evaluated in terms of their *total* effect, not just the immediate ones.

Interestingly, this exercise often will lead to a quandary that points up gaps in policy articulation and questions that are difficult if not impossible to resolve. A current example is that of alternative technologies which are generally labor intensive, small in scale and energy conserving. These also

involve massive shifts in the sociopolitical organization of American society. Most of these shifts would weaken hierarchical patterns of social control and power. (Buttel and Flinn, 1977: 13)

Another example, from the author's personal experience, is that of the establishment of textile mills in Brazil.[14] Mills for manufacturing synthetic fabric largely benefit established industries, large metropolitan areas and rural areas with plantation or agribusiness agriculture. The most marked effects of cotton mills, on the other hand, accrue to small business, individual entrepreneurs and the rural and small town economy in proximity to the towns in which the mills are located. In policy terms, then, this situation presents the classic dichotomy of either fostering development in agglomerations and assuming trickle-down effects or stimulating grass roots development under the assumption of trickle-up effects.

In the above two examples of alternative technologies and textile mills, the various outcomes associated with the diffusion of the respective innovation are simply not compatible with one another given the structure of society. There also are real and unresolvable differences of opinion. Does the path to development, for example, require exacerbating or reducing locational, economic and social disparities? And, assuming egalitarianism is not possible, which groups in society ought to be favored?[15]

It is not surprising, then, that there is rarely an articulated policy concerning welfare consequences that might guide the decisions of the diffusion practitioner. Nevertheless, even though there may be no immediate solution in a policy sense, it is important that the various effects be known and themselves articulated, and that the myopia about the consequences of diffusion be reduced.[16]

Research Methodology in a Policy Context

The material presented above provides a set of considerations pertaining to bringing about the adoption and diffusion of innovation and to the impacts of such efforts. While these considerations, in this author's estimation, represent a contribution to the prevailing ongoing perspective of public programs, they are nevertheless general and their application to the diffusion of a specific innovation requires articulating a set of day-to-day practices. To do this, questions that are drastically different from the *modus operandi* of academic and professional researchers must be addressed. How, for example, should the market be segmented for diffusing condoms? Should a similar segmentation procedure be followed for diffusing birth control pills? What will be the overall impact of each of these innovations, and which set of impacts is most desirable? As with any problem, these questions require a standard set of research procedures which would include both an indication of what questions are relevant and methods for addressing them. Presently, such procedures only are available for some aspects of the marketing portion of the perspectives articulated in this book (Kotler, 1971, 1972; Roberto, 1975; Pessemier, 1977; Britt, 1973; Ferber, 1974).

In contemplating this task, however, a paradox comes to mind. By habit, many researchers and funding agencies lead towards a quantitative methodology which concatenates with and promises to extend general theory. At the present time, however, this approach does not seem completely appropriate in that its findings are likely to be of minimal utility for formulating day-to-day diffusion strategy, and possibly in error. A more suitable methodology would render a central role to *qualitative* analysis and take a case study approach in which each particular innovation diffusion situation is treated as unique, allowing general principles to emerge inductively (if at all).

This opinion derives from the author's experience in developing the market and infrastructure perspective. There, qualitative approaches were employed to analyze the diffusion of cable television, Planned Parenthood affiliates, the bank credit card, Friendly Ice Cream (all summarized in Chapter 3) and several agricultural innovations (summarized in Chapters 4, 7 and 8). Methodologically, these studies show that the findings of standard quantitative analyses frequently could be interpreted as supporting the traditional theory of the adoption perspective, whereas considering these together with the qualitative analyses indicated that such an interpretation would be incorrect! Further, the level of detail provided by a quantitative methodology tied to general theory, or even by our qualitative methodology developed to concatenate with general theory, is not sufficient for articulating a set of practices. These methodological observations also are supported by the work of Gold (1975, 1977, 1978; Gold, Pierce and Rosegger, 1970) on technological innovations in an industrial setting.

Two other research issues also warrant attention. One is for predictive models which would permit the practitioner to evaluate the likely effects of using different diffusion strategies. A number of these have been developed in marketing as *new product growth models,* but their implementation primarily involves extrapolating a curve fit to data pertaining to the previous rate(s) of diffusion over time. The logistic is most commonly used, although other functions also are found (Dodson and Muller, 1978; Mahajan and Peterson, 1978, 1979; Bass, 1969; Kotler, 1971: 519–63; Midgley, 1977: 248–77). Another set of new product growth models are more ambitious in their conceptualization. TRACKER, for example, includes an actual component for establishing the effects of advertising, price, distribution and product attributes (Blattberg and Golanty, 1978). In implementation, however, consideration generally is given only to advertising and price, and even in that extrapolation constitutes an important basis of the prediction. Further, these models are generally oriented towards continuous innovation in a developed society, such as supermarket goods, and do not include the majority of the diffusion considerations discussed in this book. They also do not provide predictions with a spatial component.

The quandary, then, is that the extrapolation models generally are not suitable for evaluating the likely effects of different diffusion strategies, because of the lack of substantive detail, but our knowledge of diffusion process is not sufficiently extensive to enable the design and implementation of a predictive model with more substantive content. Nevertheless, the design and partial implementation of models such as TRACKER or SPRINTER (Urban, 1970) is a worthwhile task in that it illuminates parts of the relationship between diffusion strategy and outcomes of which we know little; points out data and knowledge needs; and provides a forum for adapting operations research, management analysis and related techniques to the study of innovation diffusion as broadly conceived in this book. Such tasks, then, define a research agenda which, when completed, allows modification, further articulation and calibration of the predictive model.[17]

The final research need to be discussed here is for evaluation procedures and criteria. In private sector diffusion, the criteria for success would most apparently be profit, although other, less precise criteria also can be relevant (Baumol, 1972: 310–34). In the public sector, however, the goals are not so evident. For example, family planning programs have sought to maximize the number of new adoptions, but the number of continuing users are ultimately more important (Demerath, 1976; E.M. Rogers, 1973:152–224; Mandani,

1972). Going one step further, the impact of family planning upon population growth and the economic burden of population also are significant. For an innovation related to economic endeavor, a broad criteria for success, in addition to the number of adopters or continual users, could involve equity considerations and the effects upon social and economic disparities within a population. Even if evaluation criteria are decided upon, however, what level indicates *success?* For example, what percentage of the target population ought to adopt, in what amount of time and at what amount of cost to warrant a program being judged *effective?*[18]

In summary, there have been a number of studies employing a research approach in which qualitative analysis, predictive modeling or evaluation has a central role. Nevertheless, the formulation of a research strategy that might assist in defining specific practices to diffuse innovations remains an elusive goal (Rich, 1979; Gregg, Preston, Geist and Caplan, 1979). One reason is that the earlier studies have been primarily concerned with testing conceptual or theoretical models. Another reason is that the question of day-to-day implementation in diffusion generally has been left to the business community, where it is frequently solved on intuitive grounds rather than as the result of a conscious research effort. Finally, the business research that is done embodies a pragmatism with which most professional researchers have little experience.

Nevertheless, the four perspectives of innovation diffusion presented in this book—the adoption perspective, the market and infrastructure perspective, the economic history perspective and the development perspective—together with related research, constitute a beginning for the task of articulating a set of policy-oriented research procedures such as those discussed above. Completing this task is a formidable challenge, but doing so is one of the most important needs in the context of inserting innovations into society and improving diffusion policy and practices.

AN ILLUSTRATIVE EXAMPLE: FAMILY PLANNING IN THIRD WORLD NATIONS

As a closing exercise on the topic of public sector programs of innovation diffusion, it is useful to consider the discussion of the preceding section in the context of an actual set of programs. Accordingly, attention now turns to family planning in Third World settings. These programs generally utilize the traditional, adoption-oriented, communications paradigm; have operated long enough to have a record of successes and failures; and have been extensively analyzed.[19] Demerath's (1976: 86–117) observations on

why family planning programs have failed in poor countries

provides a focus for the discussion.[20]

Demerath's first observations is that family planning programs have been obsessed with technique. In part, this is because the problem has been viewed as medical rather than social, and accordingly, the remedy has been in terms of finding a suitable inoculation or vaccine. Historically, however, lowered fertility rates have occurred without the benefit of modern techniques, relying instead upon coitus interruptus, induced abortion and the condom.

A second and related observation is that family planning practitioners have oversimplified the motivations underlying fertility behavior. They have implicitly assumed that anyone can plan their personal life and that families will choose to have fewer children if they have knowledge of the advantages of doing so and if birth control methods are made available. Demerath notes, however, that Third World persons are more likely to perceive their lives as being controlled by fate, rather than self controlled, and that the social and economic fabric in which they exist makes it reasonable to have more rather than fewer children. In India, for example, it is religiously, socially and economically important to have at least one son surviving into the parent's old age. To ensure this, however, given the (perceived) death rate, each family should have six plus children on the average (Blaikie, 1975: 16–17).[21]

Demerath's third observation is that the actual characteristics of existing social institutions and customary behavior patterns are frequently overlooked by family planners. Accordingly, the level of resistance to *innovation* is underestimated. This suggests that the level of development and the related social norms are critical elements in bringing about a lowered birth rate, as discussed in Chapter 8 (pages 264–6), and that family planning ought to be only one prong of a broad program of social and economic development that attacks the *disease of poverty* and seeks to alter the societal fabric. Ironically, this observation is consistent with the precepts of the demographer's own transition theory, but Demerath would say that it has eluded the designers of family planning programs.[22]

Demerath's fourth observation is that family planning programs in Third World nations have been designed with a built-in political impotence. Being viewed as medical rather than social programs, they typically are housed in health ministries which have little political power. Further, Demerath posits that the widespread acceptance of these programs by Third World governments is precisely because of their *don't rock the boat* character and their built-in likelihood of failure in terms of meaningful social change.

Finally, Demerath observes that family planning programs are characterized by weak management, which in essence means they are characterized by a non-business-like approach. An elaboration of this point would include the observations of Roberto (1975) regarding the utility of marketing approaches for family planning programs and the comments here regarding the policy implications of the market and infrastructure perspective.

At this juncture of policy formulation with regard to innovation diffusion in general, the study of Demerath (1976) and related works by Blaikie (1975) and Weinstein (1976) are very significant. One reason is that all three studies emphasize the importance of the practitioner having an intimate familiarity, in a case study manner, with the situation he is trying to affect. Second, all three studies point up the need for critically evaluating and rethinking the traditional communications-oriented diffusion paradigm and its related strategies. Finally, the observations of these studies are consistent with those made in this chapter, with the primary difference being that Demerath and Weinstein give more emphasis to the societal context of diffusion whereas this chapter, and Roberto (1975) on family planning, emphasize the specific means of diffusing innovations.

To illustrate the broader relevance of these observations, consider the United States program of urban renewal (Congressional Research Service, 1973). Originally, this was characterized by a technological fix or better mousetrap mentality which emphasized bulldozing and replacement with modern buildings. Faced with failure and in some cases a worsening of the situations that were to be remedied, however, these programs now emphasize maintenance of the social and physical fabric of neighborhoods and their utilization as bases for reconstruction and renewal. It is not likely, given the political realities, that the next step would be a broad program of social change, as Demerath might hope for. Nevertheless, there is a growing awareness of the neighborhood system overall and of the impacts and social effects of housing policy innovations upon American cities.

Another current example is in the development and diffusion of solar energy technology. With regard to the educational aspects of this endeavor, Burns, Mason and Armington (1979: 37) note

The adoption and development perspectives were shown to be relevant to developing general education programs aimed at potential adopters of solar energy systems and to identifying possible causes of resistance. The market and infrastructure perspective and the economic history perspective address the institutional mechanisms for and barriers to diffusion of a technological innovation. As such, they implicitly include the education and training of people involved in the production and delivery of the innovation. In addition, the economic history perspective explicitly considers the skills of the users and the skills in machine making. These two perspectives and the current attempts to define the solar energy technology delivery system (TDS) illustrate the importance of education and training in diffusing a technology and identify the various types of persons to be reached by the education and training programs (e.g. installers, building tradesman, real estate developers, loan officers, utility company planners).

In summary, then, evidence points to the importance of using all four of the perspectives presented in this book in designing programs of innovation diffusion.

OVERVIEW

This chapter begins by briefly summarizing the perspectives on innovation diffusion articulated in this book: the adoption perspective, the market and infrastructure perspective, the economic history perspective and the development perspective.

The chapter then addresses the policy implications of the comprehensive model that arises from viewing these four perspectives together. Topics addressed include the strategies employed by public programs of innovation diffusion to bring about adoption; the economic, social and development impacts of these strategies; and the design of research intended to provide guidelines for policy or program formulation. One theme of this section is that most public program practitioners are employing only a small range of the myriad of tools at their disposal, and that incorporating a wider range of tools into diffusion strategy would increase their level of effectiveness in most situations. A second theme is that public program practitioners should adopt a societal perspective. This would include tailoring diffusion programs so they are cognizant of and congruent with the values and needs of the target population, using existing societal systems to improve efficiency in the task of diffusion, and being aware of the broad societal implications and impacts of diffusion program actions.

The final section of this chapter gives detailed attention to family planning programs in Third World nations. This is intended to provide a more elaborate illustration of the policy implications discussed in the preceding section.

Contemporary research, not yet manifest in policy, reflects a growing awareness of issues such as those raised in this chapter and the book as a whole. The shift away from reliance upon the communications model of innovation diffusion, for example, is evident throughout social science, as is the concern with the impacts of innovations and of the strategies by which they are diffused. It is likely, therefore, that the theories, models, collective findings and programs of innovation diffusion of the future will look quite different from those of the present. It is hoped that this book will facilitate that progress.

NOTES

1 Helpful comments pertaining to the policy issues raised in the remainder of this chapter were provided by Kevin R. Cox and Fred Day of the Ohio State University Department of Geography; David Roessner, formerly with the Office of Policy Research and Analysis of the National Science Foundation and now with the Georgia Institute of Technology, Department of Social Science; Patricia McWethy, formerly with the Social Science Division of the National Science Foundation and now with the Association of American Geographers; and Jay Weinstein of the Georgia Institute of Technology Department of Social Science.
2 A comprehensive treatment of this theme can be found in Rein (1976).
3 It should be noted that the efficacy of family planning programs has been the subject of much debate, and recent evidence casts more favorable judgement on this point. For further discussion, see note 20 of this chapter.
4 See, however, Rich (1979), Rossini and Bozeman (1977), Winner (1977), and Gregg, Preston, Geist and Caplan (1979).
5 Others have been more strident in their criticism. For example, Weinstein (1976: 3) provides the following from the *New York Times* of August 6, 1973

India's soaring birth rate has been unchecked by family planning drives in recent years. There are 57,000 Indian babies born daily. . . . Originally the Government's target was to reduce the birth rate from 41 per thousand population in 1968 to 25 by 1976. The Government has now extended the target date to 1980. The birth rate is now 38 per thousand.

To place this observation in perspective, Demerath (1976: 59) notes that

The Government of India in 1952 was the first in the world to adopt family planning as a national policy. No other nation has received so much money, technical assistance, and equipment from the family planning establishment. And no other nation has spent so much of its own funds on family planning.

However, there also is a set of more optimistic views on this question, which are discussed in note 20 below.
6 For a detailed discussion of some ways in which diffusion agency establishment considerations apply to public sector diffusions, see Meyer and Brown (1979: 247–8).
7 There are, however, exceptions to this observation. In India, Sri Lanka and Kenya, for example, the commercial condom distribution program has operated in conjunction with, and sometimes as a part of, the Government's program. The

Nirodh program of India is discussed extensively by E.M. Rogers (1973: 352–63); the *Preethi* program of Sri Lanka is discussed by Davies and Louis (1977); and Black (1976) and Black and Harvey (1976) discuss the Kenya program. There also are *community-based* distribution programs which represent a hybrid of the commercial and the traditional communications-oriented programs (Davies and Rodrigues, 1976; Echeverry, 1975). These references, together with Roberto's work (1975, 1976, 1977), should provide much useful information for other public sector or non-profit motivated diffusions.

8 This is particularly so in that the development of practical knowledge relevant to innovation and new product diffusion has largely reflected the prevailing concern with adoption and consumer behavior. Accordingly, these efforts have primarily focused on problems such as the effects of various mixes of promotional communications or the determination of consumer preferences. For a more complete discussion of the techniques developed in this context, see Kotler (1971, 1972), Roberto (1975); Pessemier (1977), Britt (1973) and Ferber (1974).

9 Examples of such an enquiry for agricultural activity include Hightower (1973) and Hayami and Ruttan (1971).

10 The viewpoint implied in this question is found in some public programs, as indicated by the inventory of Hough (1975), but it does not appear to be generally recognized as an integral part of diffusion strategy.

11 Another important set of diffusion programs to which such parallels also apply are these concerned with innovations adopted by communities. Recent studies of these include Bingham (1976), Perry and Kraemer (1978), Agnew, Brown and Herr (1978), Feller, Menzel and Kozak (1976), Lambright (1977) and Yin (1978).

12 How diffusion strategy would vary from innovation to innovation is a related question to which no attention has been given here. This neglect is largely because little research has been done on the topic, which is unfortunate since it is an important consideration for the practitioner. There has, however, been work on innovation characteristics which can be seen as an initial step towards differentiating diffusion strategies (E.M. Rogers and Shoemaker, 1971: 134–72). Characteristics noted as important in a diffusion context include an innovation's *relative advantage, compatability, complexity, observability, triability* and *communicability*. Also relevant is Robertson's (1971: 7) classification of innovations as either *continuous, dynamically continuous* or *discontinuous*, summarized in Chapter 1. Also see Zaltman, Duncan and Holbeck (1973).

13 Another dimension of this is that Columbus is presently being used to commercially test the educationally valuable innovation of two-way or participatory (viewer accessible) cable television (Beerman, 1977; Lachenbruch, 1977; Wood, 1978), but the cable company carrying out this test does not serve the portion of the city largely comprised of black households.

14 In June 1977 Howard Gauthier of the Ohio State University Department of Geography and the author prepared a report reviewing the activities of the Social Science Section of the Brazilian Institute of Geography and Statistics. The Brazilian textile mills example was used in that report, where it is elaborated in greater detail than here.

15 Examples of social policies which represent responses to questions such as these include special educational programs for deprived minorities in the United States, and the triage approach to the world food problem whereby countries are divided into those which will improve without assistance, those which require assistance and those which would not be significantly improved were any amount of assistance given (Knight and Wilcox, 1975).

16 For a related discussion, see Winner (1977), Garrison (1978), Rich (1979), Gregg, Preston, Geist and Caplan (1979).

17 For a comprehensive discussion of new product growth models in marketing see Kotler (1971: 119–63), Midgley (1977: 248–77), Robertson (1971: 249–94) and

Pessemier (1977). Incidently, the PROMAR model presented in this book (pages 57–9) could be seen as an example of a new product growth model.

18 A comprehensive discussion of evaluation procedures in family planning programs can be found in Roberto (1975: 111–14). This ought to be relevant to designing evaluation procedures for other innovation diffusion programs.

19 Also, these are the only diffusion programs to have all of these characteristics.

20 There are least two schools of thought on the reasons for fertility decline. One, of which Demerath is representative, views this as a response to societal conditions. The second school sees fertility decline more narrowly as a technological issue akin to the prevention of disease. Accordingly, the *societalists* generally would advocate broadly focused family planning programs that are concerned with the social context as well as birth control *per se,* whereas the program format advocated by the *technologists* would primarily consist of the latter concern. Since most Third World programs of family planning have been implemented on the technologists' model and since little abatement of the population problem of the Third World has occurred, there has been an apparent justification for the societalists' view of programmatic failure. However, recent evidence indicates a marked decline in the fertility level of several Third World countries and traces this, at least in part, to the influence of the ongoing family planning programs (Tsui and Bogue, 1978; Mauldin and Berelson, 1978; Knodel, 1978). Irregardless of the philosophical origins of Demerath's observations, however, they complement the perspective of this book as it pertains to the design of diffusion programs in general. Thus, Demerath's observations are employed purely for illustrative purposes, and there is no intent to promote either the societalist or the technologist viewpoint.

21 To illustrate the importance of sons, Blaikie (1975: 17) states the following. First, sons are required to perform the last funeral rites for parents. Second, sons attract dowries upon marriage whereas daughters require the family to give one. Third, sons provide economic security in old age. Fourth, sons stay at home after marriage (whereas daughters go with their husbands) and therefore provide emotional security in old age. Fifth, sons provide income and help in the field and house from an early age. Sixth, sons bring prestige, local political power and protection against the threat of physical force for household, kinship group and caste. In summary, then, the absence of a son in a family is a source of shame and economic, social and political vulnerability.

22 Interestingly, there has been some recent rethinking of demographic transition theory which is consistent with Demerath's observations about the importance of the societal fabric. Caldwell (1976, 1978) argues that economic development *per se* or industrialization may not be the key element in demographic transition, but rather cultural factors such as the direction of flows in intragenerational wealth. He notes that in traditional societies the flow is from younger to older generations whereas the flow is in the reverse direction in North American and Western European societies. Caldwell aruges further that related to the direction of flow in intragenerational wealth is the structure of the family. Whereas most traditional societies are characterized by extended families, modern societies are characterized by families that are highly nucleated both emotionally and economically. In a related observation, Demerath notes that Third World nations which have had successful family planning programs such as China and Sri Lanka have such a family structure and equitable, although not necessarily abundant, distribution of wealth (Demerath, 1976: 118–35, 157–90). For a related discussion, also see Weinstein (1976).

REFERENCES

Abler, R., Adams, J.S. and Gould, P.R. (1971) *Spatial Organization: The Geographer's View of the World,* Englewood Cliffs, Prentice-Hall.

Agnew, J.A. (1979) 'Instrumentalism, realism, and research on the diffusion of innovation', *Professional Geographer,* 31, 364–70.

Agnew, J.A. (ed.) (1980) *Innovation Research and Public Policy,* Syracuse, University of Syracuse Geographical Series.

Agnew, J.A., Brown, L.A. and Herr, J.P. (1978) 'The community innovation process: a conceptualization and empirical analysis', *Urban Affairs Quarterly,* 14, 3–30.

Aiken, M. and Alford, R.R. (1970) 'Community structure and innovation: the case of public housing', *American Political Science Review,* 64, 843–64.

Amedeo, D. and Golledge, R.G. (1975) *An Introduction to Scientific Reasoning in Geography,* New York, John Wiley.

Anderson, D. and Leiserson, M.W. (1978) *Rural Enterprise and Nonfarm Employment,* Washington, World Bank.

Anderson, D. and Leiserson, M.W. (1980) 'Rural nonfarm employment in developing countries', *Economic Development and Cultural Change,* 28, 227–48.

Anderson, D.L. (1970) 'A simple growth model for the diffusion of hybrid corn', *Proceedings of the Association of American Geographers,* 2, 1–3.

Anderson, D.L. (1971) 'On a class of innovation diffusion models', Ph.D. Dissertation, Evanston, Northwestern University, Department of Geography.

Arndt, J. (1967) *Word of Mouth Advertising,* New York, Advertising Research Foundation.

Aufhauser, R.K. (1974) 'Slavery and technological change', *Journal of Economic History,* 34, 36–50.

Babcock, J.M. (1962) 'Adoption of hybrid corn: a comment', *Rural Sociology,* 27, 332–8.

Bangura, J.S. (1965) 'The cooperative movement in Sierra Leone', *Bank of Sierra Leone Economic Review,* 2.

Bartholomew, D.J. (1973) *Stochastic Models for Social Processes,* 2nd edn, New York, John Wiley.

Bartos, O.J. (1967) *Simple Models of Group Behavior,* New York, Columbia University Press.

Bass, F.M. (1969) 'A new product growth model for consumer durables', *Management Science*, 15, 215–27.

Bateman, F. (1968) 'Improvement in American dairy farming, 1850–1910; a quantitative analysis', *Journal of Economic History*, 28, 255–73.

Baumol, W.J. (1972) *Economic Theory and Operations Analysis*, 3rd edn, Englewood Cliffs: Prentice-Hall.

Beckmann, M. (1968) *Location Theory*, New York, Random House.

Beer, S. (1968) *Management Science*, New York, Doubleday.

Beerman, F. (1977) 'QUBE looks for New World in Columbus: will big public pay for two-way services?' *Variety*, December 21.

Bell, S. (1965) 'The diffusion of radio and television broadcasting stations in the United States', M.A. thesis, Department of Geography, University Park, Pennsylvania State University.

Beltran, L.R. (1976) 'Alien premises, objects, and methods in Latin American communication research', in Rogers, E.M. (ed.) *Communication and Development: Critical Perspectives*, Beverly Hills, Sage.

Berg, S.V. (1973) 'Determinants of technological change in the service industries', *Technological Forecasting and Social Change*, 5, 407–26.

Berry, B.J.L. (1967) *Strategies, Models and Economic Theories of Development in Rural Regions*, Washington, US Government Printing Office.

Berry, B.J.L. (1972) 'Hierarchical diffusion: the basis of developmental filtering and spread in a system of growth centers', in Hansen, N.M. (ed.) *Growth Centers in Regional Economic Development*, New York, Free Press.

Berry, B.J.L. (1973) *Growth Centers in the American Urban Systems, Vols. I and II*, Cambridge, Mass., Ballinger.

Berry, B.J.L. and Horton, F.E. (1970) *Geographic Perspectives on Urban Systems*, Englewood Cliffs, Prentice-Hall.

Berry, B.J.L. Conkling, E.C. and Ray, D.M. (1976) *The Geography of Economic Systems*, Englewood Cliffs, Prentice-Hall.

Bingham, R.D. (1976) *The Adoption of Innovation By Local Government*, Lexington, Lexington Books.

Black, T.R.L. (1976) 'Community-based distribution: the distributive potential and economics of a social marketing approach to family planning', *Proceedings of the Royal Society of London, Series B*, 195, 199–212.

Black, T.R.L. and Harvey, P. (1976) 'A report on a social marketing experiment in rural Kenya', *Studies in Family Planning*, 7, 101–8.

Blackman, A.W., Seligman, E.J. and Sogliero, G.C. (1976) 'An innovation index based on factor analysis', in Linstone, H.A. and Sahal, D. (eds.) *Technological Substitution: Forecasting Techniques and Applications*, New York, Elsevier.

Blaikie, P.M. (1975) *Family Planning in India: Diffusion and Policy*, London, Edward Arnold.

Blattberg, R. and Golanty, J. (1978) 'TRACKER: an early test market forecasting and diagnostic model for new product planning', *Journal of Marketing Research*, 15, 192–202.

Bobek, H. (1962) 'The main stages in socio-economic evolution from a geographical point of view', in Wagner, R.L., and Mikesell, M.W. (eds.) *Readings in Cultural Geography*, Chicago, University of Chicago Press.

Bodenheimer, S.J. (1970) 'The ideology of developmentalism: American political science's paradigm surrogate for Latin American studies, *Berkeley Journal of Sociology*, 15, 95–137.

Boon, F. (1967) 'A simple model for the diffusion of an innovation in an urban system', Chicago, University of Chicago, Center for Urban Studies.

Borchert, J.R. (1972) 'America's changing metropolitan regions', *Annals of the Association of American Geographers*, 62, 352–73.

Bordenave, J.D. (1976) 'Communication of agricultural innovations in Latin America: the need for new models', in Rogers, E.M. (ed.) *Communication and Development: Critical Perspectives*, Beverley Hills, Sage.

Bordenave, J.D. (1977) 'La transferencia de technologia y la teoria general de los sistemas', Institute Interamericano de Ciencias Agricolas, Officina en Brasil.

Boughton, A.C. (1933) 'What 7309 "mothers" want', *Birth Control Review*, January, 8–11.

Bowden, L.W. (1965) *Diffusion of the Decision to Irrigate*. Chicago, University of Chicago, Department of Geography, Research Paper Series.

Bowers, R.V. (1937) 'The direction of intra-societal diffusion', *American Sociological Review*, 2, 826–36.

Bowers, R.V. (1938) 'Differential intensity of intra-societal diffusion', *American Sociological Review*, 3, 21–31.

Briscoe, G., Cannon, T. and Lewis, A.L. (1972) 'The market development of new industrial products', *European Journal of Marketing*, 6, 7–16.

Britt, S.H. (1973) *The Dartnell Marketing Manager's Handbook*, Chicago, Dartnell.

Brown, L.A. (1963) 'The diffusion of innovation: a Markov chain type approach', Evanston, Northwestern University, Department of Geography.

Brown, L.A. (1965) 'Models for spatial diffusion research: a review', ONR Spatial Diffusion Study, Evanston, Northwestern University, Department of Geography.

Brown, L.A. (1968a) *Diffusion Dynamics: A Review and Revision of the Quantitative Theory of the Spatial Diffusion of Innovation*, Lund, Gleerup, Lund Studies in Geography.

Brown, L.A. (1968b) *Diffusion Processes and Location: A Conceptual Framework and Bibliography*, Philadelphia, Regional Science Research Institute.

Brown, L.A. (1969) 'Diffusion of innovation: a macroview', *Economic Development and Cultural Change*, 17, 189–211.

Brown, L.A. (1970) 'On the use of Markov chains in movement research', *Economic Geography*, 46, 393–403.

Brown, L.A. (1974) 'Diffusion in a growth pole context', in Helleiner, F. and Stohr, W. (eds.), *Proceedings of the Commission on Regional Aspects of Economic Development of the International Geographical Union, Vol. II: Spatial Aspects of the Development Process*, Toronto, Allister.

Brown, L.A. (1975) 'The market and infrastructure context of adoption: a spatial perspective on the diffusion of innovation', *Economic Geography*, 51, 185–216.

Brown, L.A. (1977) 'Diffusion research in geography: a thematic account', Columbus, Ohio State University, Department of Geography, Studies in the Diffusion of Innovation.

Brown, L.A. (1978) 'The innovation diffusion process in a public policy context', in Radnor, M., Feller, I., and Rogers, E.M. (eds.) *The Diffusion of Innovations: An Assessment*, Evanston, Northwestern University, Center for the Interdisciplinary Study of Science and Technology.

Brown, L.A. (1980) 'The innovation diffusion process in a public policy context', in Agnew, J.A. (ed.) *Innovation Research and Public Policy*, Syracuse, Syracuse University Geographical Series.

Brown, L.A. (1981) *Innovation Diffusion: A New Perspective*, London and New York, Methuen.

Brown, L.A. and Albaum, M. (1971) 'On rural settlement in Israel and model strategy', in McConnell, H. and Yaseen, D. (eds.) *Perspectives in Geography 1: Models of Spatial Variation*, Dekalb, Northern Illinois University Press.

Brown, L.A. and Cox, K.R. (1971) 'Empirical regularities in the diffusion of innovation', *Annals of the Association of American Geographers*, 61, 551–9.

Brown, L.A. and Lentnek, B. (1973) 'Innovation diffusion in a developing economy: a mesoscale view', *Economic Development and Cultural Change*, 21, 274–92.

Brown, L.A. and Malecki, E.J. (1977) 'Comments on landscape evolution and diffusion processes', *Regional Studies*, 11, 211–23.

Brown, L.A. and Moore, E.G. (1969) 'Diffusion research in geography: a perspective', in Board, C., Chorley, R.J., Haggett, P. and Stoddart, D.R. (eds.) *Progress in Geography, Vol. 1*, London, Edward Arnold.

Brown, L.A. and Moore, E.G. (1970) 'The intra urban migration process: a perspective', *Geografiska Annaler, Series B*, 52, 1–13. Also in *Yearbook of the Society for General Systems Research*, 15, 109–22.

Brown, L.A. and Philliber, S.G. (1977) 'The diffusion of a population-related innovation: the Planned Parenthood Affiliate', *Social Science Quarterly*, 58, 215–28.

Brown, L.A., Craig, C.S. and Zeller, R.E. (1977) 'PROMAR: the new product marketing game', *Computer Applications*, 4, 677–768.

Brown, L.A., Malecki, E.J. and Spector, A.N. (1976) 'Adopter categories in a spatial context: alternative explanations for an empirical regularity', *Rural Sociology*, 41, 99–118.

Brown, L.A., Schneider, R., Harvey, M.E. and Riddell, J.B. (1979) 'Innovation diffusion and development in a Third World setting: the case of the cooperative movement in Sierra Leone', *Social Science Quarterly*, 60, 249–68.

Brown, L.A., Malecki, E.J., Gross, S.R., Shrestha, M.N. and Semple, R. K. (1974) 'The diffusion of cable television in Ohio: a case study of diffusion agency location processes of the polynuclear type', *Economic Geography*, 50, 285–99.

Brown, L.A., Williams, F.B., Youngmann, C.E., Holmes, J. and Walby, K. (1974) 'The location of urban population services facilities: a strategy and its application', *Social Science Quarterly*, 54, 784–99.

Brown, M.A. (1977) 'The role of diffusion agencies in innovation diffusion: a behavioral approach,' Ph.D. Dissertation, Columbus, Ohio State University, Department of Geography. Also in Studies in the Diffusion of Innovation, Ohio State University, Department of Geography.

Brown, M.A. (1980) 'Attitudes and social categories: complementary explanations of innovation adoption behavior', *Environment and Planning*, 12, 175–86.

Brown, M.A. and Brown, L. A. (1976) 'Innovation establishment in a rural setting: four case studies with reference to a theoretical framework', Columbus, Ohio State University, Department of Geography, Studies in the Diffusion of Innovation.

Brown, M.A. and Brown, L. A. (1976) 'The diffusion of BankAmericard in a rural setting: supply and infrastructure considerations', *Proceedings of the Association of American Geographers*, 8, 74–8.

Brown, M.A., Maxson, G.E. and Brown, L. A. (1977) 'Diffusion agency strategies and innovation diffusion: a case study of the Eastern Ohio Resource Development Center', *Regional Science Perspectives*, 7, 1–26.

Bucklin, L. P. (1967) *Shopping Patterns in an Urban Area*. Berkeley, University of California at Berkeley, Institute of Business and Economic Research.

Burke, R.V. (1979) 'Green Revolution technologies and farm class in Mexico', *Economic Development and Cultural Change*, 28, 135–54.

Burns, B., Mason, B. and Armington, K. (1979) 'The role of education and training programs in the commercialization and diffusion of solar energy technologies', Denver, Solar Energy Research Institute.

Burton, I. (1968) 'The quantitative revolution and theoretical geography', in Berry, B.J.L. and Marble, D.K. (eds.) *Spatial Analysis: A Reader in Statistical Geography*, Englewood Cliffs, Prentice-Hall.

Buttel, F.H. and Flinn, W.L. (1977) 'Social barriers to the adoption of foreign and alternative technologies by the United States', Columbus, Ohio State University, Department of Geography, Studies in the Diffusion of Innovation.

Bylund, E. (1960) 'Theoretical consideration regarding the distribution of settlement in Inner North Sweden', *Geografiska Annaler*, 42, 225–31.

Caldwell, J.C. (1976) 'Towards a restatement of demographic transition theory', *Population and Development Review*, 2, 321–66.

Caldwell, J.C. (1978) 'A theory of fertility: from high plateau to destablization', *Population and Development Review*, 4, 553–78.

Campbell, R.H. (1955) 'Developments in the Scottish pig iron trade, 1844–1848', *Journal of Economic History*, 15, 209–26.

Carey, J.H. (1971) 'Cable television: its impact upon the broadcast industry as seen by Tennessee broadcasters and cable television system operators', M.A. Thesis, Nashville, University of Tennessee.

Carlsson, G. (1966) 'The decline of fertility: innovation or adjustment process', *Population Studies,* 20, 149–74.

Carlstein, T. (1978) 'Innovation, time allocation and time-space packing', in Carlstein, T., Parkes, D. and Thrift, N. (eds.) *Human Activity and Time Geography,* London, Edward Arnold.

Carlstein, T., Parkes, D. and Thrift, N. (eds.) (1978a) *Timing Space and Spacing Time 1: Making Sense of Time,* London, Edward Arnold.

Carlstein, T., Parkes, D., and Thrift, N. (eds.) (1978b) *Timing Space and Spacing Time 2: Human Activity and Time Geography,* London, Edward Arnold.

Carlstein, T., Parkes, D. and Thrift, N. (eds.) (1978c) *Timing Space and Spacing Time 3: Time and Regional Dynamics,* London, Edward Arnold.

Casetti, E. (1969) 'Why do diffusion processes conform to logistic trends?' *Geographical Analysis,* 1, 101–5.

Casetti, E. and Semple, R.K. (1969) 'Concerning the testing of spatial diffusion hypotheses,' *Geographical Analysis,* 1, 254–9.

Casetti, E., King, L.J. and Jeffrey, D. (1971) 'Structural imbalance in the U.S. urban economic system, 1960–65, *Geographical Analysis,* 3, 239–55.

Casetti, E., King. L.J. and Odland, J. (1971) 'The formalization and testing of concepts of growth poles in a spatial context,' *Environment and Planning,* 3, 377–82.

Chappell, J.M.A. and Webber, M.J. (1970) 'Electrical analogues of spatial diffusion processes,' *Regional Studies,* 4, 25–39.

Chase, H.J. (1969) 'Cable television in Missouri,' M.A. Thesis, Columbia, University of Missouri.

Chilcote, R.H. and Edelstein, J.C. (1974) 'Alternative perspectives of development and underdevelopment in Latin America,' in Chilcote, R.H. and Edelstein, J.C. (eds.) *Latin America: The Struggle with Dependency and Beyond,* New York, Schenkman, Halstead Press.

Chisholm, M. (1974) 'Regional policies for the 1970s,' *Geographical Journal,* 140, 215–44.

Chung, R. (1970) 'Space-time diffusion of the transition model: the twentieth century patterns,' in Demko, G.J.,Rose, H.M. and Schnell, G.A. (eds.) *Population Geography: A Reader,* New York, McGraw-Hill.

Clark, D. (1974) 'Technology, diffusion, and time-space convergence: the example of S.T.D. telephone,' Columbus, Ohio State University, Department of Geography, Studies in the Diffusion of Innovation.

Clarke, D.L. (1968) *Analytical Archaeology,* London, Methuen.

Cobb, R.W. (1971) 'Black settlement in Silverton, Ohio, 1960–1967: a spatial diffusion process', M.A. Thesis, Buffalo, University of New York at Buffalo, Department of Geography.

Cochran, T.C. (1966) 'The entrepreneur in economic change', *Explorations in Entrepreneurial History,* 2nd series, 4, 25–38.

Code of Federal Regulations (1973) *Telecommunications,* Parts 70–9, Washington, US Government Printing Office.

Cohen, M.R. and Nagel E. (1934) *An Introduction to Logic and Scientific Method*, New York, Harcourt, Brace & World.

Cohen, Y.S. (1972) *Diffusion of an Innovation in an Urban System: The Spread of Planned Regional Shopping Centers in the United States, 1949–1968*, Chicago, University of Chicago, Department of Geography, Research Paper Series.

Coleman, J.S. (1964) *Introduction to Mathematical Sociology*, New York, Free Press.

Coleman, J.S., Katz, E. and Menzel, H. (1957) 'The diffusion of an innovation among physicians', *Sociometry*, 20, 253–70.

Coleman, J.S., Katz, E. and Menzel, H. (1959) 'Social processes in physicians' adoption of a new drug', *Journal of Chronic Diseases*, 9, 1–19.

Coleman, J.S., Katz, E. and Menzel, H. (1966) *Medical Innovation: A Diffusion Study*, Indianapolis, Bobbs-Merrill.

Collins, L. (1973) 'Industrial size distributions and stochastic processes', in Board, C., Chorley, R.J., Haggett, P. and Stoddart, D.R. (eds.) *Progress in Geography, Vol. 5*, London, Edward Arnold.

Congressional Research Service (1973) *The Central City Problem and Urban Renewal Policy*, Washington, US Government Printing Office.

Cooper, R.B. (1966) *CATV System Management and Operation*, Thurmont, TAB Books.

Copeland, O.B. (1966) 'Public Relations', in Sanders, H.C. (ed.) *The Cooperative Extension Service*, Englewood Cliffs, Prentice-Hall.

Cox, K.R. and Demko, G.J. (1968) 'Conflict behavior in a spatio temporal context', *Sociological Focus*, 1, 55–67.

Craig, C.S. and Brown, L.A. (1974) 'An experimental approach to the study of diffusion agency establishment processes', Columbus, Ohio State University, Department of Geography, Studies in the Diffusion of Innovation.

Craig, C.S. and Brown, L.A. (1978) 'Spatial diffusion of innovation: a gaming aproach', *Simulation and Games*, 9, 29–52.

Craig, C.S. and Brown, L.A. (1980) 'Simulating the spatial diffusion of innovation: a gaming experimental approach', *Socio-Economic Planning Sciences*, 14, 167–79.

Crain, R.L. (1966) 'Fluoridation: the diffusion of an innovation among cities', *Social Forces*, 44, 467–76.

Crain, R.L., Katz, E. and Rosenthal, D.B. (1969) *The Politics of Community Conflict: The Flouridation Decision*, Indianapolis, Bobbs-Merrill.

Davies, P.J. and Louis, T.D.J. (1977) 'Measuring the effectiveness of contraceptive marketing programs: Preethi in Sri Lanka', *Studies in Family Planning*, 8, 82–90.

Davies, P.J. and Rodrigues, W. (1976) 'Community-based distribution of oral contraceptives in Rio Grande do Norte, north-eastern Brazil', *Studies in Family Planning*, 7, 202–6.

Davis, K. (1963) 'The theory of change and response in modern demographic history', *Population Index*, 29, 345–66.

Davis, L.E. and North, D.C. (1970) 'Institutional change and American economic growth: a first step towards a theory of innovation', *Journal of Economic History,* 30, 131–49.

Davis, L.E. and North, D.C. (1971) *Institutional Change and American Economic Growth,* Cambridge, Cambridge University Press.

Day, R.H. (1970) 'A theoretical note on the spatial diffusion of something new', *Geographical Analysis,* 2, 68–76.

DeFleur, M.L. (1970) *Theories of Mass Communication,* 2nd edn, New York, David McKay.

DeJanvry, A. (1973) 'A socio economic model of induced innovations for Argentine agricultural development', *Quarterly Journal of Economics,* 87, 410–35.

Demerath, N.J. (1976) *Birth Control and Foreign Policy: The Alternatives to Family Planning,* New York, Harper & Row.

DeSouza, A.R. and Porter, P.W. (1974) *The Underdevelopment and Modernization of the Third World,* Washington, Association of American Geographers, Resource Paper Series.

DeTemple, D.J. (1971) *A Space Preference Approach to the Diffusion of Innovations: The Spread of Harvestore Systems Through Northeast Iowa,* Bloomington, Indiana University, Department of Geography, Geographic Monograph Series.

Deutschmann, P.J. and O. Fals Borda. (1962) *Communication and Adoption Patterns in an Andean Village,* San Jose, Programa Interamericano de Informacion Popular.

Deutschmann, P.J., Mendez, A. and Herzog, W. (1967) *Adoption of Drugs and Foods in Five Guatemalan Villages.* San Jose, Programa Interamericano de Informacion Popular.

Dhalla, N.K. and Mahattoo, W.H. (1976) 'Expanding the scope of segmentation research', *Journal of Marketing,* 40–2, 34–41.

Dickinson, H.W. (1939) *A Short History of the Steam Engine,* Cambridge, Cambridge University Press.

Dodson, J.A. and Muller, E. (1978) 'Models of new product diffusion through advertising and word-of-mouth', *Management Science,* 24, 1568–78.

Drucker, P.F. (1958) 'Marketing and economic development', *Journal of Marketing,* 22, 252–9.

Duncan, O.D. (1957) 'Population distribution and community structure', *Cold Harbor Springs Symposium on Quantitative Biology,* 22, 357–71.

Earickson, R.A. (1975) 'The spatial pattern of income generation in lead firm, growth area linkage systems', *Economic Geography,* 51, 17–26.

Echeverry, G. (1975) 'Development of the Profamilia rural family planning program in Colombia', *Studies in Family Planning,* 6, 142–7.

Edmonson, M.S. (1961) 'Neolithic diffusion rates', *Current Anthropology,* 2, 71–102.

Eiden, R.J. (1968) 'Innovation diffusion through the urban structure of North Dakota', M.A. Thesis, Grand Forks, University of North Dakota, Department of Geography.

Engel, J.F., Blackwell, R.D. and Kollat, D.T. (1978) *Consumer Behavior*, 3rd edn, Hinsdale, Dryden Press.

Engwall, L. (1973) *Models of Industrial Structure*, Lexington, D. C. Heath.

Enos, J.L. (1962) 'Invention and innovation in the petroleum industry', in Universities-National Bureau Committee for Economic Research, *The Rate and Direction of Inventive Activity*, Princeton, Princeton University Press.

Erickson, F.A. (1973) 'Location of a system of storage distribution terminals for agricultural ammonia in the corn belt', Ph.D. Dissertation, Urbana, University of Illinois, Department of Geography.

Evans, K.J. (1959) 'When and how should you sell through distributors?', *Industrial Marketing*, March, 41–4.

Evanson, R. (1974) 'The international diffusion of agrarian technology', *Journal of Economic History*, 34, 51–73.

Federal Communications Commission (1972) *Rules and Regulations*, vol. 3, Washington, US Government Printing Office.

Feller, I. (1966) 'The Draper Loom in New England textiles, 1894–1914: a study of diffusion of an innovation', *Journal of Economic History*, 26, 320–42.

Feller, I. (1971) 'The urban location of United States invention, 1860–1910', *Explorations in Economic History*, 8, 285–303.

Feller, I. (1975) 'Invention, diffusion, and industrial location', in Collins, L. and Walker, D.F. (eds.) *The Locational Dynamics of Manufacturing Activities*, New York, John Wiley.

Feller, I. (1979) 'Three coigns on diffusion research', *Knowledge: Creation, Diffusion, Utilization*, 1, 293–312.

Feller, I. and Menzel, D.C. with Kozak, L.A. (1976) *Diffusion of Innovations in Municipal Governments*, University Park, Pennsylvania State University, Institute for Research on Human Resources, Center for the Study of Science Policy.

Ferber, R. (1974) *Handbook of Marketing Research*, New York, McGraw-Hill.

Fiorentino, R., Pineiro, M. and Trigo, E. (1978) 'Limitations of appropriate technology as a strategy for development of the small farm sector', Instituto Interamericano de Ciencias Agricolas, Officina en Colombia.

Fischer, G.C. (1968) *American Banking Structure*, New York, Columbia University Press.

Fishlow, A.L. (1966) 'Productivity and technological change in the railroad sector, 1840–1910', in Brady, D. (ed.) *Output, Employment and Productivity in the United States after 1800*, New York, National Bureau of Economic Research.

Fogel, R.W. and Engerman, S.L. (1971a) 'A model for the explanation of industrial expansion during the nineteenth century: with an application to the American iron industry', in Fogel, R.W. and Engerman, S.L. (eds.) *The Reinterpretation of American Economic History*, New York, Harper & Row.

Fogel, R.W. and Engerman, S.L. (eds.) (1971b) *The Reinterpretation of American Economic History,* New York, Harper & Row.

Forbes, R.J. (1958) *Man the Maker: A History of Technology and Engineering,* London, Abelard-Schuman.

Foster, G.M. (1962) *Traditional Cultures and the Impact of Technological Change,* New York, Harper & Row.

Foster, G.M. (1973) *Traditional Societies and Technological Change,* 2nd edn, New York, Harper & Row.

Frank, A.G. (1967) *Capitalism and Underdevelopment in Latin America,* New York, Monthly Review Press.

Frank, R.E., Massy, W.E. and Wind, Y. (1972) *Market Segmentation,* Englewood Cliffs, Prentice-Hall.

Friedmann, J. (1972) 'A general theory of polarized development', in Hansen, N.M. (ed.) *Growth Centers in Regional Economic Development,* New York, Free Press.

Friedmann, J. (1973) *Urbanization, Planning, and National Development,* Beverly Hills, Sage.

Friedmann, J. (1975) 'The spatial organization of power in the development of urban systems', in Friedmann, J. and Alonso, W. (eds.) *Regional Policy: Readings in Theory and Application,* Cambridge, Mass., MIT Press.

Fuller, G. (1974) 'On the spatial diffusion of fertility decline: The distance-to-clinic variable in a Chilean Community, *Economic Geography,* 50, 324–32.

Gaile, G.L. (1980) 'The spread-backwash concept', *Regional Studies,* 14, 15–25.

Gale, S. (1972) 'Some formal properities of Hagerstrand's model of spatial interactions', *Journal of Regional Science,* 12, 199–217.

Garrison, W.L. (1978) 'Thinking about public facility systems', in *The National Research Council in 1978,* Washington, National Academy of Sciences.

Garrison, W.L. and Marble, D.F. (1965) 'A prolegomenon to the forecasting of transportation development', Evanston, Northwestern University, Transportation Center.

Garst, Ronald D. (1972) 'The spatial diffusion of agricultural innovations in Kisii District, Kenya,' Ph.D. Dissertation, East Lansing, Michigan State University, Department of Geography.

Garst, Ronald D. (1973) 'Spatial diffusion and information diffusion: a Kenyan example', *Proceedings of the Association of American Geographers,* 5, 75–80.

Garst, R.D. (1974a) 'Innovation diffusion among the Gusii of Kenya', *Economic Geography,* 50, 300–12.

Garst, R.D. (1974b) 'Spatial diffusion in rural Kenya: the impact of infrastructure and centralized decision making', Columbus, Ohio State University, Department of Geography, Studies in the Diffusion of Innovation.

Gauthier, H.L. (1968) 'Transportation and the growth of the São Paulo economy', *Journal of Regional Science*, 8, 77–94.

Getis, A. (1969) 'Residential location and the journey from work', *Proceedings of the Association of American Geographers*, 1, 55–9.

Gilbert, A.G. and Goodman, D.E. (1976) 'Regional income disparities and economic development: a critique', in Gilbert, A.G. (ed.) *Development Planning and Spatial Structure*, New York, John Wiley.

Gilmour, J.M. (1974) 'External economies of scale, interindustry linkages, and decision making in manufacturing', in Hamilton, F.E.I. (ed.) *Spatial Perspectives on Industrial Organization and Decision Making*, New York, John Wiley.

Glade, W.P., Strang, W.A., Udell, J.C. and Littlefield, J.E. (1970) *Marketing In a Developing Nation: The Competitive Behavior of Peruvian Industry*, Lexington, Heath Lexington.

Gladwin, C.H. (1979) 'Cognitive strategies and adoption decisions: a case study of nonadoption of an agronomic recommendation', *Economic Development and Cultural Change*, 28, 155–173.

Gold, B. (ed.) (1975) *Technological Change: Economics, Management, and Environment*, Oxford, Pergamon Press.

Gold, B. (ed.) (1977) *Research, Technological Change, and Economic Analysis*, Lexington, Lexington Books.

Gold, B. (1978) 'Some shortcomings of research on the diffusion of industrial technology', in Radnor, M., Feller, I. and Rogers, E. M. (eds.) *The Diffusion of Innovations: An Assessment*, Evanston, Northwestern University, Center for the Interdisciplinary Study of Science and Technology.

Gold, B., Peirce, W.S. and Rosegger, G. (1970) 'Diffusion of major technological innovations in U.S. iron and steel manufacturing', *Journal of Industrial Economics*, 18, 218–41.

Gold, B., Peirce, W.S. and Rosegger, G. (1975) 'Diffusion of major technological innovations', in Gold, B. (ed.) *Technological Change: Economics, Management, and Environment*, Oxford, Pergamon Press.

Gonzalez, C. (1965) 'Internal colonialism and national development', *Studies in Comparative International Development*, 1, 27–37.

Gordon, D.L. (1978) *Employment and Development of Small Enterprises*, Washington, World Bank.

Goss, K.F. (1976) 'Consequences of diffusion of innovations: the case of mechanization in U.S. agriculture', M.A. Thesis, East Lansing, Michigan State University, Department of Rural Sociology.

Gotsch, C.H. (1972) 'Technical change and the distribution of income in rural areas', *American Journal of Agricultural Economics*, 54, 326–41.

Gould, P.R. (1969) *Spatial Diffusion*. Washington, Association of American Geographers, Resource Paper Series.

Gould, P.R. and Tornqvist, G. (1971) 'Information, innovation, and acceptance', in Hagerstrand, T. and Kuklinski, A.R. (eds.) *Information Systems for Regional Development: A Seminar*, Lund, Gleerup, Lund Studies in Geography.

Gregg, G., Preston, T., Geist, A. and Caplan, N. (1979) 'The caravan rolls on: forty years of social problem research', *Knowledge: Creation, Diffusion, Utilization*, 1, 31–61.

Griffin, K. (1974) *The Political Economy of Agrarian Change: An Essay on the Green Revolution*, Cambridge, Mass., Harvard University Press.

Griffith, D.A. and Jones, K.G. (1980) 'Explorations into the relationship between spatial structure and spatial interaction', *Environment and Planning*, 12, 187–201.

Griliches, Z. (1957) 'Hybrid corn: an exploration in the economics of technological change', *Econometrica*, 25, 501–22.

Griliches, Z. (1962) 'Profitability versus interaction: another false dichotomy', *Rural Sociology*, 27, 327–30.

Gruber, W.H. and Marquis D.G. (eds.) (1969) *Factors in the Transfer of Technology*, Cambridge, Mass., MIT Press.

Grunig, J.E. (1971) 'Communication and the economic decision making processes of Colombian peasants', *Economic Development and Cultural Change*, 19, 580–97.

Guerrero, R.N. (1975) *Rural to Urban Drift of the Unemployed in Colombia*, Lund, Lund University Geography Institute.

Hagerstrand, T. (1952) *The Propagation of Innovation Waves*, Lund, Gleerup, Lund Studies in Geography.

Hagerstrand, T. (1953) *Innovationsforloppet ur Korologisk Synpunkt*. Lund, Gleerup. Translated by A. Pred as *Innovation Diffusion as a Spatial Process*, Chicago, University of Chicago Press, 1967.

Hagerstrand, T. (1957) 'Migration and Area', in Hannenberg, D., Hagerstrand, T. and Odeving, B. (eds.) *Migration in Sweden: A Symposium*, Lund, Gleerup, Lund Studies in Geography.

Hagerstrand, T. (1965a) 'A Monte Carlo Approach to Diffusion', *Archives Europeennes de Sociologie*, 6, 43–67.

Hagerstrand, T. (1965b) 'Quantitative techniques for analysis of the spread of information and technology', in Anderson, C.A. and Bowman, M.J. (eds.) *Education and Economic Development*, Chicago, Aldine.

Hagerstrand, T. (1967a) *Innovation Diffusion as a Spatial Process*, Chicago, University of Chicago Press.

Hagerstrand, T. (1967b) 'On the Monte Carlo Simulation of Diffusion', in Garrison, W.L. and Marble, D.F. (eds.) *Quantitative Geography, Part I: Economic and Cultural Topics*, Evanston, Northwestern University Press, Studies in Geography.

Hagerstrand, T. (1974) 'On socio-technical ecology and the study of innovations', *Ethnologica Europaea*, 7, 17–34.

Hagerstrand, T. and Kuklinski, A. R. (eds.) (1971) *Information Systems for Regional Development: A Seminar*. Lund, Gleerup, Lund Studies in Geography.

Haggett, P. (1965) *Locational Analysis in Human Geography*, London, Edward Arnold.

Haggett, P., Cliff, A.D. and Frey, A. (1977) *Locational Analysis in Human Geography*, 2nd edn, New York, John Wiley.

REFERENCES

319

Hakanson, S. (1974) 'Special presses in paper making', in Nabseth, L. and Ray, G.F. (eds.) *The Diffusion of New Industrial Processes*, Cambridge, Cambridge University Press.

Hall, P. and Hay, D. (1980) *Growth Centers in the European Urban System*, London, Heinemann.

Hanham, R.Q. (1973) 'Diffusion of innovation from a supply perspective: an application to the artificial insemination of cattle in southern Sweden', Ph.D. Dissertation, Columbus, Ohio State University, Department of Geography.

Hanham, R.Q. and Brown, L.A. (1972) 'Diffusion through an urban system: the testing of related hypotheses', *Tijdschrift Voor Economische en Sociale Geografie*, 64, 388–92.

Hanham, R.Q. and Brown, L.A. (1976) 'Diffusion waves within the context of regional economic development', *Journal of Regional Science*, 16, 65–72.

Hanneman, G.J., Carroll, T.W., Rogers, E.M., Stanfield, J.D. and Lin, N. (1969) 'Computer simulation of innovation diffusion in a peasant village', *American Behavioral Scientist*, 12(6), 36–45.

Hannemann, M. (1975) *The Diffusion of the Reformation in Southwestern Germany, 1518–1534*, Chicago, University of Chicago, Depart of Geography, Research Paper Series.

Hansen, N.M. (1971) *Intermediate-Size Cities as Growth Centers: Applications for Kentucky, The Piedmont Crescent, The Ozarks, and Texas*, New York, Praeger.

Harlan, J.R. and Zohary, D. (1966) 'Distribution of wild wheats and barley', *Science*, 153, 1074–80.

Harley, C.K. (1971) 'The shift from sailing ships to steamships, 1850–1890', in McCloskey, D.N. (ed.) *Essays on a Mature Economy: Britain after 1840*, London, Methuen.

Harley, C.K. (1973) 'On the persistance of old technologies: the case of North American wooden shipbuilding', *Journal of Economic History*, 33, 372–98.

Harris, S. (1952) *Economics of New England*, Cambridge, Mass., Harvard University Press.

Harvey, D. (1971) 'Social processes, spatial form, and the redistribution of real income in an urban system', in Chisholm, M., Frey, A.E. and Haggett, P. (eds.) *Regional Forecasting*, London, Butterworth.

Harvey, D. (1973) *Social Justice and the City*, Baltimore, Johns Hopkins University Press.

Harvey, D. (1974) 'Population, resources, and the ideology of science', *Economic Geography*, 50, 256–77.

Harvey, M.E. and Greenberg, P. (1973) 'Development dichotomies, growth poles, and diffusion processes', in Helleiner, F. and Stohr, W.B. (eds.) *Proceedings of the Commission on Regional Aspects of Economic Development of the International Geographical Union, Vol. II: Spatial Aspects of the Development Process*, Toronto, Allister.

Havelock, R.G. (1969) *Planning for Innovation: Through Dissemination and Utilization of Knowledge*, Ann Arbor, University of Michigan, Institute for Social Research.

Havens, A.E. and Flinn, W.L. (eds.) (1970) *Internal Colonialism and Structural Change in Colombia*, New York, Praeger.

Havens, A.E. and Flinn, W.L. (1975) 'Green revolution technology and community development: the limits of action programs', *Economic Development and Cultural change*, 23, 469–81.

Hawley, A.M. (1963) 'Community power structure and urban renewal success', *American Journal of Sociology*, 68, 422–31.

Hayami, Y. (1974) 'Conditions for the diffusion of agricultural technology: an Asian perspective', *Journal of Economic History*, 34, 131–48.

Hayami, Y. and Ruttan, V.W. (1971) *Agricultural Development: An International Perspective*, Baltimore, Johns Hopkins University Press.

Hightower, J. (1973) *Hard Tomatoes, Hard Times: A Report of the Agribusiness Accountability Project on the Failure of America's Land Grant College Complex*, Cambridge, Mass., Schenkman.

Hirschman, A.O. (1958) *The Strategy of Economic Development*, New Haven, Yale University Press.

Hjalmarsson, L. (1974) 'The size distribution of establishments and firms derived from an optimal process of capacity expansion', *European Economic Review*, 5, 123–40.

Hodgart, R.L. (1978) 'Optimizing access to public services: a review of problems, models and methods of locating central facilities,' *Progress in Human Geography*, 2, 17–48.

Holmes, J., Williams, F.B. and Brown, L.A. (1972) 'Facility location under a maximum travel restriction: an example using day care facilities', *Geographical Analysis*, 4, 258–66.

Hough, G.W. (1975) *Technology Diffusion: Federal Programs and Procedures*, Mt. Airy, Lomond Books.

Hovland, C.I., Janis, I.L. and Kelley, H.H. (1953) *Communication and Persuasion*, New Haven, Yale Univeristy Press.

Howard, J.A. and Sheth, J.N. (1969) *The Theory of Buyer Behavior*, New York, John Wiley.

Hudson, J.C. (1969a) 'A location theory for rural settlement', *Annals of the Association of American Geographers*, 59, 365–81.

Hudson, J.C. (1969b) 'Diffusion in a central place system,' *Geographical Analysis*, 1, 45–58.

Hudson, J.C. (1972) *Geographical Diffusion Theory*, Evanston, Northwestern University Press, Studies in Geography.

Hurter, A.P. and Rubenstein, A.H. (1978) 'Market penetration by new innovations: the technological literature', *Technological Forecasting and Social Change*, 11, 197–221.

Hyde, C.K. (1971) 'Technological change and the development of the British iron industry, 1700–1860,' Ph.D. Dissertation, Madison, University of Wisconsin, Department of History.

Ijiri, Y. and Simon, H.A. (1971) 'Effects of mergers and acquisitions on business firm concentration', *Journal of Political Economy*, 79, 314–22.

Ijiri, Y. and Simon, H.A. (1974) 'Interpretations of departures from the

Pareto curve firm size distributions', *Journal of Political Economy*, 82, 315–31.

Jeffrey, D. (1970) 'Economic impulses in an urban system', Ph.D. Dissertation, Columbus, Ohio State University, Department of Geography.

Jeffrey, D. (1974) 'Regional fluctuations in unemployment within the U.S. urban economic system: a study of the spatial impact of short term economic change', *Economic Geography*, 50, 111–23.

Johansen, H.E. (1971) 'Diffusion of strip cropping in southwestern Wisconsin', *Annals of the Association of American Geographers*, 61, 671–83.

Johnson, E.A.J. (1970) *The Organization of Space in Developing Countries*, Cambridge, Mass., Harvard University Press.

Johnson, P.S. (1975) *The Economics of Invention and Innovation: With a Case Study of the Development of the Hovercraft*, London, Martin Robertson.

Johnston, J.R. (1972) *Urban Residential Patterns: An Introductory Review*, New York, Praeger.

Johnston, R.E. (1968) 'The transfer of the cooperative movement to a non western environment: its development, its economic and political functions, and its role in Sierra Leone', Ph.D. Dissertation, Los Angeles, University of California at Los Angeles, Department of Agricultural Economics.

Jones, G.E. (1967) 'The adoption and diffusion of agricultural practices', *World Agricultural Economics and Rural Sociology Abstracts*, 9, 1–34.

Karlsson, G. (1958) *Social Mechanisms: Studies in Sociological Theory*, New York, Free Press.

Karr, G.R. and Bangura, J.S. (1968) 'Cooperatives and the development of a credit system for Sierra Leone agriculture', *Bank of Sierra Leone Economic Review*, 3.

Katz, E. (1957) 'The two-step flow of communication: an up-to-date report on an hypothesis', *Public Opinion Quarterly*, 21, 61–78.

Katz, E., Levin, M. and Hamilton, H. (1963) 'Traditions of research on the diffusion of innovation', *American Sociological Review*, 28, 237–52.

Kaufman, I. (1972) 'Change management: the process and system', in Zaltman, G. Kotler, P. and Kaufman, I. (eds.) *Creating Social Change*, New York, Holt, Rinehart, & Winston.

Kegerreis, R., Engel, J.F. and Blackwell, R.D. (1970) 'Innovativeness and diffusiveness: a marketing view of the characteristics of early adopters', in Kollat, D.T., Blackwell, R.D. and Engel, J.F. (eds.) *Research in Consumer Behavior*, New York, Holt, Rinehart & Winston.

Kelly, P. and Kranzberg, M. (eds.) (1978) *Technological Innovation: A Critical Review of Current Knowledge*, San Francisco: San Francisco Press.

Kennedy, D.M. (1970) *Birth Control in America*, New Haven, Yale University Press.

Kenya (1969) *Development Plan: 1970 to 1974,* Nairobi, Ministry of Economic Planning and Development.

King, L.J. (1976) 'Alternatives to a positive economic geography', *Annals of the Association of American Geographers,* 66, 293–308.

King, L.J., Casetti, E. and Jeffrey, D. (1969) 'Economic impulses in a regional system of cities: a study of spatial interaction', *Regional Studies,* 3, 213–18.

Kisii (1962) *District Annual Reports, Kisii District,* Nairobi, Department of Agriculture.

Kisii (1970) *District Annual Reports, Kisii District,* Nairobi, Department of Agriculture.

Knight, C.G. and Newman, J.L. (eds.) (1976) *Contemporary Africa: Geography and Change,* Englewood Cliffs, Prentice-Hall.

Knight, C.G. and Wilcox, R.P. (1975) *Triumph or Triage: The World Food Problem in Geographical Perspective,* Washington, Association of American Geographers, Resource Paper Series.

Knodel, J. (1978) 'Fertility transition in Thailand: a comparative analysis of survey data', Tokyo Conference on Comparative Fertility Transition in Asia.

Kochen, M. and Deutsch, K.W. (1969) 'Toward a rational theory of decentralization: some implications of a mathematical approach', *American Political Science Review,* 63, 734–49.

Kochen, M. and Deutsch, K.W. (1972) 'Pluralization: a mathematical model', *Operations Research,* 20, 276–92.

Kollat, D.T., Blackwell, R.D. and Robeson, J.F. (1972) *Strategic Marketing,* New York, Holt, Rinehart, & Winston.

Kotler, P. (1971) *Marketing Decision Making: A Model Building Approach,* New York, Holt, Rinehart & Winston.

Kotler, P. (1972) *Marketing Management: Analysis, Planning, and Control,* Englewood Cliffs, Prentice-Hall.

Kotler, P. (1975) *Marketing for Nonprofit Organizations,* Englewood Cliffs, Prentice-Hall.

Kresge, D.T. and Roberts, P.O. (1971) *Systems Analysis and Simulation Models,* Washington, The Brookings Institution.

Kuhn, T.S. (1970) *The Structure of Scientific Revolutions,* 2nd edn, Chicago, University of Chicago Press.

Lachenbruch, D. (1977) 'Will it play in Columbus?', *TV Guide,* December.

Lambright, W.H. (1977) *Adoption and Utilization of Urban Technology: A Decision Making Study,* Syracuse: Syracuse Research Foundation.

Lancaster, G.A. and White, M. (1976) 'Industrial diffusion, adoption, and communication', *European Journal of Marketing,* 10, 280–98.

Larouche, P. (1965) 'The simulation of residential land use growth in the Montreal region,' M.A. Thesis, New Haven, Yale University, Department of City Planning.

Lea, A.C. (1973a) 'Location-allocation models: a review', M.A. Thesis, Toronto, University of Toronto, Department of Geography.

Lea, A.C. (1973b) 'Location-allocation systems: an annotated bibliography', Toronto, University of Toronto, Department of Geography.

LeDuc, D.R. (1970) 'Community antenna television as a challenger of broadcast regulatory policy', Ph.D. Dissertation, Madison, University of Wisconsin.

Lentnek, B. (1969) 'Economic transition from traditional to commerical agriculture: the case of El Llano, Mexico', *Annals of the Association of American Geographers,* 59, 65–84.

Lentnek, B., Charnews, M. and Cotter, J.V. (1978) 'Commercial factors in the development of regional urban systems: a Mexican case study', *Economic Geography,* 54, 291–308.

Levison, M., Ward, R.G. and Webb, J.W. (1973) *The Settlement of Polynesia: A Computer Simulation,* Minneapolis, University of Minnesota Press.

Levitt, T. (1965) 'Exploit the Product Life Cycle', *Harvard Business Review,* 43, 6, 81–96.

Levy, G.W. (1972) *The Interactions of Science and Technology in the Innovative Process: Some Case Studies,* Washington, National Science Foundation.

Lewis, W.A. (1954) 'Development with Unlimited Supplies of Labor', *Journal of the Manchester School of Economics and Social Studies,* 20, 139–92.

Liedholm, C. and Chuta E. (1976) 'The economics of rural and small scale industries in Sierra Leone', East Lansing, Michigan State University, Department of Agricultural Economics.

Lilley, S. (1948) *Man, Machines and History,* London, Cobbett Press.

Lin, N. (1971) 'Information flow, influence flow, and the decision making process', *Journalism Quarterly,* 48, 33–40.

Lin, N. and Burt, R.S. (1975) 'Differential effects of information channels in the process of innovation diffusion', *Social Forces,* 54, 256–74.

Lin, N. and Melick, C. (1977) 'Structural effects on the diffusion of innovations', Columbus, Ohio State University, Department of Geography, Studies in the Diffusion of Innovation.

Lin, N., Hingson, R. and Allwood-Paredes, J. (1971) 'Mass immunization campaign in El Salvador, 1969', *HSMHA Health Reports,* 86, 1112–21.

Linstone, H.A. and Sahal, D. (1976) *Technological Substitution: Forecasting Techniques and Applications,* New York, Elsevier.

Littlewood, T.B. (1977) *The Politics of Population Control,* Notre Dame, University of Notre Dame Press.

Lovelock, C.H. and Weinberg, C.B (1978) 'Public and nonprofit marketing comes of age', in Zaltman, G. and Bonoma, T.V. (eds.) *Review of Marketing 1978,* Chicago, American Marketing Association.

Maddala, G.S. and Knight, P.T. (1967) 'International diffusion of technical change: a case study of the oxygen steel making process', *Economic Journal,* 77, 531–58.

Mahajan, V. and Peterson, R.A. (1978) 'Innovation diffusion in a dynamic potential adopter population', *Management Science*, 24, 1589–97.

Mahajan, V. and Peterson, R.A. (1979) 'First purchase diffusion models of new product acceptance', *Technological Forecasting and Social Change*, 15, 127–46.

Mak, J. and Walton, G.M (1972) 'Steamboats and the great productivity surge in river transportation', *Journal of Economic History*, 32, 619–40.

Mak, J. and Walton, G.M (1973) 'The persistance of old technologies: the case of flatboats', *Journal of Economic History*, 33, 444–51.

Malecki, E.J. (1975) 'Innovation diffusion among firms', Ph.D. Dissertation, Columbus, Ohio State University, Department of Geography. Also in Studies in the Diffusion of Innovation, Ohio State University, Department of Geography.

Malecki, E.J. (1977) 'Firms and innovation diffusion: examples from banking', *Environment and Planning*, 9, 1291–1305.

Malecki, E.J. and Brown, L.A. (1975) 'The adoption of credit card services by banks: a case study of innovation diffusion', *Bulletin of Business Research of the Ohio State University*, 50, 8, 1–4.

Mandani, M. (1972) *The Myth of Population Control: Caste and Class in an Indian Village*, New York, Monthly Review Press.

Mansfield, E. (1961) 'Technical change and the rate of imitation', *Econometrica*, 29, 741–66.

Mansfield, E. (1968a) *Industrial Research and Technological Innovation: An Econometric Analysis*, New York, W. W. Norton.

Mansfield, E. (1968b) *The Economics of Technological Change*, New York, W. W. Norton.

Marble, D.F. (1967) *Some Computer Programs for Geographic Research*, Evanston, Northwestern University, Department of Geography.

Marble, D.F. and Bowlby, S.R. (1968) 'Computer programs for the operational analysis of Hagerstrand type spatial diffusion models', ONR Spatial Diffusion Study, Evanston, Northwestern University, Department of Geography.

Marble, D.F. and Nystuen, J.D. (1963) 'An approach to the direct measurement of community mean information fields', *Papers of the Regional Science Association*, 11, 99–109.

Marble, D.F., Hanson, P.O., Huff, J.O., Manji, A.S. and Pacheco, E. (1970) 'A Monte Carlo model for the simulation of a distance biased interpersonal communications net', ONR Spatial Diffusion Study, Evanston, Northwestern University, Department of Geography.

Mauldin, W.P. and Berelson, B. (1978) 'Conditions of fertility decline in developing countries, 1965–75', *Studies in Family Planning*, 9, 89–148.

Mayfield, R.C. (1967) 'The spatial structure of a selected interpersonal contact: a regional comparison of marriage distances in India', ONR Spatial Diffusion Study, Evanston, Northwestern University, Department of Geography. Also in English, P.W. and Mayfield, R.C. (eds.) *Man, Space, and Environment*, New York, Oxford University Press, (1972).

Mayfield, R.C. and Yapa, L.S. (1974) 'Information Fields in Rural Mysore', *Economic Geography*, 50, 313–23.

McClelland, D.C. (1961) *The Achieving Society*, Princeton, Van Nostrand.

McGuire, E.P. (1971) *Franchise Distribution*, New York, The Conference Board, Research Report 523.

McVoy, E.C. (1940) 'Patterns of diffusion in the United States', *American Sociological Review*, 5, 219–27.

Meir, A. (1979) 'A disparity based diffusion model', *Professional Geographer*, 31, 382–7.

Menanteau-Horta, D. (1967) 'Diffusion and adoption of agricultual techniques among Chilean farmers: a sociological study on the processes of communication and acceptance of innovations as factors related to social change and agricultural development in Chile', Ph.D. Dissertation, Minneapolis, University of Minnesota, Department of Sociology.

Meyer, J.W. (1975) *Diffusion of an American Montessori Education*, Chicago, University of Chicago, Department of Geography, Research Paper Series.

Meyer, J.W. and Brown, L.A. (1979) 'Diffusion agency establishment: the case of Friendly Ice Cream and public sector diffusion processes', *Socio Economic Planning Sciences*, 13, 241–49.

Meyer, J.W., Brown, L.A. and Camarco, T.J. (1977) 'Diffusion agency establishment in a mononuclear setting: the case of Friendly Ice Cream and related considerations', Columbus, Ohio State University, Department of Geography, Studies in the Diffusion of Innovation.

Meyerhoff, A. (1980) 'Big farming's angry harvest', *Newsweek*, March 3, 11.

Midgley, D.F. (1977) *Innovation and New Product Marketing*, New York, John Wiley.

Mikesell, M.W. (1967) 'Geographic perspectives in anthropology', *Annals of the Association of American Geographers*, 57, 617–34.

Mikesell, M.W. (1978) 'Tradition and innovation in cultural geography', *Annals of the Association of American Geographers*, 68, 1–16.

Miller, A.J. (1967) 'Community Antenna Television: History and Outlook', M.A. Thesis, Urbana, University of Illinois.

Miller, J.C. (1974) *Regional Development: A Review of the State of the Art*, Washington, Agency for International Development, Bureau of Technical Assistance, Office of Urban Development.

Miller, J.C. (1979) *Regional Development: A Review of the State of the Art*, Washington: Agency for International Development, Bureau of Technical Assistance, Office of Urban Development.

Misra, R.P. (1969) 'Monte Carlo simulation of spatial diffusion: rationale and application to the Indian condition', in Misra, R.P. (ed.) *Regional Planning*, Mysore, University of Mysore Press.

Mitchelson, R.L., Brown, L.A. and Osleeb, J.P. (1977) 'Technical change in the agricultural sector: a problem in developing countries', Columbus, Ohio State University, Department of Geography, Studies in the Diffusion of Innovation.

Moore, E.G. (1966) 'Models of migration and the intraurban case', *Australian and New Zealand Journal of Sociology*, 2, 16–37.

Moore, E.G. (1970) 'Some spatial properties of urban contact fields', *Geographical Analysis*, 2, 376–86.

Moore, E.G. and Brown, L.A. (1970) 'Urban acquaintance fields: an evaluation of a spatial model', *Environment and Planning*, 2, 443–54.

Morrill, R.L. (1965a) 'Expansion of the urban fringe: a simulation experiment', *Papers of the Regional Science Association*, 15, 185–99.

Morrill, R.L. (1965b) *Migration and the spread and growth of urban settlement*, Lund, Gleerup, Lund Studies in Geography.

Morrill, R.L. (1965c) 'The Negro ghetto: problems and alternatives', *Geographical Review*, 55, 339–61.

Morrill, R.L. (1968) 'Waves of spatial diffusion', *Journal of Regional Science*, 8, 1–18.

Morrill, R.L. (1970) 'The shape of diffusion in space and time', *Economic Geography*, 46, 259–68.

Morrill, R.L. (1974) 'Growth center–hinterland relations', in Helleiner, F. and Stohr, W. (eds.) *Proceedings of the Commission on Regional Aspects of Economic Development of the International Geographical Union, Vol. II: Spatial Aspects of the Development Process*, Toronto, Allister.

Morrill, R.L. and Manninen, D. (1975) 'Critical parameters of spatial diffusion processes', *Economic Geography*, 51, 269–77.

Morrill, R.L. and Pitts, F.R. (1967) 'Marriage, migration, and the mean information field', *Annals of the Association of American Geographers*, 57, 401–22.

Moseley, M.J. (1973a) 'The impact of growth centers in rural regions—I. an analysis of spatial "patterns" in Brittany', *Regional Studies*, 7, 57–75.

Moseley, M.J. (1973b) 'The impact of growth centers in rural regions—II. an analysis of spatial "flows" in East Anglia', *Regional Studies*, 7, 77–94.

Mueller, D.C. (1972) 'A life cycle theory of the firm', *Journal of Industrial Economics*, 20, 199–219.

Murphy, J.A. (1948) 'What types of distribution setup for the new product', *Sales Management*, April, 44–50.

Myers, S. and Marquis, D.G. (1969) *Successful Industrial Innovations: A Study of Factors Underlying Innovation in Selected Firms*, Washington, US Government Printing Office.

Myrdal, G. (1957) *Economic Theory and Underdeveloped Regions*, London, Duckworth.

Nabseth, L. (1973) 'The diffusion of innovations in Swedish industry', in Williams, B.R. (ed.) *Science and Technology in Economic Growth*, New York, John Wiley.

Nabseth, L. and Ray, G.F. (eds.) (1974) *The Diffusion of New Industrial Processes: An International Study*, Cambridge, Cambridge University Press.

Nam, C.B. and Gustavus, S.O. (1976) *Population: The Dynamics of Demographic Change*, Boston, Houghton Mifflin.

Nartowitz, F. (1977) 'The diffusion of zero population growth chapters within the United States', Columbus, Ohio State University, Department of Geography, Studies in the Diffusion of Innovation.

National Academy of Sciences—National Research Council (1965) *The Science of Geography*, Washington: US Government Printing Office.

Newling, B.E. (1969) 'The spatial variation of urban population densities', *Geographical Review*, 59, 242–52.

North, D.C. (1971) 'Sources of productivity change in ocean shipping, 1600–1850', in Fogel, R.W. and Engerman, S.L. (eds.) *The Reinterpretation of American Economic History*, New York: Harper & Row.

North, D.C. and Thomas, R.P. (1970) 'An economic theory of the growth of the western world', *Economic History Review*, 23, 1–17.

Norton, R.D. and Rees, J. (1979) 'The product cycle and the spatial decentralization of American manufacturing', *Regional Studies*, 13, 141–51.

Nystuen, J.D. (1967) 'A theory and simulation of urban travel', in Garrison, W.L. and Marble, D.F. (eds.), *Quantitative Geography, Part I: Economic and Cultural Topics*, Evanston, Northwestern University Press, Studies in Geography.

Osleeb, J.P. (1973) 'A location theory for the uniform-price manufacturer,' Ph.D. Dissertation, Buffalo, State University of New York at Buffalo, Department of Geography.

Osleeb, J.P. (1974) 'The optimum size of plant for the uniform delivered price manufacturer', *Proceedings of the Association of American Geographers*, 6, 102–5.

Page, J.M. (1979) 'Small enterprises in African development: a survey', Washington, World Bank.

Paris, J.D. (1970) 'Regional structural analysis of population changes', *Regional Studies*, 4, 425–43.

Parker, J.E.S. (1974) *The Economics of Innovation*, London, Longman.

Pedersen, P.O. (1970) 'Innovation diffusion within and between national urban systems', *Geographical Analysis*, 2, 203–54.

Pedersen, P.O. (1975) *Urban-Regional Development in South America: A Process of Diffusion and Integration*, The Hague, Mouton.

Peet, R. (1975) 'Inequality and poverty: a Marxist-geographic theory', *Annals of the Association of American Geographers*, 65, 564–71.

Pemberton, H.E. (1936) 'The curve of culture diffusion rate', *American Sociological Review*, 1, 547–56.

Pemberton, H.E. (1937) 'Culture diffusion gradients', *American Journal of Sociology*, 42, 226–33.

Pemberton, H.E. (1938) 'The spatial order of cultural diffusion', *Sociology and Social Research*, 22, 246–51.

Perry, J.L. and Kraemer, K.L. (1978) *Diffusion and Adoption of Computer Applications Software in Local Governments*, Irvine, University of California at Irvine, Public Policy Research Organization.

Pessemier, E.A. (1968) 'Analyzing the economic potential for a new product', in Dickens, C.J., Kroeger, A. and Lockley, L.C. (eds.) *Readings in Marketing*, Homewood, Richard D. Irwin.

Pessemier, E.A. (1977) *Product Management: Strategy and Organization,* New York, John Wiley.

Pesson, L.L. (1966) 'Extension program planning with participation of clientele', in Sanders, H.C. (ed.) *The Cooperative Extension Service,* Englewood Cliffs, Prentice-Hall.

Petersen, W. (1975) *Population,* 3rd edn, London, Macmillan.

Peterson, R.A. and Mahajan, V. (1978) 'Multi product growth models', in Sheth, J. (ed.) *Research in Marketing,* Greenwich, Conn., JAI Press.

Phillips, M.A.M. (1972) *CATV: A History of Community Antenna Television,* Evanston, Northwestern University Press.

Pineiro, M., Trigo, E. and Fiorentino, R. (1978) 'Ideas for improving the content and process of technology development and diffusion in Latin America', Instituto Interamericano de Ciencias Agricolas, Officina en Colombia.

Pitts, F.R. (1963) 'Problems in computer simulation of diffusion', *Papers of the Regional Science Association,* 11, 111–19.

Pitts, F.R. (1965) 'HAGER III and HAGER IV: two Monte Carlo computer programs for the study of spatial diffusion problems', ONR Spatial Diffusion Study, Evanston, Northwestern University, Department of Geography.

Pitts, F.R. (1967) 'MIFCAL and NONCEL: two computer programs for the generalization of the Hagerstrand models to an irregular lattice', ONR Spatial Diffusion Study, Evanston, Northwestern University, Department of Geography.

Pred, A.R. (1966) *The Spatial Dynamics of U.S. Urban Industrial Growth, 1800–1914,* Cambridge, Mass., MIT Press.

Pred, A.R. (1973a) 'The growth and development of systems of cities in advanced economies', in *Systems of Cities and Information Flows: Two Essays by A.R. Pred and G.E. Tornqvist,* Lund, Gleerup, Lund Studies in Geography.

Pred, A.R. (1973b) *Urban Growth and the Circulation of Information: The United States System of Cities, 1790–1840,* Cambridge, Mass., Harvard University Press.

Pred, A.R. (1973c) 'Urbanization, domestic planning problems and Swedish geographical research', in Board, C., Chorley, R.J., Haggett, P. and Stoddart, D.R. (eds.) *Progess In Geography, Vol. 5,* London, Edward Arnold.

Pred, A.R. (1974a) 'Industry, information, and city system interdependencies', in Hamilton, F.E. (ed.) *Spatial Perspectives on Industrial Organization and Decision Making,* New York, John Wiley.

Pred, A.R. (1974b) *Major Job Providing Organizations and Systems of Cities.* Washington, Association of American Geographers.

Pred, A.R. (1975a) 'Diffusion, organizational spatial structure, and city system development', *Economic Geography,* 51, 252–68.

Pred, A.R. (1975b) 'On the spatial structure of organizations and the complexity of metropolitan interdependence', *Papers of the Regional Science Association,* 35, 115–42.

Pred, A.R. (1976) 'The interurban transmission of growth in advanced economies: empirical findings versus regional planning assumptions, *Regional Studies*, 10, 151–71

Pred, A.R. (1977) *City Systems in Advanced Economies: Past Growth, Present Processes and Future Development Options*, New York, Halsted Press.

Pyle, G. (1969) 'The diffusion of cholera in the United States in the nineteenth century', *Geographical Analysis*, 1, 59–75.

Rachman, D.J. (1969) *Retail Strategy and Structure: A Management Approach*, Englewood Cliffs, Prentice-Hall.

Radnor, M., Feller, I. and Rogers, E.M. (eds.) (1978) *The Diffusion of Innovations: An Assessment*, Evanston, Northwestern University, Center for the Interdisciplinary Study of Science and Technology.

Rainio, K. (1961) 'A stochastic model of social interaction', *Transactions of the Westermarck Society*, 7, Copenhagen, Munksgaard.

Rainio, K. (1962) 'A Stochastic Theory of Social Contacts', *Transactions of the Westermarck Society*, 8, Copenhagen, Munksgaard.

Ralston, B.A. (1978) 'A neoclassical approach to urban systems diffusion', *Environment and Planning*, 10, 267–73.

Ranis, G. and Fei, J.C.H. (1961) 'A theory of economic development', *American Economic Review*, 51, 533–65.

Ray, G.F. (1969) 'The diffusion of new technology: a study of ten processes in nine industries', *National Institute Economic Review*, 48, 40–83.

Redlich, F. (1953) 'Ideas, their migration in space and transmittal over time: a systematic treatment', *Kyklos*, 6, 301–22.

Rees, J. (1979) 'Technological change and regional shifts in American manufacturing', *Professional Geographer*, 31, 45–54.

Rein, M. (1976) *Social Science and Public Policy*, New York, Penguin.

Rein, M. and White, S.W. (1977) 'Can research help policy?', *The Public Interest*, 49, 119–36.

Renfrew, C. and Cooke, K.L. (eds.) (1979) *Transformations: Mathematical Approaches to Culture Change*, New York, Academic Press.

Rich, R.F. (1979) 'The pursuit of knowledge', *Knowledge: Creation, Diffusion, Utilization*, 1, 6–30.

Richardson, H.W. (1972) *Input-Output and Regional Economics*, London, Weidenfeld and Nicolson.

Richardson, H.W. (1976) 'Growth pole spillovers: the dynamics of backwash and spread', *Regional Studies*, 10, 1–9

Richardson, H.W. (1977) 'City size and national spatial strategies in developing countries', Washington, World Bank.

Richardson, H.W. (1978) *Regional Economics*, Urbana, University of Illinois Press.

Richardson, H.W. (1980) 'Polarization reversal in developing countries', *Papers of the Regional Science Association*, 45, 67–85.

Richardson, H.W. and Richardson, M. (1975) 'The relevance of growth center strategies to Latin America', *Economic Geography*, 51, 163–78.

Riddell, J.B. (1970) *The Spatial Dynamics of Modernization in Sierra Leone: Structure, Diffusion, and Response,* Evanston, Northwestern University Press.

Rink, D.R. and Swan, J.E. (1979) 'Product life cycle research: a literature review', *Journal of Business Research, 7, 219–42.*

Roberto, E.L. (1975) *Strategic Decision Making in a Social Program: The Case of Family Planning Diffusion,* Lexington, Lexington Books.

Roberto, E.L. (1976) 'The commercial contraceptive marketing program: a progress report', Columbus, Ohio State University, Department of Geography.

Roberto, E.L. (1977) 'The application of diffusion models to population programs: the Philippine case of the commercial contraceptive marketing program', Columbus, Ohio State University, Department of Geography, Studies in the Diffusion of Innovation.

Robertson, T.S. (1971) *Innovative Behavior and Communications,* New York, Holt, Rinehart & Winston.

Robinson, E.H. (1974) 'The early diffusion of steam power', *Journal of Economic History,* 34, 91–107.

Robson, B.T. (1973) *Urban Growth: An Approach,* London and New York, Methuen.

Roessner, J.D. (1977) 'Incentives to Innovate in Public and Private Organizations', *Administration and Society,* 9, 341–65.

Rogers, A. (1969a) 'Quadrat analysis of urban dispersion: 1. Theoretical techniques', *Environment and Planning,* 1, 47–80.

Rogers, A. (1969b) 'Quadrat analysis of urban dispersion: 2. Case studies of urban retail systems', *Environment and Planning,* 1, 155–72.

Rogers, A. (1974) *Statistical Analysis of Spatial Dispersion: The Quadrat Method,* New York, Academic Press.

Rogers, E.M. (1969) *Modernization Among Peasants: The Impact of Communication,* New York, Holt, Rinehart & Winston.

Rogers, E.M. (1973) *Communication Strategies For Family Planning,* New York, Free Press.

Rogers, E.M. (1976a) 'Communication and development: the passing of the dominant paradigm', in Rogers, E.M. (ed.) *Communication and Development: Critical Perspectives,* Beverly Hills, Sage.

Rogers, E.M. (1976b) 'New perspectives on communication and development: overview', in Rogers, E.M. (ed.) *Communication and Development: Critical Perspectives,* Beverly Hills, Sage.

Rogers, E.M. (1978) 'Reinvention during the innovation process', in Radnor, M., Feller, I. and Rogers, E.M. (eds.) *The Diffusion of Innovations: An Assessment,* Evanston, Northwestern University, Center for the Interdisciplinary Study of Science and Technology.

Rogers, E.M. and Agarwala-Rogers, R. (1976) *Communication in Organizations.* New York, Free Press.

Rogers, E.M. and Havens, E. (1961) 'Adoption of hybrid corn: profitability and the interaction effect', *Rural Sociology,* 26, 409–14.

Rogers, E.M. and Havens, E. (1962) 'Rejoinder to Griliches' another false dichotomy', *Rural Sociology,* 27, 330–2.

Rogers, E.M. and Shoemaker, F.F. (1971) *Communication of Innovations: A Cross Cultural Approach*, New York, Free Press.

Roling, N.G., Ascroft, J. and Chege, F.W. (1976) 'The diffusion of innovations and the issue of equity in rural development', in Rogers, E.M. (ed.) *Communication and Development: Critical Perspectives*, Beverly Hills, Sage.

Rondinelli, D.A. and Ruddle, K. (1976) *Urban Functions in Rural Development: An Analysis of Integrated Spatial Development Policy*, Washington, United States Agency for International Development, Office of Urban Development.

Rosegger, G. (1977) 'Diffusion of technology in industry', in Gold, B. (ed.) *Research, Technological Change, and Economic Analysis*, Lexington, Lexington Books.

Rosenberg, N. (1963) 'Technological change in the machine tool industry, 1840–1910', *Journal of Economic History*, 23, 414–433.

Rosenberg, N. (ed.) (1971) *The Economics of Technological Change*, New York, Penguin Books.

Rosenberg, N. (1972a) 'Factors affecting the diffusion of technology', *Explorations in Economic History*, 10, 3–33. Also in Rosenberg, N. (1976) *Perspectives on Technology*, Cambridge, Cambridge University Press.

Rosenberg, N. (1972b) *Technology and American Economic Growth*, New York, Harper & Row.

Rosenberg, N. (1976a) 'On technological expectations', *Economic Journal*, 86, 523–35.

Rosenberg, N. (1976b) *Perspectives on Technology*, Cambridge, Cambridge University Press.

Rossini, F. and Bozeman, B. (1977) 'National strategies for technological innovation', *Administration and Society*, 9, 81–110.

Ryan, B. and Gross, N.C. (1943) 'The diffusion of hybrid seed corn in two Iowa communities', *Rural Sociology*, 8, 15–24.

Sagers, M.J. and Brown, L.A. (1977) 'An economic history perspective on innovation diffusion', Columbus, Ohio State University, Department of Geography, Studies in the Diffusion of Innovation.

Sahal, D. (1976) 'The multidimensional diffusion of technology', in Linstone, H.A. and Sahal, D. (eds.) *Technological Substitution: Forecasting Techniques and Applications*, New York, Elsevier.

Salt, J. (1967) 'The impact of the Ford and Vauxhall plants on employment in Merseyside, 1962–65', *Tijdschrift Voor Economische en Sociale Geografie*, 58, 255–63.

Sandberg, L.G. (1969) 'American rings and English mules: the role of economic rationality', *Quarterly Journal of Economics*, 83, 25–43.

Sandberg, L.G. (1974) *Lancashire in Decline: A Study in Entrepreneurship, Technology, and International Trade*, Columbus, Ohio State University Press.

Sanders, H.C. (1966) 'The legal base, scope, functions, and general objectives of extension work', in Sanders, H.C. (ed.) *The Cooperative Extension Service*, Englewood Cliffs, Prentice-Hall.

Sauer, C.O. (1952) *Agricultural origins and dispersals*, New York, American Geographical Society.

Saxonhouse, G. (1974) 'A tale of Japanese technological diffusion in the Meiji period', *Journal of Economic History*, 34, 149–65.

Schmookler, J. (1966) *Invention and Economic Growth*, Cambridge, Mass., Harvard University Press.

Schneider, J.B. and Symons, J.G. (1971a) 'Locating ambulance dispatch centers in an urban region: a man-computer interactive problem-solving approach', Philadelphia, University of Pennsylvania, Regional Science Research Institute.

Schneider, J.B. and Symons, J.G. (1971b) 'Regional health facility system planning: an access opportunity approach', Philadelphia, University of Pennsylvania, Regional Science Research Institute.

Schumacher, E.F. (1973) *Small Is Beautiful*, New York, Harper & Row.

Scott, A.J. (1971) 'Dynamic location-allocation systems: some basic planning strategies', *Environment and Planning*, 3, 73–82.

Seiden, M.H. (1972) *Cable Television U.S.A.: An Analysis of Government Policy*, New York, Praeger.

Seidenberg, A. (1960) 'The diffusion of counting practices', *University of California Publications in Mathematics: New Series*, 3, 215–99.

Semple, R.K. and Brown, L.A. (1976) 'Cones of resolution in spatial diffusion studies: a perspective,' *Professional Geographer*, 28, 8–16.

Semple, R.K., Brown, L.A. and Brown, M.A. (1975) 'Propagator supported diffusion processes: agency strategies and the innovation establishment interface', Columbus, Ohio State University, Department of Geography, Studies in the Diffusion of Innovation.

Semple, R.K., Brown, L.A. and Brown, M.A. (1977) 'Strategies for the promotion and diffusion of consumer goods and services: an overview', *International Regional Science Review*, 2, 91–102.

Sexton, J.D. (1972) *Education and Innovation in a Guatemalan Community: San Juan la Laguna*, Los Angeles, University of California, Latin American Center.

Shannon, G.W. (1970) *Spatial Diffusion of an Innovative Health Care Plan*, Ann Arbor, University of Michigan, Department of Geography.

Shawyer, A.J. (1970) 'Diffusion: an appraisal', Ph.D. Dissertation, University of Nottingham, Department of Geography.

Shawyer, A.J. (1974) 'Diffusion: social process and spatial pattern', Annual Conference of the European Society of Rural Sociology.

Sheppard, E.S., (1976) 'On the diffusion of shopping centre construction in Canada', *Canadian Geographer*, 20, 187–98.

Sieling, R., Malecki, E.J. and Brown, L.A. (1975) 'Infrastructure growth and adoption: the diffusion of cable television within a community', Columbus, Ohio State University, Department of Geography, Studies in the Diffusion of Innovation.

Simon, H.A. and Bonini, C.P. (1958) 'The size distribution of business firms', *American Economic Review*, 48, 607–17.

Sloan Commission on Cable Communications (1971) *On the Cable: The Television of Abundance,* New York, McGraw-Hill.

Smith, C.A. (ed.) (1976) *Regional Analysis, Vol. I: Economic Systems,* New York, Academic Press.

Smith, C.A. (ed.) (1976) *Regional Analysis, Vol. II: Social Systems,* New York, Academic Press.

Smith, R.J. (1974) 'Shuttleless looms', in Nabseth L. and Ray, G.F. (eds.) *The Diffusion of New Industrial Processes: An International Study,* Cambridge, Cambridge University Press.

Smith, W. (1974) 'Innovation and diffusion—a supply oriented example: hybrid grain corn in Quebec', Columbus, Ohio State University, Department of Geography, Studies in the Diffusion of Innovation.

Sopher, D.E. (1979) 'Temporal disparity as a measure of change', *Professional Geographer,* 31, 377–81.

Stafford, H.A. (1972) 'The geography of manufacturers', in Board, C., Chorley, R.J., Haggett, P. and Stoddart, D.R. (eds.) *Progress in Geography, Vol. 4,* New York, St Martin's Press.

Stanislawski, D. (1949) 'The origin and spread of the grid pattern town, *Geographical Review,* 36, 195–210. Also in Wagner, P.L. and Mikesell, M.W. (1962) (eds.) *Readings in Cultural Geography,* Chicago, University of Chicago Press.

Steele, D.B. (1969) 'Regional Multipliers in Great Britain', *Oxford Economic Papers,* 21, 268–92.

Steindl, J. (1965) *Random Processes and the Growth of Firms: A Study of the Pareto Law,* New York, Hafner.

Steiner, R.L. (1973) *Visions of Cablevision,* Cincinnati, Stephen H. Wilder Foundation.

Stern, M.O., Ayres, R.U. and Shapanka, A. (1976) 'A model for forecasting the substitution of one technology for another', in Linstone, H.A. and Sahal, D. (eds.) *Technological Substitution: Forecasting Techniques and Applications,* New York, Elsevier.

Stevens, B.H. (1961) 'Linear Programming and location rent', *Journal of Regional Science,* 3, 15–26. Also in Smith, R.H.T., Taaffe, E.J. and King, L.J. (eds.) *Readings in Economic Geography,* Chicago, Rand McNally.

Stewart, W.M. (1965) 'Physical distribution: key to improved volume and profits', *Journal of Marketing,* 29, 65–70.

Stohr, W.B. (1974) *Interurban Systems and Regional Economic Development,* Washington, Association of American Geographers, Resource Paper Series.

Stone, A.H. (1967) 'Community antenna television and the Copyright Law Controversy', M.A. Thesis, Urbana, University of Illinois.

Stycos, J.M. (1977) 'The great tabu: a half century of population and family planning communication', Honolulu, The East-West Center.

Sujono, H. (1974) *The Adoption of an Innovation in a Developing Country: The Case of Family Planning in Indonesia,* Chicago, University of Chicago, Community and Family Study Center.

Sunkel, O. (1969) 'National development policy and external dependence in Latin America', *Journal of Development Studies*, 6, 23–48.

Taaffe, E.J. (1974) 'The spatial view in context', *Annals of the Association of American Geographers*, 64, 1–16.

Taaffe, E.J., Morrill, R.L. and Gould, P.R. (1963) 'Transport expansion in underdeveloped countries: a comparative analysis', *Geographical Review*, 53, 503–29.

Tanaka, H. (1971) 'The Japanese department store: spatial patterns as related to cultural change', M.A. Thesis, London, University of Western Ontario, Department Geography.

Tarde, G. (1903) *The Laws of Imitation*, New York, Holt, Rinehart & Winston.

Tate, C. (ed.) (1971) *Cable Television in the Cities*, Washington, The Urban Institute.

Taylor, C.G. (1951) 'A deep fringe area', *Electrical Merchandising*, December, 42–3.

Teitz, M.B. (1968a) 'Location strategies for competitive systems', *Journal of Regional Science*, 8, 135–48.

Teitz, M.B. (1968b) 'Toward a theory of urban public facility location', *Papers of the Regional Science Association*, 21, 35–51.

Temin, P. (1964) *Iron and Steel in 19th Century America*, Cambridge, Mass., MIT Press.

Temin, P. (1966a) 'Steam and waterpower in the early nineteenth century', *Journal of Economic History*, 26, 187–205.

Temin, P. (1966b) 'The relative decline of the British steel industry, 1880–1913', in Rosovsky, H. (ed.) *Industrialization in Two Systems*, New York, John Wiley.

Tepfer, C.S. (1964) 'Cable TV on the move', *Electronics World*, January, 40–41, 87.

Thomas, M.D. (1972a) 'Growth pole theory: an examination of some of its basic concepts', in Hansen, N.M. (ed.) *Growth Centers in Regional Economic Development*, New York, Free Press.

Thomas, M.D. (1972b) 'The regional problem, structural change, and growth pole theory', in Kuklinski, A. (ed.) *Growth Poles and Growth Centers in Regional Planning*, The Hague, Mouton.

Thomas, M.D. (1974) 'Structural change and regional industrial development', in Helleiner F. and Stohr, W. (eds.) *Proceedings of the Commission on Regional Aspects of Economic Development of the International Geographical Union, Vol. II: Spatial Aspects of the Development Process*, Toronto, Allister.

Thomas, M.D. and LeHeron, R.B. (1975) 'Perspectives on technological change and the process of diffusion in the manufacturing sector', *Economic Geography*, 51, 231–51.

Thompson, D.N. (1968) 'Franchise operations and Antitrust Law', *Journal of Retailing*, 44, 39–53.

Thorngren, B. (1970) 'How do contact systems affect regional development', *Environment and Planning*, 2, 409–27.

Tilton, J.E. (1971) *International Diffusion of Technology: The Case of Semiconductors*, Washington, The Brookings Institution.

Timms, D. (1971) *The Urban Mosiac: Towards a Theory of Residential Differentiation*, Cambridge, Cambridge University Press.

Tornqvist, G. (1967) *TV Agandets Utreckhng I Sveridge, 1956–65 (Growth of TV Ownership in Sweden, 1956–1965)*, Stockholm, Almqvist and Wiksells.

Tornqvist, G. (1970) *Contact Systems and Regional Development*, Lund, Gleerup, Lund Studies in Geography.

Tsui, A.O. and Bogue, D.J. (1978) 'Decline in world fertility: trends, causes, implications', *Population Bulletin*, 33–4.

Urban, G.L. (1970) 'SPRINTER Mod III: a model for the analysis of new frequently purchased consumer products', *Operations Research*, 18, 805–54.

Utterback, J.M. and Abernathy, W.J. (1975) 'A dynamic model of process and product innovation', *OMEGA: The International Journal of Management Science*, 3, 639–56.

Van der Laan, H.L. (1975) *The Lebanese Traders in Sierra Leone*, The Hague, Mouton.

Vertinsky, I. and Barth, R.T. (1972) 'A model of diffusion and implementation: an exploratory study of managerial innovation in Colombia', *Socio-Economic Planning Sciences*, 6, 153–72.

Wagner, H.M. (1975a) *Principles of Management Science: with Applications to Executive Decisions*, Englewood Cliffs, Prentice-Hall.

Wagner, H.M. (1975b) *Principles of Operations Research: with Applications to Managerial Decisions*, Englewood Cliffs, Prentice-Hall.

Wagner, P.L. and Mikesell, M.W. (eds.) (1962) *Readings in Cultural Geography*, Chicago, University of Chicago Press.

Waite, D. (1973) 'The economic significance of small firms', *Journal of Industrial Economics*, 21, 154–66.

Walton, G.M. (1970) 'Productivity change in ocean shipping after 1870', *Journal of Economic History*, 30, 435–9.

Walton, G.M. (1971) 'Obstacles to technical diffusion in ocean shipping, 1675–1775', *Explorations in Economic History*, 8, 123–40.

Warner, K.F. (1966) 'Visits', in Sanders, H.C. (ed.) *The Cooperative Extension Service*, Englewood Cliffs, Prentice-Hall.

Warneryd, O. (1968) *Interdependence in Urban Systems*, Goteborg, Regionkunsult Aktiebolag.

Wasson, C.R. (1974) *Dynamic Competitive Strategy and Product Life Cycle*, St Charles, Challenge Books.

Wasson, C.R. (1976) 'The importance of the product life cycle to the industrial marketer', *Industrial Marketing Management*, 5, 299–308.

Watson, W.B. (ed.) (1977) *Family Planning in the Developing World: A Review of Programs*, New York, The Population Council.

Webber, M.J. (1972) *Impact of Uncertainty on Location*, Cambridge, Mass., MIT Press.

Webber, M.J. and Joseph, A.E. (1977) 'On the separation of market size and information availability in empirical studies of diffusion processes', *Geographical Analysis*, 9, 403–9.

Webber, M.J. and Joseph, A.E. (1978) 'Spatial diffusion processes 1: a model and an approximation method', *Environment and Planning*, 10, 651–65.

Webber, M.J. and Joseph, A.E. (1979) 'Spatial diffusion processes 2: numerical analysis', *Environment and Planning*, 11, 335–47.

Webster, F.E. (1972) 'Communication and diffusion processes in industrial markets', *European Journal of Marketing*, 5, 178–88.

Webster, F.E. (1978) 'Is industrial marketing coming of age?' in Zaltman, G. and Bonoma, T.V. (eds.) *Review of Marketing, 1978*. Chicago, American Marketing Association.

Wedervang, F. (1965) *Development of a Population of Industrial Firms*, Oslo, Universitetsforlaget.

Weeks, J. (1970) 'Uncertainty, risk, and wealth and income distribution in peasant agriculture', *Journal of Development Studies*, 7, 28–36.

Weinand, H.C. (1972) 'A spatio-temporal model of economic development', *Australian Geographical Studies*, 10, 95–100.

Weinstein, J.A. (1976) *Demographic Transition and Social Change*, Morristown, General Learning Press.

West, J.S. and Pearson, M.M. (1979) 'Wholesaling in economic development: incorporating the distribution-center concept', *Bulletin of Business Research of the Ohio State University Center for Business and Economic Research*, 54, 8, 1–5.

Wilbanks, T.J. (1972) 'Accessibility and technological change in Northern India', *Annals of the Association of American Geographers*, 62, 427–36.

Wilson, G.W., Bergmann, B.R., Hirsch, L.V. and Klein, M.S. (1966) *The Impact of Highway Investment on Development*, Washington, The Brookings Institution.

Wind, Y. (1980) *Product Policy*, Reading, Addison Wesley.

Winner, L. (1977) *Autonomous Technology*, Cambridge, Mass., MIT Press.

Witthuhn, B.O. (1968) 'The spatial integration of Uganda as shown by the diffusion of postal agencies, 1900–1965', *The East Lakes Geographer*, 4, 5–20.

Wolfbein, S. (1944) *The Decline of a Cotton Textile City*, New York, Columbia University Press.

Wolpert, J. (1964) 'The decision process in a spatial context', *Annals of the Association of American Geographers*, 54, 537–58.

Wood, D.B. (1978) 'Talk back TV hits Columbus', *Christian Science Monitor*, January 17.

Woods, C.M. and Graves, T.D. (1973) *The Process of Medical Change in a Highland Guatemalan Town*, Latin American Center, Los Angeles, University of California.

Yankelovich, D. (1964) 'New criteria for market segmentation', *Harvard Business Review*, Mar.–Apr., 83–90.

Yapa, L.S. (1975) 'Analytical alternatives to the Monte Carlo simulation of spatial diffusion', *Annals of the Association of American Geographers*, 65, 163–76.

Yapa, L.S. (1976) 'Innovation diffusion and economic involution: an essay', Columbus, Ohio State University, Department of Geography, Studies in the Diffusion of Innovation.

Yapa, L.S. (1977) 'The Green Revolution: a diffusion model', *Annals of the Association of American Geographers*, 67, 350–9.

Yapa, L.S. (1979) 'Ecopolitical economy of the Green Revolution', *Professional Geographer*, 31, 371–6.

Yapa, L.S. (1980) 'Diffusion, development, and ecopolitical economy', in Agnew, J.A. (ed.) *Innovation Research and Public Policy*, Syracuse, University of Syracuse Geographical Series.

Yapa, L.S. and Mayfield, R.C. (1978) 'Non adoption of innovations: evidence from discriminant analysis', *Economic Geography*, 54, 145–56.

Yeates, M.H. and Garner, B.J. (1976) *The North American City*, 2nd edn, New York, Harper & Row.

Yin, R.K. (1978) *Changing Urban Bureaucracies: How New Practices Become Routinized*, Santa Monica, Rand Corporation.

Yin, R.K., Quick, S.K., Bateman, P.M. and Marks, E.L. (1978) *Changing Urban Bureaucracies: How New Practices Become Routinized–Appendices*, Santa Monica, Rand Corporaton.

Yuill, R.S. (1964) 'A simulation study of barrier effects in spatial diffusion problems', ONR Spatial Diffusion Study, Evanston, Northwestern University, Department of Geography.

Zaltman, G. (1979) 'Knowledge utilization as planned social change', *Knowledge: Creation, Diffusion, Utilization*, 1, 82–105.

Zaltman, G., Duncan, R. and Holbeck, J. (1973) *Innovations and Organizations*, New York, John Wiley.

Zaltman, G., Kotler, P. and Kaufman, I. (eds.) (1972) *Creating Social Change*, New York, Holt, Rinehart & Winston.

Zelinski, W. (1962) 'Has American industry been decentralizing? The evidence for the 1939–1954 period', *Economic Geography*, 38, 251–69.

Zelinski, W. (1967) 'Classical town names in the United States', *Geographical Review*, 57, 463–95.

Zeller, R.E. (1978) 'A study of the selection of multiple locations for consumer oriented facilities', Ph.D. Dissertation, Columbus, Ohio State University, Department of Geography. Also in Studies in the Diffusion of Innovation, Ohio State University, Department of Geography.

Zeller, R.E. and Brown, L.A. (1976) 'SIMMAR: a Markov chain based program for the diffusion of innovation', *Computer Applications*, 3, 441–85.

Zeller, R.E., Achabal, D.D. and Brown, L.A. (1980) 'Market penetration and locational conflict in franchise systems', *Decision Sciences*, 11, 58–80.

Zoerner, C.E. (1966) 'The development of American community antenna television,' Ph.D. Dissertation, Urbana, University of Illinois.

INDEX

Strategy and Social Norms or
Development Level, 264–5, 292

Congruence Between Innovation
and the Potential Adopter's
Ongoing Activities or Personal
Characteristics, 6–7, 29–30, 69,
168; *also see* Factors Influenc-
ing Diffusion, Consumer and
Agricultural Innovations,
Adopter Characteristics

Cost-Benefit Indices, 87

Demand for the Innovation, 217–
22

Development Level, 263–70

Diffusion Agency Characteristics,
57–9, 116–18, 150

Diffusion Agency Establishment
Policies, *see* Diffusion Agency
Establishment

Diffusion Agency Maintenance
and Operation, 56–63

Diffusion Agency Network, Existing vs. New, 54–6

Diffusion Agency Strategy, *see*
Diffusion Agency Strategy

Distance, 19–22, 22–3, 23–4, 25–
6, 29, 42, 55, 56–63, 68–74,
105–27, 213–14, 215

Elasticity of Demand for the Innovation, 107, 121–3, 231

Elasticity of Diffusion Agency
Profitability with Regard to
Urban Area Sales Potential,
62–3, 73–4

Exposure to the Innovation, *see*
Factors Influencing Diffusion,
Consumer and Agricultural In-
novations, Information

General Economic Conditions,
57–9

Human Resource Characteristics
such as Entrepreneurial Ability, 69, 70–2, 168; *also see*
Subculture of Peasantry

Information, 5–6, 8–9, 19–20,
22–3, 25–6, 30, 42, 47, 53,
68–74, 101–3, 107–10, 122–3,
149, 150–1, 168, 176, 214,
217–22, 229–30, 287–8

Infrastructure, 8–9, 30, 100, 101–

3, 103–5, 115–27, 150, 213–15,
217–22, 263–70, 290, 292

Innovation Characteristics, 62,
73–4, 96, 115–17, 150

Innovativeness, 6–7, 103, 114,
140–4, 150–1, 176, 191, 228,
264, 288

Institutional Actions or Characteristics, 72–3, 78–9, 86, 98,
188–90, 214–15, 222

Interaction Between Diffusion
Strategy Elements, *see* Factors
Influencing Diffusion, Consumer and Agricultural Innovations, Orchestration of Diffusion Strategy Elements

Location Rent, *see* Adoption
Rent, Location Rent

Logistics, 56–63, 73–4

Management Aggressiveness and
Innovativeness, 69, 79, 85, 97

Market Penetration Strategy, 30,
59–63

Market Potential, *see* Factors Influencing Diffusion, Consumer
and Agricultural Innovations,
Sales Potential

Market Selection and Segmentation, 101–3, 110–15, 115–27,
149, 150, 215, 227, 290

Modification and Adaptation of
the Innovation, 3–4, Ch. 6,
292–3

Non-Profit Motivation, 86–7

Orchestration of Diffusion Strategy Elements, 115–20, 214,
290

Order of Good of the Innovation,
62, 96, 111, 115–17

Organizational Structure, 52–6,
62, 68–74, 117–18, 217–22

Population Size of an Urban
Area, 20–2, 25–6, 29, 42, 56–
63, 70–4

Price of the Innovation, 8, 57–9,
100, 101–3, 105–7, 115–27,
149, 214–15, 217–22, 290

Product Life Cycle, 118–19

Profitability, 56–63, 68–74, 95,
97, 176–7